ZAGATSURVEY®

2002

SAN FRANCISCO BAY AREA RESTAURANTS

San Francisco Editor: Meesha Halm

Silicon Valley Editor: Mary Orlin

Local Coordinator: Maura Sell

Editor: Troy Segal

Published and distributed by
ZAGAT SURVEY, LLC
4 Columbus Circle
New York, New York 10019
Tel: 212 977 6000
E-mail: sanfran@zagat.com
Web site: www.zagat.com

Acknowledgments

We'd like to thank the more than 3,200 respondents who took the time to lower their forks and raise their pens to share with us their dining experiences on our surveys and via our Web site. Special thanks are due to: Laiko Bahrs, Jon and Olive Poe Fox, D.K. Jackson, Vincent and Conor Logan, Laura Reiley and Willow Waldeck. We are also indebted to all the industrious chefs and restaurateurs of the Bay Area, whose efforts entertain us, comfort us, nourish us and spare us from having to cook (and clean up) for ourselves.

This guide would not have been possible without the hard work of our staff, including Betsy Andrews, Deirdre Bourdet, Phil Cardone, Reni Chin, Shelley Gallagher, Natalie Lebert, Mike Liao, Dave Makulec, Rob Poole, Brooke Rein, Robert Seixas, Daniel Simmons and Sharon Yates.

Contents

What's New

What a difference a year makes. After the halcyon era of endless expansion and expense-account dinners, the dotcom crash (plus rising energy costs and rents) has made restaurant closures as common as pink-slip parties. Still, there were plenty of signs of life this past year.

• **Deluxe Debuts:** Two pricey premieres include the brazenly glam Asia de Cuba and Ozumo. And the mighty Masa's has emerged snazzier and tastier than ever, thanks to a much-needed remodeling and a menu makeover by *Iron Chef* victor Ron Siegel.

• **Value Returns:** Not surprisingly, value is back in vogue. Two of this year's freshmen, Pesce and Emmy's Spaghetti Shack, hope to lure diners with simple, affordable Italian-inflected eats. Veteran establishments, meanwhile, are scaling back, slashing menu prices – a welcome change, given that the average Bay Area meal costs $30.98 – and even reinventing themselves for an increasingly picky and parsimonious public. The once red-hot Ne O is playing it cool with a classic, cheaper Californian menu. Old-timer Bruno's is returning to its 1970s roots, offering a retro red-sauce menu – with recession-era prices to match.

• **Tops in Tapas:** The culinary zeitgeist of the year was unequivocally tapas. Basque and Ramblas pay homage to the traditional Spanish variety, while others have gone global – Isa, À Côté and Bistro Liaison proffer small plates inspired by France and Italy; Andalu, Grasshopper and Oritalia tout tapas with a taste of the Orient.

• **Out-of-Town Openings:** Many restaurateurs eschewed the over-saturated metropolis, setting up shop in the suburbs. In Berkeley, restaurateur George Wong opened La Rue, and downtown, a seafood specialist, comes from the folks behind César. Up in Napa and Sonoma Valleys, notable newcomers include the Pan-American Miramonte and the Mediterranean Manzanita.

• **Silicon Starters:** This year's *Survey* adds a new Silicon Valley section, reflecting the growing sophistication of the dining scene down south. Le Poisson Japonais offers high-end late-night dining, while Kingfish's New Orleans cuisine is letting the good times roll in San Mateo. Farther up the Peninsula, diners are putting on the Ritz (literally) at Navio, a splashy seafooder in the hotel's new resort.

• **On the Horizon:** More high-profilers are slated to open this fall, from a new Trader Vic's in Palo Alto to Charlie Palmer's Dry Creek Kitchen in Healdsburg. Clearly, reports of the death of the SF dining scene have been grossly exaggerated.

San Francisco, CA   Meesha Halm
October 1, 2001

About This Survey

For more than 20 years, Zagat Survey has reported on the shared experiences of diners like you. Here are the results of our *2002 San Francisco Bay Area Restaurant Survey*, covering some 1,078 local restaurants. This marks the tenth year we have covered restaurants in the Bay Area, extending from the wine country to the Monterey Peninsula.

By regularly surveying large numbers of avid local restaurant-goers about their collective dining experiences, we hope to have achieved a uniquely current and reliable guide. For this book, more than 3,200 people participated. Since the participants dined out an average of 3.1 times per week, this *Survey* is based on about 522,000 meals annually.

Of the surveyors, 56% were women, 44% men; the breakdown by age is 15% in their 20s, 28% in their 30s, 19% in their 40s, 21% in their 50s and 17% in their 60s or above. In producing the reviews contained in this guide, our editors have synopsized our surveyors' opinions, with their exact comments shown in quotation marks.

Of course, we are especially grateful to our editors, Meesha Halm, a nationally published restaurant critic, and Mary Orlin, food editor and dining critic for the *Palo Alto Weekly,* and to our coordinator, Maura Sell, a professionally trained chef and consultant to the specialty food industry.

To help guide our readers to the Bay Area's best meals and best buys, we have prepared a number of lists. See Most Popular (page 9), Top Ratings (pages 10–17) and Best Buys (page 18). To assist the user in finding just the right restaurant for any occasion, without wasting time, we have also provided 46 handy indexes and have tried to be concise.

As companions to this guide, we also publish the *Los Angeles/So. California Restaurant Survey* and the forthcoming *San Francisco Nightlife Survey,* as well as *Zagat Surveys* and Maps to more than 70 other markets around the world. Most of these guides are also available on mobile devices and at **www.zagat.com,** where you can also vote and shop.

To join our **San Francisco Bay Area Survey** or any of our other upcoming *Surveys,* you can request a ballot by registering at zagat.com and then selecting the survey in which you'd like to participate. Each participant will receive a free copy of the resulting guide when it's published.

Your comments, suggestions and even criticisms of this *Survey* are also solicited. There is always room for improvement with your help. You can contact us at sanfran@zagat.com or by mail at Zagat Survey, 4 Columbus Circle, New York, NY 10019. We look forward to hearing from you.

New York, NY
October 1, 2001

Nina and Tim Zagat

Key to Ratings/Symbols

Name, Address & Phone Number

Zagat Ratings

Hours & Credit Cards

F	D	S	C
▽ 23	9	13	$15

Tim & Nina's ◑ 🅂 ⌿

4 Columbus Circle (8th Ave.), 212-977-6000

◩ Open 24/7, this "crowded", "overpopular" joint started the "Swedish-Mexican craze" (i.e. herring or lox on tiny tacos with mole or chimichurri sauce); though it looks like a "garage" and T & N "never heard of credit cards or reservations" – yours in particular – "dirt cheap" tabs for *muy bien eats* draw demented "debit-account" diners to this "deep dive."

Review, with surveyors' comments in quotes

Restaurants with the highest overall ratings and greatest popularity and importance are printed in CAPITAL LETTERS.

Before each review a symbol indicates whether responses were uniform ■ or mixed ◩.

Hours: ◑ serves after 11 PM
　　　　🅛 open for Lunch
　　　　🅢 open on Sunday
　　　　🅜 open on Monday

Credit Cards: ⌿ no credit cards accepted

Ratings: Food, Decor and Service are rated on a scale of **0** to **30**. The Cost (C) column reflects our surveyors' estimate of the price of dinner including one drink and tip.

F	Food	D	Decor	S	Service	C	Cost
23		9		13		$15	

0–9 poor to fair	**20–25** very good to excellent
10–15 fair to good	**26–30** extraordinary to perfection
16–19 good to very good	▽ low response/less reliable

A place listed without ratings is either an important **newcomer** or a popular **write-in**. For such places, the estimated cost is indicated by the following symbols.

I	$15 and below	**E**	$31 to $50
M	$16 to $30	**VE**	$51 or more

Most Popular

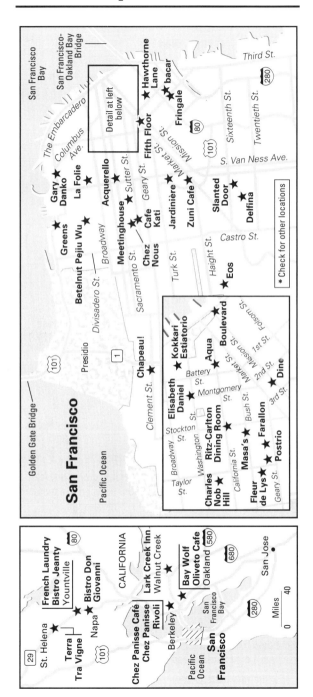

San Francisco Bay

San Francisco-Oakland Bay Bridge

Third St.

The Embarcadero

Columbus Ave.

Detail at left below

★ Hawthorne Lane
★ bacar
★ Fringale

280

Sixteenth St.

Twentieth St.

Fifth Floor
Mission St.
80
101

S. Van Ness Ave.

★ Gary Danko
★ La Folie
Sutter St.
★ Acquerello
Geary St.
★ Jardiniere
★ Zuni Cafe
★ Slanted Door
★ Delfina

★ Greens
Broadway
★ Meetinghouse
★ Cafe Kati
★ Chez Nous

Castro St.

★ Betelnut Pejiu Wu

Divisadero St.

Sacramento St.

Turk St.

Haight St.

★ Eos

* Check for other locations

101

Presidio

1

Golden Gate Bridge

Clement St.

★ Chapeau!

San Francisco

Pacific Ocean

★ Kokkari Estiatorio
★ Aqua
★ Boulevard
Folsom St.
Market St.
Mission St.
1st St.
2nd St.
3rd St.
★ Dine

Battery St.
★ Elisabeth Daniel
Montgomery St.
★ Ritz-Carlton Dining Room
Bush St.
★ Farallon

Stockton St.
California St.
★ Masa's
★ Postrio

Broadway
Washington
★ Charles Nob Hill
Taylor St.
★ Fleur de Lys
Geary St.

French Laundry
Bistro Jeanty
Yountville
80
★ Bistro Don Giovanni

CALIFORNIA

Lark Creek Inn
Walnut Creek

★ Bay Wolf
Oliveto Cafe
Oakland
580
680

San Jose •

St. Helena
★ Terra
Tra Vigne
Napa
29
101

★ Chez Panisse Café
★ Chez Panisse
Rivoli
Berkeley

San Francisco Bay

San Francisco

280

Miles
0   40

Pacific Ocean

8   www.zagat.com

Most Popular*

Each of our reviewers has been asked to name his or her five favorite restaurants. The 40 spots most frequently named, in order of their popularity, are:

 1. Boulevard
 2. Gary Danko
 3. French Laundry/N
 4. Jardinière
 5. Aqua
 6. Hawthorne Lane
 7. Fleur de Lys
 8. Fifth Floor
 9. Chez Panisse Café/E
10. Slanted Door
11. Postrio
12. Chez Panisse/E
13. Bistro Jeanty/N
14. Ritz-Carlton Dining Room
15. Tra Vigne/N
16. Fringale
17. Delfina
18. Farallon
19. Elisabeth Daniel, Rest.
20. Zuni Cafe
21. La Folie
22. Kokkari Estiatorio
23. Chapeau!
24. Lark Creek Inn/N
25. EOS
26. Terra/N
27. Chez Nous
28. Cafe Kati
29. Bistro Don Giovanni/N
30. Betelnut Pejiu Wu
31. Charles Nob Hill
32. bacar
33. Meetinghouse†
34. Greens
35. Rivoli/E
36. Bay Wolf/E
37. Oliveto Cafe/E
38. Acquerello
39. Masa's†
40. Dine

It's obvious that many of the restaurants on the above list are among the most expensive, but if popularity were calibrated to price, we suspect that a number of other restaurants would join the above ranks. Thus, for budget-conscious gourmets, we have listed 80 Best Buys on page 18. These are restaurants that give real quality at extremely reasonable prices.

* All restaurants are in the City of San Francisco unless otherwise noted (E=East of San Francisco; N=North of San Francisco; S=South of San Francisco; and SV=Silicon Valley/Peninsula).
† Tied with the restaurant listed directly above it

Top Ratings*

Top lists exclude restaurants with low voting.

Top Food Ranking

29 French Laundry/N
28 Gary Danko
   Ritz-Carlton Dining Room
   Le Papillon/SV
   Chez Panisse/E
   La Forêt/SV
   Terra/N
   La Folie
27 Fleur de Lys
   Chez Panisse Café/E
   Boulevard
   Aqua
   Masa's
   Bistro Jeanty/N
   Sushi Ran/N
   Emile's/SV
   Cheese Board/E
   Fresh Cream/S†
26 La Toque/N
   Jardinière

   Slanted Door
   Rivoli/E
   Elisabeth Daniel, Rest.
   Charles Nob Hill
   Campton Place
   Chez TJ/SV
   Fifth Floor
   Hawthorne Lane
   Cafe Jacqueline
   John Bentley's/SV
   Fringale
   Acquerello
   Sent Sovi/SV
   Erna's Elderberry/E
   Pacific's Edge/S
   Postrio
   Domaine Chandon/N
25 Kyo-Ya
   Albion River Inn/N
   Maki

Top Food by Cuisine

American (New)
29 French Laundry/N
28 Gary Danko
26 Chez TJ/SV
   John Bentley's/SV
   Postrio

American (Traditional)
27 Boulevard
24 Dottie's True Blue Cafe
   Mama's/Washington Sq.
   Gordon's/N
23 Lark Creek Inn/N

Bakeries/Delis
27 Cheese Board/E
25 Gayle's Bakery/S
24 Downtown Bakery/N
   Emporio Rulli/N
22 Liberty Cafe

Barbecue
24 Foothill Cafe/N
23 Koryo Wooden Charcoal/E
21 Brother's Korean
   Brother-in-Law's
20 Everett & Jones/E

Cajun/Creole/Southern
23 Catahoula/N
21 Kate's Kitchen
20 PJ's Oyster Bed
19 Elite Cafe
18 Nola/SV

Californian
28 Chez Panisse/E
27 Chez Panisse Café/E
26 Jardinière
   Charles Nob Hill
   Hawthorne Lane

---

* All restaurants are in the City of San Francisco unless otherwise
  noted (E=East of San Francisco; N=North of San Francisco;
  S=South of San Francisco; and SV=Silicon Valley/Peninsula).
† Tied with the restaurant listed directly above it

Top Food

Chinese
25 Tommy Toy's
Ton Kiang
Koi Palace/S
24 Yank Sing
23 Mandarin Gourmet/SV

Continental
23 Caprice, The/N
22 Dal Baffo/SV
21 Anton & Michel/S
Ovation
Bella Vista/SV

Dim Sum
25 Ton Kiang
Koi Palace/S
24 Yank Sing
23 Fook Yuen/SV
21 Hong Kong Flower/SV

Eclectic/International
25 Cafe La Haye/N
23 Firefly
22 Wappo Bar Bistro/N
21 Mixx/N
Stars

French (Bistro)
27 Bistro Jeanty/N
26 Fringale
25 Bistro Elan/SV
L'Amie Donia/SV
24 Chapeau!

French (Classic)
28 La Forêt/SV
27 Emile's/SV
26 Campton Place
Cafe Jacqueline
25 Chantilly/SV

French (New)
28 Ritz-Carlton Dining Room
Le Papillon/SV
Terra/N
La Folie
27 Fleur de Lys

Fusion
25 EOS
Roy's at Pebble Beach/S
24 House
23 Oritalia
22 Azie

Hamburgers
20 Mo's Burgers
Burger Joint
18 Balboa Cafe
17 Barney's
16 Liverpool Lil's

Indian
25 Amber India/SV
24 Vik's Chaat Corner/E
23 Shalimar
Indian Oven
22 Breads of India/E

Italian
26 Acquerello
25 Delfina
Tra Vigne/N
Bistro Don Giovanni/N
24 Oliveto Cafe/E

Japanese
27 Sushi Ran/N
25 Kyo-Ya
Maki
Kabuto Sushi
Kirala/E

Mediterranean
26 Rivoli/E
25 Bay Wolf/E
Lalime's/E
24 Chez Nous
Stokes Adobe/S

Mexican
24 Doña Tomás/E
23 La Taqueria
Las Camelias/N
Pancho Villa Taqueria
22 Aqui Cal-Mex Grill/SV

Middle Eastern/Greek
25 Evvia/SV
Kokkari Estiatorio
22 Maykedah
Truly Mediterranean
19 La Mediterranée

Pizza
27 Cheese Board/E
24 Zachary's Chicago Pizza/E
Arizmendi Bakery/E & SF
Tommaso's
22 Pauline's Pizza

Top Food

Seafood
27 Aqua
25 Swan Oyster Depot
   Pisces/SV
24 Farallon
23 Yabbies Coastal Kitchen

Spanish
22 Zarzuela
   César/E
21 Iberia/SV
20 B44
   Alegrias, Food From Spain

Steakhouses
25 Cole's Chop House/N
24 Vic Stewart's/E
   Morton's of Chicago
23 House of Prime Rib
   Harris'

Tapas
25 Isa
24 Chez Nous
20 Basque Nueva Cocina
19 Charanga
   Cha Cha Cha

Thai
25 Thep Phanom
24 Krungthai/SV
23 Marnee Thai
22 Royal Thai
21 Khan Toke

Vegetarian
27 Fleur de Lys
23 Flea St. Café/SV
22 Greens
   Millennium
19 Herbivore

Vietnamese
26 Slanted Door
25 Thanh Long
22 Ana Mandara
21 Tu Lan
   Le Cheval/E

Wild Cards
23 Helmand (Afghani)
22 Straits (Singaporean)
21 Angkor Wat (Cambodian)
20 Massawa (Eritrean)

Top Food by Special Feature

Breakfast*
24 JoAnn's Cafe/S
   Dottie's True Blue Cafe
   Mama's/Washington Sq.
   Emporio Rulli/N
   Gordon's/N

Brunch
26 Postrio
25 Wente Vineyards/E
24 Ritz-Carlton Terrace
   Viognier/SV
   Zuni Cafe

Cheese Course/Carts
28 Gary Danko
27 Boulevard
26 Jardinière
24 Zuni Cafe
21 Cosmopolitan Cafe

Hotel Dining
28 Ritz-Carlton Dining Room
   Ritz-Carlton Hotel
27 Masa's
   Hotel Vintage Ct.
26 Campton Place
   Campton Pl. Hotel
   Fifth Floor
   Hotel Palomar
   Pacific's Edge/S
   Highlands Inn

Late Night†
23 Bouchon/N
22 Taqueria Cancun
   Globe
21 bacar
   Brother's Korean

---

* Other than hotels
† Serves after 12:30 AM

Newcomers/Rated
25 Alfy's/N
   Cole's Chop House/N
24 Chez Nous
23 Jianna
   Santi/N

Newcomers/Unrated
   Asia de Cuba
   downtown/E
   Le Poisson Japonais/SV
   Miramonte/N
   Navio/S

People-Watching
27 Boulevard
26 Jardinière
   Postrio
24 Zuni Cafe
   Spago Palo Alto/SV

Tasting Menus
29 French Laundry/N
28 Gary Danko
   Ritz-Carlton Dining Room
27 Fleur de Lys
   Masa's

Wine Bars
25 EOS
21 bacar
18 Hayes & Vine
17 First Crush
14 Bubble Lounge

Worth a Trip
29 French Laundry/N
   Yountville
28 Chez Panisse/E
   Berkeley
   Terra/N
   St. Helena
27 Bistro Jeanty/N
   Yountville
26 Erna's Elderberry/E
   Oakhurst

Top Food by Location

Civic Center/Hayes Valley
26 Jardinière
24 Zuni Cafe
23 Hayes Street Grill
22 Millennium
   Bistro Clovis

Downtown/Embarcadero
27 Fleur de Lys
   Boulevard
   Aqua
   Masa's
26 Elisabeth Daniel, Rest.

Fisherman's Wharf
28 Gary Danko
22 Ana Mandara
21 Grandeho's Kamekyo
20 Scoma's
19 Mandarin

Haight-Ashbury/Cole Valley
25 Thep Phanom
   EOS
23 Indian Oven
22 Truly Mediterranean
21 Grandeho's Kamekyo

Marina/Cow Hollow
25 Isa
24 Three Seasons
   PlumpJack Cafe
23 Pane e Vino
22 Greens

Mission
26 Slanted Door
25 Delfina
24 Woodward's Garden
23 La Taqueria
   Watergate

Top Food

Nob Hill/Van Ness/Polk
28 Ritz-Carlton Dining Room
La Folie
26 Charles Nob Hill
Acquerello
24 Ritz-Carlton Terrace

Noe Valley/Castro
23 Hamano Sushi
Firefly
22 Ma Tante Sumi
Chloe's Cafe
21 Eric's

North Beach
26 Cafe Jacqueline
24 House
Mama's/Washington Sq.
Tommaso's
23 Jianna

Pacific Heights/Japantown
25 Maki
Cafe Kati
Meetinghouse
24 Chez Nous
22 Eliza's

Richmond/Sunset
25 Kabuto Sushi
Thanh Long
Ton Kiang
24 House
Chapeau!

SoMa
26 Hawthorne Lane
Fringale
25 Kyo-Ya
24 Yank Sing
Dine

East of San Francisco
28 Chez Panisse
27 Chez Panisse Café
Cheese Board
26 Rivoli
Erna's Elderberry

North of San Francisco
29 French Laundry
28 Terra
27 Bistro Jeanty
Sushi Ran
26 La Toque

South of San Francisco
27 Fresh Cream
26 Pacific's Edge
25 Club XIX
Roy's at Pebble Beach
Gayle's Bakery

Silicon Valley/Peninsula
28 Le Papillon
La Forêt
27 Emile's
26 Chez TJ
John Bentley's

Top Decor Ranking

29 Pacific's Edge/S

28 Garden Court
Ritz-Carlton Dining Room
Ahwahnee Dining Rm./E
Auberge du Soleil/N
Ana Mandara
Chateau Souverain Café/N

27 Farallon
Fleur de Lys
Ondine/N
Wente Vineyards/E
Caprice, The/N
French Laundry/N

26 Fifth Floor
Erna's Elderberry/S
Domaine Chandon/N
Jardinière
Kokkari Estiatorio
Top of the Mark
Kasbah Moroccan/N

El Paseo/N
Gary Danko
Boulevard
Nepenthe/S
Le Papillon/SV
La Forêt/SV
Rest. at Meadowood/N
Ovation
Postrio
Grand Cafe
Club XIX/S
Tra Vigne/N
Manka's Inverness/N
Compass Rose
Aqua
Roy's at Pebble Beach/S
Campton Place

25 Mikayla/N
Tommy Toy's
Cypress Club

Outdoors

Auberge du Soleil/N
B44
Bistro Don Giovanni/N
Bistro Elan/SV
Bistro Jeanty/N
Brix/N
Cafe Bastille
Cafe Flore
Cool Café/SV
Domaine Chandon/N
Empire Grill & Tap Rm./SV

Foreign Cinema
John Ash & Co./N
La Note/E
Lark Creek Inn/N
Left Bank/N
Marché aux Fleurs/N
Plouf
Ritz-Carlton Terrace
Spago Palo Alto/SV
Tra Vigne/N
Wente Vineyards/E

Romance

Acquerello
Cafe Jacqueline
Chez TJ/SV
Dal Baffo/SV
Elisabeth Daniel, Rest.
El Paseo/N
Erna's Elderberry/E
Flea St. Café/SV
Fleur de Lys
Fresh Cream/S

John Bentley's/SV
La Folie
La Fondue/SV
Maddalena's/Café Fino/SV
Manka's Inverness/N
Ovation
Perlot
Ritz-Carlton Dining Room
Terra/N
Woodward's Garden

Rooms

Ahwahnee Dining Rm./E
Ana Mandara
Aqua
Asia de Cuba
Azie
Bouchon/N
Boulevard
Cypress Club
Evvia/SV
Farallon
Fleur de Lys
Garden Court
Grand Cafe
Jardinière
Kokkari Estiatorio
La Toque/N
Le Colonial
Maddalena's/Café Fino/SV
Postrio
Ritz-Carlton Dining Room
St. Orres/N
Wild Hare/SV

Views

Albion River Inn/N
Auberge du Soleil/N
Beach Chalet Brewery
Bella Vista/SV
Caprice, The/N
Carnelian Room
Cielo/S
Cityscape
Cliff House
Domaine Chandon/N
Greens
Guaymas/N
Julius' Castle
Ledford House/N
Mikayla/N
Mistral/SV
Moss Beach Distillery/S
Navio/S
Nepenthe/S
Ondine/N
Pacific's Edge/S
Roy's at Pebble Beach/S
Sierra Mar/S
Top of the Mark

Top Service Ranking

28 Ritz-Carlton Dining Room
French Laundry/N
Le Papillon/SV
27 Erna's Elderberry/E
Fleur de Lys
Gary Danko
La Forêt/SV
26 Chez Panisse/E
La Toque/N
La Folie
Fifth Floor
Campton Place
Charles Nob Hill
Acquerello
Terra/N
Fresh Cream/S
Elisabeth Daniel, Rest.
Masa's
25 Domaine Chandon/N
Club XIX/S
Boulevard
Tommy Toy's
Ritz-Carlton Terrace
Emile's/SV
Auberge du Soleil/N
Chez Panisse Café/E
Jardinière
Pacific's Edge/S
Chez TJ/SV
Silks
24 Rest. at Meadowood/N
Aqua
Bay Wolf/E
Sent Sovi/SV
Big Four
Rivoli/E
El Paseo/N
Chapeau!
Postrio
Hawthorne Lane

Best Buys

Top Bangs For The Buck

List derived by dividing the cost of a meal into its ratings.

1. Arizmendi Bakery
2. Arizmendi Bakery/E
3. Cheese Board/E
4. Pancho Villa Taqueria
5. Burger Joint
6. Taqueria Cancun
7. El Balazo
8. La Cumbre Taqueria
9. La Taqueria
10. Truly Mediterranean
11. Downtown Bakery/N
12. Cactus Taqueria/E
13. Baja Fresh/SV
14. It's Tops Coffee Shop
15. Butler & The Chef
16. Vik's Chaat Corner/E
17. Model Bakery/N
18. Dottie's True Blue Cafe
19. Kate's Kitchen
20. Andale Taqueria/SV
21. Chloe's Cafe
22. Pork Store Cafe
23. Caffe Greco
24. Jimtown Store/N
25. Emporio Rulli/N
26. Picante Cocina Mexicana/E
27. Citrus Club
28. Pluto's
29. JoAnn's Cafe/S
30. Aqui Cal-Mex Grill/SV
31. Cafe 817/E
32. Red Tractor Cafe/E
33. Mama's Royal Cafe/E
34. Cafe Borrone/SV
35. Gayle's Bakery/S
36. Lovejoy's Tea Room
37. Café Fanny/E
38. Moishe's Pippic
39. Bette's Oceanview Diner/E
40. King of Thai

Additional Good Values

À Côté/E
Antica Trattoria
Bistro Aix
Breads of India/E
Cafe Gibraltar/S
Cha Cha Cha
Charanga
Chez Nous
Chez Panisse Café/E
Cool Café/SV
Doña Tomás/E
downtown/E
Gordon's/N
House
Hyde Street Bistro
Insalata's/N
Isa
JZ Cool/SV
Kathmandu West/SV
La Rue/E

La Villa Poppi
Le Charm
Le Soleil
Liberty Cafe & Bakery
L'Osteria del Forno
Luna Park
Marché aux Fleurs/N
Mario's Bohemian Cigar Store
Mazzini Trattoria/E
Mio Vicino/SV
Miramonte/N
Pane e Vino
Pesce
Pizzetta 211
Restaurant LuLu
St. Michael's Alley/SV
Swan Oyster Depot
Ti Couz
Tu Lan
Vivande Porta Via

Restaurant Directory

San Francisco

	F	D	S	C

Absinthe ●ⓁⓈ
| 19 | 22 | 19 | $36 |

398 Hayes St. (Gough St.), 415-551-1590

■ "Before or after the symphony", for a "swank night out" this "sumptuous", "chichi", "charming French bistro" with "art deco" decor hits all the right notes, bringing "splendid food", "amazing" cocktails and "Parisian-style glamour" to Hayes Valley; the "constant buzz" of its "hip over-30" bar scene makes it "popular" for "late-night carousing", but it's also "great for a tête-à-tête" brunch, making surveyors sigh Absinthe makes the heart grow "fonder and fonder."

Academy Grill ⓁⓂ
| 18 | 13 | 13 | $24 |

California Culinary Academy, 625 Polk St. (Turk St.), 415-292-8229

◪ "Part of the California Culinary Academy", this Tenderloin training temple teaches toques-to-be to "prepare and serve" Californian lunches and Mediterranean dinners; while the "uneven" fruits of their "good effort" "can be surprising" – "some dishes are great, others not", and "service is often clumsy" – many "find it fun to chat with" the "interesting students."

Ace Wasabi's ⓈⓂ
| 21 | 15 | 15 | $27 |

3339 Steiner St. (bet. Chestnut & Lombard Sts.), 415-567-4903

■ A "dynamite" Flying Kamikaze Roll and other "ingenious", "inventive" fin fare fashioned from "fish [as] fresh" as the "flirty waiters" lure "post-college Marina" singletons who "wait forever" for a table at this "Hard-Rock-Cafe-meets-sushi-spot"; the "cute waitresses'" cries can't compete with the cacophony of its "crowded", "chaotic" conditions, but happy-hour bingo (in which winners wangle a $20 deduction) is the Ace in the hole that "keeps it fun."

ACQUERELLO
| 26 | 23 | 26 | $53 |

1722 Sacramento St. (bet. Polk St. & Van Ness Ave.), 415-567-5432

■ For "special occasions", this Van Ness/Polk "diner's dream" "never disappoints", "setting the standard" with "heady", "heavenly", "incredibly imaginative Northern Italian food", a "world-class wine list" boasting over 750 vintages "presented in beautiful decanters", "impeccably" "gracious service" and a "posh", "polished" setting; though a paucity of patrons pooh-poohs the place as "a tad stiff by SF standards", most deem dining at this "former church" a "spiritual experience."

Alamo Square ⑤Ⓜ　　18 | 16 | 18 | $26

803 Fillmore St. (bet. Fulton & Grove Sts.), 415-440-2828
■ "Only the locals know" this French "have-it-your-way" fish house where they savor seafood grilled, sautéed, poached or blackened, then topped with their "choice of sauces"; wags warn that territorial Western Additioners "will be angry to find it listed", but "fresh" "affordable" fare and "personable" service that many label "just as good" as at "those stuffy, overpriced bistros" make this "cozy" room too fine "to keep secret."

Albona Ristorante Istriano　　22 | 15 | 23 | $35

545 Francisco St. (bet. Mason & Taylor Sts.), 415-441-1040
■ The "best part" of this "hidden gem" in North Beach is "proud" Bruno Viscovi, its "chatty", "charming proprietor" whose "friendly welcome" "makes you feel at home" (even if "your mother was never this cordial"); confident connoisseurs can cajole "him to recite the menu" then "make suggestions", but the uninitiated unfamiliar with the "pleasant surprises" and "Slavic-influenced" flavors of his "hearty", "authentic" Istrian fare ("different from" "the usual Italian") are advised to "let [him] order for you."

Alegrias, Food From Spain ⑤Ⓜ　　20 | 16 | 17 | $26

2018 Lombard St. (Webster St.), 415-929-8888
■ Though quotidian quaffers quip "after all that sangria I can't remember much", abstemious amigos admire this Spanish stalwart in the Marina for its "wonderful tapas" and "authentic paella" as well as its "friendly, down-home service"; the amorous also assess it as a "good date place" that's *muy* "romantic" and especially "fun on weekends" when "pleasant flamenco guitarists" serenade.

Alfred's Steak House Ⓛ⑤Ⓜ　　20 | 19 | 21 | $42

659 Merchant St. (bet. Kearny & Montgomery Sts.), 415-781-7058
■ "Still a happening" haven for "huge slabs", this "clubby" "classic steakhouse" (circa 1928) continues to "attract" "nostalgic" Porterhouse purists aching for some good "old-Frisco flavor" and "Caesar salad that's still prepared tableside"; though a troupe of "tradition" touters tut-tut that it "just isn't the same" since the 1997 move to its "dark" Downtown digs, and a few foes find its flesh fare "as tough as its waiters", devotees declare it's got "the meat to beat."

Alice's Ⓛ⑤Ⓜ　　18 | 16 | 15 | $17

1599 Sanchez St. (29th St.), 415-282-8999
◪ For most, this "trendy", "upscale" Chinese storefront is "worth the trip" to Noe Valley, scoring with "tasty" fare that's "always fresh and good" and a "pleasant setting"; still, "solid Californian" influences have some Sino-seekers saying it's "too Occidental", and many moan about an

"unaccommodating staff" that's "sometimes slow", sometimes "a bit hurried"; P.S. similarities to two competitors have the curious querying "are Eric's and Eliza's related?" (no, they're not).

Alioto's 🅛🅢🅜　　16　15　18　$31

8 Fisherman's Wharf (The Embarcadero), 415-673-0183
◪ For that "quintessential" cracked-crab, sourdough-bread, white-wine meal of yesteryear coupled with a "great view of the Bay", some surveyors say "get a window seat" and "dive in" at this Fisherman's Wharf "classic", a Southern Italian seafooder that's been a "SF staple" since 1935; despite the "out-of-towner" onslaught, others sigh it's grown "stale" and "shabby around the edges", with an "uninspired" staff.

Allegro 🅢🅜　　20　18　20　$34

1701 Jones St. (Broadway), 415-928-4002
■ Little-known beyond the politicos and Russian Hill royalty who frequent it, this "great neighborhood" haunt "scores" for its Italian fare, "friendly" service and "intimate" ambiance; given the high-powered clientele, it's no surprise that coddled commenters coo about the "outstanding individual attention."

Alma　　–　–　–　M

1101 Valencia St. (22nd St.), 415 401 8959
In a case of reverse gentrification, you might actually hear some Spanish at this eagerly awaited Mission newcomer, scheduled at press time to open in The Rooster's old coop; chef Johnny Alamilla is no Johnny-come-lately to the local dining scene, having turned the city on to *la cocina de la vida loca* at the short-lived Che in SoMa; expect Nuevo Latino cuisine with lots of soul (*alma* in Spanish).

Amici's East Coast Pizzeria 🅛🅢🅜　　18　11　16　$16

2033 Union St. (bet. Buchanan & Webster Sts.), 415-885-4500
■ Part of a SF chainlet, this Marina local is "thin-crust pizza paradise" for homesick Gothamites who declare it's the "closest thing to the East Coast [variety] there is"; sure, the joint "lacks atmosphere", but "the best part is that they deliver" and you can get your pie in a New York minute, thanks to "lightening fast" service.

ANA MANDARA 🅛🅢🅜　　22　28　21　$43

Ghirardelli Sq., 891 Beach St. (Polk St.), 415-771-6800
■ This "*très belle* Indochine"-inspired "stunner" "takes you away" from the Wharf with "exotic" decor (a mélange of "tropical" "lushness" and "Las Vegas" "theatricality") and "delicious" cuisine "beautifully presented" by "smiling servers"; still, some cynics say it's a touch "too pricey" for its "tad-too-tiny" portions and, like its celebrity investor, Don Johnson, it has "more glamour than taste."

Andalu ▣　　　　　－　－　－　M
3198 16th St. (bet. Guerrero & Valencia Sts.), 415-621-2211
Named for the birthplace of Spanish tapas, this casual
Mission eatery (slated at press time to open in early
September) features an assemblage of International small
plates (from spring rolls to ravioli to tuna tartare tacos) at
budget-traveler prices ($5–$12); the festive dining room
features 16-foot ceilings hung with curtains, an 18-foot-
long dazzling mural and lots of bar seating for walk-ins and
carousers from the neighborhood.

Angkor Borei ▣▣▣　　▽ 20　12　19　$17
3471 Mission St. (Cortland Ave.), 415-550-8417
■ In lower Bernal Heights, this "unusual little treasure
hidden among the salsa clubs and neighborhood markets"
pleases its few but fervent fans with "scrumptious" send-
ups of Cambodian food and an amazingly "sweet and
friendly staff"; sure, the "room is tacky and you can
hear the nightclub next door", but at these "low, low,
low prices", "I'll take it."

Angkor Wat ▣▣▣　　21　16　19　$22
4217 Geary Blvd. (bet. 6th & 7th Aves.), 415-221-7887
■ It's "fun to take off your shoes" at this Inner Richmonder
and sit lotus-style while "tasting" "outstanding Cambodian
cuisine" (including "adventurous" "spicy shark" and
"excellently prepared" curries and noodles) that's "high in
flavor" and "reasonably priced"; yes, the "gilded" decor
may "need freshening up", but "dignified", "courteous"
service and "delicious" "food make up for it"; P.S. don't
miss the traditional "dancing on [some] weekends."

Anjou ▣　　　　　22　18　21　$35
44 Campton Pl. (bet. Post & Sutter Sts.), 415-392-5373
■ "Hidden" "in a funky alleyway" "off Union Square", this
"unpretentious", "Parisian-style hole-in-the-wall" is a
"sweet little restaurant with sweet little prices" according
to the faithful who flock for its "classic", "authentically
French" bistro fare (including "good-value" fixed-price
lunches and pre-theater dinners) and "meticulous" yet
"friendly" service; *oui, oui,* the "cramped" room is "intimate
by necessity", but "who cares when the food is so good?"

Antica Trattoria ▣　　21　17　20　$32
2400 Polk St. (Union St.), 415-928-5797
■ For "true Italian food", "forget North Beach" and cancel
that "trip to Italy" declare devotees of this "exceptional"
Polk Street trattoria whose "rustic", "mouthwatering" menu,
"cute waiters" and "noisy, frenetic" atmosphere are as
"authentic" as at any "hangout in Lucca" or "neighborhood
place in Verona"; "getting a reservation can be a problem"
and "parking can be difficult to find", but the persevering
proclaim "this is the real deal."

Anzu 🅛🅢🅜
22 | 22 | 21 | $46

Hotel Nikko, 222 Mason St. (O'Farrell St.), 415-394-1100
■ A surf 'n' turfer with a twist, this "upscale" (and "pricey") Japanese-American Downtowner allows diners to delight in "delicious beef prepared by a Swiss chef" as well as "fresh" sushi that's "like buttah", all "superbly presented" by "attentive-but-not-hovering" servers; "great before the theater", it's a "quiet and classy" "place where you can have a conversation", and live "piano music in the background" makes for a "jazzy Sunday brunch."

Aperto 🅛🅢🅜
20 | 15 | 20 | $28

1434 18th St. (Connecticut St.), 415-252-1625
■ Italophiles have found their thrill on Potrero Hill at this "well-kept secret"; regulars say the "consistently tasty" "fresh pastas" are the "best [items] on the menu" but also recommend the "standout specials" (listed on a "giant chalkboard") for "something outside the usual"; with a "welcoming ambiance", it "delivers a nice experience", though some implore "spend some money on decor."

AQUA 🅛🅜
27 | 26 | 24 | $59

252 California St. (bet. Battery & Front Sts.), 415-956-9662
■ SF's ultimate "power restaurant", this top-dollar Downtowner reels in "beautiful people", "expense-accounters" looking to "impress clients" and "debonair" "seafood freaks" who all celebrate chef Michael Mina's "fabulous" "foie-gras'd", "fueled-with-flavor fish" fare that's "even richer than the clientele" and "astoundingly presented" amidst "gorgeous" minimalist decor; though a fin-icky few carp about the "chilly" service and "deafening din", Aqua-lytes say it's "worth robbing a bank" for.

Arizmendi Bakery 🅛🅢⊘
24 | 13 | 19 | $7

1331 Ninth Ave. (bet. Irving & Judah Sts.), 415-566-3117
■ It's "impossible to get just one item" at this Inner Sunset "old-world" outpost, a "cute", "quaint" "neighborhood bakery co-op" where locals "can't stop stopping" for "fabulous baked goods", including "delicious" "daily bread", "amazing scones", "addictive" "homemade pizzas" and "the world's best sourdough"; with just a few tables and a bench outside, though, it's best to "get a loaf and take it to Golden Gate Park."

Arlequin Food to Go 🅛🅢🅜
▽ 21 | 17 | 18 | $13

384B Hayes St. (bet. Franklin & Gough Sts.), 415-626-1211
■ Brought to you by the owners of nearby Absinthe, this little-known "easygoing", "European-style" spot on a trendy block in Hayes Valley is a "convenient" and "delicious" fast-food alternative, with "great sandwiches" and "quick service"; though most take out, some savor "a sunny day" in the "gorgeous little garden" over a glass of wine and a "yummy Croque Arlequin."

A. Sabella's L S M | 17 | 15 | 18 | $34 |

2766 Taylor St. (Jefferson St.), 415-771-6775

■ "For those who want the Fisherman's Wharf experience", this "friendly" veteran seafooder (afloat since 1920) "consistently" cranks out "solid" "old standbys" such as "tasty chowder" and "good, fresh" "fish dishes", while its arched windows afford "amazing views" of the "busy" bay; though some locals lament its "touristy" bent and label the food "unimaginative" and "a bit pricey for what it is", most find it a "fun place."

Asia de Cuba ◗ L S M | – | – | – | M |

Clift Hotel, 495 Geary St. (bet. Mason & Taylor Sts.), 415-929-2300

Hip hotelier Ian Schrager's new Asian-Cuban hot spot, in the $50-million renovated Downtown Clift Hotel, is splitting at the seams with an 'I'm too sexy for my shirt' crowd in search of the next new thing; colossal plates of fanciful fare served family style and specialty cocktails (think Lychee Martini) are as excessive as Philippe Starck's darkly lit dining room awash in a sea of brown velvet curtains, exaggeratedly high-back banquettes and baroque etched-mirrored communal tables (the better to see yourself in).

AsiaSF S M | 17 | 18 | 19 | $29 |

201 Ninth St. (Howard St.), 415-255-2742

■ "Hot" "boys who look like" "outrageous" girls are the "draw" at this "wildly energetic" SoMa supper club, a "campy" "crowd-pleaser" 'manned' by "phenomenal gender illusionists"; when not "dancing on the bar" and "shocking" the out-of-towners, these "friendly-as-can-be" "lip-synchers" do double duty tending tables, "so be prepared to wait" for the Cal-Asian tapas, which are "surprisingly good" considering that "the food is secondary" to the "fun, fun, fun show."

Asqew Grill L S M | – | – | – | I |

1607 Haight St. (Clayton St.), 415-701-9301
3348 Steiner St. (Chestnut St.), 415-931-9201

There's nothing askew at this Cal dinner-on-a-stick duo in the Haight and Marina specializing in skewered grub of all stripes in an upscale, fast-food setting (there's even a grilled banana split); sides are included, so you can fill your belly for about 10 bucks in about 10 minutes.

Avenue 9 L S M | 19 | 14 | 18 | $27 |

1243 Ninth Ave. (bet. Irving St. & Lincoln Way), 415-664-6999

◪ "Interesting", "inventive" New American "food is the best part of this" "high-end" Inner Sunset "neighborhood haunt" fans feel, followed by "friendly service" and "funky decor"; however, some are "not impressed" by the "sometimes-too-creative" kitchen, while others deplore the "dim light and cramped seating"; still, most agree the "gourmet food at bargain prices" is a "great value."

Azie 🆂🅼   22 24 20 $50

826 Folsom St. (bet. 4th & 5th Sts.), 415-538-0918
☑ LuLu's "high-energy" sister, this "upscale" SoMa expense-accounter draws "dressed-down millionaires" and "Silicon Valley nerds with a splash of hip" who pose before "brilliant decor" and savor "sublime to sassy" to "spectacular" Asian-French cuisine; detractors declare the "downsides" are "over-the-top Disney" digs, the "din of the bar scene" and dropping "maximum" dollars for "miniscule portions"; at least recent "dot-com eliminations" mean "you can now get a table."

BACAR ◑🅻🆂🅼   21 24 20 $47

448 Brannan St. (bet. 3rd & 4th Sts.), 415-904-4100
☑ "You could get lost for days" in this "sprawling", "dazzling" SoMa "work in progress" that's "three stories tall, a thousand wines rich" and fast becoming a "trendy" favorite of the "Gen X" "dot-commie crowd"; the vinaceous variety at this "by-the-glass mecca" generates much "hype", but many say chef Arnold Eric "Wong is Right" on track with his "innovative" New American "nibbles" as well; almost all agree the place "still needs to smooth some kinks" in service and sound levels.

Backflip ◑   13 20 13 $28

Phoenix Hotel, 601 Eddy St. (bet. Larkin & Polk Sts.), 415-771-3547
☑ "Playful" "retro decor", "potent drinks", "thundering music" and a "wickedly crowded dance floor" are "what you go for" at this "groovy", "ultra-hip" aquateria in the "terrible" Tenderloin's "fun" Phoenix Hotel; few fans flip for its "finger food", though, with some saying the ambient "eye candy" is better than the Cal-Japanese Cocktail Cuisine Menu; regardless, reviewers rave that the regular "pool parties are epic."

Baker Street Bistro 🅻🆂   19 14 18 $27

2953 Baker St. (bet. Greenwich & Lombard Sts.), 415-931-1475
■ "Delicious", "down-home", "authentic French food" "with no bells and whistles" and "charming, friendly service" are the draws at this "terrific" "sleeper" "tucked away in Cow Hollow"; "whether you think it's cozy" and "cute" or "dingy" and "drab", "expect to be eavesdropped on" as the "tables are too" "tight"; still, wallet-watchers say that "unbelievable prices" (especially for the prix fixe dinner) "justify the leg cramps."

Balboa Cafe 🅻🆂🅼   18 17 18 $28

3199 Fillmore St. (Greenwich St.), 415-921-3944
■ "Where the elite eat their meat", this "famous" "old faithful" "anchoring the ["yuppie" bar–riddled] triangle" is "a solid" "standby" "for society watching", where

"SUV-driving" singletons sup on "consistently good if unimaginative" American fare (most say stick to the "scrumptious burgers"); some can't "deal with the loafer-wearing Cow Hollow crowd" and "men's locker room" atmosphere, but most enjoy this "slice of SF."

Baldoria 🅂🅜　　　20｜18｜19｜$28

2162 Larkin St. (Green St.), 415-447-0441

■ The name means 'noisy fun', but it might as well stand for "great neighborhood place", as in this Van Ness/Polk "gem" where "lovely" Italian classics at "reasonable prices" delight diners and "the scent of garlic" permeates the air; it's a "charming setting for first dates", but be warned that some wonder "what's better looking . . . the food or the waiters?"; P.S. savvy surveyors suggest you "cab it."

Barney's
Gourmet Hamburger 🅛🅂🅜　　17｜11｜13｜$13

3344 Steiner St. (Chestnut St.), 415-563-0307
4138 24th St. (Castro St.), 415-282-7770

■ "This isn't your typical burger (but then this isn't your typical town either")" note noshers about this Bay Area chain, known for "about a million varieties" of "creative and decadent" patties and a "fantastic array of toppings"; "something about sitting outside makes the burgers even better" (maybe since the "decor's unappetizing"); however, the "unresponsive" staff needs to beef up its training.

Basil 🅛🅂🅜　　　20｜17｜17｜$22

1175 Folsom St. (bet. 7th & 8th Sts.), 415-552-8999

■ Supplicants of this "scrumptious", "sophisticated" SoMa Siamese are hardly tongue Thai'd in expressing their "compliments" for the "flair" of its "delightful", "imaginative" fare, with some even reporting "taste buds screaming in ecstasy" (though a few grumble that the "classics" on offer have been "Westernized"); the "delightful ambiance" of its "refreshingly modern setting" also scores with a "hip" crowd.

Basque Nueva Cocina Vasca 🅂🅜　20｜16｜19｜$27

398 Seventh St. (Harrison St.), 415-581-0550

■ Chef Barney Brown is hitting his stride at this "promising" SoMa "newcomer" with his "innovative" menu of "delicious" Spanish and French dishes emphasizing "tasty" Basque tapas that are "as good as they are different"; sharing the "reasonably priced" plates makes for "good group dinners" and a "fun" "night out", prompting "young, hip" patrons to proclaim "what a find!"

Beach Chalet Brewery 🅛🅂🅜　12｜18｜13｜$23

1000 Great Hwy. (bet. Fulton St. & Lincoln Way), 415-386-8439

◪ Some surveyors suggest you "grab a table by the window", drink in a "magnificent" "view of the sunset" and chase it with a "good" "housemade" English-style beer at this brewpub overlooking Ocean Beach; others opine, though, that the "awesome location" and "beautiful WPA-era murals" can't "make up for" the "uninspired" American food, "shoddy service" and "hectic" atmosphere.

Bella Trattoria 🄻🅂🄼   21 17 21 $29
3854 Geary Blvd. (3rd Ave.), 415-221-0305
■ Nothing takes the chill out of a "cold, foggy Inner Richmond evening" better than "a belly full" of "sensational" "fresh pasta" (or other Italian "delights") at this "homey" "corner" storefront trattoria, complemented by "doting" service from a "welcoming staff" that "makes you feel like you're one of the family"; "*mama mia*" the devoted declare, "is this Roma or is it heaven?"

BETELNUT PEJIU WU 🄻🅂🄼   22 22 17 $31
2030 Union St. (Buchanan St.), 415-929-8855
☑ The crowds of "beautiful people" "dreaming about" small plates of "great Pan-Asian fare" can make this "stylish" Cow Hollow beer house a "hard-to-get reservation"; "you still must wait" at the "bustling bar", so knock back a "fun girlie drink" and brace yourself for the "inconsistent", often "arrogant" service; N.B. the food rating may not reflect a post-*Survey* chef change.

B44 🄻🄼   20 17 18 $33
44 Belden Pl. (bet. Bush & Pine Sts.), 415-986-6287
■ Catalonian-cuisine cognoscenti claim chef-owner Daniel Olivella's "large selection" of "delicious paellas" and other "rustic, hearty" dishes "full of passion and garlic" are so "authentic" "you'll swear you're in Barcelona" rather than his "lively Spanish bistro" Downtown; but though the "to-die-for sangria" may "bring back memories", many would like to forget the "deafening" "din" of the "crowded", "industrial" dining room.

Big Four 🄻🅂🄼   22 25 24 $45
Huntington Hotel, 1075 California St. (Taylor St.), 415-771-1140
■ Named for the four fat cats who built the Southern Pacific railroad, this "plush", "clubby", "elegant" Nob Hill New American will "make you feel like a robber baron" with its "dignified service" worthy of a "private club"; advocates insist a "quiet rendezvous" here, supping on chef Gloria Ciccarone-Nehls' "superior" cooking, is the "best cure for excessive exposure to dot-commers."

Biscuits & Blues 🅂🄼   13 13 14 $22
401 Mason St. (Geary St.), 415-292-2583
☑ True-blue Biscuit believers boast "if you like the blues" and "good, low-down home cooking for next to nothing", this popular Downtown subterranean spot "is the place to

go"; others say that "great music" is "the main attraction" and scoff that the "Southern-style food" is "just ok"; but even if "it's not a place for fine dining", all agree it's "meant to be fun, and is!"

Bistro Aix ⑤Ⓜ 21 | 18 | 19 | $30

3340 Steiner St. (bet. Chestnut & Lombard Sts.), 415-202-0100

■ "A standout in the Marina", this "tucked-away" Med is no longer a carefully "kept secret" thanks to exuberant Aix-philes extolling its "creative, tasty", "fairly priced" fare and "amicable staff"; regular visitors to this outpost of "Provence in SF" recommend you avoid the "noisy", "cramped interior" by "sitting outside" on the "romantic", "adorable patio" in the tented, "heated back garden."

Bistro Clovis ⓁⓈⓂ 22 | 17 | 20 | $31

1596 Market St. (Franklin St.), 415-864-0231

■ "So perfectly French it's hard to describe in English" fawn flummoxed followers inflamed with feeling for this "humble", "homey" Hayes Valley "sleeper"; "delicious" bistro offerings and an "excellent" "wine-tasting" sampler make it an "inexpensive way to recreate your vacation to France" (sans the "attitude"); P.S. an "easy walk from the opera house", it's a "perfect" "pre-performance choice."

Bix ⓁⓈⓂ 22 | 25 | 21 | $42

56 Gold St. (Montgomery St.), 415-433-6300

■ "Secreted" like a "speakeasy" in a dark Downtown "alley", this "swank", "still-happening" supper club so drips with "1940s Hollywood" "glamour" that you'll "picture Ginger Rogers and Fred Astaire at the bar" as waiters in "spiffy" "white dinner jackets" "armed with the best martinis" around serve "great" Traditional American fare; it's the "live jazz singer and piano player", though, who "make it truly memorable."

Bizou ⓁⓂ 23 | 19 | 21 | $38

598 Fourth St. (Brannan St.), 415-543-2222

■ Peddling "tender beef" cheeks before they were trendy, chef-owner Loretta Keller continues to "interest" SoMa folk with her "mix of traditional", "rustic French" fare and "innovative cooking"; the resulting "robust" eats are served by a "knowledgeable, accommodating staff" at "closely spaced tables" in a "charming, unpretentious" environment that's "what a bistro should be: noisy, casual and fun."

Black Cat ◗Ⓜ 15 | 18 | 15 | $37

501 Broadway (Kearny St.), 415-981-2233

◥ Reed Hearon's "re-engineered" "see-and-be-seen" North Beach hot spot/jazz bar ("check the table next to you for a celebrity") is "now on its third life in three years", having jettisoned its multiculti menu for a French bistro focus and undergone a "charming" Provençal remodeling; many feel "its latest incarnation really works", but "surly staffers" prompt disappointed hep cats to hiss they're "not going to cross this path again."

Blowfish, Sushi To Die For L S M | 22 | 20 | 15 | $32 |
2170 Bryant St. (20th St.), 415-285-3848

◪ If you like your "sushi with a scene", you'll probably think this Mission "hipster" hot spot "rocks" thanks to "enticing", "consistently fresh" (and "pricey") creations, "daring sake mixed drinks", "ultra-modern decor" featuring "weird" "Japanese animation" cels and a "high-energy", "techno-charged" atmosphere; know, though, that the "pounding music" can reach "ear-splitting" levels and some "aloof staffers" are about "as warm as the fish"; N.B. despite the name, the bill of fare is usually fugu-free.

Blue L S M | 16 | 14 | 16 | $20 |
2337 Market St. (bet. Castro & Noe Sts.), 415-863-2583

◪ This "relaxed" storefront in a "great location" draws Castroites with "honest", "homestyle" American "comfort food" at "good prices" served by "cute waiters" who provide "friendly, if not particularly efficient, service"; despite "bland decor" and "cramped" conditions, it remains a popular "see-and-be-seen" scene.

Blue Plate, The M | 18 | 15 | 17 | $26 |
3218 Mission St. (29th St.), 415-282-6777

◪ Bernal Heights diners are divided on whether this "unpretentious", "hip" hangout "hidden" in a "not-so-great" area is "a real find" or just a place with "potential" that "tries hard but doesn't quite make it"; devotees dig the "amazing", "ever-changing seasonal" Cal-American menu, "funky decor" and "great music (with actual LPs spinning)", but detractors dis the "disinterested" staff and wonder "aren't blue-plate [specials] supposed to be a deal?"

Bocca Rotis S M | 18 | 15 | 17 | $27 |
1 W. Portal Ave. (Ulloa St.), 415-665-9900

◪ Rejoicing regulars "thank God for this" "hip" spot for "families and friends" in West Portal, a "charming Italian-French" bistro with "more style than most" serving "hearty", "aromatic" chow (the sweet-toothed suggest you "save room" for the "gooey rich desserts"); but doubters deride the kitchen's "lack of consistency" and say the "spacious, sunny dining room" can get too crowded" and "noisy."

Bontà Ristorante S | 19 | 16 | 21 | $32 |
2223 Union St. (bet. Fillmore & Steiner Sts.), 415-929-0407

■ "Enthusiastic owners" preside over a staff of "friendly, knowledgeable" waiters at this "quaint", "cute-as-a-button" Cow Hollow Italian serving "scrumptious" "hand made pastas" and "great risottos"; as long on "romantic" "ambiance" as it is short on space, it's a "charming" "favorite" of the "Union Street crowd" (who "wants it kept a secret") and considered by many the "ultimate" "neighborhood" "date place."

BOULEVARD 🅛🅢🅜   27 26 25 $52
1 Mission St. (Steuart St.), 415-543-6084

■ "A feast for the palate and the eyes", this "bustling" "top-drawer" Embarcadero American known for its "impeccable everything" is the Most Popular spot for the fifth consecutive *Survey*; it's "sure to impress" with chef Nancy Oakes' "mouthwatering" "extravagant food" (is the "fish flown in from heaven?"), a "fabulous wine selection", designer Pat Kuleto's "knockout" "belle époque decor" and "first-rate" service; it's "the consummate dining experience – hard to get in, expensive, worth every penny."

Brandy Ho's 🅛🅢🅜   18 11 14 $20
217 Columbus Ave. (bet. Broadway & Pacific Ave.), 415-788-7527

◪ "When you order" remember "hot means hot" caution constant customers of this Chinatowner that "continues its tradition of spicy food" – otherwise "be ready" to "cool the burn" from its "consistently" "satisfying" fiery Chinese fare offered at rock-bottom prices; a less committed clientele calls it a "greasy spoon" with an "uninspired" menu, "no ambiance" and "assembly line" service.

Brazen Head ●🅢🅜⧥   19 18 19 $30
3166 Buchanan St. (Greenwich St.), 415-921-7600

■ You might "walk past it a hundred times", since it "doesn't have a name on the door", but those who've "discovered this secret" Cow Hollow haunt say it's "everything a neighborhood tavern should be"; named after the oldest pub in Ireland, it offers "stick-to-your-ribs" American food, "excellent service from Eddie [Savino], proprietor extraordinaire", a "comfortable, dark" interior and a kitchen that stays open until 1 AM; P.S. "no reservations."

Brother-in-Law's Bar-B-Que 🅛🅢   21 4 11 $14
705 Divisadero St. (Grove St.), 415-931-7427

■ "It's hard to resist the aroma" "wafting" from this "funky" Western Addition "hole-in-the-wall" "rib joint" that draws people from across the city looking to "pig out" on its famous "finger-licking" barbecue and "down-home" greens; make no bones about it, "the place is a dump", so getting it "to go is a good idea."

Brother's Korean Restaurant 🅛🅢🅜   21 6 12 $20
4128 Geary Blvd. (bet. 5th & 6th Aves.), 415-387-7991 ●
4014 Geary Blvd. (bet. 4th & 5th Aves.), 415-668-2028

■ Wondering "where the Koreans eat"? – head to this duo of "do-it-yourself" late-night barbecues in the Inner Richmond serving "smoking-good" Seoul food; be prepared for "abrupt service", though, and "wear something machine washable", as you'll "come out smelling like a house afire"; P.S. the 4014 branch is "quieter."

Bruno's ●   – | – | – | M
2389 Mission St. (20th St.), 415-648-7701
As we go to press, this landmark Mission chameleon is changing its color again; proprietor Jon Varnadoe (of Foreign Cinema) plans to offer simple retro Italiano grub in the spirit of its original '70s incarnation, with recession-era prices to match; although dinner will be served Tuesday–Saturday, the hip-as-ever adjoining nightclub and lounge will feature live music seven days a week.

Bubble Lounge ●M   14 | 22 | 14 | $34
714 Montgomery St. (bet. Jackson & Washington Sts.), 415-434-4204
◪ Self-proclaimed "champagne sluts" love this "beautiful" Downtown lounge for sparkling wines and cocktails best described as "bubblicious" (the name of one peachy concoction); but bubble-bursters foam that it's saddled with a "staff [whose] attitude" borders on "rude" that serves up "plain" appetizers worth "skipping" ("they have food?" "who notices?")

Buca di Beppo ◪S◪   15 | 18 | 17 | $23
855 Howard St. (bet. 4th & 5th Sts.), 415-543 7673
See review in Silicon Valley/Peninsula Directory.

Buca Giovanni S◪   19 | 18 | 19 | $33
800 Greenwich St. (bet. Columbus Ave. & Mason St.), 415-776-7766
◪ For many, this Italian with a "romantic", "subterranean" setting still looks and feels like "North Beach out of central casting", with "tasty", "old-fashioned" pastas and "friendly service"; other veterans sadly suggest "its reputation exceeds its execution", though the "very good rabbit" dishes are still "favorites", as they were in the days when founder Giovanni Leone raised the bunnies himself.

Burger Joint ◪S◪≠   20 | 14 | 15 | $10
807 Valencia St. (19th St.), 415-824-3494
◼ Decked out in "cute" "retro diner decor", this "casually hip" Mission "walk-up" "hits the spot" with what many deem "the best damn burgers in the city" ("great milkshakes" too); since the "grilled" patties are fashioned from "juicy Niman Ranch" "hormone-free" beef, "you don't feel [as] guilty" indulging that "PMS-requisite" red-meat urge.

Butler & The Chef Cafe, The ◪◪   18 | 20 | 19 | $15
155A South Park St. (bet. 2nd & 3rd Sts.), 415-896-2075
◼ "Very French in every way but the attitude" (and "the cigarette smoke"), this "charming", "welcoming" South

Park spot where the Gallic-minded "breakfast daily" on "yummy pastries" and "grab" "great sandwiches" (such as the Croque Provençale) has many saying "we need more like it"; P.S. culinary collectors should note that elements of the "beautiful antique decor", on loan from an affiliated Potrero Hill store, are for sale.

butterfly ❂ — 18 | 20 | 15 | $36

1710 Mission St. (bet. Duboce Ave. & 14th St.), 415-864-5575

◪ "Relentlessly hip" (and "loud"), this Mission supper club that recently winged its way onto the scene draws an "arty-gone-dot-com crowd" like moths to a flame with its "imaginative" tapas-style Pacific Rim fare ("it's all about the fish tacos"), potent drinks that "will put butterflies in your belly" and a "cool DJ/live-jazz vibe"; critics gripe that "slow service", "tiny portions" and "out-of-control prices" mean it "isn't *that* cool"; N.B. a recent chef change may outdate the food score.

Cafe Bastille 🄻 Ⓜ — 17 | 16 | 17 | $26

22 Belden Pl. (bet. Bush & Pine Sts.), 415-986-5673

◼ Replete with "fresh-from-France" waiters, "authentic" bistro fare and "Frenchy" decor, this "chic" Downtown cafe feels "right from the Left Bank"; "office workers storm the place on sunny days to eat a Croque Monsieur", but at night "yuppies on dates" come out to soak up the strains of live jazz (Thursday–Saturday); P.S. patriots praise its Bastille Day bash, billed as the "biggest in the U.S."

Café Claude 🄻 Ⓜ — 16 | 16 | 15 | $24

7 Claude Ln. (bet. Grant Ave. & Kearny St.), 415-392-3515

◪ Yet another "très français" bistro "with back-alley appeal" and "live jazz" on the weekends, Claude (as insiders call it) "seems to have imported everything from Paris", including the "haughty waiters" and "good" (if "pedestrian") Gallic fare; although it's a perennially popular place for a "cozy lunchtime rendezvous" Downtown, wallet-watchers hasten here for the "three-course prix fixe" on Saturday nights.

Cafe Cuvée Ⓢ — 20 | 16 | 17 | $25

2073 Market St. (14th St.), 415-621-7488

◼ A "lovely oasis of calm" in the bustling Castro, this "small" storefront corner cafe whips up a "changing menu" of "beautifully updated classic dishes", such as honey-lavender roast chicken, using "high-quality", often organic ingredients; despite downsides of "slow service" and long waits for brunch ("go early"), it remains a "favorite secret place" for a small posse of surveyors.

Cafe de la Presse 🄻 Ⓢ Ⓜ — 14 | 13 | 12 | $21

352 Grant Ave. (Bush St.), 415-249-0900

◪ Adjacent to the Triton Hotel, this wine bar/cafe/newsstand "exists for homesick French tourists" who don't mind "paying Paris prices for a cappuccino" and Union Square shoppers who want to grab a "quick snack" and catch up on "foreign magazines"; although there's a more formal dining room, critics say stick to "people-watching" and a "glass of wine."

Cafe de Paris L'Entrecôte 🄻🄢🄼   16 | 16 | 18 | $33

2032 Union St. (bet. Buchanan & Webster Sts.), 415-931-5006
◪ "Great entrecôte and pommes frites" are the hallmarks of this "bustling" Cow Hollow "hangout" serving otherwise "variable", "uncomplicated bistro fare"; sidewalk seating makes "a good place for people-watching on Union Street" as well as an alternative to an interior that "lacks a sense of excitement."

Cafe Flore 🄻🄢🄼⇴   15 | 17 | 13 | $16

2298 Market St. (Noe St.), 415-621-8579
■ Though the American fare on offer is "surprisingly good", "it's not about the food, darling!" says the "hip, [mostly] gay" clientele that flocks to this "hectic" corner cafe "in the heart of the Castro"; "it's about the sights", so snag a coveted seat on the patio, "have a latte" "and sip it all in."

Cafe For All Seasons 🄻🄢🄼   19 | 14 | 19 | $24

150 W. Portal Ave. (bet. 14th Ave. & Vicente St.), 415-665-0900
■ This "always reliable", "always crowded" standby "in a good West Portal location" is as "comfortable" as a worn glove, thanks to a "friendly staff" and "good old Americana" food fashioned from "high-quality, fresh ingredients"; some "wish they would take reservations" and tone down the "daunting noise level", but others "wouldn't change a thing"; P.S. "great weekend brunch."

CAFE JACQUELINE 🄢   26 | 20 | 21 | $39

1454 Grant Ave. (bet. Green & Union Sts.), 415-981-5565
■ "You owe it to yourself" to visit this "endearing", "all-soufflé, all-the-time" French "gem" where "too-cute-for-words" chef-owner Jacqueline Marguiles turns out "airy" "works of art" ("both savory and sweet") that are "always perfect in texture and flavor"; although dinner can be a "pricey" ("the eggs aren't the only things inflated") "two to three-hour experience" and service a bit "snooty", it's "still one of the quaintest places to eat" in North Beach.

CAFE KATI 🄢   25 | 19 | 21 | $42

1963 Sutter St. (bet. Fillmore & Webster Sts.), 415-775-7313
■ "Everything comes piled high" at this "trendy" Japantown "joint" known for chef Kirk Webber's "edible architecture" – an "excellent fusion" of East-meets-West flavors resulting in "towering creations" that "taste as good as they look"; as with the "exquisite" Californian cuisine and "incredible wine list", fans find the "first-class" service "a delight", though the "crammed dining room" gets "loud."

Cafe Marimba L S M   19 17 14 $25
2317 Chestnut St. (bet. Divisadero & Scott Sts.), 415-776-1506
■ For "distinctive" "Oaxacan moles" and other "real" "regional" south-of-the-border food "without leaving the Marina", surveyors swear by this "spirited spot" with a "deafeningly loud" "in-your-face atmosphere" that's "always hopping" thanks to "funky" "Day of the Dead" decor and "twentysomethings" swilling strong drinks that "will spank you!"; others wish the "inattentive staff" was half as "lively" and complain of "nightmare weekend" waits.

Cafe Monk   20 21 18 $33
564 Fourth St. (bet. Brannan & Bryant Sts.), 415-777-1331
■ Devotees declare "break your vows" of abstinence at the "30-foot refectory table" in this "hip" SoMa spot, then genuflect to its new chef, Randy Windham, who resurrected its kitchen last fall with a "small", "daily changing menu" comprised of "wonderful" Cal-Med cuisine complemented by "well-chosen wines"; "sleek" "industrial" trappings (by the Limn design firm) give it a "cool" "vibe", but some complain the "munchkin portions" are as "minimalist" as the decor.

Café Mozart S   18 21 21 $38
708 Bush St. (Powell St.), 415-391-8480
◨ Lovebirds longing for a "romantic" rendezvous to celebrate a "special occasion" "go for the atmosphere" afforded by this "intimate", "charming" "little piece of Europe" on Nob Hill serving "pleasant" Californian-French fare to the mellifluous strains of the master himself; even rivals (Filet Mignon Salieri, anyone?) concede "the service is excellent" but say the "schmaltz" is "getting old and tired."

Café Niebaum-Coppola L S M   15 18 14 $26
916 Kearny St. (Columbus Ave.), 415-291-1700
◨ Those who "can't get to the Napa Valley" but yearn for a taste of the Coppola empire enjoy "alfresco dining" at this "cute" corner cafe in North Beach; a "potential glimpse of Francis serving bruschetta" and the family "wines are the draw" here, since the "touristy" Southern Italian fare "does not compare to the movies he makes" ("pizza is the best bet") and "the staff could benefit from [his] direction."

Cafe Riggio S M   18 16 18 $28
4112 Geary Blvd. (bet. 5th & 6th Aves.), 415-221-2114
◨ For "dependable" "traditional Italian" chow that's "authentic yet inventive", Inner Richmond regulars report this "unpretentious" and "comfy" (albeit "noisy") trattoria is a "pillar of the community"; non-locals, though, lament that "unimaginative" fare, "long waits" and erratic service (the "staff is practically in your lap or forgets you exist") make this "out-of-the-way" spot "not worth the trip."

Café Tiramisu ⬛Ⓜ　　　20 | 18 | 17 | $31
28 Belden Pl. (bet. Bush & Pine Sts.), 415-421-7044
■ "As the name says", "the secret to this place" is the "to-die-for" dessert, but amici of this Downtown "power-lunch spot" enjoy the "flavorful" Italian savories as well; avoid the "cramped" dining room and "sit in the wine cellar", or "on a warm summer night", experience the *molto romantico* "European feel of the alley."

Caffe Centro ⬛Ⓜ　　　18 | 15 | 16 | $16
102 South Park St. (bet. 2nd & 3rd Sts.), 415-882-1500
■ The "ridiculously long lines" "have died down" "with the last dot-bombs", but this "so-cool-it-hurts" cafe is still techie central for "great mocha lattes" and a "quick", "quality" European-style lunch; despite the "nice rotating artwork inside", most "urban hipsters" prefer the sidewalk seating or the take-out window for lunch on the grass and "good people-watching in South Park."

Caffe Delle Stelle ⬛ⓈⓂ　　　17 | 15 | 16 | $26
395 Hayes St. (Gough St.), 415-252-1110
◪ Culture vultures insist this perennially "peppy" Hayes Valley trattoria is the ticket to "a bit of Italy" "before the symphony"; amid its "jolly atmosphere", "charming waiters" relay "reliable", "rustic" Northern Italian pastas at prices that "won't make your banker nervous", though diners who put their money where their mouths are "wouldn't go out of the way to eat here."

Caffè Greco ⬤⬛ⓈⓂ⇴　　　17 | 15 | 15 | $13
423 Columbus Ave. (bet. Green & Vallejo Sts.), 415-397-6261
■ "Touted as having the best cappuccino in town", this North Beach "happening hangout" is "considered the standard" for "consistently tasty" Italian desserts; it "feels like a European" "retreat from the maddening crowds" when you linger at a sidewalk table "people-watching" over wine served by "authentic" old-world waiters.

Caffe Macaroni Ⓜ⇴　　　20 | 14 | 18 | $25
59 Columbus Ave. (Jackson St.), 415-956-9737
■ This bite-size North Beach trattoria is "like eating in a Southern Italian mother's kitchen" – if her kitchen's got a drop ceiling, that is; though "truly funny waiters" straight out of a "*Saturday Night Live* sketch" keep the "energy level high", "tall people" "need to do some serious ducking" before tucking into "fabulous", "cheap" eats from the toe of The Boot.

Caffè Museo ⬛ⓈⓂ　　　18 | 16 | 12 | $16
San Francisco Museum of Modern Art, 151 Third St. (bet. Howard & Mission Sts.), 415-357-4500
◪ On an "afternoon at the SF MOMA", this "hectic" "haven for hungry art lovers" serves "arty" Mediterranean

"snacks" and "delicious sandwiches" "at fair prices"; though the "bare-bones decor" is "not as innovative as the museum architecture", if you can "find a seat" inside or on the sidewalk, it's a "pleasant way" to "satisfy your palate after feeding your eyes."

Caffe Sport L ⊄   17 | 15 | 13 | $28
574 Green St. (bet. Columbus & Grant Aves.), 415-981-1251
◪ "Bring teens" and "tourists only" to North Beach's "wild", "crazy" "classic" so they can "learn to eat with and love their neighbors" in its "cramped and crowded" confines beneath dozens of "doodads hanging over their heads"; as you shovel down the "hearty" Southern Italian fare ("we need a great garlic fix now and then"), don't expect "to be pampered" by the "loud, rude" servers.

CAMPTON PLACE L S M   26 | 26 | 26 | $57
Campton Place Hotel, 340 Stockton St. (bet. Post & Sutter Sts.), 415-955-5555
◼ "Camp yourself here" fawn fans of this Downtown boutique-hotel haven "epitomizing fine dining"; expect a "superb experience in all respects", from chef Laurent Manrique's "magical" French feasts to the "uncluttered elegance" of the "civilized surroundings" to the "absolutely stellar service"; it's "worth refinancing the home" for "scrumptious" "power breakfasts", "romantic dinners" and "upper-crust" "special occasions."

Capp's Corner L S M   16 | 14 | 16 | $22
1600 Powell St. (Green St.), 415-989-2589
◼ If this "old-time joint" "looks like it's been there 40 years", that's because it has, representing "what North Beach is supposed to be", with its "abundant portions" of "passable", "family-style", "old-school Italian" fare ; best of all, you can "hobnob with the locals" over a $15 "all-inclusive meal" that's "perfect" before *Beach Blanket Bingo* next door.

Carême Room L M   ▽ 20 | 15 | 15 | $31
California Culinary Academy, 625 Polk St. (Turk St.), 415-292-8229
◼ Staffed by "students [who] do their best" toquing and toting "innovative" Asian lunches and Classic French dinners, this Tenderloin California Culinary Academy venue mainly makes the grade, though some say "uneven food" and "hit-or-miss" service from "the oft-overworked" apprentices mean it's "like Russian roulette"; still, those "on a budget" appreciate the "appealing" Thursday and Friday night buffets ("great value").

Carnelian Room S M   19 | 25 | 21 | $48
Bank of America Ctr., 555 California St., 52nd fl. (bet. Kearny & Montgomery Sts.), 415-433-7500
◼ Experiencing the "drop-dead" panoramic "view of the city" from this 52nd-floor Downtown perch may be "the

closest thing to flying", but most say the Californian "food isn't as spectacular", despite nosebleed prices; nevertheless, "business diners" and others looking to "impress" "out-of-towners" say the "high wow factor" and "white-glove service" "make this room in the clouds worth a visit"; N.B. jackets (but not ties) required.

Carta L S M   18 | 17 | 18 | $33
1760 Market St. (bet. Gough & Octavia Sts.), 415-863-3516
☑ The seasonally "new temptations" of its "imaginative" "revolving menu" and a "varied" international selection of "wines by the glass" make dining at this Eclectic Upper Market "neighborhood spot" a great "way to" "travel the globe" "on a budget without leaving the city" for many; others say the "too ambitious" cooks "exhaust themselves trying" to do "too many things" to "get it right every" time; service comments (from "marginal" to "superior") are also all over the map.

Casa Aguila L S M   19 | 13 | 17 | $20
1240 Noriega St. (bet. 19th & 20th Aves.), 415-661-5593
■ "Refreshingly original" "combinations" of "delicious" "Mexican food like no other in the city" served in "huge portions" make supping sensualists in the Sunset feel like extras in *Like Water for Chocolate*; after a swig of the "swell sangria" and a taste of the "nice [complimentary] mini-tamale" appetizers, you "won't notice" the "snail-paced service and cheesy decor."

Cha Am Thai L S M   18 | 12 | 14 | $19
701 Folsom St. (3rd St.), 415-546-9711
Cha Am Thai Express L M ⇗
307 Kearny St. (Pine St.), 415-956-8241
☑ Opinions diverge wildly over the food at this "inexpensive" Thai duo; while proponents praise the pad Thai and the "smile-inducing yumminess" of the curries, critics counter the Siamese savories are "so-so", "one-sauce" wonders; all agree, however, about the "disappointing", "drab" decor and "rushed" "oblivious staff" ("slow down, let me eat"); N.B. the Kearny Street branch is takeout only.

Cha Cha Cha L S M   19 | 17 | 15 | $22
1801 Haight St. (Shrader St.), 415-386-5758
Cha Cha Cha @ Original McCarthy's S M
2327 Mission St. (bet. 19th & 20th Sts.), 415-648-0504
☑ With "killer sangria, plantains to die for and packed houses year-round", this "hip" "Haight hangout" and its Mission sibling – purveyors of "tasty" "tapas"-style Caribbean treats – remain some of the "liveliest" "scenes" in SF despite "noise levels" that are "louder than the tacky decor" ("Carnivale would be quieter"); the antsy argue "it's not worth" the "interminable waits on weekends" ("take reservations", *por favor*).

CHAPEAU! S
24 │ 17 │ 24 │ $41

1408 Clement St. (15th Ave.), 415-750-9787

■ Ecstatic eaters tip their hats to this "wonderful" "hidden Richmond gem" known for its "sensuous" French bistro fare, and "charming", "gracious" "husband-and-wife owners" (he's a "wine genius" who oversees the "brilliant list") though a few are "disappointed" by the recent "chef change", most maintain the "delicious food" and "exemplary service" continue to "compensate for the" "elbow-bumping" dining room.

Charanga
19 │ 15 │ 18 │ $23

2351 Mission St. (bet. 19th & 20th Sts.), 415-282-1813

■ "Ay, Charanga!" exclaim amigos of this "fun" Mission "neighborhood favorite" where chef Gabriela Salas "is always" exercising her "creative spirit" by "cooking up new and fabulous" Caribbean tapas at "unbeatable prices"; the storefront space may be "a bit homely", but "everything from the music" that "rocks" to partner Rita Abraldes' "killer" pitchers of "both red and white sangria" "promises a lively evening."

CHARLES NOB HILL S
26 │ 24 │ 26 │ $67

1250 Jones St. (Clay St.), 415-771-5400

■ "Synchronized" "ballet-style" wait service, "exquisite" Californian-Gallic creations that are as "rich" as the clientele, "incredible tasting menus" and a "top-flight wine list" prompt patrons to dub this "posh" 'n' "pricey" place the "French Laundry of Nob Hill"; though some say the atmosphere's "stuffy", most maintain "you'll fall in love" with this pampering hideaway; P.S. food rating may not reflect chef "Ron Siegel's departure" in early 2001.

Charlie's L S M
18 │ 20 │ 17 │ $37

1838 Union St. (bet. Laguna & Octavia Sts.), 415-474-3773

◪ This "happening" initial public offering from Michael Schwab (heir to trading guru Charles) and buddy Jeff Silver is banking on "ultra-hip decor" and "great" Californian-Eclectic eats to attract a "frat row" Cow Hollow crowd; still, some speculate it's having an "identity crisis" – is it a "restaurant or a bar"?

Chaya Brasserie L S M
21 │ 23 │ 20 │ $46

132 The Embarcadero (bet. Howard & Mission Sts.), 415-777-8688

◪ With a "knockout view" of "the Bay Bridge", a "tony" "high-tech" interior and a mix of Japanese favorites like "flawless sushi" and "innovative" French fare that's as "beautiful" as the "swarms" of yuppies on cell phones, this "stunning" "waterfront" expense-accounter on The Embarcadero offers Northern Cals a taste of its famed "Southern Cal siblings"; unfortunately, cynics contend, "they've also imported the LA attitude" and "high prices."

Chaz Restaurant S
▽ 23 | 18 | 22 | $42

3347 Fillmore St. (bet. Chestnut & Lombard Sts.), 415-928-1211
■ "Charles Solomon is a food wizard" declare groupies of the "former chef of The Heights" who's "back" and casting a spell over the Marina with his "excellent", "beautifully balanced" New American–New French dishes; although it's "not yet discovered", "friendly service" and a "comfortable" room where "you can talk in a normal voice" have some predicting "soon you won't be able to get a table" at this "new neighborhood favorite"-to-be.

Cheers L S M
18 | 15 | 18 | $20

127 Clement St. (bet. 2nd & 3rd Aves.), 415-387-6966
■ "Three cheers" for the three square meals at this "reasonably priced" Inner Richmonder best known for its "superb" Californian "breakfasts" and "fab" "Sunday brunches" enjoyed on a "unbeatable" "sunny patio"; with "barely a soul in the place for dinner", locals are happy to have this "friendly", "sleepy" spot all to themselves.

Cheesecake Factory, The L S M
16 | 17 | 14 | $22

Macy's Union Sq., 251 Geary St., 8th fl. (bet. Powell & Stockton Sts.), 415-391-4444
◪ "Attention Macy's shoppers", a variety of "over-the-top cheesecakes" and other "fabulous desserts" make this perpetually "busy" Downtowner a sweet-tooth's "paradise", and its "roof deck" sports a "fantastic view of Union Square"; still, many mark down this "tourist trap" for "wastefully" "humongous portions" of "basic American food", "factory-style service" and "ridiculously long waits."

Chenery Park S M
20 | 19 | 21 | $32

683 Chenery St. (Diamond St.), 415-337-8537
■ "Finally, a really good place we can walk to" rejoice local lovers of this notable neophyte, an "oasis in the desert of Glen Park" that's "off to an exciting start" with "delightful service [that] complements" "marvelous" New American fare; though a few find its "prices high" and its "upscale decor" "rather posh" "for the neighborhood", most are happy to park it here for a night out.

Chevys Fresh Mex L S M
13 | 13 | 14 | $19

2 Embarcadero Ctr. (Sacramento St.), 415-391-2323 ⊟
Stonestown Galleria, 3251 20th Ave. (Winster Dr.), 415-665-8705
201 Third St. (Howard St.), 415-543-8060
590 Van Ness Ave. (Golden Gate Ave.), 415-621-8200
◪ Dishing out "cheap" and "humongous portions" of "passable Tex-Mex" and "fast service", this ever-expanding chain is popular with "crying babies" and "teenagers" who get a kick watching "el machino form fresh tortillas", but the *enfant*-intolerant gripe that the "free chips and salsa" and "abundant margaritas" are the

"only reasons to go", saying "even the birthday song lacks enthusiasm (can't even embarrass anyone anymore)".

CHEZ NOUS **L** **S**   24 | 17 | 20 | $29

1911 Fillmore St. (bet. Bush & Pine Sts.), 415-441-8044

■ Folks are making a "big fuss" over the "amazing small plates" of "inventive" Med meze at this "happening" "grazer's paradise" on Upper Fillmore; a staff that's "(gasp) friendly, helpful and polite" adds to the "great atmosphere", but "hellish waits" and a "jammed", "noisy" dining room have some saying "please", can't you "make it bigger and take reservations"? N.B. the food rating may not reflect a post-*Survey* chef change.

Chloe's Cafe **L** **S** **M** ⊘   22 | 14 | 18 | $15

1399 Church St. (26th St.), 415-648-4116

■ "Be prepared for" "big waits" at this "small" but "cute" Noe Valley "neighborhood place" with "consistently" "excellent" "Americana" "breakfasts", "dreamy brunches" and "great" lunches; though most would prefer to skip the "awful lines" ("where do all the people come from?"), few "waffle" over whether the "stellar omelets" and "divine banana walnut pancakes" are worth it.

Chow **L** **S** **M**   18 | 14 | 17 | $19

215 Church St. (Market St.), 415-552-2469

◪ Chowhounds find "something for everyone" in the Eclectic "comfort food" of this casual Castro "favorite", insisting "you can't beat" it for filling your belly without "emptying your wallet"; others find the "bland offerings" some of "the most overrated in town"; either way, expect "long waits"; N.B. ratings may not reflect the arrival of chef Laurence Jossel (ex Chez Nous).

Citizen Cake **L** **S**   20 | 18 | 16 | $23

399 Grove St. (Gough St.), 415-861-2228

◪ "Citizen Cake is to" dessert "what *Citizen Kane* is to the film industry – a legend" sigh surveyors swooning over the "brilliant" "baked goods" (such as the Rosebud crème brûlée tart) at Elizabeth Falkner's "hip" Hayes Valley pastry shop/eatery; though the "pricey" treats "trump" the "minimal menu" of Californian cuisine (and "Marie Antoinette would scorn" the not-so-sweet service), most find it "an excellent place to break your diet."

Citrus Club **L** **S** **M**   20 | 16 | 17 | $16

1790 Haight St. (Shrader St.), 415-387-6366

■ Soba sophisticates say this "Asian fusion noodle house" serving "great heaps of" its "amazing" signature dish is "the best one on Haight Street" (ok, so it's "the only one on Haight Street"); "friendly service" and "rock-bottom prices" ("for $6 you get a meal to eat and one to take home") cement its popularity among the "groovy" locals.

Cityscape 🅂🅼
– | – | – | E

Hilton San Francisco, 333 O'Farrell St. (bet. Mason & Taylor Sts.), 415-923-5002

Floating 460 feet above the ground, this Downtown American aerie offers jaw-dropping panoramic views of the SF cityscape, the Bay and the Bridges from every table; although locals think of it as a "kind of touristy" place, "friendly service" and chef Tal Franbuch's seasonally driven Californian menu live up to the enchanted setting; high-flyers insist the lavish Sunday buffet brunch featuring live jazz is the "best in the city."

Clémentine 🅂
22 | 20 | 21 | $36

126 Clement St. (bet. 2nd & 3rd Aves.), 415-387-0408

■ For a "feeling of the Left Bank" without the hassle of "the exchange rate", Francophiles flock to this "elegant" yet "charming bistro" in the Inner Richmond offering "very good" "Classic French cuisine" and – "can you believe it?" – "truly caring service" *sans* Gallic "attitude"; all of this at "surprisingly reasonable prices" has nationalists exclaiming "*vive la France.*"

Cliff House 🅻🅂🅼
14 | 20 | 16 | $29

1090 Point Lobos Ave. (Great Hwy.), 415-386-3330

◪ "Go for the view, stay for the view" josh jaded jurors of this "historic" "grand ol' dame", the "classic" place to drag "your visitors from the prairies" and "watch the Pacific" crashing on the cliffs below; though brunching bus-"loads of tourists" seem happy to overlook this ocean overlook's "average American" fare, most natives prefer to limit their intake to "a drink" and a "mesmerizing" sunset.

Cobalt Tavern 🅂🅼
20 | 18 | 19 | $38

1707 Powell St. (Union St.), 415-982-8123

■ Though it "will always be the Washbag" to some, "nice" husband-and-wife owners Guy and Rose Ferri "have done a great job" transforming this famous space into a North Beach "jewel" that's a "worthy successor" thanks to "solid American fare" ("this Guy can cook"), "courteous service" and "live jazz" on weekends; the "monotonous" "cobalt interior", however, has some depressives feeling "too blue."

Compass Rose 🅻🅂🅼
18 | 26 | 21 | $35

Westin St. Francis Hotel, 335 Powell St. (bet. Geary & Post Sts.), 415-774-0167

◪ Natives and tourists from all points navigate to this "gorgeous", "elegant" Downtown salon in the Westin St. Francis Hotel, a "great place" to sup on "afternoon tea" "after a full day of shopping" or take a "martini break with the girls"; though surveyors say they "rarely" go for the "rather expensive" Asian-American fare, "old-world luxury" makes the "beautiful bar" "still the place for cocktails in SF."

Coriya Hot Pot City ◑ L S M   15 9 10 $16
852 Clement St. (10th Ave.), 415-387-7888

◪ "Bring only grungy clothes" to this "fun, all-you-can-eat" Inner Richmond Taiwanese barbeque joint where guests "cook it themselves" "tabletop" using heaps of "raw, marinated meats", seafood and a "sparse selection of vegetables"; gung-ho groups find it a "great value" and an "amusing" "adventure", though others grouse that "after the novelty" "wears off, you notice" you're "paying to work."

Cosmopolitan Cafe L S M   21 22 19 $39
Rincon Ctr., 121 Spear St. (bet. Howard & Mission Sts.), 415-543-4001

◪ "It's worth the push through the" "hopping bar" "packed with" "now-broke" "young dot-commers" to get to the "gorgeous", "swank" dining room at this "smashing" SoMa yearling that "may be the salvation for" a "jinxed location"; some say the "stunning" decor "is a touch better than the food", but most find chef Steven Levine's New American nibbles "inspired", though the hard-of-hearing harp it's "way too noisy."

Crustacean L S M   22 16 18 $39
1475 Polk St. (California St.), 415-776-2722

◼ The "amazing", "finger-licking" "roasted crab" and "to-die-for garlic noodles" "reel you in hook, line and sinker" at this "pricey" Euro-Asian seafooder on Polk Street, but the "tacky" "over-glitzy" "neon" decor and "perfunctory service" "may make you crabby"; be "prepared to have the maitre d' look you over to see if you're dressed" suitably (collared shirts suggested).

Curve Bar & Restaurant L S M   – – – M
747 Third St. (King St.), 415-896-2286

Just a curve ball away from Pac Bell Park, this rookie is the latest venture of erstwhile bartender-around-town Johnny Love; chef Amy Dittmar (ex Cafe Kati) is expected to hit homers with her approachable, affordable all-American fare (such as beer-battered calamari), and when the Giants are in town, lunch and dinner will be scrapped for a special, speedier Game Day Menu.

Cypress Club S M   20 25 20 $47
500 Jackson St. (bet. Columbus Ave. & Montgomery St.), 415-296-8555

◪ You'll feel like you're "dining in a scene from *Alice in Wonderland*" rather than Downtown SF at this "opulent", "whimsical" "supper club" with "breast-shaped light fixtures", a "phallic" sculpture and other "surreal", "elephantine" design elements; although the "sensuous decor" and "fabulous [nightly] live jazz" trump the "very good" New American cuisine, boosters boast the "wonderful room" is "holding up pretty well."

Delancey Street 🅛🅢   17 | 17 | 21 | $25

600 The Embarcadero (Brannan St.), 415-512-5179

◪ "Knowing" you're "doing good while eating well" makes the "straightforward, reliable" American fare "taste even better" at this Embarcadero establishment "run by a rehab program" and staffed by "friendly" "ex-cons" and recovering addicts who "bend over backward to please"; recent "improvements in decor" and "moderate prices" "make up for the" "predictable food", and besides, "it's all for a good cause."

DELFINA 🅢🅜   25 | 18 | 22 | $37

3621 18th St. (bet. Dolores & Guerrero Sts.), 415-552-4055

◼ Craig Stoll and Anne Spencer's "rockin'", "trendy" Mission "trattoria" continues to surprise and delight" "hip"-sters and "foodies" with a one-two punch of "deceivingly" simple, "masterful" "melt-in-your-mouth" "authentic" "Italian" dishes and "exceptional", "energetic service"; while it now "has more breathing room" and a new "buzzing" bar, it's as "noisy" as ever, and reservations and parking are still "darn hard to get."

Desiree 🅛🅜⇸   – | – | – | I

39 Mesa St. (Lincoln Blvd.), 415-561-2336

Those desiring to know the whereabouts of chef Anne Gingrass (ex Hawthorne Lane) can find her cloistered at this Lilliputian cafe in the Presidio's International Film Society Building; returning to her roots (and fruits and vegetables), she whips up an ever-changing Californian farmers' market menu of breakfasts and box lunches, which can be taken out or enjoyed in-house on handcrafted pottery; N.B. closed weekends.

Destino 🅜   ▽ 20 | 20 | 20 | $30

1815 Market St. (bet. Guerrero & Valencia Sts.), 415-552-4451

◼ For "something festive, delicious and different", visit this "raucous" "newcomer" featuring "imaginative" South American tapas (such as seviche *a la peruana,* empanadas and churrasco), "personal yet professional service" and live flamenco guitarists and tango dancers; though a "tough location" on Upper Market "hides this gem" from most, the banditos who've been there say "we are so lucky to have this place."

DINE 🅜   24 | 20 | 19 | $43

662 Mission St. (Annie Alley, bet. New Montgomery & 3rd Sts.), 415-538-3463

◼ An exercise in opposites, this SoMa "mad house" hosts a "high-tech" "Gen X" crowd that feasts on "gigantic portions" of "fabulous" American "comfort food" "like mom never made" while holding "cell phone conversations" in the "sleek" dining room; a few foes find the experience "disappointingly" "utilitarian" and are turned off by the "deafening" "bar scene"; N.B. ratings may not reflect opening chef Julia McClaskey's post-*Survey* departure.

Dot Restaurant M ▽ 17 │ 22 │ 17 │ $37

Radisson Miyako Hotel, 1611 Post St. (bet. Buchanan & Laguna Sts.), 415-922-7788

▪ A "super-cool", "multi-level design" lures "in-the-know" "hipsters" to this Johnny-com-lately "hidden in Japantown", the brainchild of Joe Boxer C.U.O. (Chief Underpants Officer) Nick Graham; although most say chef Noel Pavia's "creative" New American food is "good enough", Dot-dissers suggest you "skip dinner" and go "upstairs" (climb those 12 steps) "for a drink" and "a hoot" at the "quirky Lord of Balls lounge."

Dottie's True Blue Cafe L S M 24 │ 15 │ 17 │ $15

522 Jones St. (bet. Geary & O'Farrell Sts.), 415-885-2767

▪ "If you can handle the wait to enter this tiny dive", "you're in for some great" traditional American eats; true, the "snug" storefront has "no atmosphere" and the "marginal location" ("in the heart of the Tenderloin") can be a turnoff, but Dottie devotees declare the "outstanding" breakfasts, "quality" lunches and "good service" "make it all worthwhile"; N.B. no dinner.

Dragon Well L S 20 │ 16 │ 18 │ $20

2142 Chestnut St. (bet. Pierce & Steiner Sts.), 415-474-6888

▪ Those "looking for more than kung pao chicken at the local take-out joint", this "yuppie" Marina Asian will suit you well; the "top-notch", "healthy" "nouveau Chinese" fare (including "delicious vegetarian options") is served in a "simply done" dining room by an "attentive" staff "that seems to care about pleasing" patrons; "reasonable prices" keep converts "coming back."

Dusit Thai L S M ▽ 20 │ 14 │ 18 │ $18

3221 Mission St. (bet. 29th & Valencia Sts.), 415-826-4639

▪ "Heavenly leg of lamb" and other "wonderful Thai" dishes ("try the rock shrimp and fried basil") do it for the small band of Bernal Heights denizens who "enjoy" this often "overlooked", "well-run" "neighborhood favorite"; swell prices and a welcoming staff that "treats you like family" make the "faithful" "forget the decor."

E&O Trading Co. L S M 18 │ 21 │ 17 │ $32

314 Sutter St. (bet. Grant Ave. & Stockton St.), 415-693-0303

▪ A jumble of "Far East" knickknacks gives this "big and noisy" Downtown Pan-Asian a "fun escapist atmosphere" reminiscent of a 19th-century trading house; the menu borrows from Indonesia, Malaysia, India and Vietnam, so it's best to "graze" your way through lots of "innovative" "small plates"; foes feel "the entrees pale in comparison" and the "aloof service" mars "the experience", but it's still "yuppieville" "after work" due to "great happy-hour prices" for their tropical "infusion" elixirs.

E'Angelo ⑤⊘   20 | 10 | 19 | $24

2234 Chestnut St. (bet. Pierce & Scott Sts.), 415-567-6164
■ "Was I in Italy?" wonder would-be wanderers after a visit to this "unpretentious" Marina "mainstay" that loyalists laud as "old-line Italian in the best sense"; ravioli revelers rejoice that its "reliably" "awesome" "homemade pasta" is served "piping hot" and complemented by "friendly service", while "cheap" prices have economical eaters exclaiming "wow, what a bargain!"

East Coast
West Delicatessen 🄻🅂🄼   – | – | – | I

1725 Polk St. (bet. Clay & Washington Sts.), 415-563-3542
After years of kvetching that you can't get a good nosh in these parts, Polk Streeters now have this deli that hawks all the delicacies of NY's Lower East side: mile-high pastrami sandwiches, latkes and even chopped liver; purportedly, there's even a real Jewish grandmother supervising the kitchen, so what else can we tell you?

Eastside West ⑤🄼   19 | 20 | 20 | $34

3154 Fillmore St. (Greenwich St.), 415-885-4000
■ Transplanted Yankees and other fans of this "sexy" Marina "hot spot" report that it "has hit its stride" thanks to "beautiful decor", a "cozy", "cool atmosphere", "friendly service" that "has improved over the last few years" and "fantastic live jazz" Thursday–Saturday that "doesn't overwhelm your conversation"; many say the American cuisine – "stunningly fresh" "seafood specialties" coupled with an "expansive raw bar" – is often "underestimated."

Ebisu 🄻⑤🄼   24 | 13 | 17 | $29

1283 Ninth Ave. (Irving St.), 415-566-1770
■ Sushi lovers savor "melt-in-your-mouth" maki and "top-grade" sashimi at this "always-hopping" Inner Sunset spot named for a Japanese kitchen deity; though a few nonbelievers say it's "not the religious event locals make it out to be" ("service, drab decor, etc. are standard"), most maintain "this place" "would be an everyday destination" "if only it were bigger" and the "horrendous" lines "shorter"; N.B. a to-go branch is now open at the SF International Airport, Terminal G.

El Balazo 🄻⑤🄼   19 | 12 | 11 | $10

1654 Haight St. (bet. Belvedere & Clayton Sts.), 415-864-8608
■ Haight Street hippies and "all-day shoppers" "get a fix" of Mexican fare at this colorful bi-level taqueria pumping out "wonderful giant burritos packed with ultra-fresh

ingredients" that are "head and shoulders above the average"; considering the high quality and "huge portions", it's a "definite price performer", and though there's plenty of seating upstairs, "quick" takeout is also available.

ELISABETH DANIEL, RESTAURANT ▣

26 | 24 | 26 | $75

550 Washington St. (bet. Montgomery & Sansome Sts.), 415-397-6129
■ Dining at this "elegant", "understated", "serene oasis" amid the Downtown "bustle" is a "superlative" experience thanks to chef Daniel Patterson's "imaginative", "incredibly delicious" (if "excruciatingly expensive") New French prix fixe meals, as well as his "terrific tasting menus" balanced "to symphonic perfection" with "matching wines"; co-proprietor Elizabeth Ramsay and her "superb" staff make it "all the more pleasurable."

Elite Cafe ▣▣

19 | 19 | 18 | $31

2049 Fillmore St. (California St.), 415-346-8668
■ "Bustling" "Bourbon Street" atmosphere, "swanked-up" "New Orleans specialties" and a "fab Sunday brunch" make this "fun Cajun" "hangout" on Upper Fillmore the "next best thing to being down South"; insiders suggest you "escape" the "noisy" "crowds" of yuppies by "reserving one of the" "cool" "high-back wooden booths"; N.B. ratings may not reflect the recent arrival of chef Lalo Valenzuela.

Eliza's ▣▣▣

22 | 19 | 17 | $22

2877 California St. (bet. Broderick & Divisadero Sts.), 415-621-4819
1457 18th St. (bet. Connecticut & Missouri Sts.), 415-648-9999
■ "Creative" Mandarin fare "with a twist" combined with "stylish" "non-traditional" interiors at this Pacific Heights and Potrero Hill pair manages to "convert" even "those who don't like Chinese" (though purists who "prefer the real thing" pontificate "puh-lease, when did 'Americanized' become 'inventive'?"); most say the "staff isn't friendly", but all agree "it's fast" (and there's always takeout); N.B. despite some similarities, Alice's and Eric's are not related.

Ella's ▣▣▣

21 | 16 | 18 | $22

500 Presidio Ave. (California St.), 415-441-5669
◪ "If there's a better" breakfast spot, "I want to know" demand devotees of this "quintessential all-American" "famous for" its "out-of-this-world" chicken hash and banana pancakes but also offering ("since the expansion") a "hearty" "supper menu"; though Presidio Heights "yuppies" and "moms who brunch" queue in "discouragingly long lines", not everyone thinks "it's worth the wait" – though those who do suggest you "go early."

Emma
22 | 20 | 19 | $37

San Remo Hotel, 2237 Mason St. (bet. Chestnut & Francisco Sts.), 415-673-9090

■ Tucked into the "historic" San Remo Hotel, this North Beach yearling may be a "well-kept secret" to most, but fans who know it adore chef Mark Lusardi's "fantastic, flavorful Cal-Ital food" served in a "charming", "comfortable room" and at the "restored" "turn-of-the-century" "beautiful bar"; though a handful complain they "haven't worked out the service" yet, most say it's a "sweet spot off-the-beaten-path" that's "waiting to be discovered."

Emmy's Spaghetti Shack ●⑤Ⓜ⊄ _ | _ | _ | |

18 Virginia Ave. (Mission St.), 415-206-2086

Just in time for the dot-bomb implosion comes this no-frills Bernal Heights newcomer, whipping up simple plates of Italian grub (think spaghetti and meatballs) in a funky setting; featuring live DJs on the weekends and a kitchen that actually stays open late (2 AM Friday–Saturday, midnight midweek), it's the anti–Pasta Pomodoro for the late-night clubber set.

Empress of China ⓁⓈⓂ
16 | 18 | 17 | $30

838 Grant Ave. (bet. Clay & Washington Sts.), 415-434-1345

☑ Some "still love" this "old standby", a "throwback to Chinatown dining in the '60s", whose "beautiful view" of the Bay and "decor like an imperial palace" continue to lure "tourists from Nebraska" to experience its "good food and service"; however, many locals lament its "faded beauty" and "uninspired, Americanized" fare.

Enrico's Sidewalk Cafe ●ⓁⓈⓂ
17 | 20 | 16 | $31

504 Broadway (Kearny St.), 415-982-6223

■ This "legendary" North Beach cafe is "ground zero" "for people-watching" while sitting on the "patio (the best thing about it)", tossing back some "awesome mojitos" and "eyeballing the passing parade" on honky-tonk Broadway; although the Cal-Med "food is secondary" to the scene, it's "surprisingly good for a jazz bar"; unfortunately, the same can't be said for the "clueless service."

EOS RESTAURANT & WINE BAR ⓈⓂ
25 | 20 | 21 | $43

901 Cole St. (Carl St.), 415-566-3063

■ Don't let the remote Cole Valley "neighborhood location" fool you – Arnold Eric Wong's original restaurant is still at "the epicenter of great food and wine" in SF with "amazing", "innovative" Asian "fusion-without-confusion" dishes that "are as beautiful as they taste" and one of "the best wine bars in the city"; from the "warm host" to the "decadent dessert tray", it's "a winner", but do yourself a favor: "take a taxi", as street parking is difficult.

Eric's 🄻🅂🄼   21 | 15 | 17 | $19
1500 Church St. (27th St.), 415-282-0919
■ Those "in Outer Noe Valley" craving "great Chinese food" line up at this "always-packed" "neighborhood spot" that delivers "healthy" renditions at "bargain prices" in a "classy" (yet "cramped") atmosphere; a few critics contend that the service is "hasty" ("too bad delivery isn't an option") and the food "over-sauced", but "the crowds tell [a different] story."

Esperpento 🄻🅂🄼   17 | 14 | 14 | $22
3295 22nd St. (Valencia St.), 415-282-8867
◪ "For a dose of Spain", Missionites head to this Iberian serving "good portions" of "tasty tapas" and "great sangria" at "prices that can't be beat"; "fun, funky", "colorful" decor (after all, the name means 'absurdity'), "flamenco dancers and a mariachi band" create an "exuberant" atmosphere, but "servers who seem to be on siesta" make "peak hours" a zoo.

FARALLON 🄻🅂🄼   24 | 27 | 23 | $52
450 Post St. (bet. Mason & Powell Sts.), 415-956-6969
■ "Fill yourself to the gills" at designer Pat Kuleto's "dazzling" Downtown "Atlantis" featuring an "over-the-top", "under-the-sea" "atmosphere that complements" chef Mark Franz's "swimmingly good" coastal cuisine; though foes deem the decor "splashy to a fault" ("I needed scuba gear") and the fare a tad "hoity-toity", they're drowned out by fin-atics who swear it's "worth every Benjamin."

Faz 🄻🄼   18 | 19 | 17 | $32
Crocker Galleria, 161 Sutter St. (bet. Kearny & Montgomery Sts.), 415-362-0404
◪ Tehran-born owner (and occasional chef) Faz Poursohi offers his unique brand of Italian-Med cuisine for worker bees at this "luncheon haven" (don't miss the rooftop garden) in "bustling Downtown SF"; although most patrons praise the "good prices and pleasant atmosphere", some sniff the food is "ho-hum, no sizzle", and everyone is Fazed by the "slow service."

FIFTH FLOOR 🄼   26 | 26 | 26 | $70
Hotel Palomar, 12 Fourth St. (Market St.), 415-348-1555
■ Chef "George Morrone" "is back", "chatting" up the "venture capital crowd" that "drops in" for his "wildly styled" New French dishes that "push the envelope of creativity" and are "equally matched" by an "eye-popping", "incredibly diverse wine list"; add in the kind of "impeccable service" that "fine diners pray for and almost never get" and a "quiet", "stylish" atmosphere "that envelops you from the moment you walk in", and you have satisfied surveyors advising you to "liquidate your portfolio" – this Downtowner is "seventh heaven."

Fior d'Italia ⓁⓈⓂ   17 | 18 | 19 | $34
601 Union St. (Stockton St.), 415-986-1886
■ Founded in 1886, this North Beach landmark claims to be the "oldest Italian restaurant in America" and most agree "it feels that way", but whether that's good or bad is a matter of perspective; loyalists "still love" the "surly but professional waiters" and "Rat Pack–esque setting", claiming the "big portions" of "old-country" fare "are lost on trendy San Franciscans", but others contend this "dated" "institution" is "past its prime."

Firecracker Ⓢ   21 | 18 | 17 | $26
1007½ Valencia St. (21st St.), 415-642-3470
■ This "fun, festive and upbeat" "neighborhood" "find" entices youthful "new-wealth" "Mission dwellers" with its "upscale", "gourmet" "take on Chinese food" – "spicy" and "delicious dishes" with "oomph" that "tickle the tongue" and ignite the palate; fire-eaters "love the sumptuous red decor" and "attentive service", but a few foes burned by the "crowded and noisy" atmosphere wonder whether it's "worth the chaos and price."

Firefly ⓈⓂ   23 | 19 | 21 | $33
4288 24th St. (Douglass St.), 415-821-7652
■ Combining "small-town intimacy" with "big-city" savoir faire, this Noe Valley "treasure" is "everything a restaurant should be" – chef-owner Brad Levy's "delicious" "Eclectic" "comfort foods" from around the globe "capture the essence of each" cuisine, the "friendly staff" delivers "damn" "good" service and the "fanciful down-home decor" is a "nice change from all the business" spots.

Firewood Café ⓁⓈⓂ   16 | 14 | 14 | $17
DSF Galleria, 233 Geary St. (Stockton St.), 415-788-3473
4248 18th St. (bet. Collingwood & Diamond Sts.), 415-252-0999
Sony Metreon Ctr., 101 Fourth St. (Mission St.), 415-369-6199
■ Fans get "fired up" about this set of "reasonably priced" "self-service" Americans for their "good" "rotisserie chicken", "yummy" "thin-crust pizzas" and "big fresh salads"; some say they're "essentially fast-food" places (though the "free" "spiced olives on the table" are a "nice" touch), "the decor is nothing special" and the service is "impersonal", but since both the Castro and SoMa branches are conveniently located near cinemas, they're a "good choice" for a "quick bite" "before or after the movie."

First Crush ●ⒿⓈⓂ   17 | 14 | 18 | $34
101 Cyril Magnin St. (bet. Mason & Powell Sts.), 415-982-7874
■ "Great fun for oenophiles", this theater-district Downtowner satisfies grape expectations with its "redone" "upstairs" wine bar, which claims the largest selection of Cal wines in SF; though opponents opine the

vino "outshines" the victuals and the "claustrophobic" "basement dining room", the elaborate New American "tasting menu" of "great new chef" Jennifer Biesty (ex Bizou) might warrant a second look.

FLEUR DE LYS Ⓜ   27 | 27 | 27 | $72 |

777 Sutter St. (bet. Jones & Taylor Sts.), 415-673-7779
■ If you "want to impress" "sophisticated clients" or that someone "special", head Downtown and experience Alsace-born Hubert Keller's "consistently brilliant" New French fare and the "gracious" staff's "impeccable yet unobtrusive" service; supping under the "circus"-like "tented ceiling" may be "more akin to" attending a culinary "performance than a mere dinner", but fans insist this "mercifully quiet" "cocoon" is "still the pinnacle of Bay Area romantic dining – if you're willing to pay the big bucks."

Florio Ⓢ Ⓜ   19 | 20 | 19 | $35 |

1915 Fillmore St. (bet. Bush & Pine Sts.), 415-775-4300
■ "Like a sidewalk bistro without the sidewalk", this "stylish" and "noisy" Upper Fillmore spot has "terrific ambiance", a "friendly owner who looks after you" and "good, heavy, seriously intense" fare, even if folks have to "keep going back" to figure out "is it Italian or is it French?" (actually, it's both).

Fly Trap Ⓛ Ⓢ Ⓜ   19 | 18 | 19 | $35 |

606 Folsom St. (2nd St.), 415-243-0580
◪ "Don't let the name" of this historic haunt "deter you", "nostalgists" advise – it may have "been around the block, but it still" serves "good traditional" American fare (aka "old fogies' food") such as celery Victor (a salad of eggs, poached celery and anchovy vinaigrette); trend-followers find it "tired" and "stodgy" but that doesn't seem to faze SoMa "business lunchers" or the "older crowd" who patronize it for dinner.

Fog City Diner Ⓛ Ⓢ Ⓜ   18 | 20 | 18 | $30 |

1300 Battery St. (bet. Greenwich St. & The Embarcadero), 415-982-2000
◪ Sporting a shiny "chrome" exterior and a "retro" "wood-paneled" interior, this Embarcadero "institution" is "still fun after all these years"; its "hodgepodge" of "good" New American small plates is "by no means diner food", but some complain that the "elevated prices" are equally "upscale"; still, even those who haven't the foggiest notion why it's "a SF landmark" concede it's "a must-see" "for out-of-towners."

Foreign Cinema Ⓢ   19 | 24 | 17 | $39 |

2534 Mission St. (bet. 21st & 22nd Sts.), 415-648-7600
◪ This "gimmicky" Missionite is "two restaurants in one" – the "stylish interior" offers "fine dining" on "surprisingly

good" fare, while the "heated" patio hosts "hipsters and Francophiles" who share "long, wooden" "communal tables" and watch "obscure arty or foreign flicks" "projected on the wall"; though some say it's "too hip for it's own good", "the I-wear-Prada-and-you-don't" crowd loves it; N.B. a post-*Survey* switch to a seasonal Cal-Med menu may outdate the food score.

42 Degrees   21 | 21 | 19 | $41
235 16th St. (3rd St.), 415-777-5559
◪ Owner and original chef James Moffat is back at the stoves at his "ultra hip", bi-level supper club, cooking up "pricey" but "sublime" Mediterranean dishes; although "you really have to make an effort to get to this" "hideaway" tucked among warehouses near "Lower Potrero Hill", a "cool atmosphere" and hot "nightly jazz" make it "worth the hunt" (just be prepared for a little "attitude").

Fountain Court L S M   19 | 13 | 16 | $24
354 Clement St. (bet. 4th & 5th Aves.), 415-668-1100
■ Considered by many to be one of the "best Chinese on Clement Street", this "favorite" Inner Richmond "fallback" serves "great Shanghainese food" (including "daily specials that really are"); however, an "ordinary" interior that "has seen better days" and "slack" service have many dumpling devourers opting for the "great delivery."

Fournou's Ovens L S M   20 | 21 | 20 | $43
Renaissance Stanford Court Hotel, 905 California St. (Powell St.), 415-989-1910
◪ This "sedate" stalwart in the Renaissance Stanford Court atop Nob Hill offers "steady" Cal-Med "hotel-dining" standbys from its signature "working" wood-burning oven ("if you like lamb, this is the place") and a "quiet", "old-school" "elegance"; although the combination is enough to lure a "mature crowd", adventure-seekers deem the whole "experience" a bit "dull."

Frascati S M   21 | 17 | 20 | $36
1901 Hyde St. (Green St.), 415-928-1406
■ Russian Hill residents say they'll take this "darling neighborhood" "sleeper" any time "over many a fancy restaurant" – "this beats most of 'em", partly because of the "delicious Mediterranean food", "friendly service" and "quaint atmosphere", but "more so because it is not overwhelmed by the see-and-be-seen crowd"; P.S. take a taxi, as parking is a bear in this neighborhood.

FRINGALE L M   26 | 19 | 22 | $42
570 Fourth St. (bet. Brannan & Bryant Sts.), 415-543-0573
■ "*Magnifique*" moules and steak frites are just a few of the draws at this snug SoMa bistro that "takes you back to the Basque country"; "masterful" chef Gerald Hirigoyen's

"fantastic food" ("so good we bought the cookbook") is "much better than at other places that are twice the price"; though some wonder "is it worth" "waiting among the hordes for a table" in the "cramped quarters", most surveyors say "*absolument!*"

Frjtz Fries L S M   ▽ 20 | 19 | 16 | $13

579 Hayes St. (Laguna St.), 415-864-7654
Woolin Bldg., 900 North Point St. (Bay St.), 415-928-1475
■ For a blast of Benelux culture, head to this "hip" Hayes Valley cafe/teahouse/art gallery (or its Ghirardelli Square sib) that serves "tasty crêpes", a slew of Belgian beers and "yummy frites" with "awesome" dipping sauces; DJs spin electronica and down-tempo on Saturday and Sunday in the art-filled interior, and both branches boast "great" garden patios where you can smoke (preferably, Galoises).

Galette L S M   ▽ 21 | 16 | 17 | $19

2043 Fillmore St. (bet. California & Pine Sts.), 415-928-1300
■ The latest outpost of Pascal Rigo's burgeoning bakery/restaurant empire (Bay Breads, Chez Nous), this "brand-new" Breton on Fillmore Street garners bons mots for its beguiling collection of "delicious buckwheat crépes" (or *galettes* in Brittany), "satisfying salads" and shellfish appetizers; lending an "authentic" air are framed French newspapers celebrating soccer triumphs, "accented waiters" and a broad selection of Belgian booze.

Ganges S   20 | 14 | 18 | $20

775 Frederick St. (Arguello Blvd.), 415-661-7290
■ Inner Sunsetters welcome the new management at this dal house that offers "really delicious", "creative" regional Indian specialties such as savory stuffed bananas; although the menu is still meatless, they "now serve nonvegetarian dishes" if requested ahead of time; everything else remains pretty much the same, from the long, low-slung tables to live music on Saturday nights.

GARDEN COURT L S M   19 | 28 | 22 | $40

Palace Hotel, 2 New Montgomery St. (Market St.), 415-546-5010
■ Since "the turn of the last century", the Palace Hotel's "impressive" "afternoon high tea" and Sunday breakfast buffet have been SF traditions; the "dazzling" stained-glass ceiling and marble columns of its "elegant" interior make this "serene oasis" one of "the most beautiful restaurants in the entire state", though the disappointed wonder "why, oh why" isn't the "expensive" Californian food "up to the level" of the "spectacular setting?"

Garibaldis on Presidio L S M   22 | 21 | 20 | $38

347 Presidio Ave. (bet. Clay & Sacramento Sts.), 415-563-8841
■ For over a decade, this "rollicking, rocking" neighborhood place has been a "dependable" favorite for Presidio Heights

denizens wanting "sophisticated" Cal-Med fare in a "smart setting"; now the Oakland sib is fast becoming a favorite for East Bayers, who experience the same "first-rate" cuisine, "chic" decor and, unfortunately, "deafening acoustics."

GARY DANKO 🅂🅼

28 | 26 | 27 | $75

800 North Point St. (Hyde St.), 415-749-2060

■ For "people who live to eat", "Gary Danko's reputation" (both the man and his Wharf establishment) "stretches far and wide" thanks to a novel "flexibility" in ordering that lets you "mix and match" the "artfully prepared" "nouvelle" French-American cuisine to create your "own prix fixe tasting menu" (hint: "don't miss the cheese course"); "VIP" service, an "extensive" wine list and the "exquisite setting" all prompt sighs "I'd be here weekly if I could afford it"; P.S. the full menu is available at the bar to "walk-ins."

Gaylord India 🅻🅂🅼

18 | 16 | 16 | $30

1 Embarcadero Ctr. (bet. Battery & Sacramento Sts.), 415-397-7775
Ghirardelli Sq., 900 North Point St. (bet. Larkin & Polk Sts.), 415-771-8822

◪ This set of "upscale" Indians Downtown and on the Wharf garners opinions as mixed as a vegetable curry; aficionados assert "when [the kitchen] is on", it rivals any "in the city"; but it ain't on very much deem "disappointed" dissenters, who pronounce it "average" at best and "overpriced" for such "miniscule portions"; you're probably safe if you "stick to the lunch buffet."

Giorgio's Pizza 🅻🅂🅼

21 | 13 | 17 | $17

151 Clement St. (bet. 2nd & 3rd Aves.), 415-668-1266

■ Inner Richmond "families" flock to this "old-time" Italian, which remains "deservedly crowded" for "wonderful" wafer-thin "New York–style pizza" that's got the "crust of all crusts"; kids dig the "real pizzeria-place feeling" (red vinyl booths, a jukebox and plastic grapes hanging from trellises on the ceiling).

Gira Polli 🅂🅼

20 | 14 | 17 | $22

659 Union St. (bet. Columbus Ave. & Powell St.), 415-434-4472

■ It's the chicken, stupid ("does anyone get anything else?") that draws crowds to this "incredible" "inexpensive" Italian wood-roasted rotisserie; although the "early-bird special" (no pun intended) is a real "bargain", most surveyors see this poultry purveyor as an "exceptionally run take-out operation" and eschew the "basic", "boring" dining room.

Globe ◗🅻🅂🅼

22 | 18 | 18 | $38

290 Pacific Ave. (bet. Battery & Front Sts.), 415-391-4132

◪ "For a slice of" "suave" Manhattan in SF's Downtown, globe-trotters gallop to chef-owner Joseph Manzare's "hip hangout"; although foodies feel his "fabulous" New

American fare "should be enjoyed in a less frantic atmosphere", the "NYC West" formula – "spartan" digs (think "exposed brick walls" and "deafening noise"), "young snobbish servers" and a kitchen that serves until 1 AM ("pretty rare" in this town) – is a big hit among media mavens, "restaurant people" and other night crawlers.

Godzila Sushi 🅂🅼　　　20 | 10 | 14 | $23
1800 Divisadero St. (Bush St.), 415-931-1773

■ "Cheap prices" help explain the cultlike appeal of this "shoebox"-size Pacific Heights Japanese that draws "long lines"; clearly the stars here are the "huge spicy tuna rolls" and "sashimi that melts in your mouth without burning a hole in your pocket"; the "nonexistent service" and "dumpy atmosphere" can be beastly, but with sushi this "damn good", afishionados say "it doesn't matter."

Golden Turtle 🅂　　　19 | 16 | 18 | $26
2211 Van Ness Ave. (bet. Broadway & Vallejo St.), 415-441-4419

◪ For "good, solid" Vietnamese vittles "without the snob factor of The Slanted Door", this venerable Van Ness resident fits the bill; fans report the Imperial Rolls and myriad of seasonal crab dishes (sauteed, pan-fried or roasted) "remain sublime after all these years"; however pho foes reveal that all that glitters isn't gold here, dissing the decor (despite the "hand-carved wooden wall" paneling) and griping about service that runs at "a turtle's pace."

Gordon Biersch Brewery 🅻🅂🅼　14 | 15 | 14 | $24
2 Harrison St. (The Embarcadero), 415-243-8246
See review in Silicon Valley/Peninsula Directory.

Gordon's House of Fine Eats ◑🅻🅂🅼　21 | 20 | 18 | $37
500 Florida St. (bet. 18th & Mariposa Sts.), 415-861-8900

■ Clearly "the place to be seen" in the Mission's "multimedia" gulch, this "high-energy" (aka "noisy") warehouse-turned-eatery "understands how to balance hip and tasty"; the "whimsical" New American menu offers "something to please even the pickiest palate" ("who [else] would have thought" to put "a plate of doughnuts" and "yummy scallops" on the same menu?), and when novices ask "what kind of restaurant is this?", regulars respond it's one that "can swing both ways – casual and upscale."

Grand Cafe 🅻🅂🅼　　　20 | 26 | 21 | $40
Hotel Monaco, 501 Geary St. (Taylor St.), 415-292-0101

◪ "What to say about this Goliath of a place" Downtown?; loyalists can't lavish enough praise on the "unbelievably elegant", "beautiful sweeping space" with "30-foot ceilings" and a "very classy bar" that makes you "feel like you're in an old French movie" and "sets the stage for thoughtful service"; "it's great for stylish pre-theater dining" – even though the less-enamored lament "if only the Californian–New French food was as grand as the dining room"; N.B. ratings may not reflect the arrival of new chef Victor Scargle (ex Pisces).

Grandeho's Kamekyo L S M | 21 | 15 | 19 | $26 |

943 Cole St. (bet. Carl St. & Parnassus Ave.), 415-759-8428
2721 Hyde St. (bet. Beach & North Point Sts.), 415-673-6828
■ "Buy the chef a beer for special treatment", i.e. making you "rolls not on the menu", suggest devotees of this duo of "friendly neighborhood" sushi bars featuring "fresh, awesome" raw fish and "cooked dishes" at "honest prices" that might "change the way you think of Japanese food"; best of all, you don't have to worry about parking, as both the Cole Valley and Wharf branches are conveniently located off trolley lines.

Great Eastern ◗ L S M | 21 | 11 | 14 | $27 |

649 Jackson St. (bet. Grant Ave. & Kearny St.), 415-986-2500
■ For "superb" seafood, insiders head for this bi-level "Hong Kong–style" eatery where "fish from the tanks" is often "brought over to your table for approval" before cooking (now that's "fresh"!); the "extensive" menu also ranges from the "elaborate" to the "ordinary", so "ask the waiter" to recommend; the ornate dining room may explain why the food is "several dollars more expensive" than that of nearby Chinatown "holes-in-the-wall."

GREENS L S M | 22 | 23 | 20 | $33 |

Ft. Mason Ctr., Bldg. A (Buchanan St.), 415-771-6222
◪ "Visiting vegetarians" will "think they've died and gone to the Garden of Eden" at this Marina meatless mecca; the "upscale" "Zen-like atmosphere" is enhanced by the "unparalleled" panorama of the Bay outside and rough-hewn "redwood tables" within; and if cynics crack that the 22-year-old greens seem a little wilted ("really slow service", "seems to be resting on its laurels"), most maintain this is "still a standard-bearer for herbivores."

Hahn's Hibachi L M | 15 | 9 | 13 | $15 |

1305 Castro St. (24th St.), 415-642-8151 S
525 Haight St. (Fillmore St.), 415-864-3721 S
535 Irving St. (bet. 6th & 7th Aves.), 415-731-3721 S
1710 Polk St. (bet. Clay & Washington Sts.), 415-776-1095 S
3318 Steiner St. (bet. Chestnut & Lombard Sts.), 415-931-6284
◪ Even "Korean-food snobs have grown to love this" chain of "holes-in-the-wall" that dish up "bounteous servings" of "satisfying" BBQ and "delicious kimchi" at "bargain" prices; detractors deem the dishes too "Americanized"

and the "decor too close for comfort", shrugging "you get what you pay for" (yeah, that's the point, regulars retort).

Hamano Sushi 🆂🅼   23 | 13 | 13 | $28
1332 Castro St. (24th St.), 415-826-0825
◪ This "neighborhood" Noe Valleyite is where maki mavens "bring Japanese friends who are homesick for the real deal": "huge pieces" of "succulent" sushi that "are unmatched anywhere outside of Tokyo"; they line up despite the "sterile atmosphere" (which "reminds one of a motel lobby") and the "rude staff", although some say the table "service has improved noticeably under new ownership" (which has also introduced more modern cooked items to the menu).

Harbor Village 🅻🆂🅼   20 | 18 | 16 | $31
4 Embarcadero Ctr. (Sacramento St.), 415-781-8833
◪ If you want your *shu mai* with a view, this Downtown "white-tablecloth Chinese" is the place to go – even though it may take more than a Village waiter to explain the "fresh, dizzying variety of dim sum"; the "eye-catching", "opulent setting" is a good spot for splurging for an "outrageously expensive" group banquet, but doubters declare this large vet is now "worn at the edges": "you can find better" (and cheaper) elsewhere.

Hard Rock Cafe 🅻🆂🅼   11 | 17 | 13 | $22
1699 Van Ness Ave. (Sacramento St.), 415-885-1699
◪ The Van Ness "music memorabilia mecca" follows the same formula as all the others around the world – "cool" rock 'n' roll tchotchkes, "fun music videos" to "look at" and "pricey" "burgers and shakes" – which still lures tourists and teens; grownups, however, grouse "it doesn't have the same impact as when one was 13" and wonder, unless you're in between a rock and a hard place, "why bother?"

Harris' 🆂🅼   23 | 20 | 21 | $47
2100 Van Ness Ave. (Pacific Ave.), 415-673-1888
◪ "Passersby meditating in front of the windows where the beef is aged" are your first clue that this Van Ness/Polk spot is a carnivore's clubhouse; the "good ol' boys" like the primo prime rib ("like butter in your mouth") and "famous" "icy martinis" in the "old-school atmosphere" of the dining room or the Pacific Lounge, however the less starry-eyed prefer to "pick up a steak to go", deeming the decor "dark and gloomy"; some "steer clear" of it altogether, stating this "staid" operation has passed its prime.

HAWTHORNE LANE 🅻🆂🅼   26 | 25 | 24 | $53
22 Hawthorne St. (bet. 2nd & 3rd Sts.), 415-777-9779
◼ Although founding chef "Anne's gone", the "quality lingers" on at this sophisticated "haven from the 'in' spots" of SoMa; the "creative" yet "comforting" "Asian-

Californian cuisine" (where dumplings and pizza happily coexist) still gets "high marks", as does the "elegant dining room" (exposed beams and an open working kitchen with "magnificent" artwork and flowers) and the "polished, professional staff"; while "not for the faint of wallet", it remains one of SF's "paragons of fine" business dining.

Hayes & Vine Wine Bar ◗🅢🅜 | 18 | 21 | 19 | $25 |

377 Hayes St. (bet. Franklin & Gough Sts.), 415-626-5301
◪ This "cool", "minimalist" Hayes Valley half-pint is an "oenophiles' delight" with an inventory of over 1,000 labels (40 of which are available by the glass or half glass); it also lures "ladies" and Civic Center season ticket holders looking to wet their whistle and "snack on cheese and charcuterie plates"; however, many hunger for "more food choices" (there are "no real meals") and scoff at the "attitude" of the "knowledgeable staff."

Hayes Street Grill 🅛🅢🅜 | 23 | 17 | 21 | $38 |

320 Hayes St. (bet. Franklin & Gough Sts.), 415-863-5545
◪ Savvy seafood and symphony subscribers return to this 21-year-old "no-nonsense" American in Hayes Valley specializing in "simple preparations" of "pristine" fin fare that changes daily with the local catch (it's one of the few places where you can find "great sand dabs"); but while traditionalists find it "as comfortable as an old shoe", epicureans expecting something more daring (given that it's owned by food critic Patricia Unterman) say it's "a lot of money for" "grilled fish."

Helmand, The 🅢 | 23 | 17 | 20 | $30 |

430 Broadway (bet. Kearny & Montgomery Sts.), 415-362-0641
■ Even though it's located "near the strip clubs" of North Beach, entering into this "exotic" Afghani oasis "feels like you're walking into a different world" and an introduction to "a genre rarely tried in SF"; "take your deprived Midwestern visitors" for the "novelty" of a "tangy" "blend of Middle Eastern spices", "lovely lamb dishes" and "superb" "spiced pumpkin appetizers"; the decor is "simple and unassuming" at best, but where else can you get such "fabulously different tastes" at such "reasonable prices"?

Herbivore 🅛🅢🅜 | 19 | 16 | 15 | $17 |

983 Valencia St. (21st St.), 415-826-5657
◪ Although tree huggers dig the "concept" of this Mission "no-meat" mecca where "pierced twenty-somethings" "pig out on" the "diverse" selection of dairy-free vittles and fresh "organic juices", the kitchen's labor harvests a mixed response: the addicted attest the "extremely reasonably priced" "food is so good you wonder what herbs they put in it", but skeptics suggest that while it's "great for vegans", "very little is superlative" enough on "the static menu" to appeal to "everyone else."

Hotei **L S M**   16   14   15 $17
1290 Ninth Ave. (Irving St.), 415-753-6045

■ "For a piping hot bowl of soup" "on a cold day" or a big pile of "satisfying", "slurpy" udon served in a "pleasant" Japanese "country setting", this "economical" Inner Sunset haunt does the trick; discriminating dissenters, however, denounce this "Ebisu offshoot" as "a disappointment", pronouncing the "flavors" "flat" as a noodle.

House **M**   24   17   20 $33
1230 Grant Ave. (bet. Columbus Ave. & Vallejo St.), 415-986-8612 **L**
1269 Ninth Ave. (bet. Irving St. & Lincoln Way), 415-682-3898 **S**

■ This Asian-Californian duo is home to fusion fare "without the pretentiousness" or prices of more "hip" brethren; worshipers would swim upstream for the "absolutely stunning" fish dishes (the "Chilean sea bass rocks") and caution you not to "go gaga" over "the appetizers, as you need to leave room for dessert"; while the "industrial" "decor isn't great" and shouting above the noise"will leave you hoarse", the "exciting" eats makes it all worthwhile.

House of Nanking **L S M**   20   6   10 $16
919 Kearny St. (bet. Columbus Ave. & Jackson St.), 415-421-1429

◪ To some, the popularity of this infamous "Americanized Chinese" "is befuddling", considering the staff that "orders you what they please" ("unless you can make up your mind in two minutes"), the cramped, "dingy surroundings" and the "100 percent Caucasian" clientele ("which should have been a warning in Chinatown"); yet getting "yelled at" is "part of the charm" for fans, as are the "huge amounts" of "good", "greasy" food at "bang-for-your-buck" prices.

House of Prime Rib **S M**   23   18   21 $38
1906 Van Ness Ave. (Washington St.), 415-885-4605

■ For over 50 years this "clubby" "old-school" Van Ness vet has "stuck to a formula" of roasting "satisfying slabs" of beef and "carving" them tableside from an "Airstream of a serving cart"; the "super" rehearsed service ("where else is a baked potato an event?") includes serving a "freshly mixed tossed salad" and "authentic Yorkshire pudding", all of which is included in the "great price"; while modernists find the old act "almost laughable", cheerleaders counter "they do one thing, but they do it so well."

Hunan **L M**   20   10   15 $20
1016 Bryant St. (8th St.), 415-861-5808
110 Natoma St. (bet. New Montgomery & 2nd Sts.), 415-546-4999
674 Sacramento St. (bet. Kearny & Montgomery Sts.), 415-788-2234
924 Sansome St. (Broadway), 415-956-7727 **S**

■ "There's a reason they have red peppers on the signs" at this chainlet of Hunan haunts, highly regarded as "still the hottest" in town; so "ignore" the "thrift-store" decor and sink your chopsticks into owner Henry Chung's "fantastic" fiery fare, which has been "a SF tradition for more than 20 years" (as the displayed 1970s *New Yorker* write-ups attest).

Hunan Home's Restaurant 🄻🄂🄼 | 21 | 9 | 16 | $21 |

622 Jackson St. (bet. Grant Ave. & Kearny St.), 415-982-2844
■ Although less-known than its neighbors, this "solid" "authentic" eatery gets dubbed the "dark-horse victor in the Chinatown Hunan" competition; true, it's got "no ambiance" and the elapsed time from food "order to delivery is suspiciously short", but no one argues with the fact that it serves "consistently" "yummy, spicy" Chinese ("love the honey walnut prawns") at a good "value."

Hungarian Sausage Factory & Bistro 🄂 | ▽ 17 | 13 | 16 | $20 |

419 Cortland Ave. (bet. Bennington & Wool Sts.), 415-648-2847
■ You better "be hungary" when you come to this "tiny joint"/sausage factory in Bernal Heights, because the "authentic homestyle cooking" ("yummy goulash") "is rich" and "high in cholesterol"; regulars warn "don't expect anything resembling service" and "forget the decor", but do "stay" for the "neighborhood flavor" and the nightly "live jazz piano performances."

Hyde Street Bistro 🄂 | 22 | 18 | 21 | $33 |

1521 Hyde St. (bet. Jackson & Pacific Sts.), 415-292-4415
■ It "feels like Paris" assert *amis* of this "Russian Hill enclave", a "well-hyden secret" among locals for its "true bistro food and atmosphere"; even if the "fairly priced French" fare ("great bouillabaisse", "wonderful" cherry clafoutis) "weren't as good as it is", the "warm greeting" of chef/co-owner Fabrice Marcon and pastry chef/wife Betty alone "would be worth the visit."

I Fratelli 🄂🄼 | 19 | 18 | 19 | $31 |

1896 Hyde St. (Green St.), 415-474-8240
◪ Just a few steps off the Hyde St.-Powell St cable car line, this twentysomething "neighborhood haunt" continues to serve Russian Hill locals and birthday party celebrants with "consistent", "kind-of-simple" trattoria fare; aside from the "delicious pastas", made on the premises daily, the food is "nothing special", but the "brother/owners (*i fratelli*) make the restaurant with their gracious hospitality"; cynics, however, say "it's suffering from chain-itis" since opening out-of-town branches.

Il Fornaio ●🄻🄂🄼 | 19 | 20 | 19 | $33 |

Levi's Plaza, 1265 Battery St. (bet. Greenwich & Union Sts.), 415-986-0100
■ Part of an ever-expanding chain, this Downtown spot remains "true to its Northern Italian roots", delivering

"predictable but nicely done" standards such as pasta and pizzas and "professional service"; everyone seems to know about the "wonderful outdoor seating" and the freshly baked items made "in-house" ("I could go just for the aroma"), but it's the "monthly regional special menus" that keep regulars "coming back."

Indian Oven 🆂🅼 | 23 | 16 | 17 | $23 |

233 Fillmore St. (bet. Haight & Waller Sts.), 415-626-1628
■ This frenetic, "packed Indian" curries contentment among masala mavens with its "amazing naans", "excellent chutneys" and other "skillfully prepared", "delicious" Delhi dinner items; despite its "funky location" in the Lower Haight, this "non-dive" has a considerably "fancier ambiance" than your typical buffet palace; "the service is scattered", but "when there's a line out the door on a Monday night, you know it's good."

Indigo 🆂 | 22 | 20 | 21 | $36 |

687 McAllister St. (bet. Franklin & Gough Sts.), 415-673-9353
■ When you're in the mood for a "delicious" dinner "without all the attitude", try this "perfect charmer"; although "not red-hot", it's a true-blue "alternative" in the Civic Center area for culture vultures needing a pre-performance Californian–New American meal; oenophiles who can wait until after 8 PM show up for the three-course "prix fixe" menu "which includes all-you-can-drink wine by the glass" (from a pre-selected list).

Infusion Bar & Restaurant 🄻🆂🅼 | 18 | 17 | 18 | $30 |

555 Second St. (bet. Brannan & Bryant Sts.), 415-543-2282
■ One glance behind the bar and you'll understand why this "trendy" Pac Bell Parker is dubbed a "vodka haven" – it's the dizzying display of home-brewed, "excellent fruit-infused" liquors (ranging from cinnamon apple to Serrano chili, depending on the season); beyond the martinis, the "Cajun-influenced" New American fare "is surprisingly good", "the atmosphere is authentic dot-com" and the "music in the loft isn't bad either."

Irrawaddy Burmese Cuisine 🆂 ▽ | 20 | 17 | 21 | $19 |

1769 Lombard St. (bet. Laguna & Octavia Sts.), 415-931-2830
■ Named for the river that irrigates Burma's plains, this "fun little place" is often "overlooked" in the Marina, but those who have found it enjoy the "wonderfully different" fare that combines Chinese and Indian techniques; the somewhat "skimpy portions" are served "family"-style at sunken tables by the "charming owners" and staff.

Isa 🆂 | 25 | 18 | 20 | $40 |

3324 Steiner St. (bet. Chestnut & Lombard Sts.), 415-567-9588
■ "Take your friends and order everything" on chef/co-owner Luke Sung's "exquisitely prepared" "New French

tapas" menu at this Marina "find of the year", "part of the small-plate craze" among SF eateries; just "don't show up famished", as the "prices quickly add up" if you're hoping to make a "man's meal"; since the petite "dining room is almost in the kitchen", insiders suggest "sit out back" on the heated patio.

Isobune Sushi 🄻🅂🄼   16 13 14 $23

Japan Ctr., 1737 Post St. (Buchanan St.), 415-563-1030
◸ "If you like your sushi right off the boat, this is the place for you", as the main "gimmick" of this kitschy Japantown joint is plates of pre-made hand rolls and *nigiri* that "float" around the mechanical bar; although the "average-to-decent" offerings are "not the best in town" (the wary warn "watch out for" fish that has been "circling for a while") and the "service is weak", it still reels in "out-of-towners" and kids who insist it's "definitely the most fun."

It's Tops Coffee Shop ◗🄻🅂🄼   17 15 18 $13

1801 Market St. (bet. Guerrero & Valencia Sts.), 415-431-6395
■ "A diner straight out of *Twin Peaks*", this "retro" Upper Market coffee shop (featured in many films) run by the same family since 1952 draws long lines for its flapjacks ("I defy you to find a fluffier buckwheat pancake") and the usual "classics – burgers, fries, shakes"; although the prices are decidedly new millennium, the "greasy" grub is "perfect for that middle-of-the-night, gotta-have-it bite"; N.B. the kitchen serves breakfast til 3 AM (except Sunday).

Izzy's Steak & Chop House 🅂🄼   20 16 19 $36

3345 Steiner St. (bet. Chestnut & Lombard Sts.), 415-563-0487
■ "For a good steak", "to-die-for" potatoes (prepared au gratin) and "fun bartenders who know how to keep your drinks fresh", Marina meat eaters stake their claim on this "casual" chophouse with a Prohibition-era, saloon-like "funky atmosphere" ("feels like a place for politicians and fistfights"); unlike swankier steakhouses, here "you don't have to worry about spilling sauce on your Armani."

Jackson Fillmore Trattoria 🅂🄼   21 13 17 $30

2506 Fillmore St. (Jackson St.), 415-346-5288
◸ "Tasty" "straight-ahead Italian" ("mostly Southern") and a sassy "neighborhood character" "are the hallmarks" of Jack Krietzman's perpetually "packed" "noisy" Upper Fillmore "cramped pasta heaven" that's "almost a landmark"; regulars insist the "amazing complimentary bruschetta" compensates for the "way-too-long waits", "surly" service and "nondescript decor."

JARDINIÈRE 🅂🄼   26 26 25 $57

300 Grove St. (Franklin St.), 415-861-5555
■ When "you really want to wow" someone, "take them" to this "jazzy" Hayes Valley supper club that's "*the* social"

stop "for pre- and post-symphony, opera and ballet" dining ("the people-watching is almost as good as the oysters"); co-owner Pat Kuleto's "champagne-motif", "magnificent surroundings" "pull you" in, then chef/co-owner Traci des Jardins' "orgasmic" Cal-French "garden of earthly delights" "elevates [you] to royal heights"; as for the "time-sensitive" service, "you'll only find better" "in heaven."

Jianna ●ⓈⓂ
23 | 21 | 21 | $42

1548 Stockton St. (bet. Green & Union Sts.), 415-398-0442

■ "It's about time" North Beach got "a restaurant that offers great food in a casual" "yet stylish" atmosphere carol converts; the kitchen "exceeds expectations" by delivering "innovative" New American cuisine, great wines (many available in half bottles) and "amazing" "mini-desserts"; it all comes at really "reasonable prices" and is served by a "friendly", "professional" staff to boot.

Johnfrank ⓈⓂ
21 | 19 | 19 | $42

2100 Market St. (bet. Church & 14th Sts.), 415-503-0333

■ While there are "boys, boys everywhere", this "really loud" Upper Market spot is "no longer" considered "a gay hangout but a dining destination" now that chef Lance Velasquez (ex Ne O) is manning the stoves – "everything" from his "creative" New American menu "is on the money" (he "could make you love Brussels sprouts"); however, "the bar rivals the dining" scene at times.

John's Grill ⓁⓈⓂ
17 | 18 | 17 | $33

63 Ellis St. (bet. Powell & Stockton Sts.), 415-986-0069

■ *Maltese Falcon* buffs and "a mostly older crowd" migrate to this 1908 Downtown chophouse that was a favorite hangout of Dashiell Hammett; although it's no great mystery that they "go for the nostalgia" (a warren of memorabilia-packed rooms) and "not the food", some relish the American classics, including "fresh liver with bacon and onions, an item as hard to find these days" as that jeweled bird statue.

Joubert's Ⓢ
▽ 19 | 15 | 22 | $27

4115 Judah St. (46th Ave.), 415-753-5448

■ Although "vegetarian South African food" may sound like an "oxymoron", chef-owner Patrick Joubert Conlon is out to show the kebab-conscious otherwise; adventure seekers who trek to his hideaway in the hinterlands of the Sunset are treated graciously by his "warm", "friendly staff" and treated to an array of "unusual", "tasty" specialties from 11 different regions, plus native wines – all of which "makes up for the lackluster decor."

Juban ⓁⓈⓂ
18 | 16 | 15 | $28

Japan Ctr., 1581 Webster St. (bet. Geary Blvd. & Post St.), 415-776-5822

See review in Silicon Valley/Peninsula Directory.

Julius' Castle 🆂Ⓜ 17 | 25 | 20 | $47
1541 Montgomery St. (Union St.), 415-392-2222
◪ Dining at this "enchanting" 1922 landmark aerie "tucked away" in Telegraph Hill "can be amazingly romantic" report love birds, thanks to one of the "best views of the Bay" from intimate seating areas that "allow you the privacy" "to keep kissing your partner all night long"; the less passionate, however, point out that the New American–French– Northern Italian mélange of pricey, "so-so" fare just proves the old adage "the better the view, the worse the food."

Kabuto Sushi 25 | 11 | 18 | $34
5116 Geary Blvd. (15th Ave.), 415-752-5652
■ This small spot "feels like Japan without the cigarette smoke" thanks to sashimi "so fresh it leaps off your chopsticks"; one school of surveyors says "sit at the bar" for the best view of chef-owner Sachio Kojima (aka "The Machine") wielding the "fastest sushi knife in the West", while another suggests "the tatami rooms for best atmosphere"; although both "are a bit dog-eared", "Avenue locals and the faithful" ask "with food this good, who comes for the decor?"

Kan Zaman ●Ⓛ🆂Ⓜ 18 | 22 | 17 | $21
1793 Haight St. (Shrader St.), 415-751-9656
■ Commenters have "one word to describe" this Haight-Ashbury bit of "Baghdad by the Bay": "fun!"; bands of birthday parties and "big groups on a budget" "sit cross-legged on the floor", "drink spiced wine" and "watch belly dancers" while dipping into dishes of "delicious baba ghanoush" and other Middle Eastern munchies; capping off the evening, they Kan smoke fruit-flavored tobacco "hookah pipes to chill out."

Kate's Kitchen Ⓛ🆂Ⓜ⇥ 21 | 11 | 17 | $14
471 Haight St. (bet. Buchanan & Fillmore Sts.), 415-626-3984
■ "You never walk away hungry" proclaim Kate's cheering committee, who withstand "long waits" for "mm-mm pancakes", "wonderful biscuits" and other "Southern specialties" ("any place that offers French Toast Orgy wins my vote") at this "funky" breakfast/brunch "hangover" hangout on Lower Haight; however, they like the "large portions" – "share a plate unless you're starving" – "more than the neighborhood" or the equally "plain atmosphere."

Katia's Russian Tea Room Ⓛ🆂 19 | 16 | 18 | $24
600 Fifth Ave. (Balboa St.), 415-668-9292
■ For a taste of the Old Country in "this country", comrades beat a path to this sunny Inner Richmond Russian where chef-owner Katia Troosh whips up "good" "homey" renditions of traditional fare, shuttled to your table by "slow servers (but with a smile)"; "live music" on the guitar and accordion lends an "authentic" air to the whole affair.

Kelly's Mission Rock L S 13 | 17 | 13 | $23
817 China Basin St. (Mariposa St.), 415-626-5355

▣ Sitting on the "open deck" of this bi-level China Basin spot and watching the "working waterfront" below "is great for playing hooky on a sunny weekday afternoon" or partying "after work" fans maintain; but critics caution "stick to drinks and appetizers" because the view, as nice as it is, "doesn't make up for the very mediocre, basic" American food and "hit-or-miss service."

Khan Toke Thai House S M 21 | 23 | 19 | $25
5937 Geary Blvd. (bet. 23rd & 24th Aves.), 415-668-6654

◪ "Wear socks" counsel connoisseurs, since "you will need to lose the shoes" before slinking into the sunken tables and enjoying "delish" dishes at this "lavish" Thai in the Richmond; the festive atmosphere is "good for groups of friends"; as for those curmudgeons who complain the "service is haphazard" and the low-slung "seating is uncomfortable", they can always "order takeout."

King of Thai ● L S M ≠ 19 | 6 | 13 | $12
639 Clement St. (bet. 7th & 8th Aves.), 415-752-5198

■ "Superlative noodles" and other "large portions" of "amazingly good" "Thai street food" are king at this Inner Richmond resident known for "super-speedy service" and "dirt cheap" prices that even a pauper could love; true, there's "no atmosphere", but at 1:30 in the morning, who's looking?

KOKKARI ESTIATORIO L M 25 | 26 | 23 | $45
200 Jackson St. (Front St.), 415-981-0983

■ To get a taste of Samos "in San Francisco", homesick Hellenists and Downtown businessmen book reservations at this "totally fun" taverna sporting a "spacious high-ceilinged" "timbered" interior that "takes you back to the Aegean"; fans insist the "upscale Greek" repertoire is "food elevated to an art"; although the tab is "a bit pricier than you expect" ("that's an expensive bowl of moussaka"), even Zorba would feel "welcome" "sitting in the front room" by the "roaring fire" or sipping retsina at the "spirited" bar.

Kuleto's L S M 20 | 20 | 19 | $36
Villa Florence Hotel, 221 Powell St. (bet. Geary & O'Farrell Sts.), 415-397-7720

◪ For 25 years, this "hectic" hotel "favorite" has held its place in Union Square, and although "nothing here is the best", "everything taken together" – Pat Kuleto's "striking decor" (fresco-like ceilings and whole sal*amis* dangling above a 40-foot mahogany bar), "friendly staff" and "consistently good" "midpriced" "standbys" – makes this Italian a "steady performer" for a "pre-theater" bite or a "post-shopping snack;" N.B. if you're in a hurry, order appetizers at their new next-door wine bar, Enoteca.

KYO-YA L 25 21 24 $52
Palace Hotel, 2 New Montgomery St. (Market St.),
415-546-5090

■ "Superb" sashimi, shabu-shabu and sake (11 different brands) are the hallmarks of this "serene", sophisticated SoMa sushi bar, which caters to well-to-do tourists willing to spend for what's "easily the best" (and certainly the most "expensive") "Japanese food in town"; if you're fishing for more than the raw deal, splurge for a "refined" "kaiseki dinner", "a seven-course, beautifully prepared gourmet experience" "that's worth" the Tokyo tariff.

La Cumbre Taqueria L S M 21 9 13 $10
515 Valencia St. (bet. 16th & 17th Sts.), 415-863-8205

◪ This "endlessly busy" cheap taqueria "in the heart of the Mission" is a "lunchtime" and late-dinner "staple" known for the "best burritos bar none" and other "delicious" (if "greasy") plates of "authentic Mexican" fare; "the decor is non-existent", but sated surveyors smile "the buxom lady on the wall mural makes my super taco taste all the better."

La Felce L S M 19 13 19 $32
1570 Stockton St. (Union St.), 415-392-8321

■ Dating back to 1974, this "authentic Italian" is "one of the last survivors of North Beach", and according to acolytes it'll "make you never go to a trendy place again"; the "traditional homestyle fare" (think veal saltimbocca) is served in a "low-key" dining room filled by a "real local crowd" and serviced by a "friendly staff"; the five-course prix fixe is "like a Florida early-bird special" without the "time constraints."

LA FOLIE M 28 24 26 $70
2316 Polk St. (bet. Green & Union Sts.), 415-776-5577

■ Francophiles and foodies alike lionize Lyonnaise "master chef"-owner Roland Passot's "beautiful, if a bit cozy", Polk Street bistro as "heaven on earth"; the whimsical "jester/clown theme" lends a sense of theater but "pales in comparison" to "artfully presented" "artery-clogging", "magical modern French" "concoctions" (the "Discovery Menu is highly worth the extra bucks"); an "accommodating but not cloying" staff "seduces you" with "Gallic charm."

Laghi S 20 15 19 $32
2101 Sutter St. (Steiner St.), 415-931-3774

◪ At this Pacific Heights trattoria, ever-ardent amici report that chef-owner Gino Laghi's renditions of Emilia Romagna cuisine is "the same good Northern Italian food", with the "wonderful, imaginative" pasta made on the premises and service that "makes you feel like family"; but adversaries argue the "waiters seemed stretched thin" after a recent move to "big new quarters", which they lament are *così così* and "no longer cozy."

La Méditerranée 🅛🅢🅜   19 14 17 $19
2210 Fillmore St. (Sacramento St.), 415-921-2956
288 Noe St. (bet. Market & 16th Sts.), 415-431-7210
◾ This pair of "hallway-size" Upper Fillmore and the Castro eateries lures dolmas devotees with "reliable" Middle Eastern–Mediterranean meals at "prices that seem stuck in the last decade"; unfortunately, so do "the menu and decor" dis detractors, who gripe the service is "zoo-like" and you "feel like you're sitting on top of each other"; P.S. the "sample platters" "to go" are "always party pleasers."

La Palma Mexicatessen 🅛🅢🅜   ▽ 23 9 13 $10
2884 24th St. (Florida St.), 415-647-1500
◾ You "can't get any fresher Mexican" fare than the tamales, *carnitas* and *pupusas* patted out at this "local market" and take-out joint where you can "watch the tortillas being made" by hand (one of the only places in the city that grinds its own corn for its masa); just don't expect any kind of seating or service, because this "Mission District jewel" is primarily a "place to stock" up on "bulk chile powder", hominy and other Latin ingredients.

Lapis Restaurant 🅛🅜   22 24 21 $45
Pier 33, The Embarcadero (Bay St.), 415-982-0203
◾ "Everything falls into place" at this Embarcadero "jewel", from the "swank", "airy warehouse-like interior" featuring lapis-blue walls, bronze velvet curtains and a wall of windows that afford "dramatic views of the Bay" to chef Thomas Ricci's "innovative combinations of Mediterranean" Rim flavors; it's all brought together by a "positive and attentive staff"; P.S. the adjoining "intimate lounge" is a great place "to enjoy a drink."

La Rondalla ●🅛🅢≠   13 15 13 $17
901 Valencia St. (20th St.), 415-647-7474
◾ For a "fun" night of Mexican revelry, this kitschy Mission dive "is the real thing"; "outlandish decor" (where tinsel hangs from the ceilings and "Christmas lights are on all year"), "very cheap, very potent pitchers of margaritas" and roving mariachis attract a post-bar dinner and drinking crowd (until 3 AM); true, "service is nonexistent" and the Tex-Mex menu is "mediocre at best", but after a few "killer" drinks, who cares?

La Scene Café & Bar 🅢🅜   20 20 23 $37
Warwick Regis, 490 Geary St. (Taylor St.), 415-292-6430
◾ While this "undiscovered" eatery "hidden in" Downtown's theater district "isn't a star", stage-mothering surveyors say it "deserves more recognition for its good" Mediterranean fare; as it is, ticket-holders return each season for its "good-value" pre-performance prix fixe and "friendly and efficient service" that gets you to the "show on time."

La Taqueria ⌊ⓈⓂ≠   23 | 9 | 13 | $11

2889 Mission St. (25th St.), 415-285-7117

■ "Could be the mother of all taquerias" brag boosters of this Missionite that "invented the excellent burrito" ("nothing else has ever come close to the heavenly taste"); the kitchen also "cranks out" "numero uno" tacos and "delicious *aguas frescas*" at cheapo prices, making this hole-in-the-wall "the only $10 destination food spot in the city"; you "don't expect any atmosphere" or service, but still, hooked hombres "hope it stays forever", because if it "ever closed, I would never recover."

La Vie ⓈⓂ   21 | 8 | 17 | $22

5830 Geary Blvd. (bet. 22nd & 23rd Aves.), 415-668-8080

■ "When you can't get into The Slanted Door", *c'est La Vie*, a "lovely and quiet" French-Vietnamese sleeper in the Richmond; despite the "simple decor", impressed eaters "would absolutely return" for the "wonderful selection" of "superior" Saigon specialties and the "helpful" service.

La Villa Poppi   ▽ 23 | 16 | 20 | $38

3234 22nd St. (bet. Mission & Valencia Sts.), 415-642-5044

■ This "exceedingly cute" nugget-size Tuscan trattoria in the heart of the Mission, run by "friendly talented chef" Greg Sweeting and wife Roselynn, garners "wonderful food" comments, indicating the success of the new exclusively prix fixe plan (where guests design their own multi-course "wine pairing" meals); though this 18-seater suffers from "cramped quarters", "romantics" reckon it's the "total date place"; N.B. Wednesday–Saturday only.

Le Bistrot ⓈⓂ   20 | 19 | 18 | $40

1177 California St. (Jones St.), 415-474-2000

◩ "Where else can you have French bistro cuisine" with a side of sashimi wonder wowed reviewers who've discovered this Nob Hill nouveau-comer sequestered in a condo complex; early dismissers suggest the kitchen and service are off to a "spotty" start, but at these "shockingly low prices" all is "forgiven" most say; although the "attractive" interior is "evocative of a Parisian brasserie", the sight of "its own sushi bar" and "a great view of Grace Cathedral" ground you back in SF.

Le Central Bistro ⌊Ⓜ   20 | 19 | 20 | $36

453 Bush St. (bet. Grant Ave. & Kearny St.), 415-391-2233

◩ After 25-plus years, this "old-fashioned" "unpretentious" Downtown bistro is "like a faithful friend", continuing to offer "straightforward French fare" (think cassoulet and "fantastic *poulet*") "served with a minimum of fuss"; although some say the interior feels like a "Denny's dining room" and regulars concede it's pretty much the "same old, same old", you can always count on "an interesting crowd" (it is, after all, "da mayor's secret hideout").

Le Charm French Bistro 🇱🇲 | 22 | 16 | 20 | $32 |
315 Fifth St. (bet. Folsom & Harrison Sts.), 415-546-6128

■ "Believe the name" insist those enchanted by this "utterly charming" bistro that feels "more like the 8th arrondissement" than SoMa, thanks to "marvelous" "authentic" French fare at "prices that won't leave your wallet empty"; despite the occasionally "annoying Gallic" service and the "plain room" (clearly the weakest link here, though the patio "is a plus"), "cheapskates of the world" concede "it's hard to beat" the "fabulous three-course prix fixe" for $25.

Le Colonial 🇸🇲 | 21 | 25 | 19 | $43 |
20 Cosmo Pl. (bet. Post & Sutter Sts.), 415-931-3600

☑ The "stunning tropical" "colonial setting" and "delish" "upscale New French–Vietnamese" vittles send San Franciscans on a sentimental journey to old Saigon when they visit this Downtowner; although anti-imperialists insist that bigger portions are available "at one-tenth of the price a few blocks away" and the service is "too snooty", the "sexy" atmosphere attracts "a real scene", prompting the starstruck to swagger "if it's good enough for Mick Jagger", it's good enough for them.

Left at Albuquerque 🇱🇸🇲 | 15 | 15 | 15 | $23 |
2140 Union St. (bet. Fillmore & Webster Sts.), 415-749-6700
See review in Silicon Valley/Peninsula Directory.

Le Krewe 🇱🇸🇲 | – | – | – | I |
995 Valencia St. (21st St.), 415-643-0995

A crew of refugees from PJ's Oyster Bed are hoping to let the good times roll again at this colorful new N'Awlins-style eatery strewed with Mardi Gras beads and other Bayou tchotchkes and serving authentic Cajun-Creole fare such as jambalaya, sweet-and-sour alligator and fluffy beignets; hopefully, the owners can work some voodoo on the formerly jinxed Mission space.

Le Soleil 🇱🇸🇲 | 20 | 12 | 16 | $22 |
133 Clement St. (bet. 2nd & 3rd Aves.), 415-668-4848

■ "Surprisingly" "light" and "high-quality" "Vietnamese food" that's "a whole different world for those who are used to greasy-spoon pho and lemongrass fare" is served at this "very pleasant, sunny" (and "surprisingly affordable") Inner Richmond sleeper; "ok, it's not a hip and trendy place" confess commentators, "but that's its charm."

Lhasa Moon 🇱🇸 | 17 | 13 | 19 | $20 |
2420 Lombard St. (bet. Divisadero & Scott Sts.),
415-674-9898

☑ For "the next best thing to a trip to Tibet", armchair travelers suggest heading to this Marina "rarity" known for its "wonderful butter tea", "unfiltered rice wine" and "yummy" dumplings served in a "relaxed setting" that conjures up the region; but foes fail to moon over the "simple" cuisine ("bland flavors from a colorful country"): "there's a reason it's the only Tibetan place around."

Liberty Cafe & Bakery **L S**   22 16 19 $28
410 Cortland Ave. (bet. Bennington & Wool Sts.), 415-695-8777

◪ 'Give me Liberty or give me death' remains the marching cry at this 26-seat Bernal Heights New American "loaded with" Victorian "charm"; "eat anything with a crust on it" is the mantra here, be it "the champion chicken pot pies" or the "outstanding banana cream" dessert (but don't miss "the excellent Caesar salad" either); "long waits" are common, so try to "relax at the wine bar/bakery out back"; N.B. a chef change just before press time may outdate the above food score.

Little Joe's **L S**   17 11 17 $21
523 Broadway (bet. Columbus Ave. & Kearny St.), 415-433-4343 **M**
2642 Ocean Ave. (bet. Junipero Serra Blvd. & 19th Ave.), 415-564-8200

◪ This 30-year-old North Beach "institution" (with a Sunset sib) is "still cranking out" "large plates" of "old-time" "no-frills Italian food" (think veal parmigiana, chicken marsala); natives note it's a "good place to take out-of-towners" "with no budget" "to get loud and crazy" thanks to the exuberant line cooks who "always" put on "a show"; critics, however, warn this "dumpy dive" is "way past its prime."

Livefire Grill & Smokehouse **S M**   16 18 17 $35
100 Brannan St. (bet. 1st St. & The Embarcadero), 415-227-0777
See review in North of San Francisco Directory.

Liverpool Lil's **◐ L S M**   16 16 17 $26
2942 Lyon St. (bet. Greenwich & Lombard Sts.), 415-921-6664

◼ It's "still 1973" at this "friendly" "neighborhood pub" whose "dark-wood-and-brassy interior" is covered with photos of old sports heroes; the "good-for-what-it-is" American "pub grub" is equally "trapped in time", so it naturally attracts "older-timers and a trendy younger set" seeking refuge "from the ruckus" of Cow Hollow to knock back a pint or grab "a last-minute burger" after-hours (the kitchen serves till 1 AM).

L'Olivier **L M**   20 20 22 $38
465 Davis Ct. (Jackson St.), 415-981-7824

◪ "Elegant" and "*très* French", this throwback "hidden" in a Downtown high-rise complex continues to lure the nostalgic set with its "impeccable service", "charming country fare" and a "cozy atmosphere", making it possibly the "quietest spot in town"; although the three-course "prix fixe" lunches and dinners are a "great" value, thoroughly modern Millies maintain this "fussy" veteran is "passé."

London Wine Bar 🛇Ⓜ
13 | 14 | 16 | $25

415 Sansome St. (bet. Clay & Sacramento Sts.), 415-788-4811
☑ Before wine bars were the rage, this dark, clubby Financial District "gathering place" was the only spot in SF with an extensive array of vino by the glass; these days it's not the "hippest" place around, but it still pulls in suits "after work"; the 1,100-bottle cellar (with 50 varietals available in 8-ounce pours) remains impressive, but the consensus is skip the "so-so" Californian victuals.

Long Life Noodle Company & Jook Joint 🛇Ⓜ
13 | 11 | 11 | $15

Sony Metreon Ctr., 101 Fourth St. (bet. Howard & Mission Sts.), 415-369-6188 Ⓢ
139 Steuart St. (bet. Howard & Mission Sts.), 415-281-3818
☑ A bevy of "basic" noodles, along with other "inventive-sounding" dishes, is the draw at these Embarcadero and SoMa and Asians; obviously "there's a reason there are long lines" (they're "cheap, fast"), but most noses are out of joint, maintaining all you get is "big bowls of bland stuff" and suggesting "life is too short to eat here."

L'Osteria del Forno 🛇ⓈⓂ⇗
23 | 15 | 19 | $24

519 Columbus Ave. (bet. Green & Union Sts.), 415-982-1124
■ "More proof that good things come in small packages", this "matchbox" "charmer" in North Beach cranks out "ultra-thin pizza" and "wonderful focaccia sandwiches"; amici "wish it were easier to get in" but withstand the wait because it "feels like Italy", and at these "embarrassingly cheap prices" it's "one of the best buys for your money."

Lovejoy's Tea Room 🛇Ⓢ
18 | 21 | 20 | $18

1351 Church St. (Clipper St.), 415-648-5895
■ For a taste of "the English countryside" in Noe Valley, Darjeeling devotees dovetail it to this "quirky place" that serves afternoon tea amid a jumble of knickknacks and antiques; tea-totalers attest it's the "perfect place" for "bridal showers" "when you can't afford the Ritz-Carlton" but recommend sticking with the "buttery scones" and Devonshire cream over the heartier West End standards.

Luna Park 🛇ⓈⓂ
21 | 18 | 18 | $27

694 Valencia St. (18th St.), 415-553-8584
☑ "The secret is out" about this "fun" "hipster hangout in the Mission", thanks to its interactive eclectic (French-Italian, with American influences) fare – "gotta have" the goat cheese fondue and "make-it-yourself s'mores"; a

"louder-than-a-rocket" "bar scene" dominates the racy red room, but Lunatics shrug it off and insist the "personable service" and "affordable prices" are "surprising for such a busy place"; P.S. lunch is calmer and easier to get into.

Macaroni Sciue Sciue 🅛🅜   ▽ 18 | 15 | 18 | $25

124 Columbus Ave. (bet. Jackson & Kearny Sts.), 415-217-8400
■ Compared to bigger sibling Caffe Macaroni, this casual North Beach cafe is still relatively "undiscovered", but it serves "the same" good food continuously from 10 AM until closing at "budget prices"; "you know it's authentic Italian when you can watch the waiters smoking and flirting while you're enjoying your meal."

MacArthur Park 🅛🅢🅜   17 | 18 | 17 | $32

607 Front St. (bet. Jackson St. & Pacific Ave.), 415-398-5700
◪ Many a San Franciscan "grew up on the BBQ ribs and mud pies" served at this "plantation-size" institution, a "dependable" Downtowner that still lures families and some suits with "huge portions" (as well as those fondly remembered crayons) at "reasonable prices"; single folk are less nostalgic about the "unimaginative, traditional American fare" and "tired decor" but concede there's a "great happy-hour" bar scene.

Magnolia Pub & Brewery 🅛🅢🅜   15 | 14 | 16 | $18

1398 Haight St. (Masonic Ave.), 415-864-7468
◪ This "funky" "Haight place" is a favorite "friendly gathering spot" ("and you don't even have to have purple hair to fit in") best known for its "awesome" "handcrafted" ales and "beers on tap" (also used to steam the signature mussels); but the American grub "is definitely hit or miss", so "stick with the yuppie burgers" and the microbrews.

Maharani 🅛🅢🅜   18 | 15 | 17 | $26

1122 Post St. (bet. Polk St. & Van Ness Ave.), 415-775-1988
◪ She'll feel like a maharani at this ornate pink palace in Van Ness/Polk whose "above-average Indian" cuisine "curries you home to Old Bombay"; some say the food's a tad "tired", so for a hot date, order an extra spicy dish and ask the "friendly hosts" for a booth in the bead-curtained Fantasy Room.

MAKI 🅛🅢   25 | 17 | 21 | $37

Japan Ctr., 1825 Post St. (Webster St.), 415-921-5215
■ "So different from the ordinary Japanese" marvel maki mavens about the signature *wappa-meshi* (a wooden basket filled with veggies, meat and steamed rice) and other "unique" specialties at this "tiny jewel" hidden on the second floor of the Japan Center; although the 17-seat dining room is incredibly "tight", the owner who "greets and bids" guests seems to compensate for it, as does the "variety of cold sakes."

Mama's on
Washington Square L S ⊄
24　16　17　$19

1701 Stockton St. (Filbert St.), 415-362-6421

■ "Not even my mama makes better French toast" confess homebodies about this "North Beach tradition" that draws "long lines" for its "heavenly breakfast" and brunch, featuring such American treats as "fluffy omelets" and "excellent crumb cakes"; be sure to "bring your coffee, a date and your Sunday paper to read while waiting"; just don't go at night, as they don't serve dinner.

Mandalay L S M
20　10　16　$20

4348 California St. (6th Ave.), 415-386-3895

■ Many a fan fawns that this Inner Richmond "old standby" serves "the best Burmese food I've ever had" ("ok, it's the only Burmese I've ever had"); the "unique tea leaf salad" and other specialties are "wonderful" "taste sensations", but there's "no ambiance whatsoever", so if you can't "ignore the decor", it might be "better for takeout."

Mandarin, The L S M
19　20　18　$39

Ghirardelli Sq., 900 North Point St. (bet. Larkin & Polk Sts.), 415-673-8812

◪ "If your out-of-town guests insist on eating at the Wharf", this "elegant" upscale Chinese aerie overlooking San Francisco Bay is a good option; guests gush "what a setting" – now if only the "mundane menu" "would match it", particularly at these "expensive" prices.

Mangiafuoco S M
19　18　18　$31

1001 Guerrero St. (22nd St.), 415-206-9881

■ Mission munchers maintain they *mangia bene* at this "low-key" "authentic" trattoria ("Italians actually work here") that serves reasonably priced "homemade pastas" (including "gnocchi so good I wish I could sleep on them"); though the place gives most a "warm feeling", a few fault "hit-or-miss" service.

Manora's Thai Cuisine L S M
21　14　17　$22

1600 Folsom St. (12th St.), 415-861-6224

◪ Dating back to the days when there wasn't a Thai on every corner, this SoMa standby stands out for its expansive menu offering "a spectacular variety" of "consistently good" – though "no longer" "the best" – traditional eats; despite digs about the "dated decor", it manages to provide a "great atmosphere for entertaining", making it a perennial "favorite" for "lunchtime" or before hitting the clubs.

Mario's Bohemian
Cigar Store Cafe ◕ L S M ⊄
19　15　15　$16

566 Columbus Ave. (Union St.), 415-362-0536

■ "Gazing out the windows to Washington Square Park" while eating a "meatball focaccia sandwich might be a [viable] choice for a last supper" declare devotees of this "legendary" "old-style" Italian cafe; don't expect much in the way of service or space – just savor the local flavor from "one of the last authentic North Beach joints left."

Marnee Thai 🇱🇸🇲 | 23 | 14 | 17 | $22 |

2225 Irving St. (bet. 23rd & 24th Aves.), 415-665-9500

✓ "Moody" Marnee, the "grande dame proprietor" and self-professed psychic (who feels enThaitled to "order for you") provides "entertainment all by herself" at this veteran Sunset Siamese; the scene's often "crowded and rushed" "but worth it" for the cuisine of her husband and chef Chai Siriyarn, who prepares "heavenly angel wings" and other "excellent" fare from his native Bangkok.

MASA'S | 27 | 24 | 26 | $82 |

Hotel Vintage Court, 648 Bush St. (bet. Powell & Stockton Sts.), 415-989-7154

■ SF's "formal" Downtowner is "back and the best again" since the arrival of *Iron Chef* victor Ron Siegel (ex Charles Nob Hill); his "beautifully arranged and magnificently prepared" New French cuisine "revolutionizes the way you look at food", while the "stunning" remodel ("a beautiful blend of modern art and traditional toile") and the "telepathic yet unobtrusive" waiters make a visit "like going to heaven" (only "it's easier to do, especially more than once"); just be aware "financing should be offered to pay the tab."

Massawa 🇱🇸 | 20 | 13 | 18 | $16 |

1538 Haight St. (bet. Ashbury & Clayton Sts.), 415-621-4129

■ "Adventurous diners" scoop up the "delicious hot" and "spicy Eritrean food" and wash it down with a glass of "honey wine" at this "funky" cheapo Haight Street haunt where dog-eared travel posters are the "bare-bones setting's" only attempt at decor; just "don't expect to get silverware" – not because the service can be "very, very slow" but because you eat East African–style: with *injera* (spongy bread) and your fingers.

Ma Tante Sumi 🇸🇲 | 22 | 19 | 20 | $35 |

4243 18th St. (bet. Castro & Diamond Sts.), 415-626-7864

■ The "inventive" (though "not overly intimidating") Asian-Californian fare at this "charming" sleeper is easily "the best in the Castro", made "more so by" the recent arrival of Brenda Buenviaja (ex Oritalia) who maintains owner Sumi Hirose's East-West vision; the "intimate" dining room with "cross-cultural accents" is a "peaceful" "little haven" from the ruckus of the neighborhood bars.

Matterhorn Swiss Restaurant 🇸 | 19 | 17 | 18 | $32 |

2323 Van Ness Ave. (bet. Green & Vallejo Sts.), 415-885-6116

■ "Save yourself a trip to Switzerland" and trek over to this "fondue heaven" on Van Ness that replicates a meal in the

Alps with belly-busting portions ("come hungry") of bubbling cauldrons of cheese, chocolate or meat, served by "waiters in traditional attire" in a "pseudo–ski lodge atmosphere."

Max's Diner L S M　　　16 | 14 | 16 | $21
311 Third St. (Folsom St.), 415-546-0168

☑ "As an ex-NYC cab driver can vouch", this "remember-the-'50s" SoMa diner is "not up to par but is as close as you can find out here" to a traditional deli; "pretty good corned beef, root beer floats" and other Jewish "comfort foods" are doled out in "obscene portions" ("with prices that reflect that"); however, dieters and other detractors dis it as a "Denny's in disguise"; N.B. breakfast is served all day.

Max's on the Square Restaurant L S M　　　16 | 13 | 16 | $22
Maxwell Hotel, 398 Geary St. (Mason St.), 415-646-8600

■ The Downtown offshoot of Max's formulaic Jewish deli chainlet features "gigantic" sandwiches with "the works", zaftig cheesecakes and "friendly service"; though portions, like prices, are "sometimes overwhelming", it's "close to everything", hence a "handy" choice for Union Square "shoppers" or "pre- or post-theater" diners.

Max's Opera Cafe L S M　　　16 | 15 | 16 | $23
Opera Plaza, 601 Van Ness Ave. (Golden Gate Ave.), 415-771-7300

☑ "Singing waiters" are the main shtick at this Opera Plaza Jewish diner that's "sort of a Lindy's West"; although locals "craving matzo ball soup" and a decent Reuben in this otherwise "deli-free zone" don't mind paying "big bucks" for "big plates" ("enough for at least four meals"), rebels retort "once you taste the food, you won't care that you got a ton of it."

Maya L M　　　21 | 21 | 19 | $38
303 Second St. (bet. Folsom & Harrison Sts.), 415-543-2928

☑ To compare this "high-class" Mexican in SoMa to what you typically find in the Mission "is like calling the Golden Gate Bridge a causeway" declare disciples who adore the "innovative" "complex" cuisine; the "gorgeous" ironwork, "outstanding collection of tequilas" and "truly accommodating service" are other pluses; even so, the bargain police wonder "is it legal to charge that much for a burrito?"

Mayflower L S M　　　20 | 11 | 13 | $24
6255 Geary Blvd. (27th Ave.), 415-387-8338

■ "Fantastic dim sum" by day and "awesome seafood" by night are "always pleasers" at this large Hong Kong–style Richmonder whose low, "low prices" make up for the "banal setting."

Maykedah **L S M** 22 | 17 | 19 | $29
470 Green St. (bet. Grant Ave. & Kearny St.), 415-362-8286

■ This North Beach "treasure" ranks as the "best Persian in the city" – perhaps even "in Northern California" – thanks to its "marvelous" signature kebabs, "exotic stews" and basmati rice; "moderate prices" make it a "great deal", even if the decor is a tad "stuck in the '80s."

McCormick & Kuleto's **L S M** 19 | 22 | 19 | $37
Ghirardelli Sq., 900 North Point St. (bet. Larkin & Polk Sts.), 415-929-1730

◪ "The view's the thing" at this "huge" "tourist-infested" Ghirardelli Square "waterfront" seafooder that, thanks to the tiered setting, "doesn't have a bad seat in the house"; although critics carp about "small portions, big prices" and "fairly ordinary" fare, insiders insist "stick to the oysters" and signature crab cakes and you should be safe.

mc² **L M** 21 | 22 | 19 | $44
470 Pacific Ave. (Montgomery St.), 415-956-0666

◪ A "sleek" Downtown "design-district" spot suits the "see-and-be-seen" set with its cool – some say "icy" – "minimalist decor" (a juxtaposition of exposed brick and aluminum chairs) and chef Yoshi Kojima's "primped and prettified" Californian-French food that's "fusion at its trendiest"; although skeptics find the setting and the service just "too 'too'" for their tastes, most feel that "E [for "excellent"] equals mc²."

Mecca **S M** 20 | 23 | 17 | $40
2029 Market St. (bet. Dolores & 14th Sts.), 415-621-7000

◪ "All are welcome" to join the "eclectic SF mix" at this Upper Market supper club, which is "great for cruising and dining" alike, thanks to a "bar that glows literally and figuratively" and "creative", if "unbelievably pricey", New American (with Asian detours) cuisine; although critics say it "tries too hard to be hip", advocates argue the atmo contains enough "eye candy to keep the meal moving."

MEETINGHOUSE, THE **S M** 25 | 21 | 23 | $42
1701 Octavia St. (Bush St.), 415-922-6733

■ Pacific Heights' "neighborhood keeper" (and sleeper) specializes in "superlative" "jazzed up" American "home cooking" "that you wish your mom had known how to make"; it starts with "stupendously flaky biscuits", "ends with" a "yummy" "homemade peppermint ice cream sandwich" and "strikes a chord" with "everything in between"; although the snug "old apothecary turned Shaker-style" room can "lead to long waits", a "very caring staff" compensates.

Mel's Drive-In ●**L S M**⊅ 12 | 15 | 14 | $16
3355 Geary Blvd. (bet. Parker & Stanyan Sts.), 415-387-2255
2165 Lombard St. (Steiner St.), 415-921-2867

(continued)
Mel's Drive-In
801 Mission St. (4th St.), 415-227-4477
Richelieu Hotel, 1050 Van Ness Ave. (Geary St.),
415-292-6357
◪ This chain of "kitschy" "'50s-retro" American diners ("did the Fonz just walk by?") keeps rockin' around the clock with teens "nostalgic for a time and place they never knew", as well as "clubbers sobering up" at 1 AM; although fans find the service is "like the good old days", modernists mutter that the throwback grub – "greasy burgers and fries" and "old-fashioned milkshakes" – simply "gets the job done" without warranting the "tourist prices."

Memphis Minnie's BBQ Joint L S   20 | 11 | 16 | $16
576 Haight St. (Fillmore St.), 415-864-7675
■ Billed as SF's home of swine dining, Bob Kantor's infamous barbecue shack is "resurrected yet again" (this time "looking like a cheesy theme restaurant"); Lower Haight locals lament it "stinks up the neighborhood", but there's nothing off-putting about "succulent" slow-cooked smoked meats, notably the 18-hour brisket ("best of my life"), and Southern sidekicks.

Merenda L S M   – | – | – | M
1809 Union St. (bet. Laguna & Octavia Sts.), 415-346-7373
Chef-owner Keith Luce (ex PlumpJack Cafe) and his wife Raney have struck out on their own at this value-oriented homespun Cow Hollow newcomer that, at press time, plans to be part trattoria, part enoteca and part rosticceria; the sit-down dining room will showcase Northern Italian fare, and true to the name (which translates as 'snack'), the wine bar and gourmet take-out counter (offering roasted meats and fresh pastas) will serve continuously 11 AM–10 PM.

Mescolanza S M   21 | 16 | 20 | $25
2221 Clement St. (bet. 23rd & 24th Aves.), 415-668-2221
■ Specializing in "fresh salads", "good thin-crust pizza" and both "classic and unusual pastas" in a "cozy (or too snug?)" dining room, this "homey" "reasonably priced" trattoria is your typical "wonderful neighborhood Italian" – except that it's located in a "predominantly Asian neighborhood" of the Richmond, which may explain why it's always "super busy", even on weekdays.

Michelangelo   17 | 16 | 16 | $22
Restaurant Caffe S M ⊅
579 Columbus Ave. (Union St.), 415-986-4058
◪ "Bring cash – and patience" to this bite-size trattoria that always has "a line out the door"; it's full of fun-seeking tourists gunning for "cheap, big portions of pasta" and equally gigantic "porcelain goblets of wine"; however, discriminating diners dis the place as "basically Pasta

Pomodoro with kitschy decor", saying the gratuitous "Gummi Bears are a great change of pace if you don't mind sharing one bowl with all of North Beach."

Mifune ⅃Ⓢ Ⓜ   19 | 11 | 14 | $16

Japan Ctr., 1737 Post St. (bet. Buchanan & Webster Sts.), 415-922-0337

■ Expect "noodles, noodles and more noodles" at this "authentic" soup shop ("am I in Tokyo?" – no, just the Japan Center) "serving up soul-warming" bowls that are so "tasty" they "will make you slurp some more"; although "service leaves a little to be desired" ("if you don't want to see your server, this is the place to go") and the decor is at best "nondescript", it's the ideal "quick" solution for "a post-movie" bite or "for colds and cold days."

Millennium Ⓢ Ⓜ   22 | 20 | 22 | $34

Abigail Hotel, 246 McAllister St. (bet. Hyde & Larkin Sts.), 415-487-9800

☑ "Even the most zealous of carnivores" enjoy this "sophisticated" "gourmet vegetarian" ("SF's solution to mad cow disease") in the Civic Center culture gulch, where "animal lovers rejoice" over chef Eric Tucker's "delicious", environment-friendly fare (even the wines are organic) delivered by "courteous" waiters; although the "basement setting" isn't as lofty as the "inventive combinations" of flavors (which critics carp "compete against one another"), most say this Y2K hideaway is A-ok.

Miss Millie's Ⓢ   20 | 18 | 17 | $23

4123 24th St. (bet. Castro & Diamond Sts.), 415-285-5598

■ "The wait is long, but the rewards are great" at this "quaint" Noe Valley venue that's "preferred" for the "splendid brunch" (for which it doesn't take reservations) but also serves a "homey" New American supper (for which it does); the "adorable" retro dining room, with ivy-covered, hand-painted wooden booths and a tented, heated patio, fills up with a 24th Street crowd and the heavenly aroma of "big cinnamon buns" baking.

Moishe's Pippic ⅃ Ⓜ ⊄   16 | 9 | 15 | $13

425A Hayes St. (bet. Gough & Octavia Sts.), 415-431-2440

■ "Everything is exactly as it should be" at this "good, basic" "classic Jewish deli": "corned beef piled high", Dr. Brown's Cream Soda and enough "entertaining Windy City memorabilia" "to make an ex-Chicagoan cry" – or at least, head to Hayes Valley.

Mom is Cooking ⅃ Ⓢ   17 | 8 | 11 | $17

1166 Geneva Ave. (bet. Edinburgh & Naples Sts.), 415-586-7000

☑ "If mom cooks, it's good" at this Excelsior eatery, but it's unclear when chef Abigail Murillo is in the kitchen, as her "down-home Mexican" fare "has declined" since last year's *Survey*; patrons are also losing patience with the notoriously "slow service" and "dingy decor"; still, it's "hard not to enjoy yourself in the back patio", especially after a shot of one of the 100 tequilas on hand.

MoMo's 🇱🇸🇲   17 | 19 | 17 | $34
760 Second St. (The Embarcadero), 415-227-8660
▰ Though it's a fly ball away from Pac Bell Park, going "on a Giants game day" can be "a no-no at MoMo's" unless you love a crush of sports fans; it's also "a scene" after 5 PM, when "twentysomething singles" crowd the bar and "chill on the sunny patio" to enjoy "great appetizers and drinks"; however, there's less rooting for the "overpriced New American food", and the service strikes out too.

Montage 🇱🇸🇲   15 | 17 | 15 | $32
Sony Metreon Ctr., 101 Fourth St. (Mission St.), 415-369-6111
▰ While it's "a great concept" (a serious eatery inside the Sony Metreon), the "splashy bar" and "good-looking room are the best this place has to offer"; reviewers roast the seasonally focused Californian menu as "corporate cuisine" and say service "is AWOL" "even when [the room's] empty; N.B. a post-*Survey* chef change may outdate the food score.

Moose's 🇱🇸🇲   21 | 21 | 20 | $40
1652 Stockton St. (bet. Filbert & Union Sts.), 415-989-7800
■ "Not many places can pull off [having] the NCAA tournament in the bar, a jazz piano tinkling and scrumptious Sunday brunch", but this "lively" "North Beach hangout" does; the "sunny windows overlook Washington Square Park", but the real show is the "people-watching" inside – the sight of SF's "elite" wolfing down the "best burgers in town" and other American fare; P.S. although meet-and-greet meister Ed Moose is cutting back, new chef Jason Miller is "one of SF's rising stars."

Morton's of Chicago 🇸🇲   24 | 21 | 22 | $55
400 Post St. (bet. Mason & Powell Sts.), 415-986-5830
▰ When carnivores "really need a hunka, hunka burnin' beef" they head to this steakhouse chain's "clubby" Downtown outpost; apparently size does matter ("the 48-ounce porterhouse could feed a family of seven"), because despite digs about the service (a "corny", "show-and-tell" "menu presentation") and the tariff ("could fly to Chicago for the price of dinner"), prime-ribbers call it "paradise."

Mo's Burgers 🇱🇸🇲   20 | 10 | 14 | $16
Yerba Buena Gardens, 772 Folsom St. (bet. 3rd & 4th Sts.), 415-957-3779
Mo's Grill 🇱🇸🇲
1322 Grant Ave. (bet. Green & Vallejo Sts.), 415-788-3779
■ Mo' better burgers ("thick, juicy" and "cooked the way you want") accompanied by a mess of "curly fries" and a

milkshake make the meal at this duo; neither the North Beach nor SoMa locales have more than "no-frills" decor (although the latter boasts a "great view of the skyline"), but they're "speedy" and "cheap."

Narai **L S**   ▽ 22 12 20 $22

2229 Clement St. (bet. 23rd & 24th Aves.), 415-751-6363
■ This "real sleeper" is "still *the* place to eat near the California Palace of The Legion of Honor", thanks to what's "quite possibly the best Thai food" in the Richmond ("vegetarians should head straight for the spicy tofu"); "good service" compensates for the "plain atmosphere."

Neecha Thai Cuisine **L S M**   19 13 19 $20

2100 Sutter St. (Steiner St.), 415-922-9419
■ A veritable "vegetarian utopia" (nearly half of the menu is comprised of plant-based and mock-meat dishes) sets apart this "storefront" Pacific Heights Thai; enthusiasts insist it "should have a line around the block", but since they also "don't tell anyone" about it, it never does.

Ne O **S**   _ _ _ M

1007 Guerrero St. (bet. 22nd & 23rd Sts.), 415-643-3119
While not exactly a neophyte, this Missionite after a short-lived spin as a white-hot spot under Lance Velasquez and an even shorter spurt as a not-so-hot high-end Asian-French has resurrected itself with a classic Californian menu executed by a sous-chef under Velasquez; as if to emphasize the new deal, the infamous snow-white walls are now painted in primary colors and nothing costs over $15.

Nob Hill Café **L S M**   20 16 20 $28

1152 Taylor St. (bet. Clay & Sacramento Sts.), 415-776-6500
■ Two desparate storefronts will lead you into the lair of this "cozy" "neighborhood" trattoria "well loved by" Nob Hill-ites for its "simple pizzas and pastas" (particularly the one with "pesto sauce of the gods") and "friendly service", which "comes with a genuine smile"; the only thing it doesn't offer is reservations, so "go early or be prepared" to "wait forever" outside.

North Beach Pizza **L S M**   17 9 13 $16

1499 Grant Ave. (Union St.), 415-433-2444 ◗
1310 Grant St. (Vallejo St.), 415-433-2444
1649 Haight St. (Belvedere St.), 415-751-2300 ◗
715 Harrison St. (3rd St.), 415-371-0930 ◗
4787 Mission St. (bet. Persia & Russia Aves.), 415-586-1400
Pier 39 (bet. Grant & Stockton Sts., off The Embarcadero), 415-433-0400
800 Stanyan St. (Haight St.), 415-751-2300 ◗
3054 Taraval St. (41st Ave.), 415-242-9100
◪ "Pizza the way it should be: big, cheesy and saucy" proclaim patrons of this pie-purveying chain, while foes

(predictably "spoiled East Coasters") whine it's "West Coast pizza at its worst"; although several branches offer sit-down dining, most folk just "speed-dial" for delivery ("they have an indoor place?").

North Beach Restaurant ◖ L S M ⬛ 19 | 16 | 17 | $34

1512 Stockton St. (bet. Green & Union Sts.), 415-392-1700
◪ "When you want a taste of the Old Country", this 31-year-old North Beach Italian is the place, thanks to "solid" standards (notably housemade pasta and "very fresh fish"), "prompt waiters" and an "amazing" 500-bottle wine cellar to boot; despite a recent redesign, "disappointed" detractors deem it's "getting tired" and "doesn't [even] seem as much a value as before."

Northstar L S M ⬛ 19 | 18 | 19 | $30

288 Connecticut St. (18th St.), 415-551-9840
◪ Locals insist that this "charming", petite "Potrero Hill eatery" with a "homey" "Martha Stewart minimalist decor" is "a good choice if you're in the neighborhood"; but since founder Brad Levy sold out, reports of "spacey" "inexperienced service" and "uneven, uneven" New American fare abound, leading critical commuters to conclude there's "no reason [to] come from elsewhere."

One Market L M ⬛ 22 | 21 | 21 | $46

1 Market St. (Steuart St.), 415-777-5577
◪ It might be called One Market, but diners are of two minds about Bradley Ogden's big New American sporting "a panoramic view of the Ferry Building"; the positives proclaim it's "making a comeback" thanks to "fantastic new chef Adrian Hoffman", who has "brought the food on track", and an "attentive staff"; naysayers insist, however, "it's as pricey" and "boring" as a "bank lobby" (which at least explains why it's a popular "business lunch" destination).

Original Joe's ◖ L S M ⬛ 19 | 14 | 19 | $24

144 Taylor St. (bet. Eddy & Turk Sts.), 415-775-4877
◪ Owned and operated by the same average Joe (actually Tony) since 1937, this Tenderloin "tradition" "never changes", and that's just fine with loyalists who "brave the neighborhood" for the "old-fashioned" Italian eats, "crusty atmosphere" and "raffish" "cast of characters"; grimacing at the "greasy" grub, *au courant* clients complain "tradition can only take you so far"; P.S. the "San Jose institution" of the same name and similar menu is actually unrelated.

Oritalia L S M ⬛ 23 | 22 | 21 | $46

Juliana Hotel, 586 Bush St. (Stockton St.), 415-782-8122
■ This avatar of "marvelous" east-meets-west fusion cuisine reopened in the summer of 2001 after its hotel landlord underwent seismic renovations; the "elegant" "upscale" dining room remains untouched, but chef Jon

Nelson now offers a graze craze–oriented menu (not fully reflected in the food score) that features an expanded offering of Zen Tapas, aka small plates, served continuously throughout the day.

Osteria S　　　　23　17　22　$29

3277 Sacramento St. (Presidio Ave.), 415-771-5030

◪ "A home away from home" is how devotees describe this "convenient" Presidio Heights trattoria serving "rock-solid" Northern Italian standbys (including a "luscious calamari steak"); there's nothing chic or "cutting edge" here (perhaps why it's "a favorite" of one surveyor's "89-year-old neighbor"), but a few gripes about "jam-packed" seating and "loud" "noise level" suggest the appeal might be "for regulars only."

Ovation S M　　　　21　26　20　$50

Inn at the Opera, 333 Fulton St. (Franklin St.), 415-553-8100

◪ The "beautiful", finely appointed dining room, replete with "live piano music", "roaring fireplace" and "quiet atmosphere", "deserves an ovation" at this "formal" Hayes Valleyite; unfortunately the "pricey" Continental–New French fare "doesn't measure up", but it's "very convenient" to theaters, and once the "pre-opera, -symphony and -ballet crowd" leaves, "it turns into the most romantic restaurant in the city."

Ozumo L S M　　　　–　–　–　E

161 Steuart St. (bet. Howard & Mission Sts.), 415-882-1333

One of the season's hottest players is this high-end Embarcadero rookie brought to you by U.S.-born Japanese baseball star Jeremy James; the modern tea garden-esque dining room sports the biggest sushi bar in SF, but another draw is the extensive selection of small plates from the robata grill executed by former *ozumo* (championship sumo) wrestler Koji Makiyama; small wonder the sake set (the bar pours 30 varieties) is already stopping by.

Pacific L S M　　　　25　21　24　$48

Pan Pacific Hotel, 500 Post St. (Mason St.), 415-929-2087

■ "Why is no one talking about this place?" beseech baffled buffs of this "unbelievably uncrowded" Downtown refuge; after all, it showcases "spectacular" Californian fare ("try the tasting menu") "complemented" by an "attentive staff" in a "quiet, beautiful room"; sure, the "setting shouts HOTEL", but most maintain this "unhurried experience" is the "best-kept secret in Union Square."

Pacific Café S M　　　　20　15　20　$28

7000 Geary Blvd. (34th Ave.), 415-387-7091

◪ For 25 years, this family-friendly "fish spot" in the Richmond has been luring locals with a passel of "far from adventurous, but impeccably prepared" seafood (including little-seen sand dabs) proffered by "nice service folk" who "make you feel like family"; contrarians carp it's "overpriced" for "extremely mediocre" fare and are "baffled" by its popularity (well, does the phrase "free wine while you wait" mean anything?)

Palatino L S M   – – – M

803 Cortland Ave. (Ellsworth St.), 415-641-8899
Named after one of the seven hills of Rome, this piccolo 34-seat trattoria located atop up-and-coming (and equally hilly) Bernal Heights lures locals with its nice selection of Italian classics in a cozy, rustic red-painted dining room, outfitted with copper-topped tables and rough-hewed wooden benches; it's owned by the folks who run Ristorante Milano on Russian Hill (another one!).

Palio d'Asti L M   20 20 20 $38

640 Sacramento St. (bet. Kearny & Montgomery Sts.), 415-395-9800
■ Food, service and decor are neck and neck (and neck) at this "high-end" Financial District mainstay (named for, and decorated in honor of, a medieval bareback horserace); although the place rides on its reputation as an "excellent" "business lunch" spot, the "creative Italian cuisine", bounteous wine bar and "great service" are just as "good at dinner", when it's considerably less hectic.

Palomino ● L S M   18 21 18 $35

345 Spear St. (bet. Folsom & Harrison Sts.), 415-512-7400
◪ "It may be touristy", but this "spacious" Cal-Med on the Embarcadero, with perhaps SF's largest outdoor heated patio, is a "great place to eat" "highly recommended appetizers" and savor the "yupfest" bar scene "after a Giants game"; although locals lament "service can be slow" and the main courses "uninspired", others retort "you can overlook the faults" when you've got such a "nice view" overlooking the Bay Bridge.

Pancho Villa Taqueria ● L S M   23 10 15 $10

3071 16th St. (bet. Mission & Valencia Sts.), 415-864-8840
■ "The line out the door" at this "scruffy" Mission Mexican proves its popularity; "don't worry, it moves quickly" as an "eclectic crowd" chooses between the "biggest, baddest burritos" in the barrio and a "spicy chicken in red sauce" that's "the best thing that ever happened to a taco"; the "fluorescent lights" are a bit much at midnight but illuminate the local art hanging on the walls; P.S. suburbanites can go to the San Mateo location, which has "better ambiance."

Pane e Vino L S M   23 19 20 $36

3011 Steiner St. (Union St.), 415-346-2111
■ This "highly spirited" "Cow Hollow institution" is "delicious on all fronts", from the "fabulous pastas" and

"beyond-belief stuffed artichokes" "down to the cafe latte"; an animated, accented staff makes guests "feel at home, even if you're not Italian"; although all the hustle-and-bustle means you "can't hear yourself chew", amici are happy to spend their hard-earned *pane* here.

Paragon **L M**   15 | 18 | 17 | $34
701 Second St. (Townsend St.), 415-537-9020
◪ The "bar scene" at this "simultaneously hip and elegant" South Beach sophomore attracts the last remaining dot-commers at happy hour and Giants fans due to its "great location"; however, they seem to "pass on dinner" ("very average" New American fare) as they pass by and warn that "in this city", "location won't carry you" for very long.

Park Chow **L S M**   19 | 16 | 18 | $20
1240 Ninth Ave. (bet. Irving & Lincoln Sts.), 415-665-9912
◪ An "inexpensive" Inner Sunset Eclectic ("specializing in everything and nothing") "should be called Park Chow Down" according to the hungry hounds of "cheapskates" who pack the place for "decent" "comfort food" at "unbelievable prices"; the cozy fireside and "roof deck" evoke a "more upscale" feel than at sibling Chow, but the "hip singles scene" is equally "fun to watch."

Park Grill **L S M**   23 | 23 | 22 | $42
Park Hyatt Hotel, 333 Battery St. (Clay St.), 415-296-2933
■ This "sophisticated Downtowner" is the "ultimate biz restaurant": "quiet", "classy", "clubby" with "respectful service"; though well-known for expensive-account "power breakfasts" and "civilized lunches", it's also the "best-kept secret" for a New American "dinner on short notice."

Parma **M**   20 | 15 | 20 | $27
3314 Steiner St. (bet. Chestnut & Lombard Sts.), 415-567-0500
■ "Quintessential Northern Italian hole-in-the-wall" in the Marina presided over by "gracious owner and host" Pietro Elia, who welcomes guests "with [traditional] greetings", then rewards them with "big portions" of "unadulterated heavy, wonderful" fresh pastas, a "killer Caesar salad" and "service with a kiss."

Pasta Pomodoro **S M**   15 | 12 | 15 | $16
2027 Chestnut St. (Fillmore St.), 415-474-3400 **L**
598 Haight St. (Steiner St.), 415-436-9800
816 Irving St. (9th Ave.), 415-566-0900 **L**
2304 Market St. (Castro St.), 415-558-8123 ◐ **L**
1865 Post St. (Fillmore St.), 415-674-1826 **L**
4000 24th St. (Noe St.), 415-920-9904 **L**
655 Union St. (Columbus Ave.), 415-399-0300 **L**
1875 Union St. (Laguna St.), 415-771-7900 **L**
■ "The Gap of food" – "bland and everywhere" – is how most surveyors describe this string of "spaghetti factories"

that's taken its formula of "bargain-basement, made-to-order" Italian fare in "stripped-down" "unspectacular settings" to every corner of the Bay Area; despite the digs, commentators concede it's "decent, convenient and fast" – a real "godsend for parents", "before the movie" or when "you're just too tired to cook."

Pastis L M   23   20   22 $40
1015 Battery St. (Green St.), 415-391-2555
■ "When you can't get a table at Fringale, come here" fawn fanciers of this off-the-beaten-path Downtowner, aka "Gerald Hirigoyen's other restaurant"; this "beautiful" bistro serves "similar delicious" New French fare "in a more spacious setting", which includes a "lovely" "zinc bar" for "sipping pastis" that will make you "feel like you're back in Cannes"; overall, "the ambiance is inviting, although sometimes the waiters are not."

Pauline's Pizza   22   14   17 $20
260 Valencia St. (bet. Duboce & 14th Sts.), 415-552-2050
■ The avatar of "gourmet pie in this town", this "civilized" pizzeria in a "scary" stretch of the Mission ("don't be afraid of the bars on the window") proffers the most "creative combinations" slathered atop "delightfully" "thin crusts" (the "pesto is absolutely the best"), along with homegrown veggies and "sublime sorbets"; "if only they delivered" sigh stay-at-home types.

paul K S   20   17   19 $33
199 Gough St. (Oak St.), 415-552-7132
■ It's definitely "not the same old Mediterranean food" being served up at Paul Kavouksorian's "inventive" Hayes Valley sophomore (where pomegranate scents a duck sauce as well as a vodka martini); a cadre of "informative and friendly" waiters deftly explains the "interesting combos" in an "intimate" (i.e. "a little crowded") space.

Pazzia L M   ▽ 21   16   19 $25
337 Third St. (bet. Folsom & Harrison Sts.), 415-512-1693
■ Pizza baked in a wood-burning oven, "thin and crispy just like in Italy", is the pull of this "high-energy" "small Italian" not far from the SF MOMA and Moscone Center; though short on space, it's as long on "charm" thanks to an "incredibly attentive (and incredibly good-looking) staff" and a warm "owner who goes out of his way" to accommodate.

Peña Pachamama S   ▽ 19   19   16 $26
1630 Powell St. (bet. Green & Union Sts.), 415-646-0018
■ Once the stomping ground for Joe DiMaggio and Marilyn Monroe, this bi-level North Beach space is now the nexus of "Andean culture", run by the founder of Sukay, a music ensemble from that region; it is also "San Francisco's most fun underground [club]", featuring "creative, tasty organic

Bolivian food" such as *salteñas* (savory turnovers) that's "surprisingly" good for what's essentially a live world music and dance venue.

Perlot 🖪🄼 ▽ 19 | 24 | 20 | $52

Hotel Majestic, 1500 Sutter St. (Gough St.), 415-441-1100

◪ Sporting a new name and a gussied-up interior, the Hotel Majestic's elegant eatery retains the majestic Edwardian "great decor" and live piano music that made it one of the most romantic rooms in the city; new chef Geoffrey Blythe is clearly "not afraid to experiment", offering his New American dishes, such as signature green tomato 'tarte tatin', in prix fixe and tasting menus; they're complemented by a California-heavy wine list and "lovely service."

Perry's 🄻🖪🄼 15 | 15 | 16 | $27

1944 Union St. (bet. Buchanan & Laguna Sts.), 415-922-9022

Perry's Downtown ◗🄻🖪🄼

Galleria Park Hotel, 185 Sutter St. (bet. Kearny & Montgomery Sts.), 415-989-6895

◪ A "middle-aged" "city crowd" frequents this pair of "white-collar burger places"/pubs Downtown and in Cow Hollow to engage "in lively conversation" and tuck into "reliable but nothing special" American fare; aside from the "cheap" Lobster Madness Nights on Wednesdays and Saturdays, young'uns wonder "why this place is so popular."

Pesce 🄼 ▽ 21 | 18 | 19 | $31

2227 Polk St. (bet. Green & Vallejo Sts.), 415-928-8025

▉ This newly spawned, anchovy-size seafooder with a Northern Italian bent is a "refreshing" "addition" to Van Ness/Polk Street, luring "fish lovers" with "simple" but "very fresh" preparations at prices that are "such a good value", they can afford to pack themselves to the gills.

Piaf's 🖪 17 | 20 | 18 | $38

1686 Market St. (Gough St.), 415-864-3700

◪ You can "feel Edith Piaf's presence" at this "very purple" Hayes Valley cabaret plastered with a passel of photos of the chanteuse and patronized by a largely gay clientele; since the owners recently jettisoned the "way too limited" French Bistro menu for a trendier tapas-style one (a move unreflected in the ratings), expect that *escargots in beurre blanc* to be as petite as the Little Sparrow herself.

Picaro 🖪🄼 17 | 15 | 15 | $22

3120 16th St. (bet. Guerrero & Valencia Sts.), 415-431-4089

◪ "Tasty tapas", "great sangria" and a "fun atmosphere" make this funky Mission Spanish ("the lesser half of Esperpento" nearby) a popular spot for "groups" of hipsters "before films" at the Roxie; fans find that "nice-size portions" and short waits compensate for the "prickly service" and what some Iberian addicts avow are "disappointing" "attempts at traditional" fare.

Pier 23 Cafe L S M　　　12 | 16 | 13 | $24
Pier 23, The Embarcadero (Greenwich St.),
415-362-5125
◪ This "gritty" seafood "shack" jutting out on an old Embarcadero pier reels in "bikers" and "the khakis-and-cell-phone crowd" alike; although aficionados assert "the only reason to visit is to sit out back, drink" and listen to the live jazz, they agree it is "absolutely the best place to" do so; besides, after "you have a few", who cares about lackluster service and "what the food tastes like"?

Pizzetta 211 L S ⇗　　▽ 25 | 17 | 22 | $20
211 23rd Ave. (California St.), 415-379-9880
■ "The familiar ambiance is deceptive" at this "fun, out-of-the-way" Richmond pizzeria that bakes up "amazing" individual-size "thin, crisp crust" pies topped with "organic", "fresh, unusual toppings" (the signature's a farm-egg version); and if it isn't the "best in the city", it's certainly "the friendliest"; just be ready for "self-service."

PJ's Oyster Bed S M　　　20 | 15 | 17 | $31
737 Irving St. (bet. 8th & 9th Aves.), 415-566-7775
◪ In the Inner Sunset, "every day is Mardi Gras" at this "happening" "neighborhood fish house" with a "fun and upbeat" (and "loud") atmo; Bayou buffs recommend you "bring Handi-Wipes" to deal with the "great" finger-lickin' "Cajun/Creole seafood" and "drinks that would fell a sailor"; party-poopers point out "service is iffy" and feel the "heavy-handed food doesn't live up to the hype."

Planet Hollywood L S M　　9 | 15 | 10 | $24
2 Stockton St. (Market St.), 415-421-7827
■ "Look at the memorabilia, then leave" advise antagonists about this "gimmicky" Downtown "tourist trap" "where everything's a commercial and for sale"; they concede it's "great for" "foreign visitors" and kids but "not much else" and are as silent as a Buster Keaton movie when it comes to the American fare.

Plouf L M　　　22 | 17 | 17 | $33
40 Belden Pl. (bet. Bush & Pine Sts.), 415-986-6491
■ "Delicious mussels [on the plate] and muscles on the yummy waiters" are the pull at this *très français* Downtown seafooder that's *magnifique* when there's "sunshine in the alley" of Belden Place; although service is "what you'd expect" from the aforementioned "absurdly French staff" – equal parts flirty and surly – "close your eyes" and you'll "feel like you're in Paris"; P.S. "even if you don't like *moules*", "be sure to get extra bread to dunk in the broth."

PlumpJack Cafe 🅛🅜   24 21 23 $46

3127 Fillmore St. (bet. Filbert & Greenwich Sts.), 415-563-4755

■ "You can't beat the deals" at this Cow Hollow cafe harboring "the finest wine list in the city, perhaps the country", that's "not only inventive" "but priced at retail"; there's also plenty of "praise" for "perfect" Mediterranean fare and "professional service"; now if only they could plump up the "warm, intimate" dining room – "it's so small, it's already too hard to get a table"; N.B. post-*Survey* changes in chef and prices may outdate the food and cost scores.

Pluto's 🅛🅢🅜   18 12 13 $13

627 Irving St. (bet. 7th & 8th Aves.), 415-753-8867
3258 Scott St. (Chestnut St.), 415-775-8867

■ Far out, cry fans of this chainlet of "chic *hofbraus*" in the Marina and Inner Sunset that are "like college cafeterias" only "healthier"; the "happy cooks" "behind the counter" "do it your way", loading you up with "amazing salads" ("with a capital S", thanks to "huge portions"), Thanksgiving fixings or other "good" traditional American chow to "pick and choose from"; the "great value" and "generous portions" make up for "the decor, or lack of it."

Ponzu ◗🅢🅜   20 21 19 $38

Serrano Hotel, 401 Taylor St. (bet. Geary & O'Farrell Sts.), 415-775-7979

◪ "Groovy, hip" decor paired with the "riot of flavor combos" that typifies chef "John Beardsley's fun take on Pan-Asian" plates are both indicators that this eatery in the Serrano is not your father's hotel dining room; "if you're over 25", the "steady thump, thump, thump" from the DJ booth and "spotty service" might not be your cup of tea, but most maintain this "pre-theater" spot named for a Japanese dipping sauce is "worth every" yen.

Pork Store Cafe 🅛🅢🅜   21 12 16 $14

1451 Haight St. (bet. Ashbury & Masonic Aves.), 415-864-6981

■ "Greasy-spoon breakfast at its best" is what makes locals happier than pigs in heaven at the Haight's oldest free-standing eatery (decorated with old photos from when the joint was a pork manufacturer), which flips "huge" servings of "thick bacon, amazing buttermilk biscuits and the best hash browns in SF" (and does so till closing); free coffee placates hopefuls waiting for a coveted seat.

POSTRIO 🅛🅢🅜   26 26 24 $54

Prescott Hotel, 545 Post St. (bet. Mason & Taylor Sts.), 415-776-7825

■ "Trendy restaurants come and go, but few can match" the staying power of owner Wolfgang Puck's Downtown "power place"; in the kitchen, the brothers Rosenthal "consistently put out" "inventive, outstanding" New

American dishes that "match" "the glamorous decor" ("walking down the staircase feels like going to the ball"); there's also plenty of "people-watching" at the upstairs bar where you can order "great gourmet pizza" (what else?) till midnight.

Potrero Brewing Company �LSM | 16 | 16 | 15 | $24 |

535 Florida St. (bet. 18th & Mariposa Sts.), 415-552-1967
■ "Great boutique beer", pool tables galore and a "roof deck with killer views of the Mission" make this "spacious" Potero Hill hangout "truly a find if you can find it" say hopheads; however, teetotalers retort the American grub "is kind of like every other brewery's": "not that good."

Powell's Place �LSM | 19 | 10 | 14 | $16 |

511 Hayes St. (bet. Laguna & Octavia Sts.), 415-863-1404
■ It's the "superb fried chicken" at this "funky" Hayes Valley Southern soul fooder, owned by Gospel Elite choir leader Emmit Powell, that has surveyors singing his praises; "nothing else matters" croon the converted, not the "stripped-bare" setting or the "slow service"; in fact, it's all the more refreshing "in a city that's gentrifying by the nanosecond."

Prego Ristorante ◑LSM | 17 | 17 | 18 | $33 |

2000 Union St. (Buchanan St.), 415-563-3305
■ "Well-above-average" "wood-burning-oven Italian" fare "served by very professional career waiters" makes ciao-ing down at this "comfortable" Cow Hollow trattoria "a solid dining experience"; although a few find it "way too overpriced for a chain", neighbors with short attention spans appreciate that it's "easy to get in" here.

Primo Patio Cafe �LSM | ▽ 17 | 11 | 15 | $15 |

214 Townsend St. (bet. 3rd & 4th Sts.), 415-957-1129
■ On sunny days, lunchtimers line up for this "funky little hole-in-the-wall" in SoMa, "a great bargain" in Caribbean-Mexican fare (with the "best jerk chicken around" clearly the primo choice); the dining area, a "cheerful patio", prevents folks from feeling jerked around by the notoriously island-time service; N.B. normally closed at 4 PM, the kitchen stays open late on Giants game nights.

Puccini & Pinetti �LSM | 14 | 16 | 16 | $30 |

Monticello Inn, 129 Ellis St. (bet. Mason & Powell Sts.), 415-392-5500
■ This "very lively, happening place" Downtown attracts "families going to the theater", as "all ages can find something they like" on the "decent menu" of Italian eats and the staff sets a "fun, fun, fun" tone; however, purists "pass it by", pronouncing this Kimpton Group–owned eatery a clunker because of its "small portions" of "plain food."

Ramblas ⓈⓂ
▽ 22 | 22 | 22 | $23

557 Valencia St. (bet. 16th & 17th Sts.), 415-565-0207
■ The folks behind the Thirsty Bear Brewing Co. couldn't help but lap up this "fun" and "stylish" Mission eatery, rechristening it after a popular neighborhood in Barcelona and instituting a menu of more than 20 hot and cold tapas that are "authentic" and wallet-friendly; not surprising, it offers six Thirsty Bear microbrews (as well as Belgian brands) along with "sangria to-die-for" and nicely priced Spanish and California wines.

R & G Lounge ⓁⓈⓂ
20 | 10 | 15 | $25

631 Kearny St. (bet. Clay & Sacramento Sts.), 415-982-7877
■ You "feel like you've entered an Amy Tan novel" when you step inside this Chinatown seafood house replete with Cantonese families sharing platters of the "signature salt-and-pepper-roasted crab dish" (downstairs) and a "fish tank in the middle of the dining room" (upstairs); the "SF cognoscenti" sit in the latter, where the same food is served on "white tablecloths" for the "same price" (though we can't guarantee service will be any less "rushed").

Rasselas Ethiopian ⓈⓂ
▽ 17 | 13 | 15 | $22

2801 California St. (Divisadero St.), 415-567-5010
1534 Fillmore St. (bet. Geary Blvd. & O'Farrell St.), 415-346-8696 ◑
◪ There are "no utensils required" and "no reservations taken" at this Pacific Heights jazz club and its Western Addition sib that books some "fantastic" acts; supporters scoop up the "delicious spicy hand food" before the show, but protestors "go for the music" only, declaring if this is authentic fare, "I don't think I'll ever be visiting Ethiopia."

Red Herring ⓁⓈⓂ
19 | 20 | 19 | $41

Hotel Griffon, 155 Steuart St. (bet. Howard & Mission Sts.), 415-495-6500
◪ "Seafood lovers" lap up the "great" "water views of the Bay Bridge" afforded from a few coveted tables at this whimsical spot overlooking the Embarcadero; although cynics carp the "very creative" fin fare (e.g. tandoori snapper) is "not as good since [chef] James Ormsby" went upstream, the "incredibly varied wine list" and "witty staff" assure that it's still a fine catch.

Restaurant LuLu ⓁⓈⓂ
21 | 20 | 18 | $37

816 Folsom St. (bet. 4th & 5th Sts.), 415-495-5775
◪ Wood "ovens firing, servers bustling and voices roaring" characterize this SoMa stalwart whose menu offers a "portal to Provence"; "take a group and tuck into" a passel of "lusty" "rotisserie goodies" served "family-style" (iron skillet "mussels are required eating"); detractors declare the "multi-decibel din" and "attitude at the door" are

getting "tired", but they don't deter, just "go early" or plan to wait in the "buzzing bar."

Rick's S M   ▽ 16   16   18 $25

1940 Taraval St. (30th Ave.), 415-731-8900

◪ To have a taste of Honolulu in the Sunset, head to this "fun" "local haunt" where the "always friendly servers" proffer "huge portions" of "New American comfort food with a Hawaiian flair"; although protestors poi-poi it as "very basic", everyone comes to Rick's on weekends for the live island music and on the first Monday of every month for Luau Platters featuring 'Kahlua pork' and all the fixin's.

Ristorante Bacco S M   21   17   20 $33

737 Diamond St. (bet. Elizabeth & 24th Sts.), 415-282-4969

■ Experts eschew "the hustle of the main restaurants in Noe Valley" for this "neighborhood" trattoria, which offers "non-trendy Italian food" (the "homemade pasta is a plus"), a "gracious staff that spends a lot of time fussing over favorite customers" and a "great wine list" to boot; although the "minimal decor" and "so-so atmosphere" pale in comparison to its big-name brethren, "take it from an Italian citizen – this is as authentic as it gets."

Ristorante Ideale S   21   16   21 $32

1309 Grant Ave. (bet. Green & Vallejo Sts.), 415-391-4129

■ For an "authentic" Roman holiday without the airfare, "this undiscovered North Beach gem is worth seeking out"; "listening to the funny waiters yelling at each other as they rush sumptuous fare" ("knockout pastas" and "unbelievable lasagna") to the tables is an ideal way to feel like you're dining near the Spanish Steps (as opposed to the strip clubs of Broadway).

Ristorante Milano S   22   15   22 $32

1448 Pacific Ave. (bet. Hyde & Larkin Sts.), 415-673-2961

■ "The warmth of the staff, especially the owners, is only rivaled by the excellence" of the Northern Italian cuisine ("the best housemade pasta bar none") at this Russian Hill "hole-in-the-wall"; small wonder neighborhood habitués "squeeze in" "at least once or twice a month", while non-locals sigh "wish it was around the corner from me."

Ristorante Umbria L M   21   17   20 $29

198 Second St. (Howard St.), 415-546-6985

■ Although this SoMa Italian is "absolutely overrun by dot-commers" and "business travelers" confabbing at the nearby Moscone Center, "locals too" appreciate the "very good" Umbrian specialties and "comfortable atmosphere"; P.S. it's run by "two very friendly Italian brothers" – so ladies, don't take umbrage at their flirty "welcome."

RITZ-CARLTON DINING ROOM Ⓜ 28 | 28 | 28 | $72

Ritz-Carlton Hotel, 600 Stockton St. (bet. California & Pine Sts.), 415-773-6198

■ "It's impossible to leave" this Nob Hill "over-the-top treat" not feeling like a VIP – albeit an "overstuffed VIP" sigh satiated surveyors; the atmosphere of "extreme elegance", the cadre of "tuxedoed waiters" delivering "incomparable service" (which again scores No. 1 in the *Survey*) and chef Sylvain Portay's "sublime" New French cuisine (a "perfect blend of creative flavors") are "just what you'd expect from a hotel whose first name is Ritz"; so "don't wait for a special occasion, go now!"

Ritz-Carlton Terrace Ⓛ Ⓢ Ⓜ 24 | 25 | 25 | $47

Ritz-Carlton Hotel, 600 Stockton St. (bet. California & Pine Sts.), 415-773-6198

■ This "little brother to the Dining Room" atop Nob Hill "is definitely a worthy alternative", especially for the "most sumptuous Sunday brunch" and "extravagant Friday night seafood buffet"; while the cuisine is Mediterranean, the dining room "feels like an English country house" and sitting on the namesake terrace is "heaven"; expect "a Ritzy experience" with "gracious service" and prices that will make you "feel like you underwent a walletectomy."

Rocco's Seafood Grill Ⓢ Ⓜ 19 | 17 | 18 | $33

2080 Van Ness Ave. (Pacific Ave.), 415-567-7606

■ For a taste of "old SF" specialties such as cioppino and "big portions" of other "basic seafood" (plus prime rib), this "reasonably priced" American "over on Van Ness, far from the madding crowd" does the trick; apparently "free parking across the street" outweighs the "lack of atmosphere and decor" for the tourists and "the cast of *The Wild One,* 30 years later" who populate the place.

Roosevelt Tamale Parlor Ⓛ Ⓢ ⊅ 17 | 8 | 13 | $15

2817 24th St. (bet. Bryant & York Sts.), 415-550-9213

■ "Make the trek" to this family-run "authentic Mexican" located "off-the-beaten-path in the Mission" to "get your fill (and you will)" of its "bomber"-size "fresh, homemade tamales"; although some dub it "El Funko" for its "hole-in-the-wall" atmosphere and "gritty" locale, it's a "tradition" that's "been there forever" (actually, just since 1922).

Rose Pistola Ⓛ Ⓢ Ⓜ 21 | 20 | 18 | $40

532 Columbus Ave. (bet. Green & Union Sts.), 415-399-0499

◪ Owner Reed Hearon's "high-energy" North Beach seafooder is still "hot as a pistol" as the throng of tourists and "young lively" locals wait to enter to "share lots of tasty small plates" and mix-and-match their fish with sauces and sides; optimists opine the "very good" Northern Italian specialties "are well worth screaming over the crowd for", but the less-impressed insist that the "cool and bored servers" and "hit-or-miss cuisine" signal this "rose is definitely wilting."

Rose's Café 🄻🅂🄼   19 | 17 | 15 | $26

2298 Union St. (Steiner St.), 415-775-2200

■ This "casual" Cow Hollow cafe is a "yummy little sister to Rose Pistola" that offers "similar" "very tasty Northern Italian" fare but is decidedly less "crowded"; the coveted sidewalk seating is ground zero for yuppies "watching the world go by" and doing brunch, but locals report the "greatly improved" dinner menu "is [also] a solid bet" – "just expect the service to be as slow as molasses."

Rotunda 🄻🅂🄼   20 | 23 | 19 | $34

Neiman Marcus, 150 Stockton St. (Geary St.), 415-362-4777

■ "Rise above the crazed crowd in Union Square" at this "spectacular" domed-ceilinged New American aerie on top of Neiman Marcus that's an "elegant stop" for "lunch with the girls" when on a "shopping break" or for "afternoon tea"; "demand a booth" or a "table with a view" charge the choosy clientele, who rave about the "killer lobster club" and "amazing popovers" but mark down the "slow service."

Royal Thai 🄻🅂🄼   22 | 16 | 19 | $24

951 Clement St. (11th Ave.), 415-386-1795

See review in North of San Franscisco Directory.

Roy's 🄻🅂🄼   22 | 22 | 20 | $44

101 Second St. (Mission St.), 415-777-0277

◪ "Finally Roy Yamaguchi has opened" proclaim patrons of the peripatetic chef's brand of "beautifully presented" "creative Euro-Asian cuisine" being wokked up in the "open kitchen" at his spacious "see-and-be-seen" outpost; however, hype-haters hiss that the staff's "cheery" "aloha attitude" is "grating" and the "quirky" "food combos don't always work" in SoMa like they do in Hawaii (maybe "a day in the sun changes things").

Rubicon 🄻🄼   24 | 21 | 23 | $50

558 Sacramento St. (bet. Montgomery & Sansome Sts.), 415-434-4100

■ "Like DeNiro" (a minority investor), this "high-power dining" spot Downtown delivers "a consistently good performance"; new chef "Denis Leary really knows how to wow his guests", offering "something for nearly everyone" on his Cal–New French menu, and the "professionally trained staff is willing to go out of its way"; although skeptics sniff at the "somewhat stuffy surroundings", this is "a good place for entertaining", especially given the "wonderful wine list" crafted by sommelier Larry Stone.

Sam's Grill & 　　　21 | 16 | 19 | $35
Seafood Restaurant 🄻🄼

374 Bush St. (bet. Kearny & Montgomery Sts.), 415-421-0594
☑ "Nothing changes" at Downtown SF's oldest "old-men's club" : not the "solid seafood dishes", nor the American sides ("damn good onion rings") or the "wisecracking" waiters that are "as crusty as the great sourdough"; still, modernists moan that while the fish "is the freshest, the patrons are not"; same goes for the "bare-bones room."

Sanraku Four Seasons 🄻🅂🄼 　　22 | 13 | 16 | $31

Sony Metreon Ctr., 101 Fourth St. (Mission St.), 415-369-6166
704 Sutter St. (Taylor St.), 415-771-0803
■ "After eating" the "melt-in-your-mouth sushi and exquisite rolls" at this Downtown Japanese (with a younger Sony Metreon sibling) "you won't be asking why such a plain-looking [place] has a line out the door"; however, the sometimes "slow and dazed" service doesn't go over so "swimmingly well" with fish fans.

Savor 🄻🅂🄼 　　　17 | 15 | 15 | $20

3913 24th St. (bet. Noe & Sanchez Sts.), 415-282-0344
■ In Noe Valley, this "create-your-own-crêpe" French-Med bistro "is best on a sunny day", when you can partake of the "outdoor seating"; savvy souls savor the "good breakfast" (offered all day) over dinner but gripe "you could die of malnutrition waiting to be served."

Scala's Bistro ◗🄻🅂🄼 　　23 | 22 | 20 | $38

Sir Francis Drake Hotel, 432 Powell St. (bet. Post & Sutter Sts.), 415-395-8555
■ "When all else fails", there's this "happening" Italian-French Downtowner that serves continuously until midnight; so whether it's for a "fabulous pick-me-up lunch", post-"shopping therapy" or an "elegant dinner", the "gorgeous decor" (oversized booths, checkered tiles, gilt mirrors) will make you feel "like you're part of something" ("SF's best can be seen [here] frequently"); only catch: it's "impossible to carry on a conversation" over the "lively" bar din.

Schroeder's 🄻🄼 　　　13 | 15 | 14 | $25

240 Front St. (bet. California & Sacramento Sts.), 415-421-4778
☑ Crammed with "instant nostalgia", this "SF institution" Downtown serves (somewhat "slowly") potato pancakes and other "homey" and "heavy" "German standards" "like it did 100 years ago"; while kitsch-lovers say "don't miss polka nights", the irreverent answer "oompah-pah! I think someone's stepped on my Wiener schnitzel."

Scoma's 🄻🅂🄼 　　　20 | 18 | 18 | $35

Pier 47 (bet. Jefferson & Jones Sts.), 415-771-4383
☑ Since 1965, this "vintage Bay Area seafood house" has served up "heaping portions" and "gorgeous waterfront

views" of "what's left of the fishing industry"; though gripers grouse it's "become more tired than the structure that houses it", with "ridiculous prices" and "long waits", supporters say it remains "surprisingly good after all these years" and "one of the better Wharf places to bring visitors."

Sears Fine Food ⬛⬛⬛⬛⊘   17 | 11 | 16 | $17 |
439 Powell St. (bet. Post & Sutter Sts.), 415-986-1160
◪ "Step back into the '50s" when you enter this Union Square coffee shop ("more pink than a Victoria's Secret store") that serves "old-fashioned Ah-mur-kin breakfasts" and lunches; skeptics may sniff that "Sears Fair Food is more like it" ("the legendary" "silver dollar pancakes" are the "only thing worth ordering"), but tell that to "the line of tourists out the door."

Shalimar ⬛⬛⬛⊘   23 | 3 | 8 | $14 |
532 Jones St. (Geary St.), 415-928-0333
■ For an authentic "Third World experience", brave hearts and bargain-hunters head to this Tenderloin "hole-in-the-wall", a counter-service "dive" whose "spicy and scrumptious Indian-Pakistani food" (including "the best naan this side of the Indian Ocean") is "better than most expensive" eateries of its ilk; "takeout is a good option for the genteel crowd" that can't ignore the "abysmal decor."

Shanghai 1930 ⬛⬛   20 | 23 | 18 | $42 |
133 Steuart St. (bet. Howard & Mission Sts.), 415-896-5600
◪ Descending into this "sexy" SoMa spot "makes you feel like you've stepped back in time" to the "1930s and the Paris-of-the-East" thanks to "gorgeous decor", a swank bar mixing up "excellent cocktails" and live music serenading the room on weekends; despite digs about "small portions" for big prices, the "high-end Chinese" chow rates well, but time-sensitive suppers sigh "if they could only shanghai some attentive waiters."

Silks ⬛⬛⬛   24 | 25 | 24 | $55 |
Mandarin Oriental Hotel, 222 Sansome St. (California St.), 415-986-2020
■ "Stunning" Asian-Californian food (the "'dayboat scallops' are phenomenal"), an "unbeatable wine list", "silky smooth service" and a "sumptuous wealthy room that oozes class" are a winning combo that should make the Downtown Mandarin Oriental Hotel's "elegant" eatery "packed", so "why, why, why doesn't anyone dine here?" its fervent followers fret.

SLANTED DOOR, THE ⬛⬛   26 | 18 | 20 | $34 |
584 Valencia St. (17th St.), 415-861-8032
◪ "Absolutely epic" attest epicures about this "hip minimalist" Mission spot where chef Charles Phan's "sublime" "California take" on traditional Saigon street

eats ("the 'shaking beef' will leave you shaking with pleasure") is paired with a "brilliant yet unusual wine list"; the "unbelievable noise level", "arrogant service" and "legendary wait for reservations" admittedly are "drawbacks", but "hey, it was good enough for Clinton" (we bet *he* didn't have to wait two months for a table); P.S. "go for lunch", a much easier ticket.

Slow Club 🄻🅂🄼　　　　21 | 18 | 18 | $30
2501 Mariposa St. (Hampshire St.), 415-241-9390
■ The epitome of "SF cool", this "loud" Mission supper club serves "stylish" New American food and "mean and strong drinks" to a hipster crowd; the "mysteriously dark", "sexy" industrial environs make it "hard to see your food" but also "the perfect date place"; reservations aren't taken, so "get a Lemon Drop at the bar (assuming you can get to the bar)" and settle in for a "slow" wait.

Sno-Drift　　　　　　14 | 21 | 10 | $27
1830 Third St. (16th St.), 415-431-4766
🄴 *Wallpaper**meets Potrero Hill at this "oh-so-cool" club/restaurant; hipsters and the bridge-and-tunnel crowd dig the "super cocktail menu" and "fun" '60s "ski lodge" decor, replete with cone fireplace, frosted white vinyl padded bar and Orange Crush–colored see-through walls; a limited Californian menu ("excellent grilled flatbread") is served Wednesday–Saturday, but most "skip the food and hit the" dance floor.

South Park Cafe 🄻🄼　　　21 | 18 | 18 | $33
108 South Park St. (bet. 2nd & 3rd Sts.), 415-495-7275
■ Snare an "outdoor seat" on the sidewalk and "pretend you're in Paris" when you visit this "quintessential bistro" whose "quaint setting on the park" (South Park, that is) makes it a "great getaway from Downtown"; "nicely executed basics" are proffered by "charmingly French" waiters in what some call a "supremely romantic setting" but carpers just call "cramped."

Splendido 🄻🅂🄼　　　18 | 19 | 17 | $38
4 Embarcadero Ctr. (Sacramento St.), 415-986-3222
🄴 "One of the only Embarcadero [eateries] without the feel of a chain", this "lovely" locale ("beautiful Bay view") is a mainstay for "power dinners" thanks to its "dependably good, if never great", Italian fare and location "convenient" to the Financial District; however, naysayers note that "poor service" and "shabby upholstery" suggest that it's "not so Splendid anymore."

Stars ●🄻🄼　　　　21 | 22 | 20 | $46
555 Golden Gate Ave. (Van Ness Ave.), 415-861-7827
🄴 A "star is reborn" thanks to the combination of a new chef – Amaryll Schwertner, whose Cal-Med-International

cuisine is realized in "very creative presentations and combinations" – and "the same great atmosphere"; since it's "near Civic Center", culture vultures find it "always perfect before the opera or symphony", and although nostalgics note "it's no longer the supernova" it was in the '80s, a new generation welcomes the "reincarnation."

Stinking Rose 🄻🅂🄼   15 | 16 | 16 | $26

325 Columbus Ave. (bet. Broadway & Vallejo St.),
415-781-7673

☑ It's "major garlic headquarters" at this North Beach theme restaurant that blooms with a kitschy "interior that straddles the line between fun and cheesy" and a "shticky staff" that serves a passel of "potent food" (from bread to ice cream) prepared with the "vibrant herb"; although it attracts "throngs of tourists", locals "turn up their noses" (literally and figuratively), sniffing the place "lives up to its name" – and they don't mean the rose part.

Straits Cafe 🄻🅂🄼   22 | 18 | 17 | $31

3300 Geary Blvd. (Parker Ave.), 415-668-1783

■ "Open your mind and mouth to creative Singaporean food" – an "interesting fusion" of Indian, Indonesian and Chinese "bold flavors", "served family-style" – that breaks the monotony of typical Asian eats but "won't break your wallet"; "great tropical drinks" ("ginger martini", anyone?) and a "distinctive setting" make you "feel like you're in" the heart of the tropics instead of Inner Richmond; however, many say the service is in dire straits ("the rice may come tomorrow").

Suppenküche 🅂🄼   21 | 17 | 18 | $27

601 Hayes St. (Laguna St.), 415-252-9289

■ For "a visit to Germany", "beer and brat" buffs head to this "hip" Hayes Valley "*gasthaus*" where "Euro-babe waitresses" serve "simple" yet "delicious" "stick-to-your-ribs" Bavarian fare on "wood-plank tables" and picnic benches; despite the monastic setting, the room roars like a beer hall and the atmosphere is "jovial" due to "groups of friends" (bring your own or "make them here") drinking native brews from das communal boot.

Sushi Groove 🅂🄼   23 | 20 | 17 | $30

1516 Folsom St. (11th St.), 415-503-1950 ◗
1916 Hyde St. (bet. Green & Union Sts.), 415-440-1905

■ A "mix of funky techno music" and "designer sushi" lends a "fun party" vibe to this "trendy" Japanese duo; the "hip" decor and "stuck-up service" "can be a bit of a scene", but once the "really fresh, creatively presented fish" arrives, you "won't notice"; Hyde Streeters knock back "sake martinis" in the "wine bar" next door as they wait, while the SoMa branch eases the delay with a DJ.

Swan Oyster Depot ⓛ Ⓜ⊄   25 | 13 | 22 | $25

1517 Polk St. (bet. California & Sacramento Sts.), 415-673-1101

■ Bivalve buffs "could consume oysters, sourdough and Anchor Steam all day long" at Polk Street's "no-frills seafood counter", a "treasured time warp" (founded 1912) that's "so old-fashioned it's almost stylish"; despite a perennial wait for one of the 20 "shaky stools", once in, the "fun servers" and SF's "best clam chowder" compensate.

Tadich Grill ⓛ Ⓜ   20 | 19 | 20 | $33

240 California St. (bet. Battery & Front Sts.), 415-391-1849

◪ "Welcome to" "old-time SF" and the "no muss, no fuss" "fresh seafood" (including such exotics as "petrale sole and sand dabs with legendary tartar sauce") meted out by this Downtown "alpha restaurant" dating back to 1849; but while nostalgics wax it's "tradition on a plate", cynics snap that "good food is a thing of the past here" – and they can "skip the merchandizing" and "sassy service" too.

Taiwan Ⓛ Ⓢ Ⓜ   19 | 8 | 13 | $17

445 Clement St. (6th Ave.), 415-387-1789

■ The "pot stickers are deservedly famous" at this Inner Richmond "throwback to the dumpling houses of Taipei" that serves dim sum (*sans* those rolling carts) and other "authentic Chinese" specialties throughout the day; sure, it's a "hole-in-the-wall" with a "run-down" atmo, but the steamed goodies are tasty and prices "very affordable."

Takara Ⓛ Ⓢ Ⓜ   ▽ 22 | 12 | 13 | $33

22 Peace Plaza (Geary Blvd.), 415-921-2000

■ Nestled in Japantown's Peace Plaza, this "underrated", underrepresented yearling is "not your run-of-the-mill" Nipponese; true, they serve "some of the best sushi" and "great tempura", but it's the various intriguingly named rice dishes (Iron Rice Pot, Basketly) and savory custards that make eating here "like being in Japan."

Taqueria Cancun Ⓛ Ⓢ Ⓜ⊄   22 | 8 | 11 | $9

1003 Market St. (6th St.), 415-864-6773
3211 Mission St. (Valencia St.), 415-550-1414 ◓
2288 Mission St. (19th St.), 415-252-9560 ◓

■ This cult taqueria trio draws gringos to its "dicey neighborhoods" for "cheap, satisfying and fast" Mexican fare "made with love"; "super burritos" – "carne" or "veggie" versions – are considered among "the best north of the border", thanks to lightly grilled tortillas and "fresh avocado to top them off"; P.S. "the jukebox rocks out" late into the night.

Ten-Ichi Ⓛ Ⓢ Ⓜ   21 | 15 | 19 | $28

2235 Fillmore St. (bet. Clay & Sacramento Sts.), 415-346-3477

■ Finatics "make a trip" to this Upper Fillmore mainstay "just for the Indian summer roll" (tempura green beans with barbecued eel), enjoying the "terrific sushi and even better donburi" while they're at it; the "happy" staff is "the sweetest" and so is the "mochi ice cream", which may explain why the place has "been around for 23 years."

Terra Brazilis ⑤　　　　19 │ 18 │ 18 │ $29

602 Hayes St. (Laguna St.), 415-241-1900

■ It's "worth the visit" to this "warm, bright and cozy" Brazilian in Hayes Valley for the "new menu" that chef Michael Cook (ex Campton Place) has cookin'; even if it's a bit "uneven", it still offers an "adventure for your palate" ("they do great things with yucca"); of course, "it would taste better if your neighbors weren't in your plate"; P.S. only beer, wine and a "tasty sangria" are served.

Thai House ⑤Ⓜ　　　21 │ 14 │ 17 │ $21

2200 Market St. (bet. 15th & Sanchez Sts.), 415-864-5006 Ⓛ

151 Noe St. (Henry St.), 415-863-0374

■ "Wonderful curries, excellent service and a surprisingly "good wine selection for a Thai" place make these "reasonably priced Castro haunts" "reliable destinations" and "everyone's favorite"; P.S. the Noe Street original has a more quaint, "neighborhood feel."

Thanh Long ⑤　　　25 │ 15 │ 18 │ $38

4101 Judah St. (46th Ave.), 415-665-1146

■ "Ready a bib and dig in" to the "to-die-for garlic noodles" and "world-famous roasted crab" ("more addictive than crack") that are the pull at this Sunset Vietnamese seafooder (a lowbrow version of its sister Crustacean); the hooked confess it's "hard to stray" from those signature dishes but admit they get "a bit crabby about" the "high prices" and "waits that can be more than Long."

Thanya & Salee ⓁⓈⓂ　　▽ 20 │ 14 │ 16 │ $21

1469 18th St. (Connecticut St.), 415-647-6469

■ Locals "never get sick of this place", "one of the few Thai" eateries serving "good duck *larb*" (and the only Thai, period, on Potrero Hill); since "it's connected to the Lilo Lounge" next door, a faux tropical bar that's open till 2 AM, "it's easy to spend the whole evening here."

Thep Phanom Thai Cuisine ⑤Ⓜ　25 │ 15 │ 19 │ $25

400 Waller St. (Fillmore St.), 415-431-2526

■ The name may be "hard to pronounce", but the eats are "easy to swallow" at this "reigning champ" in the Lower Haight, with an "exhaustive selection" of "Phanomenal" dishes that are "some of the best you'll find east of Bangkok"; although surveyors voted it "best Thai in town", it's definitely not "superior" "in terms of decor, service" and ambiance, which is "festive or noisy, depending on how you look at it."

Thirsty Bear Brewing Co. 🅛🅢🅜   16 | 14 | 13 | $25
661 Howard St. (bet. New Montgomery & 3rd Sts.),
415-974-0905
◧ This "bustling" SoMa Spaniard serving "interesting
tapas" (fish cheeks, blood sausage) and "beer brewed
on the premises" packs in "the few remaining dot-com
yuppies jabbering loudly into cell phones" and "frat boys"
thirsty for a "happy-hour hangout place after work";
but others can't bear the "sleepwalking waiters" and
"noisy", "cavernous" interior.

Three Seasons 🅢🅜   24 | 16 | 19 | $27
3317 Steiner St. (bet. Chestnut & Lombard Sts.),
415-567-9989
■ Celebrating its first season in a formerly jinxed location,
this yearling is "the Marina's answer to The Slanted Door"
boasting nine different types of spring rolls, a half-dozen
satay selections and other "unique twists" on traditional
"Vietnamese dishes"; though the "hit-or-miss service"
and grotto-like atmosphere don't live up to the "vibrant
flavors", this is "a place to watch for sure."

Ti Couz 🅛🅢🅜   21 | 16 | 16 | $21
3108 16th St. (bet. Guerrero & Valencia Sts.),
415-252-7373
■ A visit to this "fun and happening" budget Missionite
is like taking a "youth-hostel trip to the Brittany coast";
"yummy buckwheat crêpes" filled with "unusual sweet
and savory" fillings (the "banana and Nutella [version]
yum"), in addition to "seafood platters", "continue to
fortify hipsters" who contend that the quaint "village
atmosphere" and wide selection of "hard ciders on
tap" make the "Gen-X style service" and "devastatingly
long waits" "bearable."

Timo's 🅢🅜   17 | 14 | 15 | $24
842 Valencia St. (bet. 19th & 20th Sts.), 415-647-0558
◧ "Live" flamenco guitarists and "great" pitchers of sangria
make this "funky" Spaniard a "fun" favorite "in the
over-tapas-ized Mission" for many amigos (especially
vegetarians); however, critics cry the "decor is like a
dungeon" and "prices are too high for what you get"
("the menu said tapas, not tidbits"), warning "if you're too
hungry you can rack up a steep bill."

Tin-Pan Asian Bistro 🅛🅢🅜   19 | 19 | 19 | $25
2251 Market St. (bet. Noe & Sanchez Sts.), 415-565-0733
◧ It's a real "scene" at this late-night Pan-Asian bistro in
the Castro that "looks promising", thanks to its "inviting
atmosphere", "nice table settings" and wide variety of
"East/West" noodle dishes "to select from" ("try the
chocolate-raspberry won ton"); however, foes pan the
fusion fare as having "fused into mediocrity."

Tita's L S M
▽ | 18 | 15 | 19 | $17 |

3870 17th St. (bet. Noe & Sanchez Sts.), 415-626-2477
■ For a "little bit of Honolulu in SF", natives hang ten at this Castro eatery that delivers "an oasis of island tranquility in a restless neighborhood"; the "Hawaiian-style plates" (such as the "great Kahlua pork") served by a "staff that shows lot of aloha spirit" make homesick Islanders feel "very *o'hana* (home)", especially "when a trip is a ways off."

Tokyo Go Go S
23 | 21 | 17 | $31 |

3174 16th St. (bet. Guerrero & Valencia Sts.), 415-864-2288
■ Fin fans seeking a raw deal head to this "cool" Japanese in the Mission featuring "huge slices of fresh fish" and "inventive [sake] drinks" in a "60s mod–meets–George Jetson" atmosphere; although "well-prepared" "innovative sushi rolls are their forte", the kitchen "puts out some really yummy small plates" such as the "to-die-for miso-marinated sea bass"; so don't let the "annoying wait" and "impossible parking" deter you from Go-ing.

Tommaso's S
24 | 16 | 20 | $25 |

1042 Kearny St. (bet. Broadway & Pacific Ave.), 415-398-9696
■ "One of the few joints in North Beach that's not a tourist attraction", this "family-run" Southern Italian has a devout following that insists "anything from the original wood-burning oven [circa 1935] is a must" – particularly the thin-crust pizza, which is arguably the "best in the city"; while there's "friendly service", the decor seems lifted "from a Scorcese film."

Tommy's Joynt ◐ L S M⊄
14 | 13 | 13 | $16 |

1101 Geary Blvd. (Van Ness Ave.), 415-775-4216
◪ "Step into the Twilight Zone at this Van Ness" German-American "*hofbrau*" that's "home" to "a lot of weird stewed items" (buffalo, oxtail, brisket) and "pitchers of beer from around the world"; night crawlers and bargain hunters "don't come here for the atmosphere" but for the "unbelievable prices"; even history buffs hedge "it's a landmark, but just for the building" (circa 1947), not for the "greasy-spoon" grub.

Tommy Toy's
Cuisine Chinoise L S M
25 | 25 | 25 | $53 |

655 Montgomery St. (bet. Clay & Washington Sts.), 415-397-4888
■ With its "fascinating" fare ("it's not Chinese, not nouvelle French", but a hodgepodge of both), "fabulous decor" reminiscent of the Empress Dowager's sitting room and impeccable service ("throw your fork on the floor and watch 10 waiters run to pick it up"), this formal Downtowner is "the standard-bearer" for business dining; it's "too dark", "too expensive" ("do they charge for the celebrity pics on the wall?") and "yes, the staff pushes the prix fixe too much" – but "they're right to."

Tonga Room ⑤Ⓜ   11 | 24 | 15 | $32
Fairmont Hotel, 950 Mason St. (California St.), 415-772-5278
■ "Who cares what the food is like when it's raining inside?"
josh fans of this Nob Hill "tropical" paradise; it's the
"kitschiest place in town", replete with tiki huts, "volcanic
drinks", a floating barge/bandstand for the live Polynesian
combo and fake "storms" that erupt every half hour;
residents recommend "skip the overpriced Asian entrees
and come during the all-you-can-eat buffet happy hour."

Ton Kiang Ⓛ⑤Ⓜ   25 | 13 | 17 | $24
5821 Geary Blvd. (bet. 22nd & 23rd Aves.), 415-387-8273
■ Dumpling devotees declare this "bustling" Richmond
Chinese offers the "best dim sum in SF" thanks to the
rapid stream of "fresh, hot and uniquely tasty" "goodies"
proffered by "efficient" "non-English speakers who laugh
as you try to interpret" what's "parading in front of your
table"; the "terrific Hakka" dinner specialties add to its
status as "a destination" "worth the trip out of tourist
land"; P.S. "go with a big group to make reservations or
brave huge lines."

Top of the Mark ⑤   19 | 26 | 20 | $43
*Mark Hopkins Hotel, 1 Nob Hill, 18th fl., (bet. California &
Mason Sts.), 415-616-6916*
☑ It's "swing time with a view" for the "over-45-year-
old" set "on show at this Nob Hill sky lounge" featuring
"incredible views" of SF from the "newly renovated 18th
floor" of the Mark Hopkins Hotel; predictably, the "average"
Californian dinners and "extravagant Sunday brunches"
"don't live up" to the vistas, but "romantics" rave "there's
no better place for a drink on a special occasion" – or to
display "dance steps of old."

Town's End   20 | 16 | 19 | $25
Restaurant & Bakery Ⓛ⑤
2 Townsend St. (The Embarcadero), 415-512-0749
■ "Come for the bread basket, stay for the brunch", "then
walk it off with a nice Embarcadero stroll" suggests the
carbo-loading clientele of this "sunny" New American; the
"blow-your-mind baked goods" are the be-all and end-all
here, drawing long lines on weekend mornings and "lifting
up" the otherwise "average food" at dinner; P.S. opt for a
sunny patio seat over the "noisy dining room."

Trattoria Contadina ⑤Ⓜ   22 | 17 | 22 | $28
1800 Mason St. (Union St.), 415-982-5728
■ Technically in North Beach but "tucked far away enough
to find parking", this "venerable" "homey" trattoria is
"everything a neighborhood Italian should be" – the
"wonderful servers" "treat you like family", the kitchen
prepares "excellent", "hearty" standards and the dining
room is filled with a "good mix of locals and tourists."

Truly Mediterranean ●ⓁⓈⓂ 22 7 14 $10

1724 Haight St. (Cole St.), 415-751-7482
3109 16th St. (Valencia St.), 415-252-7482 ⊟

■ These "hole-in-the-wall" shacks offer truly "tasty", "authentic" Med–Middle Eastern fast food; aside from the "great" signature schwarma, surveyors sigh "happiness is their homemade falafel" – which "they grill", making it "nice and crispy on the outside"; there's limited seating and dismal decor at both the Haight and Mission branches, so most folks order their gyros "to go."

Tu Lan ⓁⓂ⊟ 21 3 9 $11

8 Sixth St. (Market St.), 415-626-0927

■ "Refreshingly generous portions" of "fabulous" and "cheap" Vietnamese food are "worth climbing over the bums for" at this SoMa "dive"; "your bravado will be rewarded when you taste their curry fried rice or those luscious Imperial Rolls", just be warned "service is whatever" and "decor is slum dump"; P.S. "the faint of heart" can "order to go."

21st Amendment Brewery Cafe Bar ⓁⓈⓂ 17 17 16 $24

563 Second St. (bet. Brannan & Bryant Sts.), 415-369-0900

■ "Good microbrews" and "better-than-average" "bar food" make this yearling brewery "one of the [more desirable] new eating and drinking spots" near Pac Bell Park; the "hip, lofty" warehouse interior fits right in with the neighborhood, resembling the office spaces of the dot-commers who employ the joint as their "after-work hangout"; fans feel it's best (and less crowded) "when the Giants are out of town."

Twenty Four ⓁⓈⓂ 19 22 19 $36

Pacific Bell Park, 24 Willie Mays Plaza (bet. King & 3rd Sts.), 415-644-0240

■ "Only in SF would there be such a good restaurant at a ball park" swear supporters of this "surprising classy" American seafooder celebrating its first season at bat; sports aficionados say "the food and the service hit a home run whether the Giants are in town or not", and even critics concede that it "sure beats hot dogs" in the stands.

2223 Restaurant ⓈⓂ 21 18 19 $36

2223 Market St. (bet. Noe & Sanchez Sts.), 415-431-0692

■ This "trendy" yet "low-key" New American is the "exception to the general rule that if it's in the Castro it doesn't have to be good"; the "comfort food" is "solidly terrific" and the "pretty waiters" deliver "consistently good service" to the "beautiful" customers who consider it "wonderful" for Sunday brunch and a "great" place to "meet a friend or find a lover."

Universal Cafe ⚫🆂
22 | 17 | 19 | $32

2814 19th St. (bet. Bryant & Harrison Sts.), 415-821-4608
■ "Tucked away" in "nowhere land" in the "gentrified" Mission, this "small" "industrial chic" "treasure" earns universal applause for its "laid-back" yet "urban" vibe and new chef Peter Erickson's "delicious" New American fare; even enthusiasts, however, could do without the "uncomfortable chairs" and "somewhat snobby staff."

Venticello 🆂🅼
22 | 22 | 21 | $40

1257 Taylor St. (Washington St.), 415-922-2545
■ A roaring "fireplace, cable cars driving by and great views of the Bay" make this "intimate" Nob Hill Northern Italian "wonderful" for a "romantic" dinner or to "meet fellow San Franciscans, since you practically sit on top of your neighbors"; either way, the "remarkable fare" makes this trattoria – "hidden" "away from the busy tourist spots" – "a nice place for locals to enjoy a special evening."

Venture Frogs Restaurant 🆂🅼
12 | 12 | 13 | $24

1000 Van Ness Ave. (O'Farrell St.), 415-409-2550
☑ With its "computer chip–embedded glowing bar" and "plasma TVs", this Civic Center Pan-Asian is the apotheosis of "dot-com excess"; the digerati dig the "hi-fi" decor and "friendly staff" that "treats you like family", calling it "awesome for dinner and a movie"; however, the less bullish berate "uninspired food", "unreliable service" and "unappetizing" "corporate"-named dishes that just "remind you that the party is finally over."

Via Vai Trattoria ⚫🆂🅼
18 | 16 | 18 | $31

1715 Union St. (bet. Gough & Octavia Sts.), 415-441-2111
☑ This "pleasantly low-key" Cow Hollow Italian is a specialist in "great thin-crust pizza" and "simple pastas" at "reasonable prices"; amici insist it's a "good alternative to [sib] Pane e Vino" "because there's never a wait", but even they admit it shares the same flaws – "tight quarters" and "noisy atmosphere"; P.S. "check out the patio."

Vicolo ⚫🆂🅼
21 | 11 | 12 | $18

201 Ivy St. (bet. Franklin & Gough Sts.), 415-863-2382
■ "Hidden" in an alleyway (*vicolo*), this "informal" Italian in Hayes Valley is a "real find" for a "quick bite" "before the opera, symphony or ballet"; the "fabulous" deep-dish pizza "sets the standard" ("the secret is the cornmeal crust") and the "salads couldn't be bigger or fresher", which is why most don't mind that there's "no atmosphere to speak of"; N.B. half-baked pies are available to go.

Vivande Porta Via ⚫🆂🅼
21 | 15 | 18 | $33

2125 Fillmore St. (bet. California & Sacramento Sts.), 415-346-4430
☑ For admirers of cookbook author Carlo Middione's "authentic Italian" cuisine, his "dependable" Upper

Fillmore "eat-in or take-out" gourmet shop-cum-trattoria is the only place to be (since his more formal Vivande went south last year); some say it's "overpriced" for the "down-home deli setting", but fettuccine freaks fawn "his [homemade] pasta dishes can't be beat."

V Restaurant & Wine Bar M　▽ 23 | 22 | 23 | $55

Orchard Hotel, 665 Bush St. (bet. Powell & Stockton Sts.), 415-837-1680

■ This "elegant" Cal-French yearling may be the "jewel" in the crown of Downtown's Orchard Hotel, but it sure doesn't serve "your usual hotel fare", offering instead "excellent" "cutting-edge" five- and eight-course tasting menus (as well as à la carte); service is equally top shelf, and the wine bar offers a "great selection" (27 varieties by the glass); though it's not yet widely known, fans fear once "the word gets out, it will be impossible to get a reservation."

Walzwerk　20 | 16 | 22 | $24

381 Van Ness Ave. (bet. 14th & 15th Sts.), 415-551-7181

■ The "striking Amazons" who own and run this "spartan" sprocket-looking haus of brats and bier cast a spell over das diners who single them out as the Mission joint's best asset; although ratings for the "authentic" "rib-sticking" East German "comfort food" have gone sauer since our last *Survey*, herring hounds still consider it "a gem."

Waterfront Restaurant & Cafe L S M　20 | 23 | 19 | $43

Pier 7, The Embarcadero (Broadway), 415-391-2696

◪ "Breathtaking views of the SF Bay" are afforded by this 36-year veteran – actually two eateries in one: the top floor offers "top-shelf" Cal-French fare and "more refinement", while the downstairs cafe offers "midpriced seafood" and "an outdoor deck"; critics carp about "slower-than-a-slug" service and cry "you're paying for" the panorama, but locals with "out-of-town guests" are "happy to return."

Watergate S M　23 | 19 | 21 | $39

1152 Valencia St. (bet. 22nd & 23rd Sts.), 415-648-6000

■ In the Mission, this "understated", "undiscovered" New French–Asian has built up a loyal local clientele by offering "outstanding" "haute cuisine" and "orgasmic tea" at "value prices" (especially the prix fixe menus); "cheery" and "attentive" service is an added bonus.

We Be Sushi L M　16 | 10 | 15 | $17

3226 Geary Blvd. (bet. Parker & Spruce Sts.), 415-221-9960
94 Judah St. (6th Ave.), 415-681-4010
538 Valencia St. (bet. 16th & 17th Sts.), 415-565-0749 S
1071 Valencia St. (22nd St.), 415-826-0607 S ⊄

◪ To wallet-watchers, this mini-chain of "poor man's sushi" joints serving maki 'like mom used to make' is the "right spot to get your weekly fix"; pickier palates, on the other hand, point out that "the quantity-to-price ratio is excellent, but the quality passable."

Woodward's Garden S   24 | 15 | 20 | $43
1700 Mission St. (Duboce St.), 415-621-7122
■ "Who thought you would find" such "delicious", "rock-solid" New American food "under the freeway" marvels the mostly coupled crowd that flocks to this "cozy", "romantic" Mission "hideaway"; devotees attest that "big flavors and portions" make up for "snug" quarters and shrug "who cares about decor when it tames the prices?"

Xyz L S M   19 | 22 | 17 | $45
W Hotel, 181 Third St. (Howard St.), 415-817-7836
◪ This "hip" SoMa Californian ("wear black to fit in") is a "people-watching dreamland", attracting a "socially fabulous" crowd to its "glamorous" dining room with plush "high-back booths" and "swank" upstairs martini bar; to many, the "creative" seasonally changing cuisine is "as beautiful as the art" in the neighboring SF MOMA (with a price tag to match); however, cynics complain about "teeny portions" and "big-ego'd servers", claiming a case of "style over substance."

Yabbies Coastal Kitchen S M   23 | 18 | 20 | $37
2237 Polk St. (bet. Green & Vallejo Sts.), 415-474-4088
■ "Fresh seafood cooked to perfection" is the hook at this "amazing" Polk Street New American restaurant and raw bar ("the tuna poke is a gift from God" – Neptune, we assume); despite its "sleeper" status, seafaring surveyors swear its piscatorial pleasures are as "good as the bigger names" in town and the "outstanding service" and "awesome wine list" blow them out of the water.

Yank Sing L S M   24 | 16 | 18 | $28
Rincon Ctr., 101 Spear St. (bet. Howard & Mission Sts.), 415-957-9300
49 Stevenson St. (bet. 1st & 2nd Sts.), 415-541-4949
■ "It's hard to stop ordering" at these "superb" SoMa dim sum parlors where "cart after cart laden" with a "great variety" of "delicious" "delicacies" that really sing (including Peking duck by the slice) roll by; vets report that it's "much fancier" and "more expensive than Chinatown", but the "quality and taste are [also] much higher"; P.S. "devastated" Downtowners mourn the closure of the original Battery Street branch.

Yokoso Nippon L M ≠   ▽ 18 | 10 | 13 | $20
314 Church St. (15th St.), no phone
■ "Cheap, fast" and "decent" slabs of "fresh" fish reel in the "budget-constrained" to this "cramped" Upper

Market/Church Street hole-in-the-wall Japanese, aka 'No Name Sushi', as it has no phone and no sign (which might explain the low response rate); however, since it has the "lowest prices around", surveyors "can't complain."

Yoshida-Ya 🇱🇸🇲　　　　21 | 18 | 18 | $32
2909 Webster St. (Union St.), 415-346-3431
■ Although voters "love the sushi" at this "reliable" Cow Hollow Japanese, it's the *yakitori* (traditional barbecue) menu that sets it apart; the private tatami room upstairs, where you sit on the floor, offers a "relaxed atmosphere" and is a "fun" option for a repast "with a group."

Yuet Lee ●🇱🇸🇲⊄　　　　20 | 6 | 12 | $21
1300 Stockton St. (Broadway), 415-982-6020
■ "Wear eyeshades and enjoy" the "wonderful" "authentic" seafood at this cash-only Chinatown "dump" that's "all about flavor and nothing else"; addicts assert the "sublime" "salt-and-pepper prawns and crabs are worth" the "bleak" decor (a particularly atrocious lime-green) and service, especially at 3 AM, when it's one of the few still serving.

Yukol Place Thai Cuisine 🇸🇲　　∇ 20 | 13 | 19 | $22
2380 Lombard St. (bet. Pierce & Scott Sts.), 415-922-1599
■ For its few but fervent fans, this is *the* Thai place in the Marina, a favorite with temple-like ornamentation that makes for a "great atmosphere", accommodating service and tasty, well-priced renditions of Siamese standards.

Zante's Indian Cuisine & Pizza 🇱🇸🇲　　19 | 6 | 10 | $15
3489 Mission St. (30th St.), 415-821-3949
■ "Who would have thought Indian pizza" "would taste so good"?; those who've tried this Bernal Height dal house's "bizarre" combination of tandoori chicken, cauliflower, ginger, green onions and garlic slathered and baked on top of naan ("a stroke of genius"), that's who; unfortunately, the "surly service" and garish pink decor don't curry the same admiration, so most get their Delhi dinners to go.

Zao Noodle Bar 🇱🇸🇲　　　15 | 13 | 15 | $17
2406 California St. (Fillmore St.), 415-345-8088
2031 Chestnut St. (Fillmore St.), 415-928-3088
822 Irving St. (bet. 8th & 9th Aves.), 415-682-2828
3583 16th St. (bet. Market & Noe Sts.), 415-864-2888
◧ This fast-expanding chain of "fusiony" Asian noodle and soup shops is "a cute concept" – sort of a House of International Noodles for the "yuppie set"; admirers appreciate the "heaping servings" for a "fast, fresh, inexpensive" "carbo shot in the arm", but phos who are familiar with "the real thing" call the "concoctions" "disappointing" and "bland."

Zaré **L M**
23 21 22 $39

568 Sacramento St. (bet. Montgomery & Sansome Sts.), 415-291-9145

■ "Host-with-the-most" Hoss Zaré sets apart this "little jewel box" from the other "uptight", "overpriced" "options in the Financial District"; his "personal touch" is evident throughout, from the "homey Med" fare to his regular schmoozing with customers; N.B. the new billowy decor has breathed new life into the dining room.

Zarzuela
22 17 20 $31

2000 Hyde St. (Union St.), 415-346-0800

■ Seville-savvy surveyors say this Castilian is "as Spanish as a flamenco guitar", with an "impeccable" staff serving "a huge variety" of "outstanding" tapas ("go with a group to sample it all") and the "best sangria" in town to wash it all down; now, "if only they took reservations and would park your car" on Russian Hill.

Zax
23 19 21 $40

2330 Taylor St. (Columbus Ave.), 415-563-6266

■ Hidden "away from the tourists" but well "worth the detour", this "small" "husband-and-wife-run" bistro serving "serious" French-Mediterranean fare is "North Beach's best-kept secret"; locals love the "changing menu" but are relieved that the "heavenly" signature "goat-cheese soufflé is always on it"; a "caring staff" and "romantic, quiet atmosphere" make it a "great date" place before "heading to" nearby clubs.

Zazie **L S M**
20 19 18 $23

941 Cole St. (bet. Carl St. & Parnassus Ave.), 415-564-5332

■ The "cornerstone of Cole Valley", this "unpretentious", "cozy" French bistro is consistently packed for its "great little breakfasts" and "straightforward and downright tasty" food; *amis* advise "stop to smell the honeysuckle" on your way to the "sunny patio" and turn the other cheek when it comes to the "harried service."

Zinzino **S M**
19 18 17 $29

2355 Chestnut St. (bet. Divisadero & Scott Sts.), 415-346-6623

■ This "dependable, reasonably priced" Italian in the Marina specializes in Neapolitan-style thin-crust pizza in "odd shapes" and parchment-baked spaghetti and meatballs; the front bar, festooned with vintage Italian street posters, is a "fun" place to "relax, drink a glass of wine and watch a foreign film on TV"; N.B. as we go to press, the place has been sold and is in transition.

Zodiac Club, The **M**
17 20 17 $32

718 14th St. (bet. Church & Sanchez Sts.), 415-626-7827

■ "Take a date" to this "trendy", "swanky" Upper Market astrologically oriented bar/restaurant serving "good vibes" along with Mediterranean-inflected Californian cuisine into the witching hour; the "cosmic" "horoscope beverages help you get out of your drink box", and the first-come, first-serve curtain-ensconced Lion's Den, if you're lucky enough to snag it, is a "great place for a birthday party."

ZUNI CAFE ●🌓L S
24 21 19 $39

1658 Market St. (bet. Franklin & Gough Sts.), 415-552-2522 ■ Chef-owner Judy Rodgers' "notoriously hip" and "hyped" Hayes Valley spot has been the "epitome of the SF restaurant scene" since opening in 1979; the "gorgeous" "overcrowded bar" – home of "outrageous [balsamic-spiked] Bloody Marys" and an amazing array of "fresh oysters" – is ground zero for "people-watching"; although the Northern Italian–Med menu "changes daily", few venture beyond the "signature roast chicken, hamburgers and Caesar salad" that are "the yardstick" by which all others are judged.

East of San Francisco

	F	D	S	C

À Côté ◑ **L S** ▽ 25 | 24 | 23 | $31
5478 College Ave. (Taft St.), Oakland, 510-655-6469
■ Located *à côté* (next door) to its progenitor Citron, Chris Rossi's "wonderful new Rockridge bistro" offers a "stunningly delicious" and "nicely presented" French-inspired "all tapas, all the time" menu (don't miss the "fabulous" baked mussels with Pernod); a "fun", albeit chaotic, ambiance and "eclectic wine list and cocktail selection" solidify its status as "the 'in' place" in the East Bay, and although patient patrons "wish they did reservations", they concede it's "worth the long wait."

AHWAHNEE DINING ROOM, THE L S M 19 | 28 | 22 | $45
The Ahwahnee Hotel, 1 Ahwahnee Rd., Yosemite National Park, 209-372-1489
■ With "the magnificence of Yosemite" visible through the floor-to-ceiling windows and giant pine beams supporting the "stately" dining room (dating back to 1927), visitors to the national park feel "it's a privilege to eat" here during their stay; not surprisingly, the "spectacular setting outshines" the pricey High Sierra cuisine (a heartier take on Californian), but most assert "it's an experience that everyone should have in this lifetime."

Ajanta L S M 22 | 17 | 18 | $25
1888 Solano Ave. (bet. Alameda & Colusa Aves.), Berkeley, 510-526-4373
■ This "family-run" "sophisticate" is "the *ne plus ultra* of great Indian dining" in Berkeley thanks to chef-owner Lachu Moorjani's "wonderful regional dishes that you won't find elsewhere" and a "rotating seasonal menu" that ensures "you're always pleasantly surprised"; "erotic murals" depicting the naked figures of the Ajanta caves "add to your date" and neutralize quibbles about "micro-portions"; N.B. join their mailing for monthly special alerts.

Arizmendi Bakery L M ⌁ 24 | 11 | 17 | $9
3265 Lakeshore Ave. (bet. MacArthur & Mandana Blvds.), Oakland, 510-268-8849
■ The *Survey*'s Best Bang for the Buck, this funky Oaklander is "not a restaurant" per se, but its signature "melt-in-your-mouth" "pizza rivals" the best, and the "fabulous breads, scones, muffins and biscotti" "make you glad to be alive"; do-goodniks report it's "one of the few collectives left", so "it's worth stopping by and supporting it."

Autumn Moon Cafe L S M　　18　16　17　$24
3909 Grand Ave. (Sunny Slope Ave.), Oakland, 510-595-3200
■ A "cleverly converted home in the attractive Grand Avenue area" of Oakland is an appropriate setting for this "casual" American that draws "hour-long waits on the weekends" for its "excellent pancakes", challah French toast and other homespun breakfast and brunch "comfort foods"; "friendly service" and an outdoor patio add to the appeal, but surveyors are less moony over the dinner fare.

Barney's Gourmet Hamburger L S M ⌿　　17　11　13　$13
1600 Shattuck Ave. (Cedar St.), Berkeley, 510-849-2827
1591 Solano Ave. (Tacoma Ave.), Berkeley, 510-526-8185
5819 College Ave. (Chabot Rd.), Oakland, 510-601-0444
4162 Piedmont Ave. (Linda Ave.), Oakland, 510-655-7180
See review in San Francisco Directory.

Battambang L M　　21　13　17　$18
850 Broadway (9th St.), Oakland, 510-839-8815
■ An "unsung" "find" offers Oaklanders "truly excellent Cambodian" delicacies and "friendly service" at "low prices"; the "beautiful food" ("steamed rice custard dessert is presented in an origami-like banana leaf box") stands in stark contrast to the "ugly room", but insiders insist it's the "best deal" in town.

BAY WOLF L S M　　25　21　24　$42
3853 Piedmont Ave. (Rio Vista Ave.), Oakland, 510-655-6004
■ "You can always count on chef Michael Wild for a great meal" bay boosters of this "top" Oakland Cal-Med that's been an "East Bay staple" since 1975; "everything sparkles" – from the "elegantly relaxed setting" to the "excellent service" to the "sublime" signature duck dishes; "other places come and go, this one gets better and better."

Bette's Oceanview Diner L S M　　21　16　17　$17
1807 Fourth St. (Hearst Ave.), Berkeley, 510-644-3230
■ You might have to "sleep outside the previous night to get in line for Sunday brunch" at this "cute retro" diner in Berkeley that whips up "interesting twists on traditional breakfast fare" ("soufflé pancakes, anyone?"); the eggstatic also espouse the "unusual selections on the jukebox" and "good service despite massive table competition"; a few patrons pout "what, no ocean view?" (nope, and there's no dinner either).

Bighorn Grill L S M　　18　21　19　$33
2410 San Ramon Valley Blvd. (Crow Canyon Rd.), San Ramon, 925-838-5678
◪ Designer Pat Kuleto's hunting-lodge decor creates "a nice atmosphere" for indulging in steaks washed down with "big martinis" at this San Ramon grill, a cinema paradiso

for ticket-holders of the nearby theater; however, the meat elite beef "too bad the food doesn't match the decor" and say "save your money until you can afford a trip to the city."

Bistro Liaison L S M   ▽ 24 | 24 | 24 | $24
1849 Shattuck Ave. (Hearst Ave.), Berkeley, 510-849-2155
■ Locals are already having a love affair with this "brand-new" Berkeley bistro where French-inspired "reasonably priced" "*petit plats*" (small plates) rule; chef-owner Todd Kneiss (ex Left Bank) covers familiar terroir with his "very Parisian" menu (think coq au vin and tarte tatin) as well as more unusual dishes such as roasted quail stuffed with black-truffle risotto; "delightful decor" and "spectacular service that other restaurants should strive for" have kept it "packed" since day one.

Blackhawk Grille L S M   22 | 22 | 20 | $40
The Shops at Blackhawk, 3540 Blackhawk Plaza Circle (Camino Tassajara), Danville, 925-736-4295
☑ You can't beat "eating by the waterfalls and overlooking the fountains" at this "upscale" spot in suburban Danville; cosmopolites claim that since new chef Daniel Amaya (an underling at Gary Danko) nested here, the Californian fare has soared to "exceptional" heights, but the hawkish snipe it's "too pricey" and "snooty" "for an East Bay" "shopping center"; still, it's a great repose "after visiting the car museum" nearby – and besides, there aren't "a lot of choices in this neck of the woods."

Blue Nile L S   19 | 17 | 15 | $17
2525 Telegraph Ave. (Dwight Way), Berkeley, 510-540-6777
☑ "What fun!" rave reviewers after a hands-on dinner at this "family-style" Ethiopian staffed by "women in authentic garb"; the "adventurous" get a kick out of "grabbing bites" of the "really tasty" stews ("eating with your fingers makes for a great icebreaker on a first date") and swilling the "homemade honey wine" in the "funky" dining room ("love those '60s beaded curtains"); nonetheless, nile-hilists gripe this "bland" Berkeley vet is no longer "the best African in the area."

Bollinger Bar & Grill L S M   ▽ 18 | 24 | 18 | $40
680 Bollinger Canyon Way (1½ mi. east of I-680), San Ramon, 925-968-1500
☑ A curvaceous dining room maximizes the "great views" of San Ramon at this massive newcomer where seasoned restaurateur Faz Poursohi offers a "hugely portioned" New American potato-skins-and-babyback-ribs repertoire paired with a mostly California wine list; but while satisfied suburbanites "feel it's like going to the city without going to the city", dissenters dig that the "disappointingly" "under-flavored" "food doesn't justify the beautiful location."

Brazio **L S M**   ▽ | 20 | 21 | 21 | $41 |

The Shops at Blackhawk, 3421 Blackhawk Plaza Circle (Camino Tassajara), Danville, 925-736-3000
■ Bravo to chef-around-the-Bay Fred Halpert (of Livefire Grill fame) whose Northern Italian steakhouse in Danville "continues to improve" as the "terrific grilled meats and fish" and service inch closer to the heights of the "lovely atmosphere" – an elegant environment with tiled columns and "terraces overlooking a duck pond"; it's "reminiscent of the Tuscan countryside without the language problem."

Breads of India & Gourmet Curries **L S M ⊬** | 22 | 10 | 15 | $19 |

2448 Sacramento St. (Dwight Way), Berkeley, 510-848-7684
■ "As their name says", the "breathtakingly aromatic" "wide selection of breads is the highlight" at this "hole-in-the-wall in the middle of Berkeley" that also serves a "daily rotating menu" of "wonderful subtle tastes" of India; naan partisans posit that the "shared tables in the crowded dining room are part of the experience, along with long lines"; however, the "decor falls flat in comparison" and "the 'screw you' attitude" of the service doesn't curry any favor with critics.

Bridges Restaurant **L S M** | 23 | 25 | 23 | $48 |

44 Church St. (Hartz Ave.), Danville, 925-820-7200
■ This "beautiful and refined" Californian-Asian serves a "very suburban, very Danville" "clientele very well indeed"; the "nicely presented" gourmet "fusion food isn't groundbreaking" but it "appeals to a general audience"; the only consistent complaint is that the place has become "too pricey", although they've recently introduced "an excellent-value prix fixe" tasting menu.

Britt-Marie's **L S ⊬** | 18 | 16 | 20 | $24 |

1369 Solano Ave. (bet. Carmel Ave. & Ramona St.), Albany, 510-527-1314
■ Albany's "honest" 20-year-old stalwart is "everything a neighborhood restaurant should be": "inexpensive", with "lots of simple but good Eclectic food" and "comfy surroundings"; although critics claim the fare is "secondary to meeting the regulars", the owners must be doing something right, since this "place has stood its ground, as other places come and go."

Bucci's **L M** | 19 | 18 | 18 | $28 |

6121 Hollis St. (bet. 59th & 61st Sts.), Emeryville, 510-547-4725
■ Emeryville's best "high-tech" asset may not be Ask Jeeves (whose corporate HQ is here) but this industrial-looking longtimer serving "satisfying" "Cal-Med comfort food" and some of "the best pizza in the East Bay"; despite its slick "mod" decor, a "fun atmosphere" and its support

of "local artists" give frequenters "a warm feeling" about it, which would rise even higher "if the noise level were lower."

Cactus Taqueria L S M   20 | 11 | 14 | $11

1881 Solano Ave. (The Alameda), Berkeley, 510-528-1881
5642 College Ave. (Keith Ave.), Oakland, 510-547-1305

■ "Variety is the draw" at this set of Berkeley and Oakland Mexicans serving "more interesting" send-ups "than [your] standard taqueria"; "damn good chicken tacos", "gourmet burritos" ("get the special fillings") and a "huge variety of salsas" convert the college types who report it's the "best deal in town" for a "healthy, cheap and delicious" meal.

Cafe 817 L M   22 | 17 | 15 | $17

817 Washington St. (bet. 8th & 9th Sts.), Oakland, 510-271-7965

■ "You'd swear you're in Italy" (not Downtown Oakland) at this piccolo cafe that's developed a cult following for its "excellent breakfasts", "great salads and sandwiches" and "coffee done right"; although the "menu is limited", "everything has taste and style", and boosters "only wish it was a trifle larger"; N.B. at press time, dinner service was slated to resume in September.

Café Esin L   ▽ 24 | 16 | 22 | $30

2416 San Ramon Valley Blvd. (Crow Canyon Rd.),
San Ramon, 925-314-0974

■ The husband-and-wife team that runs this beloved Med-American cafe ought to write a book entitled *"How to Make the Best of an Odd Space" and Influence People,* as their three-year-old toddler has become a "never-miss destination" despite its "unlikely location" in a mall; "the attention to detail" is evident from the "great service" down to the "scrumptious specials" and "incredible desserts" baked daily by wife Esin herself, prompting converts to chirp "it's like Chez Panisse in San Ramon."

Café Fanny L S M   23 | 13 | 16 | $16

1603 San Pablo Ave. (Cedar St.), Berkeley, 510-524-5447

■ "Everything that Alice touches turns magical" sigh the spellbound of Ms. Waters' "peculiar but charming" stand-up cafe serving Italian and "French–themed breakfast and lunch treats" ("beignets is all I can say") made with organic ingredients à la Chez Panisse; but while it may be "the cheapest way to sample an authentic café au lait", even *amis* assert it's "way overpriced" and "the cramped quarters are no longer charming", so unless you "don't mind sitting on the curbside", "takeout is the answer."

Café Rouge L S M   20 | 18 | 17 | $34

Market Plaza, 1782 Fourth St. (bet. Hearst Ave. & Virginia St.),
Berkeley, 510-525-1440

◪ "Nothing soothes your inner carnivore like a Rouge burger complete with crispy fries" maintain meat lovers at this "hip" Berkeley bistro (complete with zinc-topped bar), located in a gourmet market that sports its own "butcher shop in the back"; but while Francophiles felicitate it for being "surprisingly good for shopper territory", "rather inconsistent food" and "inattentive, downright nasty service" have critics seeing red ("deserves its local nickname, Café Rude").

California Cafe Bar & Grill L S M | 19 | 19 | 19 | $32 |

1540 N. California Blvd. (bet. Bonanza St. & Civic Dr.), Walnut Creek, 925-938-9977
See review in Silicon Valley/Peninsula Directory.

Cambodiana L S ▽ | 21 | 15 | 20 | $20 |

2156 University Ave. (bet. Oxford St. & Shattuck Ave.), Berkeley, 510-843-4630
■ Conveniently located right in Downtown Berkeley, this Cambodian sleeper is the "perfect place for academic visitors" or for a "pre–Berkeley Rep dinner"; top honors are handed out for the "great" specials such as salmon Mekong and "tasty" marinated and grilled lamb chops at "very reasonable prices", however set designers sneer there's "not much in the ambiance department."

Carrara's L M | – | – | – | M |

2735 Broadway (27th St.), Oakland, 510-663-2905
Paul Carrara's recently relocated cafe (after ten years in Emeryville) literally "comes with that new-car smell" – it's situated at the far end of a working Chrysler dealership on Oakland's Auto Row; so although the dining area with two-story-high ceilings and large picture windows is separated by a bank of potted plants, you can kick the tires on a shiny new PT Cruiser (a plus for restless kids) while test-driving the sophisticated Mediterranean menu.

Casa Orinda S M | 18 | 18 | 19 | $31 |

20 Bryant Way (Moraga Way), Orinda, 925-254-2981
■ You'd half expect to see Roy Rogers and Dale Evans walk through the doors at this "one-of-a-kind" Orinda "landmark" that's a "throwback" to the '50s; while today's urban "cowboys" go for the traditional American grub like "a really good steak" and "great fried chicken" (as well as some Italian staples), the heaping sides of "nostalgia" and the "campy Western charm are worth the visit" alone; P.S. don't miss the "fantastic gun display."

César ◗ S M | 22 | 21 | 18 | $28 |

1515 Shattuck Ave. (bet. Cedar & Vine Sts.), Berkeley, 510-883-0222
■ Although the "trendy young crowd" is "Berkeley chic" and the owners pedigreed from Chez Panisse, this "fun and happening" bar offers the holy Spanish trinity of "*tapas, vino y sol*"; the "limited" but "seductive" selection

of "outstanding" "small plates" served at "shared tables" "with old and new friends" ("the way food should be eaten") is "perfect for after a movie or anytime you want a little meal"; but hungry hippos warn "the bill easily catches up with you."

Cha Am Thai L S M | 18 | 12 | 14 | $19

1543 Shattuck Ave. (Cedar St.), Berkeley, 510-848-9664
See review in San Francisco Directory.

CHEESE BOARD COLLECTIVE, THE M⇄ | 27 | 11 | 20 | $12

1504 Shattuck Ave. (Vine St.), Berkeley, 510-549-3183
CHEESE BOARD PIZZA COLLECTIVE, THE L M⇄
1512 Shattuck Ave. (Vine St.), Berkeley, 510-549-3055
■ These two "institutions" only "do a few things, but they do them exceptionally well": the original Collective is a veritable "living cheese museum" ("you've heard of it? they've got it") and "great bakery" (the "chocolate thing brioche" is so good); the spin-off several doors down serves the "best damned pizza this side of capitalism", even if it's only "one flavor a day" and usually vegetarian ("sooo Berkeley"); though they dish up "service with a smile", "neither is a restaurant", but then "they don't have to be."

Chevys Fresh Mex L S M | 13 | 13 | 14 | $19

2400 Mariner Square Dr. (opp. Jack London Sq.), Alameda, 510-521-3768
1890 Powell St. (Frontage Rd.), Emeryville, 510-653-8210
4685 First St. (Hwy. 580), Livermore, 925-960-0071
650 Ellinwood Way (Ellinwood Dr.), Pleasant Hill, 925-685-6651
5877 Owens Dr. (Hopyard Rd.), Pleasanton, 925-416-0451
3101 Garrity Way (Hilltop Mall Rd.), Richmond, 510-222-9802
Bay Fair Mall, 312 Bay Fair Dr. (Hesperian Blvd.), San Leandro, 510-276-0962
Bollinger Crossings Plaza, 18080 San Ramon Valley Blvd. (Bollinger Canyon Rd.), San Ramon, 925-327-1910
See review in San Francisco Directory.

CHEZ PANISSE M | 28 | 25 | 26 | $66

1517 Shattuck Ave. (bet. Cedar & Vine Sts.), Berkeley, 510-548-5525
■ "Alice for President" chant constituents of the owner of this Berkeley landmark where "excellence meets ethics and enterprise"; the "daily changing menu" of "revolutionary Cal-Med cuisine" is "cooked perfectly in a manner that allows its best qualities to shine" and doled out at a "civilized pace" by the "unpretentious" staff in a "cozy, intimate" setting; a few inevitably just "do not get it", but the only real downside is the "Russian roulette reservations" game, which locks you into an unknown fixed menu in advance.

CHEZ PANISSE CAFÉ L Ⓜ | 27 | 23 | 25 | $41 |
1517 Shattuck Ave. (bet. Cedar & Vine Sts.), Berkeley, 510-548-5049

■ "If you can't afford" Alice Waters' "famous kitchen" downstairs, keep climbing to her "casual" upstairs; the "California-on-the-plate" menu (with Med touches) is "essentially the same quality seasonal food" "but with a wider choice" and an equally "strong wine list"; in fact, many Berkeleyites "prefer" this sibling for its more "low-key" ambiance and "unpretentious" yet "impeccable service" and delight that "now that they take reservations" ("one month in advance"), you can "enjoy it more often."

Christopher's Ⓢ Ⓜ | 19 | 18 | 17 | $31 |
1501A Solano Ave. (Curtis St.), Albany, 510-525-1668

■ "Thank goodness he's back" cry clients of Christopher Cheung, who's once again wokking up his brand of "Cal cuisine with an Asian twist" at this "popular" Albany spot; while his "inventive dishes" "generally hit" but "sometimes fail", his equally famous "great hamburger" is always safe; the "simple decor attracts the locals" even if the high ceilings and hard surfaces make the place "too loud."

Citron Ⓢ Ⓜ | 24 | 21 | 22 | $45 |
5484 College Ave. (bet. Lawton & Taft Aves.), Oakland, 510-653-5484

■ "Is this Oakland?" demand disoriented diners visiting chef-owner Chris Rossi's "very French" spot where a "hearty", ever-changing menu (emphasizing "housemade charcuterie"), "caring staff" and "comfy" (but "perhaps too simple") decor add up to "the definition of a neighborhood bistro"; some sourpusses whine about the pricey "limited menu" ("if you like their selections, you're fine").

Doña Tomás | 24 | 20 | 20 | $29 |
5004 Telegraph Ave. (bet. 49th & 51st Sts.), Oakland, 510-450-0522

■ "Step into a bit of authentic Mexico in Oakland" at this "upscale" yearling, a "cute storefront" whose "phenomenal" culinary offerings "go beyond the usual burritos and tacos"; the "marvelous mojitos and margaritas warm you up" for "perfect carnitas" and "seasonally changing" moles; best of all, "the staff is starting to get it."

downtown ● L Ⓢ | – | – | – | E |
2102 Shattuck Ave. (Addison St.), Berkeley, 510-649-3810

Located in an airy and sprawling 150-seat restored century old building in the heart of Berkeley's arts district, this new sib of César's is being hailed as "a welcome necessity" thanks to its "fish-focused" Mediterranean menu, which includes a variety of raw and roasted preparations, an extensive wine list (including many half-bottles) and its first-rate lineup of live jazz Wednesday–Saturday.

Duck Club ⓁⓈⓂ　　　21 | 21 | 21 | $38
Lafayette Park Hotel, 3287 Mt. Diablo Blvd. (Pleasant Hill Rd.),
Lafayette, 925-283-3700
See review in Silicon Valley/Peninsula Directory.

ERNA'S ELDERBERRY HOUSE ⓈⓂ　26 | 26 | 27 | $77
48688 Victoria Ln. (Hwy. 41), Oakhurst, 559-683-6800
■ Forget El Capitan – "Yosemite's best secret" is this
"wonderful old-world" retreat; the Cal-French prix fixe
tasting menus offer "sublime, unbelievable meldings of
local ingredients" and an incredible wine list that
"includes some Sierra finds"; but to many, the insanely
"attentive service" – "after a while you start thinking of
things to ask for just to see how pampered you can get" –
and "castle-like setting" are what make it "worth the
drive, wherever you live."

Everett & Jones Barbeque ⓁⓂ　20 | 11 | 13 | $18
296 A St. (Myrtle St.), Hayward, 510-581-3222 ●Ⓢ⇆
126 Broadway (2nd St.), Oakland, 510-663-2350 Ⓢ
2676 Fruitvale Ave. (bet. Davis & 27th Sts.), Oakland,
510-533-0900 Ⓢ⇆
3415 Telegraph Ave. (34th St.), Oakland, 510-601-9377 ⇆
■ "The real deal in BBQ" is available at this soulful chain;
the "outrageous beef links", "addictive greens" and
"finger-licking good ribs" are "as delicious as they are
messy"; the decor is what you'd expect, "which is to say
[there is] none", but most branches only have limited
seating anyway, so queue up and get your 'cue for the road.

FatApple's ⓁⓈⓂ　　　18 | 13 | 16 | $17
1346 Martin Luther King Jr. Way (bet. Berryman &
Rose Sts.), Berkeley, 510-526-2260
7525 Fairmount Ave. (bet. Colusa & Ramona Aves.),
El Cerrito, 510-528-3433
■ Berkeley's vintage "all-American diner" (circa 1969) and
its newer sibling in El Cerrito continue to dish out "burgers,
shakes and fries" that, along with "quick service", are
"much better than your average coffee shop's" – making
these "good places to take the children"; however, it's
the "delectable pastries" (including the signature apple
pie) that make 'em a "great place to sin."

Faz ⓁⓈⓂ　　　18 | 19 | 17 | $32
600 Hartz Ave. (School St.), Danville, 925-838-1320
5121 Hopyard Rd. (bet. Gibraltar & Owens Drs.),
Pleasanton, 925-460-0444
See review in San Francisco Directory.

Garibaldis on College ⓁⓈⓂ　22 | 21 | 20 | $38
5356 College Ave. (bet. Clifton & Hudson Sts.), Oakland,
510-595-4000
See review in San Francisco Directory.

Ginger Island L S M   17 17 16 $29

1820 Fourth St. (bet. Cedar St. & Hearst Ave.), Berkeley, 510-644-0444

☑ Strategically located on the chi chi shopping corridor of Berkeley's 4th Street, this New American is a surefire choice for refueling; "the relaxed atmosphere and pretty dining area" make it a perfect spot to kick back and sip on a zingy "homemade ginger ale", but the unimpressed gingerly point out that the menu "sounds more adventurous than it really is" and the "service is as slow as molasses."

Grasshopper S   –   –   –   M

6317 College Ave. (Claremont Ave.), Oakland, 510-595-3559
Brought to you by a coterie of Café Rouge alumni, this "terrific" newcomer features a tapas-style menu, only the "out-of-this-world" "small plates" are Asian-inspired and all washed down with an "extensive" selection of 20 premium sakes and cuisine-appropriate wines; unfortunately, the "lovely" warehouse-like room really gets hopping (and noisy) when "the beautiful people of Oakland congregate (yes, there are beautiful people in Oakland)."

Hotel Mac L S M   19 19 19 $35

50 Washington Ave. (Park Pl.), Point Richmond, 510-233-0576
■ Set in a turn-of-the-century hotel, this historical "dinner house" (food critic Duncan Hines ate here) is a "popular" "special-occasion place" that's "always full of locals (a good sign)"; however, outsiders observe it's "well worth the trip out to Point Richmond", thanks to "consistent" Continental fare and "warm, old-world" atmosphere that lends itself to sipping "12-year-old tawny while cozying up on the love seat with a beau."

Il Fornaio L S M   19 20 19 $33

1430 Mt. Diablo Blvd. (bet. Broadway & Main St.), Walnut Creek, 925-296-0100
See review in San Francisco Directory.

Isobune Sushi L S M   16 13 14 $23

5897 College Ave. (south of Chabot Rd.), Oakland, 510-601-1424
See review in San Francisco Directory.

Italian Colors L S M   7   17 18 $31

2220 Mountain Blvd. (bet. Park Blvd. & Snake Rd.), Oakland, 510-482-8094
■ This "dependable" "no-frills" Oakland Cal-Italian represents a "weekly pleasure" for a "basically local" crowd; the "simple yet enjoyable food" won't cause a "culinary freak-out" but, when paired with attentive waiters and "warm comfortable atmosphere", inspires pretty colorful comments such as "do not leave without trying the gooey warm chocolate cake."

Jade Villa L S M　　17 | 10 | 11 | $21
800 Broadway (bet. 8th & 9th Sts.), Oakland, 510-839-1688
◪ Jaded judges rule "it's no Yank Sing", but dumpling devotees declare "one look at the clientele will tell you you've found the best dim sum in the East Bay" at this "crowded, noisy" cavern in Oakland's Chinatown; one look will also explain why "it's best if you speak Cantonese" to deal with the notoriously inattentive staff.

Jimmy Bean's L S M　　19 | 12 | 13 | $16
1290 Sixth St. (Gilman St.), Berkeley, 510-528-3435
◪ There's more than just java (though they've got that too) at this modest but "friendly" "breakfast/lunch hangout" brought to you by the same folks behind Lalime's; the slightly "different" offerings – organic salads, tortilla eggs and sandwiches laced with caramelized onions and romesco sauce – appeal to advocates, but the blasé Berkeleyites blast it as a "default choice."

Jojo　　23 | 18 | 20 | $40
3859 Piedmont Ave. (Rio Vista Ave.), Oakland, 510-985-3003
◪ "Extremely cozy in all senses of the word", this "little bistro" is making big waves since its Oakland opening; enthusiasts enjoy its "smashing" "simple and fresh Country French cuisine", "delightful service" and "inviting atmosphere" (not to mention co-owner Mary Jo Thoresen's desserts); some say "NoNo", griping that "tiny space" + "tiny portions" = "tiny value", but they're outnumbered; just be prepared for a "wait, even with reservations."

Jordan's L S M　　▽ 22 | 24 | 20 | $41
Claremont Resort & Spa, 41 Tunnel Rd. (Claremont Ave.), Berkeley, 510-549-8510
◼ "Classy" and "romantic", this Claremont Resort eatery shines thanks to the "incredible" "astronaut's view of the Bay Area" and also to the "very good" Pacific Rim fare, "great desserts" and "attentive service" – all of which makes folks "feel very special to dine there."

Juan's Place L S M　　18 | 12 | 16 | $16
941 Carleton St. (9th St.), Berkeley, 510-845-6904
◼ This "family-run" "Berkeley institution" "that hasn't changed in nearly 30 years" is "everybody's idea of a Mexican" eatery – "yummy margaritas", "huge portions of cheap food", "kitschy decor" and a "noisy" dining room that's "so loud you can't hear the kids yelling"; sated surveyors scream a "meal will last you a month", which may explain why it's a mainstay for "starving students."

Kensington Circus Pub S M　　▽ 16 | 19 | 21 | $17
389 Colusa Ave. (Kensington Circle), Kensington, 510-524-8814
◼ East Bay parents looking for a little stimulation (plus libation) schlep to this child-friendly Kensington hangout

for a pint and some "good English" grub or the "best burgers"; there are toys for the tots as well as darts for their pops, so "even if you take the kids, it still feels like a pub."

Kirala L S M　　　　25　17　17　$31

2100 Ward St. (Shattuck Ave.), Berkeley, 510-549-3486
■ "The new sake bar [pouring 30 different varieties] is cute" and all, but the crowds gather at "Berkeley's landmark" Japanese for the "fresh, beautifully presented sushi" ("hands down the best in the East Bay") and "especially good robata yaki"; sensitive types fear the "ridiculously" "long lines" ("can you say reservations? they can't") and "loud space may scare all the fish away", but it certainly doesn't deter determined devotees who manage to "stomach the wait" and "harried service."

Koryo Wooden　　　　23　9　11　$21
Charcoal BBQ ◐ L S M

4390 Telegraph Ave. (Shattuck Ave.), Oakland, 510-652-6007
■ Follow the smoke to this "fun", "noisy" "down-home" dive in Oakland specializing in "awesome Korean BBQ"; "yes, the charcoal comes to your table and you do the cooking", but surveyors still feel like the staff should be doling out more attention.

Lalime's S M　　　　25　21　23　$43

1329 Gilman St. (bet. Neilson St. & Peralta Ave.), Berkeley, 510-527-9838
■ "It doesn't look like much", but this converted home in a "funky" stretch of North Berkeley houses "a gastronomic giant" that amazes with its ever-changing "innovative" Cal-Med menu, including "duck cooked to perfection", that showcases "fresh ingredients"; toss in a "class wine list", "relaxing atmosphere" and "unpretentious" "service to match" and it's "easy to see why this is one of the best in the East Bay"; N.B. the owners have jettisoned their prix fixe–only setup for an à la carte menu.

La Mediterranée L S M　　　19　14　17　$19

2936 College Ave. (Ashby Ave.), Berkeley, 510-540-7773
See review in San Francisco Directory.

La Note L S M　　　　20　19　16　$21

2377 Shattuck Ave. (bet. Channing Way & Durant Ave.), Berkeley, 510-843-1535
■ "*Parlez-vous* delicious?" ask *amis* of this "adorable", "modestly priced" bistro offering "a slice of Provence" "in the heart of Berkeley"; its sunny decor and "lovely garden patio out back" give a sense of "walking into a Van Gogh painting", and the "creative but simple" "countryside cooking" is equally "vibrant in flavor"; the service hits the only sour note, ranging from "slow" to "downright rude"; still, the place draws "ridiculously" long lines on weekends.

Lark Creek L S M   23 23 22 $43
1360 Locust St. (Mt. Diablo Blvd.), Walnut Creek, 925-256-1234
See review in North of San Francisco Directory.

La Rue Brasserie & Bistro L S   – – – M
1428 San Pablo Ave. (Page St.), Berkeley, 510-528-5030
Last year, this Berkeley bungalow housed Bistro Viola;
now, *voilà*, there's a new tenant, a casual Cal-French
that offers such classics as crocks of cassoulet for two,
mussels steamed in red wine sauce and frites with an
array of dipping sauces; Sunday brunch features omelets
and *pain perdu*.

Le Cheval L S M   21 14 15 $22
1007 Clay St. (10th St.), Oakland, 510-763-8495
■ They don't horse around at this "lively" "barn-like"
Oakland institution serving "authentic Vietnamese cuisine"
at breakneck speed ("your order comes out almost before
you finish saying it"); sensitive types sneer you get "service
without a smile" but concede for such "delicious food at
unbelievable prices", it's the "best deal in the East Bay."

Left at Albuquerque L S M   15 15 15 $23
1824 Mt. Diablo Blvd. (California Blvd.), Walnut Creek,
925-287-8400
See review in Silicon Valley/Peninsula Directory.

Left Bank L S M   21 21 19 $38
60 Crescent Dr. (Monument Blvd.), Pleasant Hill, 925-288-1222
See review in North of San Francisco Directory.

Little Shin Shin L S M   17 10 15 $19
4258 Piedmont Ave. (bet. MacArthur Blvd. & Pleasant Valley
Ave.), Oakland, 510-658-9799
◪ "Be prepared to wait" at Piedmont Avenue's "very
popular" Chinese specializing in Mandarin and Szechuan
cuisine; the fare, which "varies from average to a sublime
symphony of flavors", is noted as being "the most authentic"
"in the area", although shunners snap that's because
"there's no competition"; since the "funky" dining room
doesn't win any beauty prizes, supporters suggest
"takeout is best."

Long Life Noodle Company &   13 11 11 $15
Jook Joint L S M
2261 Shattuck Ave. (Kittredge St.), Berkeley, 510-548-8083
See review in San Francisco Directory.

Long Life Vegi House L S M   15 9 14 $13
2129 University Ave. (Shattuck Ave.), Berkeley,
510-845-6072
■ The secret to the long life of this politically correct
eatery is "huge portions" at starving-student prices; the

"good, healthy, clean Chinese" menu offers an array of fish and faux-meat dishes (rather oddly called 'veggie beef'); while sourpusses point out "no Asian ever sets foot into this" "ugly restaurant", there's still a plethora of Berkeley undergrads who do.

Mama's Royal Cafe ⌶ Ⓢ Ⓜ ≠   20 | 13 | 15 | $15
4012 Broadway (40th St.), Oakland, 510-547-7600
■ "Don't talk to me about anything but tofu rancheros" command converts to this "Oakland institution" whose legendary "homey breakfasts" and "weekend brunches" also include the "best omelets in the world" and "coffee from the gods"; although the "kitschy atmosphere", replete with an "interesting [vintage] apron collection", isn't much, it gives you something to look at "while waiting for your table"; just don't expect royal treatment from the staff.

Max's Diner ⌶ Ⓜ   16 | 14 | 16 | $21
Oakland City Ctr., 500 12th St. (bet. Broadway & Clay St.), Oakland, 510-451-6297
2015 Crow Canyon Pl. (Crow Canyon Rd.), San Ramon, 925-277-9300 Ⓢ
See review in San Francisco Directory.

Mazzini Trattoria ⌶ Ⓢ Ⓜ   22 | 20 | 20 | $35
2826 Telegraph Ave. (bet. Oregon & Stuart Sts.), Berkeley, 510-848-5599
◪ Although it's just blocks from UC Berkeley, dining at this "sophisticated" trattoria is more akin to "visiting a friend's house in Toscana"; regulars rave that the "elegant, confident fare" is meted out by a "knowledgeable staff" in the "beautiful dining room", while the "handsomest bartenders in town" pour from the "adventurous Italian wine list"; however, a coterie of cynics sneer if "Alice Waters' brother-in-law wasn't involved" (he's co-owner), this "overpriced" place wouldn't get as many "raves."

Mezze ⌶ Ⓢ   19 | 17 | 18 | $33
3407 Lakeshore Ave. (bet. Hwy. 580 & Mandana Blvd.), Oakland, 510-663-2500
◪ This "urbane" upstart near Oakland's Lake Merritt district is making a "promising" debut with a "surprisingly sophisticated atmosphere and decor", but even ardent early adopters concede it's still "feeling its way": while "the meze platter is great", the other Mediterranean entrees are "not quite consistent enough"; and as the room fills, it grows "as loud as a train station", while the "amateur servers" get swamped.

Nan Yang Rockridge ⌶ Ⓢ   21 | 15 | 19 | $22
6048 College Ave. (Claremont Ave.), Oakland, 510-655-3298
■ "When they're good, they're very good", and when they're not, don't let the "inconsistency keep you away"

from this Oakland Burmese; seasoned eaters say ask the "gracious owner" or "waiters for suggestions" and "try a variety of things" such as the wonderful "ginger salad"; the "antiseptic room doesn't lend anything to the experience", but overall, it's a "nice change from other Asian cuisines."

Nizza La Bella L S M　19　17　18　$32
825-827 San Pablo Ave. (Solano Ave.), Albany, 510-526-2552
☑ "The jury is still out" on this year-old "slice of the Riviera" in Albany; most locals love the "earthy, rustic and delicious" fare ("think Provence mixed with Italy") and decor reminiscent of Nice, with "sidewalk seating" and zinc-topped bar; but bad-mouthers find it beleaguered by "uneven", "clunky preparations" and "surly service."

North Beach Pizza ◑ L S M　17　9　13　$16
1598 University Ave. (California St.), Berkeley, 510-849-9800
See review in San Francisco Directory.

OakTown Cafe L M　18　19　17　$27
499 Ninth St. (Washington St.), Oakland, 510-763-4999
☑ This "nice little" spot, situated in a 19th-century cigar factory "on a picturesque corner of restored Old Oakland", churns out "great pizza" and other "solid" Med-influenced American lunches from its formidable, room-dominating wood-burning oven; although naysayers note "nothing memorable", loyalists are rooting for the "friendly staff and owner"; N.B. dinner is served Wednesday–Saturday only.

O Chamé L M　22　21　19　$29
1830 Fourth St. (Hearst Ave.), Berkeley, 510-841-8783
■ It's one-stop shopping for surveyors at this "unusual" Berkeley Japanese that offers "meditation and a meal all in one" thanks to its "peaceful, minimalist, feng shui atmosphere" and "soothing", "exquisite" food; the "bowls o' noodles" are "o so good", and the "traditional scallion pancakes alone are worth the trip."

OLIVETO　24　22　21　$47
CAFE & RESTAURANT L S M
5655 College Ave. (Shafter Ave.), Oakland, 510-547-5356
☑ "Tuscany revisited" is the theme of this highly "hyped" Oakland "destination"; boosters boast that ex Chez Panisse executive chef Paul Bertolli's "straightforward approach" is the "benchmark for rustic, true Northern Italian" fare (especially the "perfectly prepared" roasted meats) served in "simple, elegant surroundings"; however, pessimists can't see past the "puny portions" and "awfully expensive prices", wondering "what is the fuss?"; P.S. you can "eat cheaper downstairs" at the lively cafe.

Paragon Bar & Cafe 🄻🅂🄼   – | – | – | M

Claremont Resort & Spa, 41 Tunnel Rd. (Domingo St.),
Berkeley, 510-549-8510
This spanking new Berkeley brasserie aims to lure the
Claremont Resort's spa-and-tennis-club set to knock back
a few martinis, munch Californian eats and watch the
game; the look is retro '40s, dominated by an impressive
marble bar and comfy cocktail lounge, but the paragon of
atmosphere is expected to be the 60-seat outdoor deck
(slated to open in October) affording sweeping views of
SF and the Bay.

Pasta Pomodoro 🄻🅂🄼   15 | 12 | 15 | $16

5500 College Ave. (Lawton Ave.), Oakland, 510-923-0900
See review in San Francisco Directory.

Phuping Thai Cuisine 🄻🅂🄼   ▽ 21 | 17 | 21 | $21

Pacific East Mall, 3288 Pierce St. (Central Ave.), Richmond,
510-558-3242
■ An odd "location in the mall doesn't" diminish the "tasty
flavors" or "caring" service of this Richmond eatery, which
some deem "the best Thai in the East Bay"; "moreover, the
splendid parking lot" makes it an enticing "alternative to
Thep Phanom", its SF-based older sibling.

Piatti 🄻🅂🄼   19 | 19 | 18 | $34

100 Sycamore Valley Rd. W. (San Ramon Valley Blvd.),
Danville, 925-838-2082
See review in North of San Francisco Directory.

Picante Cocina Mexicana 🄻🅂🄼   21 | 13 | 15 | $14

1328 Sixth St. (bet. Camelia & Gilman Sts.), Berkeley,
510-525-3121
■ The first venture in Jim Maser's (aka "Alice Waters'
brother-in-law") culinary troika (which includes Café
Fanny and Mazzini Trattoria), this "real fresh Mex" attracts
all strata of Berkeley society thanks to "homemade tortillas"
and "healthy" and "unusual" fillings that "elevate the taco to
an art form"; true, the tab is "slightly expensive", especially
since the "decor is à la school cafeteria", but amigos insist
it's one "Mexillent" place.

Pizza Rustica 🄻🅂🄼   18 | 11 | 15 | $18

5422 College Ave. (bet. Kales & Manila Aves.), Oakland,
510-654-1601
■ "Love that thin crust" proclaim pie-d pipers of this
Oakland eatery where "filling, robust pizza" fashioned
from "fresh ingredients" "dominates the menu", along
with "delectable rotisserie chicken" and "wonderful
salad"; although out-on-the-towners relish the "great
Friday night atmosphere", a good many devotees dial for
their dinner, ever so grateful that "they deliver."

Plearn Thai Cuisine ⎣⎦⎣S⎦⎣M⎦   18 | 12 | 16 | $19

2050 University Ave. (bet. Milvia St. & Shattuck Ave.), Berkeley, 510-841-2148

◪ Advocates and adversaries are tied when it comes to this nearly 20-year-old "convenient and cheap" Siamese near UC Berkeley; proponents posit it's "hard to top this Thai", while opponents opine this old spot "used to be great" but is "getting tired"; and then there are the wishy-washy centrists who say "it's satisfying at times" – guess you'll have to cast the deciding vote.

Postino ⎣⎦⎣S⎦⎣M⎦   21 | 23 | 20 | $42

3565 Mt. Diablo Blvd. (Oak Hill Rd.), Lafayette, 925-299-8700

■ "Fine dining finally comes to suburbia" in the guise of this "romantically lit" trattoria that features one of the "most unbelievable settings" around Lafayette and a "very tasty" Northern Italian menu (the "swordfish with almonds and raisins is to die for"); however, a handful argues "the postman forgot to leave" training manuals for a "staff that runs the gamut from cold to pleasant."

Prima ⎣⎦⎣S⎦⎣M⎦   23 | 22 | 22 | $41

1522 N. Main St. (bet. Bonanza & Lincoln Sts.), Walnut Creek, 925-935-7780

■ "You don't have to love wine, but it helps" if you want to appreciate this primo vino mecca in sleepy Walnut Creek; while the "excellent cellar" (1,600 labels strong – 25 of which are available by the glass and "some of which are available for sale at the shop next door") has always been the lure here, the food is "bouncing back" "thanks to new chef" Peter Chastain, whose "creative" Northern Italian menu "is giving the East Bay a lesson in fresh."

Red Tractor Cafe ⎣⎦⎣S⎦⎣M⎦   15 | 14 | 14 | $13

5634 College Ave. (bet. Keith Ave. & Ocean View Dr.), Oakland, 510-595-3500

◪ Fans of this fast-fooder that plows "big servings" of "wholesome" "farm food" for a farthing feel it's "fun for the family", as kids can feast on macaroni-and-cheese and Rice Krispie treats while coloring on paper place settings; however, skeptics see red over the fact that there's "not much to look at" (except for those placemats adorning the walls) and food that "will remind you of TV dinners."

Restaurant Peony ⎣⎦⎣S⎦⎣M⎦   19 | 13 | 12 | $26

Pacific Renaissance Plaza, 388 Ninth St. (bet. Franklin & Webster Sts.), Oakland, 510-286-8866

■ "In the heart of Oakland's Chinatown", this monster-size Mandarin attracts "big crowds" of "local Chinese" and *shu mai* mavens seeking "fabulous dim sum"; like every "authentic" spot of its ilk, the noise is "deafening on Sundays", and "unfriendly" scattered service hampers the experience; but hey, at least it has "easy parking."

Rick & Ann's L S M   21 15 17 $20
*2922 Domingo Ave. (bet. Ashby & Claremont Aves.),
Berkeley, 510-649-8538*

■ There's no place like this "homey but hectic" "East Bay establishment" offering "creative, yummy variations on traditional breakfasts" served by a "genuinely warm and friendly" staff; unfortunately "everybody knows about it" – from "the 'very Berkeley' clientele" to "the Claremont tennis set", so "get there early, then wait (and wait and wait) and drool"; others say the "comfort-food dinners are even better" (at least way "better than mom could ever hope to make").

RIVOLI S M   26 22 24 $41
*1539 Solano Ave. (bet. Neilson St. & Peralta Ave.),
Berkeley, 510-526-2542*

■ This Berkeleyite shines as "a star in the East Bay"; chef/co-owner Wendy Brucker's "marvelous" Cal-Med cuisine yields "big flavors" from "simple" ingredients, and hubby Roscoe Skipper's "gracious staff" helps you navigate some "excellent wine and food pairings"; although the dining room is a tad "cramped", there's the "memorable view of the magical garden out back where squirrels and kittens have dinner together"; the result is an "almost perfect dining experience" – one "you can actually get a reservation" for.

Rue de Main L M   ▽ 18 19 18 $39
22622 Main St. (bet. B & C Sts.), Hayward, 510-537-0812

■ "We thought we were in Paris" sigh surveyors after an evening at this "pretty", "fine-dining mainstay" in a not-so-swanky suburb ("how does it survive in Hayward?"); the "romantic" decor with murals creates a "wonderful atmosphere", augmented by the "fair French food"; some rue the fact that the eats are "expensive."

Salute Ristorante L S M   18 20 17 $31
*Marina Bay, 1900 Esplanade Dr. (Melville Sq.), Richmond,
510-215-0803*

■ Perched on a "picturesque" spot by the Richmond marina, this Italian-Mediterranean affords "fantastic views of SF and the Bay"; alas, the "always reliable" but "average food" is "nothing to get excited about" and the service seems "intrusive"; N.B. the original branch is in San Rafael.

Santa Fe Bar & Grill S M   19 20 19 $36
*1310 University Ave. (bet. Acton & Bonar Sts.), Berkeley,
510-841-4740*

■ Despite its illustrious past (Jeremiah Tower once cooked here), this erstwhile Santa Fe Railroad Company train station remains "a real sleeper"; theatergoers find it "our favorite near the Berkeley Rep" for its "fine" Californian fare that features "organic produce" grown in surrounding gardens, but dissenters deem it "disappointing."

Saul's Restaurant & Delicatessen 🄻🅂🄼
16 | 13 | 14 | $18

1475 Shattuck Ave. (bet. Rose & Vine Sts.), Berkeley,
510-848-3354

◪ "When you get the urge for real NY deli sandwiches", "latkes to die for" and kosher pickles, this "Jewish-style" storefront with "self-conscious" "Manhattan decor" in Berkeley's "gourmet ghetto" "is the place to go" (ok, so it's the "only place in the East Bay" to go); but critics cry the recent expansion has "sucked the soul out of Saul's" and the only authentic thing now is "that you pay too much for not enough, and usually get a little attitude thrown in for free."

Scott's 🄻🅂🄼
18 | 18 | 18 | $35

Jack London Sq., 2 Broadway (Embarcadero W.), Oakland,
510-444-3456
1333 N. California Blvd. (Bonanza St.), Walnut Creek,
925-934-1300

See review in Silicon Valley/Peninsula Directory.

Shen Hua 🄻🅂🄼
20 | 17 | 15 | $21

2914 College Ave. (bet. Ashby Ave. & Russell St.), Berkeley,
510-883-1777

◪ For a refreshing change from "your run-of-the-mill" moo shu shack, this Elmwood eatery "takes Chinese cuisine to a new level"; although the kitchen specializes in Beijing- and Szechuan-style fare created for the Imperial courts, don't expect the royal treatment from the staff; "extremely curt service", paired with a "screeching dining room", "makes takeout a requirement" for many subjects.

Skates on the Bay 🄻🅂🄼
17 | 23 | 17 | $32

100 Seawall Dr. (University Ave.), Berkeley,
510-549-1900

◪ "Take your out-of-town relatives" and "enjoy the sunset" at this Berkeley New American boasting "fabulous city views" and plenty of Kodak moments; Bay watchers insist "this tourist trap is still a fun" and "enjoyable place to just 'be'"; however, for sustenance, cynics say "stick to brunch" or "good" seafood appetizers, because the place seems to be skating "on location alone."

Soizic 🄻🅂
22 | 19 | 19 | $34

300 Broadway (3rd St.), Oakland, 510-251-8100

▣ "Although the outside looks like a union headquarters for local janitors", inside the "classy, creative" chef/co-owner (and painter) has transformed this Jack London Square warehouse into a "fabulous hideaway" with an "artistic vision of food and space"; a "sophisticated" "well-presented" mélange of Californian-French-Asian flavors, "attentive and informed servers" and a quiet atmosphere where (gasp!) "guests can actually hear each other" makes some Oaklanders opine it's "the Downtown's best."

Spenger's L S M
14 | 16 | 14 | $30

1919 Fourth St. (bet. Hearst & University Aves.), Berkeley, 510-845-7771

☑ Berkeley's seafood "landmark" (since 1890) remains "enormously popular", with its kitschy "nautical museum" a "must-see" for kids and fishing buffs; some old salts suggest the new owners "missed the boat", saying that "Mrs. Paul's is still in the kitchen", but a groundswell in the food and service scores suggests most swabbies feel the "much-needed makeover" has gone "swimmingly."

Spettro L S M
17 | 14 | 18 | $23

3359 Lakeshore Ave. (Mandana Blvd.), Oakland, 510-465-8320

■ This "funky" "Lakeshore institution" is as "comfy as an old slipper" for Oaklanders who call it their "weekly home away from home"; the "welcoming" staff treats everyone "like family", meting out "complimentary pizza and house red wine while you wait"; the spirited decor (tombstones and the like) is matched by an even quirkier Asian-Italian-Mex menu that ranges from coconut-lime mussels to peanut butter pizza ("sounds odd, but tastes great").

Spiedini L S M
20 | 20 | 21 | $37

101 Ygnacio Valley Rd. (Oakland Blvd.), Walnut Creek, 925-939-2100

☑ Specializing in "rotisserie meats Northern Italian-style", this trendy trattoria in Walnut Creek has been around since the mid-'80s; some say it's still "top-notch" in "food, service and the room", but longtime locals lament it has "lost its appeal" over the years; maybe it's just that the aging clientele is getting less tolerant of "noisy" atmosphere that's akin to "going to a rock concert, sitting in the front row and trying to have a nice dinner."

Tachibana L S M
22 | 17 | 17 | $28

5812 College Ave. (bet. Birch Ct. & Chabot Rd.), Oakland, 510-654-3668

■ You can still get a raw deal at this Rockridge resident that serves "consistently fresh" sushi, but why not sample the wide selection of "delicious" "yakitori and grilled dishes (such as miso-glazed salmon) that makes this one of the best Japanese around"?; toss in a "charming" Asian-esque atmosphere", 20 types of sake and "great service" and you start to see why Oaklanders call it a "weekly favorite."

Taiwan ● L S M
19 | 8 | 13 | $17

2071 University Ave. (Shattuck Ave.), Berkeley, 510-845-1456
See review in San Francisco Directory.

Townhouse Bar & Grill L M
20 | 19 | 19 | $30

5862 Doyle St. (bet. 59th & Powell Sts.), Emeryville, 510-652-6151
■ Although this townie hangout "looks like an old shrimp shack from the outside, inside" there's "surprisingly good",

"creative" Eclectic-American food ("don't miss the salads"), a "fun staff" and "a trendy Emeryville crowd" knocking back "great martinis" at the bar; there's also an outdoor terrace and "snappy jazz" on Wednesday nights, prompting proud patrons to proclaim "everybody should have such a place."

Trader Vic's L S M   20 | 23 | 22 | $43

9 Anchor Dr. (Powell St.), Emeryville, 510-653-3400

■ For "a touch of nostalgia" (with a paper umbrella hanging off it), hula over to the Emeryville marina; habitués still carry a (tiki) torch for this 1934 faux-Polynesian "institution", noting that "all the old great dishes are still here – crab rangoon, beef cho cho" – and are just "as good as the exotic drinks are fun" (especially the Mai Tai, which was born here); although a few pooh-pooh the pupu platters (shocked that "the cooking is stuck in the '60s" – duh!), there's no better place to satisfy your kitsch itch.

Trattoria La Siciliana S ⌿   ▽ 25 | 19 | 20 | $27

2993 College Ave. (Ashby Ave.), Berkeley, 510-704-1474

■ You'll feel like you've been "transported to Sicily" after breaking garlic bread "family-style" at this "excellent", "authentic" bi-level trattoria on Elmwood's restaurant row; regulahs "love this place" for its "lusty Southern Italian cooking", but fuhgeddaboudit for first dates because "when they say garlic, they mean it."

Tropix L S M   ▽ 16 | 14 | 18 | $20

3814 Piedmont Ave. (Yosemite Ave.), Oakland, 510-653-2444

■ When the urge for the tropics strikes, Oak Towners head for this festive Caribbean spot serving up "must-eat plantains" and the signature jerk chicken for little more than the cost of a rum-and-coke on the plane to Jamaica; the staff is "humorous and attentive", and best of all, there's a "secret garden" out back for chillin'; N.B. a chef change post-*Survey* may outdate the above food rating.

Uzen L M   24 | 17 | 18 | $27

5415 College Ave. (bet. Hudson St. & Kales Ave.), Oakland, 510-654-7753

■ For what some denuzens deem the "best Japanese fare in the East Bay", this "small" Oakland eatery "is where it's at", because (compared to certain others) it's "less expensive", has a "calmer ambiance" and – get this – "has no wait"; the "sleek, minimalist decor" allows the "sublime sushi", super soups ("their miso is manna") and "fat noodles" to take center stage – just "how it should be."

Venezia L S M   19 | 20 | 18 | $27

1799 University Ave. (Grant St.), Berkeley, 510-849-4681

■ Maybe the best things going for this "whimsical", "lively" Berkeley trattoria are the "decorated painted walls" and actual hanging garments that evoke wash day in an Italian piazza; although the "gimmicky" "cute decor brings 'em in", the "hand-cut pastas" and "service with a smile" are what keep 'em coming back (along with the promise that there'll be a "changing selection of laundry" overhead).

Venus L S   ▽ 24 | 18 | 20 | $17

2327 Shattuck Ave. (Durant Ave.), Berkeley, 510-540-5950
■ This "hidden gem" – or should we say planet? – first appeared on radar screens for its "interesting breakfast menu" and Eclectic lunches touted as "Berkeley's best"; though dinner is now in its orbit, it's still a relative "sleeper", so "go before people discover it and the wait gets long."

Verbena L M   — | — | — | M

Walter Shorenstein Bldg., 1111 Broadway (11th Ave.), Oakland, 510-465-9300
As we go to press, Oaklanders are getting a scent of fresh Italian fare as city slickers Gordon Drysdale (Gordon's House of Fine Eats) and the Real Restaurant Group bring their fun-lovin' Cal-Med concept to town; the 100-plus-seat venture intends to cater to the business community with a wine list that carries a strong whiff of East Bay wineries (yes, there really are worthy East Bay wineries).

Via Centro L S   22 | 19 | 20 | $35

(fka Caffe Centro)
2132 Center St. (bet. Oxford St. & Shattuck Ave.), Berkeley, 510-981-8373
■ Although the menu reads like "page 26 in the Trattorias 'R' Us catalog", "wonderful, simple food" plus "informed service" makes this Tuscan-Med "a fine addition to the Downtown dining scene", especially for patrons of the nearby Berkeley Repertory Theater; N.B. the recent arrival of chef de cuisine Kenneth Jensen (imported from sibling Santa Fe Bar & Grill) may outdate the above food rating.

Vic Stewart's S M   24 | 23 | 22 | $41

850 S. Broadway (bet. Mt. Diablo Blvd. & Newell Ave.), Walnut Creek, 925-943-5666
■ This "classic steakhouse in the 'burbs" of Walnut Creek sates carnivores' cravings with the tried-and-true formula of "hearty cocktails", "large sides", an "ample prime rib" and "a bone-in New York [strip] that melts in your mouth"; all that, plus the "lovely decor's" train-depot theme (including a 1901 Pullman car that doubles as a private dining room), makes this a real "Bay Area stop"; the "service is high-end" and – as to be expected – so are the prices.

Vik's Chaat Corner L S   24 | 5 | 10 | $10

724 Allston Way (bet. 4th & 5th Sts.), Berkeley, 510-644-4412
■ For authentic Southern Indian "street food", "those in the know" line up at this uncomely *chaat* (snack) house

hidden in an "industrial warehouse with a grocery store in the back"; although it's not for the faint-hearted ("the floor will be covered in [paper plate] trash and you will have to fight for a table"), the "incredible", "tasty morsels" at "absurdly cheap" prices are so good that possessive patrons promised they'd "pay us to keep this place a secret" (sorry, but your check never came).

Vi's L S M ⊄   20 │ 9 │ 15 │ $15

724 Webster St. (bet. 7th & 8th Sts.), Oakland, 510-835-8375
■ With pho like this, who needs friends? ask admirers of this thrifty Vietnamese in Chinatown (a stone's throw from the Oakland Museum) that also serves other "wonderful" "soulful soups" and humble Hanoi comestibles ringing with "clear intense flavors"; P.S. java judges enjoin "don't miss the iced coffee, but order it at the beginning of your meal, because the brewing (done at your table) takes a while."

Voulez-Vous S M   ▽ 12 │ 14 │ 14 │ $23

2930 College Ave. (bet. Ashby Ave. & Russell St.), Berkeley, 510-548-4708
◪ *Une petite* "pearl" in Elmwood's restaurant row, this "charming neighborhood spot promises to become a favorite if some of the rough edges mellow with time"; "falling-off-the-bone coq au vin" and other "authentic French" bistro standards paired with lots of recorded French pop music and live bands seem like "a good, fun idea" to well-wishers, but wags want none of it, saying the fare "fills you up and leaves you disappointed."

WENTE VINEYARDS L S M   25 │ 27 │ 23 │ $47

5050 Arroyo Rd. (Wetmore Rd.), Livermore, 925-456-2450
■ For a "superb" supper of "seasonal, regional" Californian cuisine "set among the vineyards", enthusiastic oenophiles "trek" to this winery restaurant located "in the tranquil Livermore Valley" ("closer then Napa"); it offers "great food-and-wine pairings", "gracious service" and "an extensive knockout" cellar; golfers can even play a few rounds on the on-site course before sitting down, preferably on the "lovely" patio.

Xanadu L S M   18 │ 21 │ 17 │ $35

700 University Ave. (4th St.), Berkeley, 510-548-7880
◪ 'In Xanadu did Kubla Kahn a stately pleasure dome decree', and in Berkeley did restaurateur George Chen turn this "funky train station" into a place with "gorgeous decor" and "exotic cuisine" billed as 'restorAsian' (restorative Asian, get it?); although the "artfully presented Asian-Californian food" "is good (depending on what you order)", "the health benefits seem more like a gimmick than a true value add"; N.B. a recent chef departure may outdate the food score.

Yoshi's at | 18 | 20 | 17 | $31 |
Jack London Square 🇱🇸🇲

Jack London Sq., 510 Embarcadero W. (Washington St.),
Oakland, 510-238-9200

◪ This "stylish" Japanese in Jack London Square lures music lovers with the promise of dinner and a show, but not everyone agrees on how well the "soy-and-samba" "formula" works; most ticket-holders suggest that while "there are better sushi" salons around, there's "no finer jazz club in the world", so it's "worth it if you need to get good seats at the evening set"; however, downbeat critics harp it don't mean a thing if the seafood doesn't sing (which they think it doesn't).

Zachary's Chicago Pizza 🇱🇸🇲⌀ | 24 | 11 | 14 | $16 |

1853 Solano Ave. (The Alameda), Berkeley, 510-525-5950
5801 College Ave. (Oak Grove Ave.), Oakland, 510-655-6385

■ "No other could top" the pizzas offered at this Berkeley and Oakland pair, clear contenders for the title of "the Bay's best" (and already the hands-down champs for "best deep-dish pie west of Chicago"); Zach's zealots warn "bring cash and 40 minutes of waiting time", or else try this "half-baked idea": "via phone, order" an unfinished pizza to heat up and "enjoy at home."

Zaika 🇸🇲 | – | – | – | ⌐ |

1700 Shattuck Ave. (Virginia St.), Berkeley, 510-849-2452
This Northern Berkeley venture, a fine-dining spin-off of the perennially bustling Breads of India, is like naan from heaven for Indian addicts; its large kitchen allows chef-owner Rohit Singh to showcase the *zaika* (or richness) of her country's diverse regional cuisine in a monthly changing menu format, along with exotic drinks and eventually, wine and beer; but what's expected to curry the most favor is that – unlike its lentil-size sibling – they've promised to accept reservations and credit cards.

North of San Francisco

| | F | D | S | C |

ALBION RIVER INN 🆂🅼　　25 | 23 | 24 | $43
3790 Shoreline Hwy./Hwy. 1 (Albion Airport Rd.), Albion, 707-937-1919
■ Finally, "food as wonderful as the view" sigh surveyors of the "fabulous" Californian fare at this inn that affords a "stunning view of the Albion River and the Pacific Ocean"; of course, it's preferable to "get there before dark" to drink in the sunset as well as the "zillions of single-malt scotches"; "warm service", "live piano" music and "one of the best wine lists on the coast" foster a "romantic" setting inside; P.S. since the hotel's "breakfast is as superb as dinner", many arrange "a trip to Mendocino just to eat here."

Alfy's 🅻🆂　　25 | 21 | 23 | $50
636 San Anselmo Ave. (Bridge St.), San Anselmo, 415-453-3407
■ "What's it all about?" – simply the "best thing to happen in Marin in a long time" reveal reviewers enamored of this "SF-caliber restaurant in the suburbs" (opened by Masa's alumni); in addition to the "top-notch" New French fare, "a scene-to-be-seen" atmosphere and "great outdoor dining add to the urban feeling" – as, unfortunately, do the "high prices"; N.B. the arrival of chef Mateo Grendados (also ex Masa) may outdate the above food rating.

Alta Mira 🅻🆂🅼　　15 | 24 | 18 | $37
Alta Mira Hotel, 125 Bulkley Ave. (bet. Bridgeway & Harrison Ave.), Sausalito, 415-332-1350
☑ "On a clear day" "you can see forever from the patio" of this "old-school glamour" hotel in Sausalito; now if only the "tired" Cal-Continental "food and service could equal the breathtaking view" sigh surveyors, who recommend you stick to Bay-watching and Sunday brunch.

Amici's East Coast Pizzeria 🅻🆂🅼　18 | 11 | 16 | $16
1242 Fourth St. (bet. B & C Sts.), San Rafael, 415-455-9777
See review in San Francisco Directory.

Applewood Inn & Restaurant　　▽ 23 | 22 | 23 | $42
13555 Hwy. 116 (River Rd.), Guerneville, 707-869-9093
■ The "lovely" dining room is a "wonderful surprise" to guests of this apple farm–turned–resort in a "rustic" Redwoodsy setting; the "elegantly prepared" Californian-French "menu changes" daily, "focusing on the seasons", and "the staff is more than accommodating"; though without a doubt "the only restaurant of its caliber in the Russian River area", it oddly doesn't get any "buzz."

Ara Wan Thai L S M ▽ | 23 | 19 | 22 | $27 |

47 Caledonia St. (Pine St.), Sausalito, 415-332-0882

■ This Sausalito Siamese draws in locals for its "yummy Thai" standards and poetic sounding specialties such as Shrimp Lost in the Woods and Spicy Angel in the Sea; the special service will ensure you make it to the show on time (it's located "right next to the movie theater").

AUBERGE DU SOLEIL L S M | 24 | 28 | 25 | $61 |

Auberge du Soleil Inn, 180 Rutherford Hill Rd. (Silverado Trail), Rutherford, 707-967-3111

■ "Overlooking the Valley floor and the gentle hills beyond", this "rustic" "romantic" Rutherford resort is about as "close to heaven as you can get"; "new chef" Richard Reddington's Provençal fare is "simply sublime", the "wine wonderful" and the service "knowledgeable"; "you'll have to cash in some of your stock options (if they're still worth anything) to pay", but where else can you "feel like royalty" and "yet dress informally"?; P.S. the budget-minded can "enjoy classy snacks [and drinks] on the deck."

Avenue Grill S M | 20 | 17 | 18 | $34 |

44 E. Blithedale Ave. (Sunnyside Ave.), Mill Valley, 415-388-6003

■ This Mill Valley "locals' hangout" delivers "consistently good, homestyle Cal-American food" "that will satisfy every family member", but it also offers enough "great people-watching" to "be a hot spot for a casual night off"; all in all, it's "a reliably good time, but you pay for it" with your wallet ("Marin-style prices") and your eardrums ("noisy, noisy, noisy").

BISTRO DON GIOVANNI L S M | 25 | 23 | 23 | $41 |

4110 St. Helena Hwy./Hwy. 29 (bet. Oak Knoll & Salvador Aves.), Napa, 707-224-3300

■ Husband-and-wife duo Donna and Giovanni Scala's (get the name now?) "high-energy" trattoria is the *Cheers* of Napa, "so good even the locals go"; the "incredible Italian food" is prepared "with lots of heart" and served on a "spectacular" "patio overlooking the vineyards"; although patronized by wine industry movers-and-shakers, it lacks the "super-pretentious" service of other establishments.

BISTRO JEANTY L S M | 27 | 23 | 24 | $42 |

6510 Washington St. (Mulberry St.), Yountville, 707-944-0103

■ Chef-owner "Philippe Jeanty's second act" in Yountville (Domaine Chandon was his first) is "the *ne plus ultra* of French bistros", offering "a virtual vacation" to "rural France" sans "the jet lag" or "the airs"; the Gallic "garage-sale decor is a perfect match for the rustic", "perfectly executed" "comfort food" at comparatively "affordable prices"; an "authentic bonhomie" is palpable in the "hectic and loud" dining rooms, which extends from the staff to "the community table" (accommodating walk-ins).

Bistro Ralph ∎⑤Ⓜ 23 | 18 | 21 | $39
109 Plaza St. (Healdsburg Ave.), Healdsburg, 707-433-1380
∎ Ralph Tingle "revolutionized the Healdsburg area's cuisine" when he opened this "smart and arty" American bistro back in 1992; while the kitchen focuses on "fresh, seasonal ingredients", regulars relate you can't go wrong with either the "chicken liver appetizer" or signature duck confit; although the bar "rightly emphasizes [local] Sonoma wines", it's also one of the few places in town where you can order a martini.

Boonville Hotel ⑤Ⓜ 21 | 20 | 19 | $37
14050 Hwy. 128 (Lambert Ln.), Boonville, 707-895-2210
◪ This funky out-of-the-way historic roadhouse serves "surprisingly fresh and very tasty" Cal–New American fare in a handcrafted Shaker-inspired dining room; it's the epicenter of culinary activity in the one-horse town of Boonville, and although the limited menu has "some hits, some misses", travelers sigh "thank God it's here", as "no place on the way to Mendocino compares"; N.B. dinner is served only Thursday–Monday.

Bouchon ◕∎⑤Ⓜ 23 | 24 | 22 | $44
6534 Washington St. (Yount St.), Yountville, 707-944-8037
∎ From the fire-engine-red painted facade to the crammed marble tables, owner Thomas Keller's bistro *français* offers Yountville "a little bit of Paris – Left Bank, of course"; some note "a bit of an attitude" and "unbearably painful [noise] levels", but they're shouted down by admirers of the "*très authentique*" fare ("wonderful mussels and frites") and the "jumping late-night scene" – one of the area's few – that attracts "other Napa Valley restaurant" folks ("a recommendation in itself").

Brannan's Grill ∎⑤Ⓜ 20 | 22 | 19 | $37
1374 Lincoln Ave. (bet. Cedar & Washington Sts.), Calistoga, 707-942-2233
∎ The "gorgeous" "Arts & Crafts interior" of this New American "that's a hop, skip and a jump from some great Calistoga spas" has always been its strongest asset, but judging from the ratings jump, this three-year-old "now has the food straightened out" ("the sea bass easily bested more expensive places"); sitting at the "accommodating" antique bar that offers a "choice of 200 wines by the glass" is a fitting way to end a day of winery visits or mud baths.

Brix ∎⑤Ⓜ 22 | 23 | 21 | $43
7377 St. Helena Hwy./Hwy. 29 (Washington St.), Napa, 707-944-2749
∎ "You won't want to return to Kansas once you've spent an afternoon on the patio" of this scenic Napa spot; indeed, the "sprawling vineyards and a delightful garden" – the source for much of the "amazing" Asian-Cal-French fusion

menu – make a "beautiful setting"; there's an "extensive wine list", and while the attached shop strikes some as too "commercial", most find it all "quite satisfying"; N.B. a late-summer chef change may outdate the food ratings.

Bubba's Diner L S M | 17 | 14 | 16 | $21 |
566 San Anselmo Ave. (bet. Tamalpais & Tunstead Aves.), San Anselmo, 415-459-6862
◪ "Good grub, Marin-style" is the hallmark of this "down-home diner" in San Anselmo whipping up "huge portions" of "classic comfort food that's farmers' market fresh"; but although "the menu's the same" since a switch in chefs, a drop in food ratings seems to corroborate voters' views that it "has gone downhill."

Buckeye Roadhouse L S M | 22 | 23 | 21 | $37 |
15 Shoreline Hwy./Hwy. 1 (west of Hwy. 101), Mill Valley, 415-331-2600
■ "Only in Mill Valley could you get away with calling this a roadhouse"; the rest of us just call it "so much fun" for its "touched-by-a-sophisticated-hand" American "smokehouse fare", "desserts pretty close to heaven", "moose-hunters ambiance" and "the kind of waitresses you'd want to steal away with"; "it'd be the perfect place if no one else had heard of it" but everyone has, so "it's always packed."

Cactus Cafe L M | ▽ 19 | 11 | 17 | $20 |
393 Miller Ave. (bet. Evergreen & Montford Aves.), Mill Valley, 415-388-8226
■ "You might have a hard time finding" this taqueria in tony Mill Valley, but "when you do", you'll be rewarded by "unique" Californian-Southwestern fare; the "great value for such creative food" and the chance to engage in "low-key celebrity spotting over shiitake tacos" easily outweigh the lack of decor; besides, doesn't "everybody know the best Mexican food is eaten on folding chairs"?

Cafe Beaujolais S M | 25 | 21 | 23 | $44 |
961 Ukiah St. (School St.), Mendocino, 707-937-5614
■ For over two decades, popular thought has been that you simply "can't go to Mendo without [having] a meal" at this "charming" Victorian farmhouse that serves "simple" yet fabulous" French–New American fare; founding chef-owner Margaret Fox has moved on, but the "same great staff" and "terrific breads" linger; satisfied surveyors happily report the "new owner has maintained the same high standards" and even with a gentle remodel, the "place remains magical as ever."

Cafe Citti L S M | 19 | 10 | 16 | $21 |
9049 Sonoma Hwy./Hwy. 12 (Shaw Ave.), Kenwood, 707-833-2690
■ Kenwood's "simple" "side-of-the-road" Northern Italian is a "one-of-a-kind bargain" dishing up "dynamite

chicken" and "large and filling" "salads and sandwiches"; there's "nothing fancy" about this "walk-up counter" – precisely why Citti slickers say wine country "needs more like this."

Cafe La Haye S   25 18 21 $36

140 E. Napa St. (bet. 1st & 2nd Sts.), Sonoma, 707-935-5994

■ This "tiny" "hidden treasure" makes big waves with locals who "are upset that the world is finding this one"; but with such "phenomenal" Eclectic–New American eats at "unbelievable prices", a "friendly staff that loves to talk about the food" and "darn fine original artwork" to boot, how could they expect to keep this place (arguably "the best in Sonoma") a secret?

Cafe Lolo L M   23 19 22 $37

620 Fifth St. (bet. D St. & Mendocino Ave.), Santa Rosa, 707-576-7822

■ Most Santa Rosa residents consider this Downtown American that delivers "consistently good food with a seasonally varied menu" a "real find"; they attribute the success to chef/co-owner Michael Quigley and his wife Lori, "who makes you feel like a guest at her home"; of course, "if you are anything above average size it can get quite cozy" (ok, "very cramped and loud"), "but good things come in small packages", right?

California Cafe Bar & Grill L S M 19 19 19 $32

The Village at Corte Madera, 1736 Redwood Hwy./Hwy. 101 (Paradise Dr.), Corte Madera, 415-924-2233
See review in Silicon Valley/Peninsula Directory.

Calistoga Inn   20 22 20 $33
Restaurant & Brewery L S M

1250 Lincoln Ave. (Cedar St.), Calistoga, 707-942-4101

■ Calistoga's first (and only) brewpub offers an "awesome patio by a creek" that provides tourists with a "romantic", "relaxing" respite from the winery-hopping hustle; but locals like it too for "interesting beers" and "wonderful" American grill grub prepared on the outdoor barbecue.

CAPRICE, THE S M   23 27 23 $46

2000 Paradise Dr. (Mar West St.), Tiburon, 415-435-3400

■ "It's not so much the [interior] as the Bay Area's natural beauty that makes this place lovely" explain Tiburon residents on why this beloved old vet remains a "place for wedding anniversaries" and "parents"; while the Californian-inflected Continental fare still plays second fiddle to the "sweeping views of SF" and "sailing races", a jump in the score indicates that "food is improving" and is now quite "delicious"; of course, the "expensive" prices remind you that you're paying for all that watery romance.

Carneros **L S M**   ▽ 24 | 20 | 18 | $40

The Lodge at Sonoma, 1325 Broadway (Leveroni Rd.), Sonoma, 707-931-2042

◪ The crown jewel of the newly built luxe Lodge at Sonoma, this highly anticipated newcomer marks the return of chef Brian Whitmer (ex SF's Moose's), preparing what he calls artisan-inspired wine-country cuisine in a Mediterranean style; you can watch him in action in the open kitchen that dominates the rustic high-ceilinged dining room; despite some service glitches, eager beavers are pronouncing it "already a classic."

Catahoula   23 | 20 | 20 | $42
Restaurant & Saloon **L S M**

Mount View Hotel, 1457 Lincoln Ave. (bet. Fair Way & Washington St.), Calistoga, 707-942-2275

■ "New Orleans comes to Calistoga, and it works" say Southern-food lovers of what is easily the "best casual dining" in the Valley; chef-owner Jan Birnbaum's "heart is as big as he is", and "you can watch him in the open kitchen" preparing the oh-"so-spicy and decadent" eats; boosters "love that gumbo" (yep, there's real rooster in that thar stew), "sexy grits" and "those [Catahoula-breed] dogs on the walls"; pity the "informal service" and industrial environs "don't live up to" the grub.

Celadon **L M**   24 | 20 | 23 | $35

1040 Main St. (bet. 1st & Pearl Sts.), Napa, 707-254-9690

■ Owner Greg Cole's cloistered New American – boasting a "small but sophisticated menu", "attentive" staff and a "great setting" overlooking the Napa River – is a "hidden gem" that's "worth the adventure to find" (hint: it's over the bridge behind the Main Street Exchange); not-so-neighborly natives ask us to "please remove from the *Survey*" – there are already "too many tourists."

Charcuterie **L S M**   ▽ 21 | 15 | 19 | $32

335 Healdsburg Ave. (Plaza St.), Healdsburg, 707-431-7213

■ This charcuterie-turned-"casual" bistro in Healdsburg serves "good", simple "French country food" – salads, sandwiches and, of course, pork tenderloin; not everyone goes hog wild over the "too small space", but it's a handy "lunch spot between wineries" and you gotta "love the pigs" (the porcine bric-a-brac) that bedeck the interior.

CHATEAU SOUVERAIN CAFÉ   24 | 28 | 22 | $37
AT THE WINERY **L S M**

400 Souverain Rd. (Hwy. 101, Independence Ln. exit), Geyserville, 707-433-3141

■ Nestled on a vineyard-covered hillside in Geyserville's Alexander Valley, this winery's "beautiful" culinary outpost affords visitors "spectacular views" and a "splendid setting" in which to test their wine-and-food-pairing skills;

the "wonderfully prepared and presented" Cal-French menu is matched by a "solicitous" staff and "impeccable service" of the all-Chateau Souverain list; N.B. an annotated alfresco menu is served on the picturesque patio from 2:30–5 PM.

Chevys Fresh Mex L S M   13 | 13 | 14 | $19
Bon Air Shopping Ctr., 302 Bon Air Shopping Ctr.
(Sir Francis Drake Blvd.), Greenbrae, 415-461-3203
128 Vintage Way (Rowland Blvd.), Novato, 415-898-7345
24 Fourth St. (Wilson St.), Santa Rosa, 707-571-1082
157 Plaza Dr. (bet. Admiral Callaghan Ln. & Turner Pkwy.),
Vallejo, 707-644-1373
See review in San Francisco Directory.

Christophe L S   21 | 17 | 21 | $32
1919 Bridgeway (Spring St.), Sausalito, 415-332-9244
◼ "Tiny and attractive", this bistro with a "very French staff" and very "traditional" menu is Sausalito's "best-kept secret"; although the "romantic spot's" "popular with the middle-aged Lexus driver" crowd, it's really the "incredibly cheap" "early-bird specials" ("the best price performer in the category") that "draw long lines" and vociferous praise.

Cole's Chop House S M   25 | 25 | 23 | $47
1122 Main St. (bet. 1st & Pearl Sts.), Napa, 707-224-6328
◼ "It's the steaks, stupid" that coral carnivores into owner Greg Cole's (of Celadon) Napa steakhouse, the prime dry-aged slabs of meat are "as good as you'll get" "west of Chicago" and a welcome change in a town where "chops aren't the usual fare"; the "very classy restored stone building" (circa 1886) is a befitting backdrop for the traditional menu where "every morsel is à la carte" – from the "incredible spinach salad" to "the best hash browns"; N.B. the wine list abounds with beefy California Cabernets.

Cucina Jackson Fillmore S   22 | 17 | 19 | $35
337 San Anselmo Ave. (Tunstead Ave.), San Anselmo,
415-454-2942
◼ This "totally happening spot" in San Anselmo follows the same "neighborhood trattoria" formula that owner Jack Krietzman employs in his similarly named city venture – "intoxicating" food (like "melt-in-your-mouth gnocchi"), "affordable wines" and a "great atmosphere"; suburban surveyors dub it the "best Northern Italian in Marin", but city slickers say "it's missing the edge of SF"; however, "bring your earplugs" because the piccolo dining room is just as "noisy."

Della Santina's L S M   21 | 20 | 21 | $32
133 E. Napa St. (1st St.), Sonoma, 707-935-0576
◼ To "dine under the trees in the garden" at this family-run trattoria "located in the heart of Sonoma" is "downright romantic"; although a "variety" of "good, plain" Northern

"Italian specialties" is available, carbo-lovers counsel "go right to the [homemade] pastas."

Deuce 🅛🆂🅼

▽ 21 | 20 | 21 | $34

691 Broadway (France St.), Sonoma, 707-933-3823

■ An "up-and-coming" spot in Sonoma pulls a one-two punch with "delicious" "innovative" New American fare (huckleberry mousse, anyone?) and "friendly, attentive service"; but its ace-in-the-hole is the "beautiful garden patio" seating "when weather permits."

Diner, The 🅛🆂⊄

– | – | – | I

6476 Washington St. (California Dr.), Yountville, 707-944-2626

This "old-style diner" whipping up "great comfort food" with an extra helping of "charm" is "an institution in Yountville" that's "still hanging onto its funky roots" despite the gourmet gentrification that surrounds it; one concession to chic is that the "good old-fashioned burgers, milkshakes" and Tex-Mex specialties are fashioned from "fresh organic ingredients"; P.S. breakfast is a "Valley tradition" here, so expect "crowds on weekend mornings."

Dipsea Cafe, The 🆂🅼

18 | 16 | 16 | $19

200 Shoreline Hwy./Hwy. 1 (Tennessee Valley Rd.), Mill Valley, 415-381-0298

■ "Hopping" with joggers and well-to-do locals, this "cheerful" coffee shop is a "great place to see a slice of Mill Valley" while consuming "truly original takes" on traditional American grub; although it's known for its "power-breakfast scene", outdoorsy types covet "sitting on the patio in the sun and devouring a delish sandwich after a great hike."

DOMAINE CHANDON 🅛🆂🅼

26 | 26 | 25 | $64

1 California Dr. (Hwy. 29), Yountville, 707-944-2892

■ For the ultimate wine-country "event", "bring [your] guests" to Moët Hennessy's "sparkling" Napa Valley showcase, the ultimate "live-it-up place" where the "phenomenal" Californian-French cuisine and "stupendous service" "are as good as the bubbles"; given such "serene surroundings" without and "outstanding architecture" within, even those who "don't like champagne love this restaurant"; P.S. for a more affordable way to enjoy the view, try "appetizers at the tasting bar."

Downtown
Bakery & Creamery 🆂🅼⊄

24 | 12 | 16 | $13

308A Center St. (Matheson St.), Healdsburg, 707-431-2719

■ "No visit to Sonoma is complete without stopping" at this "fabulous" take-out spot off Healdsburg Square (follow the "wonderful aroma when approaching the plaza"); "no, it's not a restaurant" ("a bench outside is all the seating"), but it does churn up the "best ice cream for miles around", not to mention "sublime buns" and pastries; P.S. "if you can't get to" the mother ship, their baked goodies are available at the SF Ferry Plaza farmers' market.

Duck Club 🇸🇲 | 21 | 21 | 21 | $38 |
Bodega Bay Lodge & Spa, 103 Coast Hwy. 1 (Doran Beach exit), Bodega, 707-875-3525
See review in Silicon Valley/Peninsula Directory.

El Paseo 🇸 | 23 | 26 | 24 | $46 |
17 Throckmorton Ave. (bet. Blithedale & Miller Aves.), Mill Valley, 415-388-0741
■ "Did someone order up romance?" ask starry-eyed surveyors, because this "old-fashioned" (a few say "outdated") Cal-French, situated in "charming rooms", is "still about the most romantic place around" Mill Valley; some go for the "gorgeous food" and "out-of-sight wine list", some "go for the fine service" and others just "keep going back."

Emporio Rulli 🇱🇸🇲 | 24 | 24 | 18 | $19 |
464 Magnolia Ave. (bet. Cane & Ward Sts.), Larkspur, 415-924-7478
■ There's "a little miracle in Larkspur", and it's this "one-of-kind place" that adherents assert is the "best bakery in Marin" and certainly "as good as anything in Italy"; it's "worth a drive just for" the "great coffee" and "fantastic pastries, candies, cookies, gelato" and Italian panini, which are "out of this world" and "make you feel like you are in heaven" (talk about a religious experience).

Feast 🇱🇲   ▽ | 23 | – | 19 | $32 |
714 Village Ct. (bet. Claremont Dr. & Patio Ct.), Santa Rosa, 707-591-9800
■ "Promising, talented" chef/co-owner Jesse McQuarrie has moved on up from his "homey and small" courthouse digs to this full-size Santa Rosa establishment; early enthusiasts who swooned over his "outstanding" New American food and "nice wine list" should enjoy hearing that the expanded space means practically five times the space, so all that tight-"squeeze" stuff is a thing of the past.

Felix & Louie's 🇱🇸🇲 | 16 | 16 | 15 | $31 |
106 Matheson St. (Healdsburg Ave.), Healdsburg, 707-433-6966
◪ Run by Ralph Tingle (the Ralph behind Bistro Ralph), this Healdsburg Italian-American is highly "kid-friendly", what with its "good pizzas", casual atmosphere and a "great back patio" that's "perfect" for running around "on a warm evening"; however, grown-ups gripe that the grub is "only passable" and suggest if your tots "are old enough, leave them here and eat" elsewhere.

Foothill Cafe S | 24 | 15 | 22 | $34 |

J&P Shopping Ctr., 2766 Old Sonoma Rd. (Foothill Blvd.), Napa, 707-252-6178

■ "What a find (if you can find it)" barks a bevy of barbecue boosters who insist the "great ribs and meats" at "down-home prices" in this "unpretentious" BBQ-Californian "storefront" easily "compensate for the bad location and decor"; so foot it on over to Napa and "mix with farmers, debutantes and locals" – in fact, it's hard not to, since "there's hardly any room to move."

Frantoio S M | 21 | 20 | 19 | $37 |

152 Shoreline Hwy./Hwy. 1 (west of Hwy. 101), Mill Valley, 415-289-5777

■ It's easy to overlook this upscale Northern Italian in Mill Valley "because it's in a Best Western", but most who find it are "surprised" by the "innovative pastas", "excellent pizzas" and "friendly service"; although not everyone is thrilled by the "barn-like" dining room, it's "fun to watch olive oil being made" in the on-site press in the autumn; otherwise, on warm days, the "outdoor patio is a delightful" place to be.

FRENCH LAUNDRY L S M | 29 | 27 | 28 | $102 |

6640 Washington St. (Creek St.), Yountville, 707-944-2380

■ "If heaven exists on earth, it must reside in chef-owner Thomas Keller's" Yountville New American, the *Survey's* No. 1 for Food; the enchanting "French chateau"-like building sets the stage for "over-the-top" menus that are "a revelation of whimsical presentations and sensational tastes" "from the first minute to the fourth hour"; "unerring service" rounds out a "transcendental experience" that even "jaded" folk find "worth the pilgrimage, the splurge" and the "insanity of obtaining reservations."

General's Daughter, The L S M | 20 | 23 | 21 | $38 |

400 W. Spain St. (4th St.), Sonoma, 707-938-4004

■ This Sonoma establishment resides "in a restored Victorian" home, originally built for General Vallejo's daughter; the general consensus is it's "absolutely charming", offering a "lovely outdoor porch" on which wine-country trekkers can enjoy "solid" Californian fare and a wine list that favors local boutique bottlings.

Gira Polli S M | 20 | 14 | 17 | $22 |

590 E. Blithedale Ave. (Camino Alto), Mill Valley, 415-383-6040
See review in San Francisco Directory.

girl & the fig, the L S M | 23 | 20 | 21 | $37 |

110 W. Spain St. (1st St.), Sonoma, 707-938-3634

■ Those who give a fig for this "welcoming" homespun bistro need to direct themselves to Sonoma Square, where it has relocated; but relax, girl, you'll still find the same "excellent French" bistro fare, "attractive atmosphere" and "offbeat wine selections" that shirk trendy Chardonnays and Cabernets for a "nice Rhone varietals" list (though the majority are California vintages).

girl & the gaucho, the S M

– | – | – | E

13690 Arnold Dr. (O'Donnell Ln.), Glen Ellen, 707-938-2130
Owner Sondra Bernstein is living *la vida loca,* creating a "funky" Pan-Latin cantina whose dining room (hung with glass chandeliers and a black-velvet matador painting) makes a lively backdrop for chef John Toulze's equally snazzy menu of tapas; guests can also go loco with the "large plates", mixing and matching sides and sauces from the country of their choice; the wine list includes little-known Southern Hemisphere offerings.

Glen Ellen Inn Restaurant S M

▽ 20 | 19 | 20 | $39

13670 Arnold Dr. (Warm Springs Rd.), Glen Ellen, 707-996-6409
■ "Undiscovered" in Glen Ellen, this Californian run by a husband-and-wife team sports one of the most "romantic settings" in the area; insiders insist if it's warm enough, "get a table outside" because dining "by the creek" is a "great way to end a day of wine tasting"; N.B. the place has finally made good on its name, offering rooms for rent.

Gordon's L S

24 | 19 | 19 | $26

6770 Washington St. (Madison St.), Yountville, 707-944-8246
■ Serving "great traditional American" breakfasts and lunches and "terrific down-home" Friday night dinners, owner Sally Gordon's humble Yountville "joint" would be just another "local favorite" – except these days it has "caught on" with out-of-towners and is "now crowded on the weekends" (don't you hate when that happens?).

Green Valley Cafe L

▽ 22 | 15 | 19 | $29

1310 Main St. (Hunt Ave.), St. Helena, 707-963-7088
■ This "unpretentious Northern Italian" is where "every St. Helenan eats" (and quite "often" at that); while there's nothing particularly "elegant" here, if you're lucky, you might "get a chance to see [local denizen] Francis Ford Coppola" tucking into the "ethereal lasagna" or one of their "fabulous pastas."

Guaymas L S M

19 | 22 | 17 | $31

5 Main St. (Tiburon Blvd.), Tiburon, 415-435-6300
◪ City folk with or without visitors in tow "cross the bridge" or "ride the ferry" to "escape the fog" and soak up the "fantastic Bay views" and "fiesta atmosphere" at this "fun" waterside Mexican in Tiburon; despite the touristy trappings, the kitchen prides itself on "fresh" "authentic regional cuisine"; many mutter the execution and service aren't "as good as the setting", but after a few of "those margaritas", it "doesn't matter."

Guernica S
▽ 20 | 18 | 20 | $32

2009 Bridgeway (Spring St.), Sausalito, 415-332-1512
■ Long before Basque cooking became hip, this 27-year-old "longtime favorite" in Sausalito was cooking up "belly-warming" specialties such as paella and lamb shanks braised sheepherder style (with beans); the "homey atmosphere" makes for an "intimate", almost "romantic spot" "on the cheap", although the "no-rush" service is not for everyone.

Hana Japanese L S
▽ 26 | 14 | 21 | $40

Doubletree Plaza, 101 Golf Course Dr. (Roberts Lake Rd.), Santa Rosa, 707-586-0270
■ "Don't underestimate this sushi spot" just by its location in a shopping mall: chef-owner Ken Tominaga is "an unexpected diamond in the plebian rough of Santa Rosa", catering "masterful creations" fashioned from the "freshest fish" around, along with other Japanese specialties ("try the omakase" menu), that make up for the "marginalized decor."

Il Davide L S
22 | 18 | 20 | $33

901 A St. (bet. 3rd & 4th Sts.), San Rafael, 415-454-8080
■ With murals of the Tuscan countryside in the dining room and umbrella-topped tables outside, this "attractive" trattoria delivers "consistently" "excellent" (if perhaps "predictable") Italian "food with flair" (including "melt-in-your-mouth risotto") and a "great wine list" to make it a "popular" "addition to the San Rafael scene"; P.S. "to avoid the noise", insiders "ask for the back rooms."

Il Fornaio L S M
19 | 20 | 19 | $33

Corte Madera Town Ctr., 223 Corte Madera Town Ctr. (Madera Blvd.), Corte Madera, 415-927-4400
See review in San Francisco Directory.

Insalata's Restaurant L S M
23 | 22 | 22 | $37

120 Sir Francis Drake Blvd. (Barber St.), San Anselmo, 415-457-7700
■ "Kudos to chef-owner Heidi Krahling", whose insalata getsalota nominations for "best of Marin" when "you want to go the couscous route"; that, and the rest of the "creative and hearty" Cal-Med cuisine, is served by a "well-trained staff" in a sprawling dining room decorated with "oversized [still life] paintings" and a "nice, gentle vibe" that's "comfortable enough for every day"; the San Anselmo set suggests "if it were in SF the place would be packed and the prices would be ten times higher."

Jimtown Store L S M
19 | 19 | 17 | $16

6706 Hwy. 128 (1 mi. east of Russian River), Healdsburg, 707-433-1212
■ A perfect "pit stop", this vintage-looking "farm-town store" is a real "kick", "abounding with charm", tchotchkes

and antiques; despite the "country atmosphere", it offers up "fine sandwiches" and "refreshingly innovative" "breakfast foods" to "take out or eat on the patio", making it a veritable "oasis" on an otherwise empty country back road outside of Healdsburg (no, you haven't driven past it).

Joe's Taco Lounge & Salsaria L S M
19 17 16 $16

382 Miller Ave. (Montford Ave.), Mill Valley, 415-383-8164

■ Make no mistake, this is not your average Joe's taqueria – what with "*muy bueno* fish tacos" and other "fresh" Tex-Mex with a decidedly Californian spin, legions of hot sauce, "funky" '50s-style vinyl tablecloths and kitschy "stuff on the walls"; "non-existent service" notwithstanding, it's a "great spot after a day at Stinson Beach"; just expect "long waits" with SUV-steering Mill Valleyites.

John Ash & Co. L S M
24 25 24 $49

Vintners Inn, 4330 Barnes Rd. (River Rd.), Santa Rosa, 707-527-7687

■ "The Sonoma standard" of "fine dining", this Santa Rosa "destination" "has it all" – "wonderfully presented", "delicate but delicious" Californian cuisine, "impeccable, professional service" and an eye-popping 500-plus list of labels emphasizing local vintages; but what makes it "epitomize wine country" is its "extraordinary setting in the vineyards" (visible from the outdoor patio as well as parts of the dining room); simply put, "nothing is lacking – and should not be at these prices."

Kasbah Moroccan S
23 26 23 $36

200 Merrydale Rd. (Willow St.), San Rafael, 415-472-6666

■ Advocates admit they have an "exotic" erotic ball at this "fun", "romantic" restaurant in San Rafael, "sitting on" low-slung chairs and enjoying the "great belly dancers" shaking their things in the "beautiful" Kasbah-inspired dining room; while many maintain the "very tasty Moroccan dishes" are "better than" what you'd find in Marrakech, it's the overall "great ambiance" that gets 'em.

Kenwood L S
24 22 22 $41

9900 Sonoma Hwy./Hwy. 12 (Warm Springs Rd.), Kenwood, 707-833-6326

■ For an "ideal retreat from the city", this Kenwood wine-country veteran is "an outstanding find"; "the setting is picture perfect" ("try to get a table outside or near the open window"), "as are the crispy roast duck" and other creative New French–New American fare accompanied by "intense sauces that make the small portions seem big"; why this "consistent" charmer is not better known is beyond the ken of most reviewers.

La Ginestra 🅂
| 20 | 16 | 20 | $27 |

127 Throckmorton Ave. (Miller Ave.), Mill Valley, 415-388-0224

■ "The nuevo Mill Valley crowd may not appreciate this classic old-fashioned, family-run Southern Italian, as it's not hip and trendy enough", but to plenty of "long-time locals" (one fan's been "dining here since I was a year old") and families it remains a "favorite" due to "great pizza", "to-die-for homemade ravioli" and a "down-to-earth staff."

LARK CREEK INN, THE 🅻🅂🅼
| 23 | 23 | 22 | $43 |

234 Magnolia Ave. (Madrone Ave.), Larkspur, 415-924-7766

■ "Dining's a lark" at chef-owner Bradley Ogden's "charming country house" with a "storybook setting surrounded by redwoods" in Larkspur; the "hearty" "down-home" American cuisine is laced with "little innovations" by co-chef Jeremy Sewell and matched by "great service"; "we wish it really was an inn because we didn't want to leave"; P.S. though the San Mateo and Walnut Creek spin-offs serve many of the same classics, they don't have the same wow factor "as the Marin county flagship."

Las Camelias 🅻🅂🅼
| 23 | 17 | 20 | $21 |

912 Lincoln Ave. (bet. 3rd & 4th Sts.), San Rafael, 415-453-5850

■ "From the homemade salsa and chips that greet your arrival to the portions of hearty, well-seasoned" "great moles" and other "regional" dishes that "spell *muerte* to any diet", this "family-run" San Rafael spot is considered the most "unusual and creative Mexican" in Marin, with a "friendly staff" and "pretty decor" to boot.

LA TOQUE 🅂
| 26 | 24 | 26 | $84 |

1140 Rutherford Rd. (Hwy. 29), Rutherford, 707-963-9770

■ Toques off to owner and "culinary genius Ken Frank" for offering visitors another "pinnacle of fine dining" that many frequenters feel is the "second-best wine-country restaurant" – and a "more accessible" one too; sybarites suggest "live the life of Napa" and "do the outstanding wine-pairing" option on the prix fixe–only menu that features "marvelously presented" seasonally driven New French fare; "superb service" and a "lovely room" top off the experience; N.B. jacket preferred.

Ledford House 🅂
| ▽ 22 | 22 | 21 | $41 |

3000 Shoreline Hwy./Hwy. 1 (Spring Grove Rd.), Albion, 707-937-0282

■ For a "spectacular view" and a homey dining experience, Mendo locals suggest you head here to "watch the sunset over the Pacific Ocean at the bar, then settle down for some great" Cal-Med fare (some of the most "inventive cooking on the coast"); be sure to ask "always welcoming owner" Tony "to turn you on to his latest viticultural discoveries."

Left Bank 🄻🅂🄼 21 | 21 | 19 | $38

507 Magnolia Ave. (Ward St.), Larkspur, 415-927-3331
■ You really do feel "like you're on the Left Bank" at this "high-energy bistro" that emanates "a big-city buzz" despite being in sleepy Larkspur; Lyon-born owner Roland Passot (of La Folie fame) and his entourage "cook mean [French] fare", and the "*très joli*" decor is equally "authentic"; however, the "hustle-and-bustle" can mean "inattentive service", and the "squished-together" tables can mean too much togetherness, even for touchy-feely Marinites; still, you can bank on the hours: "open all day."

Little River Inn 🅂🄼 22 | 21 | 22 | $38

7901 Shoreline Hwy./Hwy. 1 (Little River Airport Rd.), Little River, 707-937-5942
■ To experience the famous Ole's Swedish hotcakes and all the other "wonderful" morning foods that buffs boast are the "best breakfasts ever", you might have to "stay for the weekend" at this historic Mendocino resort overlooking the Little River inlet; when it comes to dinner by chef Silver Canul (considered one of the coast's culinary up-and-comers), "stick to the [signature pepper] steak" or the seafood specials caught in the nearby Noyo Harbor.

Livefire Grill & Smokehouse 🄻🅂🄼 16 | 18 | 17 | $35

6518 Washington St. (Yount St.), Yountville, 707-944-1500
◪ This large BBQ palace hawking a "variety of" "good grilled meats" and other "upscale comfort food" is certainly "not in the upper echelon of Napa Valley eateries", but the "hip-ish decor" and location within "walking distance of Yountville inns" keep it smoking; however, grumblers grill it for "spotty service" and "damn expensive [prices] for what you get", predicting in "another year, this fire will burn out."

Lotus Cuisine of India 🄻🅂🄼 ▽ 23 | 17 | 23 | $25

704 Fourth St. (bet. Lincoln & Tamalpais Aves.), San Rafael, 415-456-5808
■ San Rafaelites rave they're "transported to India" after tucking into the "superb curries", "great flavored naans" and other Delhicious items meted out by a "delightful staff"; bargain hunters should head here for the "awesome lunch buffet", as "dinner portions tend to be on the small side."

Lucy's Cafe 🄻🅂🄼 ▽ 21 | – | 18 | $22

6948 Sebastopol Ave. (bet. Main St. & Petaluma Ave.), Sebastopol, 707-829-9713
■ Although this "reliable Cal-Med cafe" lures locals out of bed for its "tasty breakfasts" and "nice" hearth-baked breads, afternoon noshers note the "delicious pizza", prepared in an open brick oven and topped with all-organic "imaginative" goodies (*so* Sebastopol), is also the "best for miles"; N.B. at press time, it's scheduled to move, which may outdate the decor score.

MacCallum House ⑤Ⓜ   ▽ 21 | 22 | 20 | $42
MacCallum House Inn, 45020 Albion St. (Lansing St.),
Mendocino, 707-937-5763

■ This bed-and-breakfast, a historic farm house complete with water towers and wraparound porch, is as "quaint as Mendocino itself"; chef-owner Alan Kantor "is a veritable Sherlock Holmes who searches out the finest regional ingredients" for his North Coast–inspired Californian cuisine, served in a beautiful Victorian dining room that offers "very warm atmosphere" and a dreamy view of gardens and the Pacific Ocean; P.S. "if the restaurant is crowded, eat in the [less formal] Grey Whale Bar."

Madrona Manor ⑤Ⓜ   23 | 23 | 23 | $47
Madrona Manor Wine Country Inn, 1001 Westside Rd.
(W. Dry Creek Rd.), Healdsburg, 707-433-4231

■ Although the romantics swoon "who cares what you're eating when you are seated on the veranda on a warm, star-filled night?", "under new chef Jesse Malgren, the [Californian–New French] food now matches the wonderful decor" at this Healdsburg historic landmark (built in 1881); the inn itself's a "perfect wine-country getaway", so why not spend the night and make it a "total experience"?

Manka's Inverness Lodge ⑤Ⓜ   24 | 26 | 21 | $53
30 Callendar Way (Argyle St.), Inverness, 415-669-1034

◪ Considered "*the* place to be in the beautiful Point Reyes National Seashore", this 1917 hunting lodge is an "eccentric destination with an eccentric family-run kitchen" cooking up Californian fare that's "so earthy it feels like eating with the *Blair Witch Project*" (whatever's roasting in the dining room fireplace may be your entree); picky eaters find the "prix-fixe menus" a "bit tricky" and the service something out of 'Hotel California', but if you "stay over", it's a "great weekend getaway" "in the woods."

Manzanita Ⓛ⑤Ⓜ   ▽ 26 | 22 | 22 | $44
336 Healdsburg Ave. (North St.), Healdsburg, 707-433-8111

■ Even though this new "classy brasserie" – brought to you by the folks behind the lateWillowside – only opened in February 2001, it "made a big splash immediately" thanks to chef Bruce Frieske's "well-seasoned Mediterranean fare" cooked in a wood-burning oven and enhanced by an "appealing atmosphere and professional service"; sighing "it's the best thing to happen to eating in Healdsburg", partisans predict it'll be "another wine-country classic."

Marché aux Fleurs Ⓛ   – | – | – | E
23 Ross Common (off Lagunitas Rd.), Ross, 415-925-9200
Named for the outdoor flower markets of Provence, this *très joli* Country French nouveau-comer in Ross lives up to its name with a gorgeous outdoor garden patio and interior dotted with floral paintings and fresh-cut flowers; the

menu features innovative twists on Gallic classics such as 'shellfish escargot' (sizzling mussels and shrimp in a traditional snails' plate) and lavender crème brûlée.

Marin Joe's ◗ L S M 　　　| 19 | 14 | 19 | $29 |
1585 Casa Buena Dr. (south of Tamalpais Dr.), Corte Madera, 415-924-2081
■ Dining at this Corte Madera institution is like taking a "trip back in time" to when "lots of old-style Italian" (we're talkin' spaghetti with meat sauce) and "real cocktails" constituted fine eats; sentimentalists say "the food, decor and service haven't changed since the '50s" (when it first opened), though even they admit the "long waits" can get "tedious."

Mariposa S 　　　| 24 | 19 | 22 | $45 |
275 Windsor River Rd. (Bell Rd.), Windsor, 707-838-0162
■ "You may want to move to Windsor" after sampling this small but "warmly hospitable" venture; the "chance-taking" chef-owners' Californian menu harbors "culinary works of art", and is paired with "patient service" and an "imaginative wine list"; although a few gripe that "it's a little too cozy", the majority rules that the "remarkable food" makes up for the "unremarkable space."

Max's Restaurant L S M 　　　| 16 | 13 | 16 | $22 |
60 Madera Blvd. (Hwy. 101), Corte Madera, 415-924-6297
See review in San Francisco Directory.

Maya L S M 　　　| 20 | 21 | 18 | $29 |
101 E. Napa St. (1st St.), Sonoma, 707-935-3500
◪ When you need a siesta from wine-tasting food, head to this "upscale Mexican" restaurant located "right on the square in Sonoma"; while fans favor the "dynamite margaritas" and "interesting" south-of-the-border *cocina*, foes find the fare only "fair"; still, most dig the delightfully "kitschy decor" (maybe it's that Mayan god perched above the 'Temple of Tequila' bar).

Meadowood Grill L S M 　　　| 22 | 24 | 23 | $44 |
Meadowood Resort, 900 Meadowood Ln. (Howell Mountain Rd., off Silverado Trail), St. Helena, 707-963-3646
■ This swanky St. Helena resort's casual eatery has "no pretensions in spite of all the reasons it could have them" – a "serene", "beautiful setting", "great Californian food" and "impeccable and completely unobtrusive service"; although some wonder "who wants to eat at a country club?", sports fans submit the balcony is a "great place to watch the action – golfing and croquet carts" driving by.

Mendo Bistro L S M 　　　| – | – | – | M |
301 N. Main St. (Redwood St.), Fort Bragg, 707-964-4974
Homespun Eclectic bistro in Fort Bragg that bills itself as an affordable dining alternative to the swankier spots to

the south, while still showcasing the bounty of the North Coast; some say the kitchen's ambitious globe-trotting menu, which ranges from fresh pasta to sushi, "just misses", but it's building a following among local wine makers and chefs.

Meritage **L S M** | 21 | 17 | 19 | $36 |
522 Broadway (Napa St.), Sonoma, 707-938-9430
■ Following the trend of giving eateries vinous names, this simple Sonoma Square sophomore merits praise for its "outstanding" Northern Italian fare and New French specialties; the "friendly, helpful staff" "readily pours" many "nice wines by the glass", creating a "very pleasant" atmosphere; aw shucks, it even has a new oyster bar.

Mikayla at the Casa Madrona **S M** | 22 | 25 | 22 | $44 |
Casa Madrona Hotel, 801 Bridgeway (San Carlos Ave.), Sausalito, 415-331-5888
■ "The view's the thing" at this "romantic" hillside hideaway in sleepy Sausalito whose "magnificent vistas of SF and environs" (on "clear days and evenings", fogheads feel compelled to note) are a "treat for out-of-towners as well as Bay Area residents"; although the setting "supercedes the food", the seasonal Cal-Med menu is "still superb"; N.B. don't miss the Sunday brunch buffet.

Miramonte
Restaurant & Café **L S M** | – | – | – | M |
1327 Railroad Ave. (bet. Adams & Hunt Sts.), St. Helena, 707-963-1200
Mira, mira, the fountainhead of New American cooking, Cindy Pawlcyn (of Mustards Grill), is at it again at this festive newcomer; served from 10 AM till 11 PM, the menu showcases foods of the Americas, from Alaska to Argentina; the interior is decked out with multicultural accents, while a patio featuring a wood-burning oven and 100-year-old fig tree firmly roots diners in St. Helena.

Mistral **L S M** | 21 | 18 | 22 | $34 |
1229 N. Dutton Ave. (College Ave.), Santa Rosa, 707-578-4511
■ This "very wine-friendly" Santa Rosa standby has always surprised surveyors with its "fab food" and "pleasant atmosphere", especially given "its office park" setting; however, change is in the wind since founder Michael Hirschberg sailed on; new management is blowing the Mediterranean menu toward traditional French sauces and sophisticated Provençal techniques, while also re-paving the cellar with more Sonoma labels.

Mixx Restaurant **L M** | 21 | 20 | 21 | $35 |
Historic Railroad Sq., 135 Fourth St. (Davis St.), Santa Rosa, 707-573-1344
◩ In Santa Rosa's Historic Railroad Square, this Eclectic-Med garners mixxed reviews: a steady clientele finds it

"friendly" and "good enough to keep going back" (praising the "delightful desserts" and "nice bar" in particular); but naysayers nix the "uneven", "unexceptional food" and prefer to leave it for the "older (very osso buco) crowd."

Model Bakery **L** **S**   21 | 15 | 15 | $14
1357 Main St. (bet. Adams & Spring Sts.), St. Helena, 707-963-8192
■ "For a sweet treat in wine country", direct your Model T to St. Helena's "hometown haunt" where a local coffee-and-cake crowd mingles at cozy communal tables to consume a morning cup of joe and "very good baked goods"; more substantial lunch offerings include "scrumptious soups and sandwiches" served on artisanal breads and little pizzas baked in its famous brick oven.

Moosse Cafe **L** **S** **M**   22 | 19 | 21 | $32
Blue Heron Inn, 390 Kasten St. (Albion St.), Mendocino, 707-937-4323
Don't let the "casual setting" fool you – this "hidden gem" set in the ground floor of Mendocino's Blue Heron Inn "tucks great surprises into seemingly straightforward [Californian] dishes", which "are as beautiful as they are delicious"; if it's not too blustery outside, "sit on the balcony" and drink in an intoxicating view of the Pacific.

Mucca **S**   ▽ 21 | 21 | 21 | $40
Jack London Village, 14301 Arnold Dr. (north of Madrone Rd., off Hwy. 12), Glen Ellen, 707-938-3451
■ Owners Joseph Manzare and Mary Klingbell's "fun" homage to the cow (*mucca* in Italian) has fast become "a favorite" in Glen Ellen's Valley of the Moo-n; grazers warn the menu is "weighted toward carnivores" ("huge portions" of "grilled meats" and not one, but four, kinds of T-bones), but most kowtow to this "real up-and-comer" for its "superb service" and "bucolic setting" in a 1860 grist mill; N.B. dinner is served Thursday–Sunday only.

Mustards Grill **L** **S** **M**   24 | 19 | 21 | $37
7399 St. Helena Hwy./Hwy. 29 (Yount Mill Rd.), Napa, 707-944-2424
■ Founding chef-owner Cindy Pawlcyn has returned to this Napa Valley New American where her "creative and clever twists on comfort food" "continue to set the standard" for "casual wine-country dining"; "it's excessively crowded" (reservations are a must), but the staff is refreshingly "laid-back" "for such an 'in' place"; so "find a wine that you've never tasted" (from the "very good local selection") and "settle in with the Mongolian pork chop."

Napa Valley Grille **L** **S** **M**   22 | 20 | 20 | $37
Washington Sq., 6795 Washington St. (Madison St.), Yountville, 707-944-8686
◪ "Locals love" this "quiet", "comfy" Californian for its "consistently good" ("and many times inspired") wine-

country fare (in particular, the "wild game is fun"); but less-sympathetic surveyors shrug this Yountville branch of a national chain is "pleasant [but] forgettable" – with "outrageous wine prices" their only outstanding memory.

Napa Valley Wine Train 🄻🅂🄼   18 │ 23 │ 19 │ $57

1275 McKinstry St. (bet. 1st St. & Soscol Ave.), Napa, 800-427-4124

◪ For "a real moving experience" (literally), hop aboard this "unique" 1917 dining locomotive that "tours Napa Valley"; while enthusiastic engineers exclaim "the cars are beautiful and the views are pretty", a few feel railroaded, raging that the Californian fare is "what you'd expect from train food" and the"service doesn't measure up to the picturesque ride"; still, "everyone should do it once."

955 Ukiah 🅂🄼   ▽ 21 │ 19 │ 21 │ $40

955 Ukiah St. (Lansing St.), Mendocino, 707-937-1955

◪ Even armed with the address, you might not easily find this little-known "family-run" establishment "that looks like a house down a pretty garden path"; but once you do, expect "fresh" New American–French fare and a very locally oriented wine list; while many maintain it's the "best restaurant in Mendocino", others 86 it, finding the food "pedestrian" and the kitchen "unable to pull off" the more ambitious combinations.

Olema Inn 🄻🅂   20 │ 20 │ 20 │ $36

10000 Sir Francis Drake Blvd. (Hwy. 1), Olema, 415-663-9559

◼ This "romantic" resident in the Olema Inn "has always been a treat" for Point Reyes Peninsula day-trippers (particularly because there are so few "choices in the area"); however, "the recent change in ownership and chefs" "has transformed" the experience into something that's now "worth the drive" thanks to a "seasonal, innovative" New American menu ("their BBQ oysters are a must"), "renovated dining room" and a "delightful patio."

ONDINE 🅂🄼   22 │ 27 │ 23 │ $57

558 Bridgeway (Princess Ave.), Sausalito, 415-331-1133

◼ "At last, a gem on the water in Marin" exclaim enthusiasts of this "elegant" redo of a Sausalito spot; the "dramatic" dining room is "surrounded by windows overlooking the Bay, the nearby islands and the SF skyline", making it ideal for a "romantic date" or impressing out-of-towners; "elegant service" helps make "every meal a treat"; N.B. the post-*Survey* arrival of John Caputo (ex Gary Danko) and a new Med menu may outdate the food score.

Pairs 🄻🅂🄼   ▽ 23 │ 21 │ 21 │ $36

4175 Solano Ave. (Wine Country Ave.), Napa, 707-224-8464

◼ Since this "St. Helena favorite moved to Napa", its "very talented" "chef-owner brothers" are "off to a good start";

the new neighbors nod approval of the "unusual" Asian-Californian menu with wine-and-food pairings and "lovely presentations"; they've even done "a good job decorating."

Pangaea S ▽ 25 19 22 $39

250 Main St. (Eureka Hill Rd.), Point Arena, 707-882-3001
■ There's "no better place to pop open an Anderson Valley Pinot Noir and watch the water greet the land" than at this Cal-International cafe in Point Arena, the southernmost town of Mendocino County; although "hard to find, it's worth it" for the "stellar culinary creations" that make "great use of local fresh fish and veggies" – all at "reasonable prices"; N.B. serves dinner only, Wednesday–Sunday.

Parkside Cafe L S M 22 18 20 $25

43 Arenal Ave. (Hwy. 1), Stinson Beach, 415-868-1272
■ Everyone's "favorite place" in Stinson, this 1940s "beach retreat" lures locals with "excellent [American] breakfast and brunch" served all day, as are sandwiches; the picnic tables on the patio are a "great place to hang out in the afternoon", but those in a rush can snag a hot dog at the concession counter located right at the entrance to the beach.

Pasta Pomodoro L S M 15 12 15 $16

421 Third St. (Irving St.), San Rafael, 415-256-2401
See review in San Francisco Directory.

Pearl L ▽ 22 18 20 $31

1339 Pearl St. (bet. Franklin & Polk Sts.), Napa, 707-224-9161
■ "This hidden gem" in the town of Napa proper is "a local favorite" thanks to the "nicest owners" who churn out "consistent" rustic Californian cuisine with "innovative" International influences; their "warm reception" and "friendly service make up for the odd location" and "quirky decor"; ask to dine on the "comfortable [covered] patio."

Pelican Inn L S M 14 23 18 $28

Pelican Inn, 10 Pacific Way (Hwy. 1), Muir Beach, 415-383-6000
■ Hawking "ales, darts" and shepherd's pie, this authentic looking British pub offers "a little bit of England by the beach"; because it's "so damn atmospheric", guests tend to overlook the "only ok" traditional fare and stick to "a snack and a beer" on the "charming" patio "after hiking in Muir Woods"; N.B. call ahead for seasonal hours.

Piatti L S M 19 19 18 $34

625 Redwood Hwy./Hwy. 101 (Seminary Dr. exit), Mill Valley, 415-380-2525
El Dorado Hotel, 405 First St. W. (Spain St.), Sonoma, 707-996-2351
6480 Washington St. (Oak Circle), Yountville, 707-944-2070
◪ "Always dependable", this chain (born and bred in the Napa Valley but now with 15 branches) delivers "honest

Italian" fare in "pleasant" environs (often offering pretty patios for alfresco dining); however, aside from the addictive "special dipping sauce" for bread (a concoction of olive oil, balsamic vinegar, chiles, basil and garlic), "the rest of the meal is nothing to brag about" and is oft hampered by "slooow service."

Piazza D'Angelo L S M | 19 | 19 | 19 | $34 |

22 Miller Ave. (Throckmorton Ave.), Mill Valley, 415-388-2000
◪ "The place to be seen in Mill Valley", this "trendy stop" is "everything a local trattoria should be" according to angels who admire its "large variety" of "consistently good" Italian food in a "happening" though "unbelievably noisy" "atmosphere"; devils declare it "wouldn't survive anywhere but Marin" ("all looks", "mediocre" eats), but survive and thrive it does.

Pinot Blanc L S M | 22 | 23 | 22 | $49 |

641 Main St. (Grayson St.), St. Helena, 707-963-6191
◼ "You forget the world when you're dining" at celeb chef-owner Joachim Splichal's St. Helena outpost; the "visually spectacular" setting, a warren of Provençal-meets-Laura-Ashley decorated rooms (plus a "primo outside patio"), is "enhanced by gracious service"; equally "impressive" is the Cal–New French menu, "a perfect blend of familiarity and innovation", and an impressive wine list that features cult California Cabs; still, a few feel it's "a bit formal for the country" – and "a bit pricey."

PlumpJack Cafe L S M | 24 | 21 | 23 | $46 |

PlumpJack Squaw Valley Inn, 1920 Squaw Valley Rd. (Hwy. 89), Olympic Valley, 530-583-1576
See review in San Francisco Directory.

Ravenous S⊘ | 24 | – | 21 | $36 |

420 Center St. (North St.), Healdsburg, 707-431-1302
Ravenette L S⊘
117 North St. (bet. Center St. & Healdsburg Ave.), Healdsburg, 707-431-1770
◼ This "idiosyncratic" Healdsburg haunt is "never full of itself and therefore always full" of "locals who love to go" to get their fill of "terrific" "homey" Californian fare at "down-to-earth prices"; after years of fans' wondering "how they make such great food in such a tiny space", the owners recently relocated to a 1930s bungalow that sports a full bar, cozy alcoves and nearly double the seating area; N.B. the old locale now houses the lunch-only Ravenette.

Ravens, The S M | ▽ 23 | 24 | 23 | $34 |

Stanford Inn by the Sea, 44850 Comptche-Ukiah Rd. (Coast Hwy. 1), Mendocino, 707-937-5615
◼ For a "nice change of pace" when all that foie gras and barrel-oaked chardonnay starts expanding your waistband,

this "great" Vegan venture serves up an ambitious eclectic menu – from Moroccan veggie curry to pistachio-encrusted tofu – and a large organic wine list; set in a sprawling seaside resort, the lovely dining room affords "terrific views of the ocean" and Mendocino coast.

Rendezvous Inn & Restaurant S   ∇ 24 | 16 | 23 | $42

647 N. Main St. (Bush St.), Fort Bragg, 707-964-8142
■ "Kim can cook" exclaim fans of Kim Badenhobs, "a French-trained chef in Fort Bragg"; though little-known (it only serves Wednesday–Sunday), her eatery-within-an-inn makes a "wonderfully reliable" rendezvous for those craving a historic dining room and wild game dishes, and it "may become a great place" on the North Coast.

Restaurant at   24 | 26 | 24 | $53
Meadowood, The S M

Meadowood Resort, 900 Meadowood Ln. (Howell Mountain Rd., off Silverado Trail), St. Helena, 707-963-3646
■ "If you're looking for a luxury place with elegant food" and "masterful service" "in the wine country, this is it"; you'll be hard-pressed to find a more "lovely outdoor setting" (overlooking manicured golf and croquet lawns), a more "perfect [rendition] of Californian cuisine" or a more exhaustive "well-priced wine list"; the whole "dining experience" is "no more or no less than you'd expect" from a swanky St. Helena resort (and no cheaper either), "the only problem is that you have to leave at the end."

Restaurant at   22 | 20 | 20 | $44
Sonoma Mission Inn & Spa S M

Sonoma Mission Inn & Spa, 18140 Sonoma Hwy./Hwy. 12 (Boyes Blvd.), Sonoma, 707-939-2415
■ This "top-notch" Sonoma spa restaurant underwent a personal makeover last year, emerging with fresh Mission-style decor and an updated Californian menu; calorie counters can still order something "delicious" off the à la carte menu (which "takes the pain out of losing weight"), while hedonists can indulge in "excellent prix fixe menus"; the inn-pressed sigh "if I could eat here once a month (along with the treatments), I'd be in heaven."

Restaurant at   ∇ 25 | 23 | 23 | $48
Stevenswood, The S M

Stevenswood Lodge, 8211 Shoreline Hwy./Hwy. 1 (2 mi. south of Mendocino), Little River, 707-937-2810
■ What sets apart this cozy Continental nestled in a "romantic getaway" just south of Mendocino Village is the hands-on approach of up-and-coming chef Marc Dym (ex Ritz Carlton in Newport Beach), who lavishes attention on the "wonderful food" while still taking time to "check on" guests in the "intimate [36-seat] dining room"; toss in a "romantic" fireplace, "great wine list" and "elegant service"

and you see why locals consider it "a coastal treasure"; N.B. days of operation vary, so call ahead to check.

Restaurant 301 S M

▽ 23 | 20 | 23 | $37

The Carter House, 301 L St. (3rd St.), Eureka, 707-444-8062

■ "Eureka!" exclaim enthusiasts who make the five-hour trek up the coast only to "discover" "a restaurant of this high caliber" near the Redwood National Forest; the "creative", seasonally driven New French–New American cuisine includes local seafood and vegetables grown in the surrounding gardens; but the hallmark here is the 2,500 wine cellar that fans feel is "better than anything you'd find in the wine country."

Rice Table S

▽ 21 | 17 | 20 | $26

1617 Fourth St. (G St.), San Rafael, 415-456-1808

■ At this "delightful" Indonesian eatery in San Rafael, everything is "very flavorful" (though "beware, some dishes are very spicy"), but the "deal of the century" is the Rice Table Dinner featuring "four courses for under $20"; the "charming owner" and his "friendly staff" "go out of their way to help with the food."

Ristorante Fabrizio L M

19 | 15 | 20 | $32

455 Magnolia Ave. (Cane St.), Larkspur, 415-924-3332

■ Host-with-the-most Fabrizio Martinelli has been pleasing Larkspur locals for 20 years at his neighborhood trattoria; there's "not much decor", but it's got "good [dare we say fab?] rustic Italian fare", a "homey feeling" and "the best price tag in Marin", prompting followers to plead "don't let this secret out"; P.S. don't miss the "fabulous lobster special" on Mondays.

Robata Grill & Sushi L S M

21 | 18 | 18 | $29

591 Redwood Hwy./Hwy. 101 (Seminary Dr. exit), Mill Valley, 415-381-8400

■ This "bustling" Japanese in Mill Valley with a pleasantly "authentic decor" is ideal for groups of diners who can't make up their minds – fish lovers will reel with delight over the "fantastic sushi" ("worth the wait"), while the good robata yaki and "great tempura" will satisfy the more squeamish; both appreciate the "fair prices" and the "very original green tea crème brûlée."

Roux

– | – | – | E

1234 Main St. (Hunt Ave.), St. Helena, 707-963-5330

Named for its *roux*-headed chef-owner (a consultant to sundry Napa Valley wineries) as well as the classic sauce thickener, this new vinous venture specializes in French–New American fare, showcased in a four-course tasting menu (with a wine-pairing option); veteran St. Helenans might recognize the spot as the site of the late Triology.

Royal Thai L S M   22 16 19 $24

610 Third St. (Grand Ave.), San Rafael, 415-485-1074
If there's better "Thai food in Marin" to be had, surveyors
certainly don't know about it, because they insist you "can't
beat" this San Rafael "old standard" for "great flavors",
"caring service" and "delightful [traditional] decor"; still,
sensitive stomachs warn "beware the medium spicy curry"
or you'll be "numb for days."

Rutherford Grill L S M   22 19 20 $32

1180 Rutherford Rd. (Hwy. 29), Rutherford, 707-963-1792
■ At this "jovial" American steakhouse in Rutherford, "the
smells alone will have you dying to get in and grab a bite"
of "the famous ribs" or "buttery rotisserie chicken"; the
"no-corkage-charge" policy is also a big lure for "real
grape guys" who hold forth at the "large busy bar"; all that,
paired with "down-to-earth service", makes this "relaxed
chain" (owned by Houston's) a "nice change from the pricey
and rich foods of Napa's gourmet" dens; P.S. reservations
aren't taken, so "the wait might be long."

Sake Tini L S M   18 13 17 $24

Bel Aire Plaza, 3900 Bel Aire Plaza (Trancas St.), Napa,
707-255-7423
■ Napa types in-the-know have noticed this newcomer
that has turned a strip-mall bowling alley into a "swinging,
hip" Asian diner and lounge; chef "Tod Kawachi of Brix
fame" cooks up a "unique menu" that ranges from bonita
flakes to burgers, from stir-fries to french fries; an erratic
entertainment schedule and late-night bar serving sake-
infused cocktails aim to make the joint a Valley hot spot,
but partiers pout the "decor is too drab for a night out."

Salute Ristorante L S M   18 20 17 $31

706 Third St. (Tamalpais Ave.), San Rafael, 415-453-7596
See review in East of San Francisco Directory.

Sam's Anchor Cafe L S M   14 21 15 $25

27 Main St. (Tiburon Blvd.), Tiburon, 415-435-4527
◪ Sun-worshipers drop anchor at this "always crowded",
80-year-old Tiburon waterside dive "to catch rays and
men" ("what the good life in California is all about", eh?);
although the interior has been "gently transformed and
upgraded", you can't beat the "God-made decor" – "drop-
dead views" of Alcatraz, Angel Island and the SF skyline;
but "stick to cocktails" and leave the "above-average
burgers" for the "seagulls to snatch up."

Sand Dollar L S M   ▽ 13 17 15 $24

3458 Shoreline Hwy./Hwy. 1 (Calle Del Mar), Stinson Beach,
415-868-0434
◪ A handful of sandy surveyors seeking a respite from
Stinson Beach comes to this casual American to "sit outside

and enjoy a beer and burger"; but most West Marinites prefer to spend their dollars elsewhere, noting that since a change of ownership, "the decor went up" but the "horrible food" and disappointing service remain; N.B. the bar stays open till 2 AM, a rarity in these sleepy parts.

Santi L S M
23 | 20 | 20 | $36

21047 Geyserville Ave. (Hwy. 101), Geyserville, 707-857-1790
■ This "splendid" nuovo-comer "hidden in" the Geyserville "hinterlands" is quite possibly the "best Italian north of the Golden Gate" Bridge; chef/co-owners Thomas Oden and Franco Dunn "can cook", and the "strong wine list" ("heavy on locals" and bottles from The Boot) is well matched to the "hearty and delicious" food; add in the "warm" taverna decor, and you've got an attractive "alternative to the snooty places in the wine country."

Scoma's L S M
20 | 18 | 18 | $35

588 Bridgeway (Princess St.), Sausalito, 415-332-9551
See review in San Francisco Directory.

Station House Café L S M
19 | 16 | 17 | $25

11180 Shoreline Hwy./Hwy. 1 (2nd St.), Point Reyes Station, 415-663-1515
■ A "gem in the wilds of West Marin", this "casual" New American cafe is a "favorite" among outdoorsy types who like to "unwind with a bucket of steamed clams or barbecued oysters after a long day on the trails at the Point Reyes Seashore"; although the "servers tend to be space cases" and the "decor a little dated", it's a vital part of the local community, especially when weekend bands entertain on "the beautiful back patio."

Stinson Beach Grill L S M
15 | 13 | 15 | $25

3465 Shoreline Hwy./Hwy. 1 (east of Fairfax Bolinas Rd.), Stinson Beach, 415-868-2002
■ One of "the only places in town", this roadside grill is as "laid-back as its namesake" seaside village; the patio is "great for sunny days after a long walk", and while the Eclectic food's a tad "nondescript", nothing beats "steamers on the way home from the beach."

St. Orres S M ≠
24 | 25 | 23 | $45

36601 Shoreline Hwy./Hwy. 1 (2 mi. north of Gualala), Gualala, 707-884-3303
■ The sudden appearance of a "wild" Russian Orthodox edifice in "the middle of nowhere" initially "draws in" travelers to this offbeat bed-and-breakfast, but chef-owner Rosemary Campiforno's "unusual" yet "fantastic" Cal creations ("polenta garnished with popcorn", "candies in the salad") are what make it "a memorable" experience; that, plus the "atmospheric" "fern-bar feeling", adds up to a delightful "North Coast secret."

SUSHI RAN 🅛🅢🅜   27 | 20 | 21 | $38

107 Caledonia St. (bet. Pine & Turney Sts.), Sausalito, 415-332-3620

■ "Attention, sushi aficionados", this "out-of-the-way Japanese" is the "best darn place in Marin" – "maybe in the entire Bay Area" – plying patrons with "melt-in-your-mouth fish", a "great variety of daring rolls" and other "fine delicacies"; although the jaded jibe it's "too much of a reservation circus", "there's a nice little wine and sake bar to wait in", and besides, it's "a haven for locals looking to get away from the tourists plaguing Sausalito."

Sushi to Dai For 🅛🅢🅜   19 | 13 | 17 | $26

869 Fourth St. (bet. Cijos St. & Lootens Pl.), San Rafael, 415-721-0392

☑ "The cute name" of this "busy" Japanese joint "says it all" to some San Rafaelites who swoon over the "exotically prepared" fish; but others say it's hardly worth dying for the "standard sushi", let alone wrestling with the crowds or the "rushed" service.

Syrah 🅛   ▽ 22 | 19 | 21 | $37

205 Fifth St. (Davis St.), Santa Rosa, 707-568-4002

■ Banking on a viticultural buzz name (syrahs are used to make Rhône Valley wines) and an urban renewal movement in Downtown Santa Rosa, this Californian-inflected French bistro opened with grape expectations and is living up to them, thanks to an "imaginative" "monthly changing menu", "good service" and "quaint atmosphere"; three guesses which varietals the wine list emphasizes.

Tastings Restaurant 🅢🅜   – | – | – | M

505 Healdsburg Ave. (Piper St.), Healdsburg, 707-433-3936

After a long day of wine you-know-what, let the pros at this modest New American show you how it's done; the hidden setting (behind a Healdsburg bank parking lot) belies the seriousness of the epicurean efforts of chef Derek McCarthy and sommelier Finn Finnegan, who collaborate on a five-course tasting menu, each dish paired with a wine from the globe-trotting list.

TERRA 🅢🅜   28 | 25 | 26 | $57

1345 Railroad Ave. (bet. Adams & Hunt Sts.), St. Helena, 707-963-8931

■ For husband-and-wife team Hiro Sone and Lissa Doumani, this "romantic restaurant" in St. Helena is a "labor of love", and surveyors are smitten after sampling the "exquisite" "medley of flavors" of the Southern French–Northern Italian fare ("did these people invent fusion?") served in "elegantly plain" surroundings; not only is dining here "a haze of incredible food, well-timed service" and a "selection of boutique wines one wouldn't have gotten to taste otherwise", it's "shockingly affordable, given the area."

Tomatina L S M
18 15 13 $20

Inn at Southbridge, 1016 Main St. (bet. Charter Oak Ave. & Pope St.), St. Helena, 707-967-9999

■ "It's all about the chicken Caesar piadine, baby" remark respondents referring to the salad-topped flatbread that's the specialty at this St. Helena pizzeria; as an "inexpensive", "informal" and "innovative Italian spiced with fun", it's an ideal place to "take the kids" or to grab "a healthy bite" on the go; however, don't expect any kind of service – "you stand in line to place your order, fast-food" style.

TRA VIGNE L S M
25 26 22 $45

1050 Charter Oak Ave. (Hwy. 29), St. Helena, 707-963-4444

■ For a taste of "Firenze in California", Italophiles make a pilgrimage to this "see-and-be-seen" "St. Helena mainstay" whose "sublime" villa-like ambiance "transports you to Tuscany" but whose "rich, flavorful seasonal" menu "epitomizes wine-country cuisine"; if you can "overlook the tourists" and sometimes "snobby waiters", travelers insist "the highlight of any Napa trip" "is to eat and drink your way through the afternoon in the courtyard."

Tuscany L S M
19 21 19 $36

1005 First St. (Main St.), Napa, 707-258-1000

◪ A "welcome addition to Napa", this Tuscan newcomer attracts an "energetic local crowd" with its "over-the-top" decor, "fun atmosphere" and "interesting" Northern Italian fare, "some of which is very good", some of which "needs work"; skeptics are waiting to see how it pans out "when the glamour has worn off", but in the meantime, the biggest downside is that they "don't take reservations" and they "need to."

Uva, Trattoria Italiana L S M
▽ 16 14 16 $27

1040 Clinton St. (Main St.), Napa, 707-255-6646

■ Although it's "not bad", "nothing except the pizzas really stands out" at this "unpretentious", "middle-of-the-road" Italian that makes its own pasta; still, many find it's a "hard-to-match value" for pricey Napa.

Wappo Bar Bistro L S M
22 20 19 $36

1226 Washington St. (Lincoln Ave.), Calistoga, 707-942-4712

■ In a true testament to "global cuisine", a meal at this "exciting" bistro "will take you from California to Vietnam to India and back"; international travelers concede while "it doesn't always work", it's "the only place to go in Calistoga on a sunny day to sit under a grapevine arbor" (the inside, by contrast, is a tad "cramped").

Willow Street Wood-Fired Pizza L S M
19 15 17 $22

812 Fourth St. (Lincoln Ave.), San Rafael, 415-453-4200
See review in Silicon Valley/Peninsula Directory.

Willow Wood Market Cafe ▮▮ ▽ | 22 | 17 | 18 | $26

9020 Graton Rd. (bet. Eddison & Ross Sts.), Graton, 707-522-8372

▪ Travelers are "surprised to discover" such "innovative food" at this "homey, funky" cafe/country store that's "pure Graton", a "hip artist community" in west Sonoma; although it "looks like a chicken house from the outside", market watchers insist it's "hard to beat for upscale" Cal-Med fare within or on the "fun, small patio" out back.

Wine Spectator Greystone ▮▮▮ | 22 | 23 | 21 | $44

Culinary Institute of America, 2555 Main St. (Deer Park Rd.), St. Helena, 707-967-1010

▪ For a "grand wine-country dining" experience, try this showcase at the CIA's St. Helena outpost; whether you sit on the patio overlooking the valley's vineyards or eat inside in "the grand old castle"-like building and "watch the chefs" at work, the Californian fare is "excellent", the "service is top-notch" and the Golden State–only wine list is "amazing"; N.B. the arrival of new chef and Food Network co-host Pilar Sanchez postdates the food rating.

Yankee Pier ▮▮▮ | 20 | 15 | 19 | $30

286 Magnolia Ave. (bet. King St. & William Ave.), Larkspur, 415-924-7676

▪ Owner Bradley Ogden's "lively" (aka "noisy") "New England seafood house" in Larkspur is "not on a pier", but its "casual" "hokey" "decor makes you feel like you're eating at a boathouse on Cape Cod"; Yankee fans concede it's a bit "pricey" for "fried food", "but it's the best you can do without flying to the East Coast"; just "beware": despite a "cheerful" staff, service is "hectic and rushed" and "the no-reservations policy means there can be quite a wait."

Zin ▮▮▮ | 22 | 18 | 19 | $34

344 Center St. (North St.), Healdsburg, 707-473-0946

▪ Familiarity breeds contentment at this "casual" spot in Healdsburg that dishes up "classy comfort food" (including a "great smoked pork chop") in a "neighborhood bar" setting where the service is friendly and everyone seems to know each other; even the "wine list" is all-American, though with such a "great selection of Zinfandels" – get the name now? – you're apt to discover something new.

zuzu ▮ | – | – | – | M

3535 Guerneville Rd. (Willowside Rd.), Santa Rosa, 707-523-4814

Seattle's husband-and-wife team John Stewart and Duskie Estes has taken over this little roadhouse (fka Willowside) outside of Santa Rosa; at press time, the dueling chefs are expected to introduce a hybrid of cooking styles – Northern Italian specialties such as steak with blue cheese ravioli (his) and playful Americana offerings like homemade Fig Newtons (hers) – that can stand up to the big, beefy Sonoma County–oriented wines.

South of San Francisco

F | D | S | C

Anton & Michel Restaurant 🄻🅂🄼 21 | 24 | 23 | $47

Mission St. (bet. Ocean & 7th Aves.), Carmel, 831-624-2406

■ For 20 years, this "Carmel institution" has lured travelers with its "gorgeous decor" and "wonderful Continental cooking"; although modernists concede there's "nothing new or exciting" about the place, there's also nothing more "peaceful" than "eating outside by the beautiful fountains."

Avanti 🄻🅂🄼 ▽ 20 | 15 | 19 | $27

Palm Ctr., 1711 Mission St. (Bay St.), Santa Cruz, 831-427-0135

◪ Boasting a large wine list and "rustic" "pastas and fish" dishes fashioned from "fresh ingredients" ("no mushy red sauce" here), this "unpretentious" spot offers "the best Italian food in Santa Cruz" avow advocates; however, "organic or not", the fare's "forgettable" to folks who can't understand "what all the fanfare is about."

Barbara's Fishtrap 🄻🅂🄼⇗ 19 | 14 | 16 | $21

281 Capistrano Rd. (Hwy. 1), Princeton by the Sea, 650-728-7049

■ Sure it's "a dive", but at least it's no tourist trap, insist day-trippers heading down the coast, who love to stop at this seafood shack "on the Princeton pier near the boats" and "grab" the "freshest fried fish and chips in the Bay Area."

Basque Cultural Center 🄻🅂 18 | 13 | 18 | $25

599 Railroad Ave. (bet. Orange & Spruce Aves.),
South San Francisco, 650-583-8091

■ Locals basque in the glow of community at this "jewel" on "the edge of industrial" South SF, where the traditional "family-style dinners" of French fare are "hearty and plentiful, the decor is dated but functional and the service is attentive"; "abundant" portions make it a "bargain."

Bittersweet Bistro 🄻🅂🄼 ▽ 23 | 20 | 20 | $41

787 Rio Del Mar Blvd. (bet. Clubhouse Dr. & Hwy. 1), Aptos,
831-662-9799

◪ Although this Aptos bistro "is noted for the best desserts from here to LA", sweethearts insist the Med-American mains are "equally fabulous" and the "wine list incredible"; but sour souls find it "too expensive" and mutter you must "take the bitter service with the wonderful sweets."

Cafe Gibraltar 🅂🄼 ▽ 27 | 18 | 23 | $29

171 Seventh St. (Hwy. 1), Montara, 650-728-9030

■ While the look is "converted gas station", the "unique" Pan-Med food at this "wonderful little find" in sleepy

Montara is "much better than you'd imagine it would be" (rock solid, we daresay), and the staff is refreshingly "friendly"; for the full effect, "sit outside" and enjoy the "great view"; locals plead "don't give away our secret", but the no-reservations policy should stave off out-of-towners.

Carmel Chop House S M — | — | — | E

5th Ave. & San Carlos St., Carmel, 831-625-1199
Chef-owner Kurt Grasing (of Grasing's Coastal Cuisine) offers Carmel this new contemporary chophouse, aided and abetted by longtime business partner and *bon vivant* radio host Narsai David; the menu features prime beef along with fresh seafood and pastas and an impressive Central and Northern Californian–oriented wine list.

Casanova L S M 22 | 23 | 22 | $46

Fifth Ave. (bet. Mission & San Carlos Sts.), Carmel, 831-625-0501
◪ Sentimentalists swoon over this 23-year-old "tradition in Carmel" where "the charm level is as high as it gets" – with two "lovely garden patios", "very good French-Italian" fare, a "fantastic wine cellar" (1,250 labels deep) and "service to please"; but the sarcastic snipe "intimate means cramped" and say, go only "if you enjoy feeling like a fleeced tourist"; N.B. Lassie lovers can lunch with their dogs on the canine-friendly patio.

Cetrella Bistro & Café S M — | — | — | M

845 Main St. (Monta Vista Ln.), Half Moon Bay, 650-726-4090
Scheduled in September to rock the sleepy coastal hollow of Half Moon Bay, this moderate rustic will showcase the coastal cuisine of France, Italy and Spain as interpreted by culinary pistol Erik Cosselmon (ex executive chef of Rose Pistola); fireplaces, an exhibition kitchen and cheese rooms add to the visuals of its 8,700-sq.-ft. historic building.

Charlie Hong Kong L S M — | — | — | I

1141 Soquel Ave. (Seabright Ave.), Santa Cruz, 831-426-5664
"Gargantuan portions of very yummy noodles" with "many choices of [organic] toppings" are the draw at this Santa Cruz Asian, although insiders suggest "take out, don't eat in", as "there's no atmosphere."

Chart House S M 17 | 19 | 19 | $36

8150 Cabrillo Hwy. (5 mi. north of Half Moon Bay), Montara, 650-728-7366
444 Cannery Row (Drake Ave.), Monterey, 831-372-3362
See review in Silicon Valley/Peninsula Directory.

Chevys Fresh Mex L S M 13 | 13 | 14 | $19

123 Crossroads Blvd. (Rio Rd.), Carmel, 831-626-0945
141 Hickey Blvd. (El Camino Real), South San Francisco, 650-755-1617
See review in San Francisco Directory.

Cielo **L S M**   ▽ 22 | 26 | 23 | $42

Ventana Inn & Spa, Hwy. 1 (30 mi. south of Carmel), Big Sur, 831-667-4242

■ Whether you're staying at the posh Ventana Inn & Spa or simply taking a "trip down the coast", time your meal "during daylight" to "sit outside on the patio" and soak up the "killer view" "overlooking Big Sur"; foodies give the kitchen "points for trying to be different" with the "diverse" Cal–New American menu and the "friendly service."

Clouds Downtown **L S M**   ▽ 19 | 19 | 21 | $32

110 Church St. (bet. Chestnut St. & Pacific Ave.), Santa Cruz, 831-429-2000

■ "As hip as it gets in Santa Cruz", this Asian-Cal draws local pols, partiers and journalists with a "captivating menu", "urbane, edgy atmosphere" and a "great bar"; but what makes folks feel like they're on cloud nine is "absolutely the warmest owner" and his "friendly, happy staff."

Club XIX **L S M**   25 | 26 | 25 | $62

The Lodge at Pebble Beach, 17 Mile Dr. (Hwy. 1), Pebble Beach, 831-625-8519

◪ Yes, "jackets are required", but this is not your father's golf-club dining room – it's "where the well-heeled go to eat fine food at Pebble Beach" and be coddled with "fine service"; with an "excellent" New French menu inspired by consulting chef Hubert Keller (of Fleur de Lys), you should "prepare to drop a fortune"; inevitably, this "decadent place" strikes some as "stiff" and "too old-fashioned."

Convivio Trattoria **S**   ▽ 24 | 20 | 21 | $37

655 Capitola Rd. (7th Ave.), Santa Cruz, 831-475-9600

■ This "lively" husband-and-wife-run trattoria in Santa Cruz wins over locals with its Cal-Italian menu (don't miss the "fabulous razor-thin pizza"), "good service" and locally oriented wine list; a wood-burning oven and rotisserie in the open kitchen adds warmth to the dining room, and Thursday night jazz makes things all the more convivio.

Covey, The **L S M**   ▽ 22 | 24 | 24 | $54

Quail Lodge Resort & Golf Club, 8205 Valley Greens Dr. (Carmel Valley Rd.), Carmel, 831-620-8860

◪ The feather in the cap of the Quail Lodge Resort is this "elegant" Carmel stalwart, dating back to 1973; while many maintain it's "not quite as good as it used to be", it remains a favorite special-occasion spot, offering a "gorgeous setting for a leisurely candlelit dinner" of Cal cuisine and Monterey County wines, supplemented by "superb service."

Crow's Nest **L S M**   16 | 21 | 17 | $32

2218 E. Cliff Dr. (7th Ave.), Santa Cruz, 831-476-4560

◪ At this recently remodeled "Santa Cruz hot spot", the surf-and-turf "food may be mediocre", but "the ambiance and view" – "overlooking the beach and the harbor" – "are not"; while some say "forget the restaurant and go upstairs for people-watching and cocktails", fans insist the patio's "heat lamps make dining outside very pleasant."

Duarte's Tavern L S M　　20　13　17　$25
202 Stage Rd. (Pescadero Rd.), Pescadero, 650-879-0464
■ "No trip down the Pacific Coast Highway is complete without a stop" at this Pescadero "institutional dive" that "reeks of Old California tradition"; the kitchen has been serving up the same "folksy" American fare since 1934, but "it's all about the artichoke or green-chile soup" and the homemade olallieberry pie.

Duck Club S M　　21　21　21　$38
Monterey Plaza Hotel & Spa, 400 Cannery Row (Wave St.), Monterey, 831-646-1700
See review in Silicon Valley/Peninsula Directory.

El Palomar L S M　　▽ 20　18　20　$22
Palomar Hotel, 1336 Pacific Ave. (Soquel Ave.), Santa Cruz, 831-425-7575
■ The "fun" Santa Cruz crowd really cooks at this "higher-end Mexican" (featuring "great fresh fish") in Downtown's Palomar Hotel; the "loud, meat-market setting" may heat things up, but the "margaritas will cool you down" and the "pretty people who work there" are the icing on *la tarta*.

Fandango L S M　　24　23　23　$40
223 17th St. (Lighthouse Ave.), Pacific Grove, 831-372-3456
■ Showcasing a "superb" Pan-Mediterranean menu and an "incredible [1,000-label] wine list", this "quaint little place" in Pacific Grove will "make you feel like you're a guest at someone's house", with a "delightful owner" and staff that "really welcomes all"; it's a "pleasant escape from the busier tourist spots of Monterey" and, judging from the jump in ratings, absolutely fandabulous.

Flying Fish Grill S M　　▽ 22　19　21　$37
Carmel Plaza, Mission St. (bet. Ocean & 7th Aves.), Carmel, 831-625-1962
■ At this "cozy" seafooder, the namesake fish hang from the ceiling while out of the "tiny kitchen" flies an "unusual Asian-Cal" cuisine, an "imaginative merge of East and West in a Carmel mall" (of all places); although a few think some dishes should be "grounded", this "nice experience" passes most surveyors' test with flying colors.

FRESH CREAM S M　　27　25　26　$56
Heritage Harbor, 99 Pacific St. (bet. Artillery & Scott Sts.), Monterey, 831-375-9798
■ After more than 20 years, this formal French standby is "still the cream of Monterey restaurants" thanks to "superb

food", "accommodating service" and a "great view" that can't be beat; be sure to "ask for a window table, as the lights of the squid boats in the Harbor provide an interesting backdrop to a romantic meal"; although a few fresh types find "that's a lot of money to look at the water", most merely moan "lovely, lovely, lovely."

Gabriella Café 🇱🇸🇲   ▽ 21 | 19 | 22 | $31
910 Cedar St. (bet. Church & Locust Sts.), Santa Cruz, 831-457-1677

⬛ While this "very Santa Cruz" cafe's name comes from the owner's daughter, the inspiration for chef James Denevan's (ex SF's Blue Plate) "healthy" yet "innovative" Cal-Ital fare springs from the bounty of the local farmers and grape growers; but while converts covet the "cozy and chatty" atmosphere, gripers grouse it's so "small and tight, you can't help but bump into your neighbor's dish, face and what-have-you."

Gayle's Bakery & Rosticceria 🇱🇸🇲 25 | 13 | 16 | $17
504 Bay Ave. (Capitola Ave.), Capitola, 831-462-1200

⬛ Savvy surveyors drive from all over to this Capitola "institution"; while some claim it's "by far the best bakery on the West Coast", huzzahs also go out to Gayle for bringing "fabulous deli fare, salads and sandwiches" – "all the fixings for a great picnic" – to "the masses"; you do have to line up "cafeteria-style" to get the goodies, but at least you can "drool over the artisanal breads" and "amazing desserts" as you wait for a seat.

Grasing's Coastal Cuisine 🇱🇸🇲 24 | 19 | 22 | $41
Sixth & Mission Sts. (opp. fire station), Carmel, 831-624-6562

⬛ "Ambitious" chef-owner Kurt Grasing's Californian eatery deals in "delicious dishes" that emphasize "fresh, seasonal local produce" and are served at "fair prices" (the "prix fixe is tops"); though "small", it's "light and airy", and its "unpretentious" "neighborhood feel" is a refreshing "addition to the less-than-exciting Carmel dining scene."

Half Moon Bay Brewing Company 🇱🇸🇲   – | – | – | M
390 Capistrano Ave. (Hwy. 1), Princeton by the Sea, 650-728-2739

A big outdoor patio with an ocean view is just one draw at Half Moon Bay's new brewpub on the block; the variety of hops (ranging from pale ale to stout) already has fans lined up before the gates of wrought-iron wheat shafts; the menu is full of standard American pub fare with a twist; N.B. look for live blues bands most weekends.

Il Fornaio 🇱🇸🇲   19 | 20 | 19 | $33
The Pine Inn, Ocean Ave. (Monte Verde), Carmel, 831-622-5100

See review in San Francisco Directory.

JoAnn's Cafe L S M ⊘   24 | 12 | 21 | $17

1131 El Camino Real (Westborough Blvd.), South San Francisco, 650-872-2810

■ "Bring a large appetite" to this South SF coffee shop where eating the "fantastic" "morning meals" is "like being home again" thanks to the staff that treats you "like family"; it's equally "amazing to watch how it runs with such small accommodations", so insiders insist "get there early" (it closes at 2:30 PM).

Koi Palace L S M   25 | 16 | 15 | $27

365 Gellert Blvd. (bet. Hickey & Serramonte Blvds.), Daly City, 650-992-9000

■ As you enter this "bustling" Daly City Chinese, the 1,500-gallon tank teeming with gilled specimens hints at the "amazing, exotic, fresh seafood" served here; but this palace is equally popular for its "varied selection" of "inventive dim sum" (beyond the "usual standards") that is so "delicate it puts some chefs in Hong Kong to shame"; "the prices may be high" and "the wait can be long, but it is well worth it" – even if it's "out of the way."

Marinus S M   ▽ 28 | 28 | 26 | $63

Bernardus Lodge, 415 Carmel Valley Rd. (Laureles Grade Rd.), Carmel, 831-658-3500

■ "'Class' is written all over this place" in Carmel Valley, where, in a "retro hunting lodge–type atmosphere", chef Cal Stamenov's "nearly flawless" Cal-French dishes are complemented by "attention to detail", "superb service" and an "impeccable" wine staff (naturally, since it's on Bernardus Winery property); of course, dining here may undo "days of [the resort's] spa and fitness treatments" – but at least your "taste buds will be doing back flips."

Mezza Luna L S M   19 | 17 | 19 | $31

459 Prospect Way (Capistrano Rd.), Princeton by the Sea, 650-728-8108

◧ Comments run half-and-half about this "oasis of Southern Italia in the South Bay"; the Luna-struck claim that dining at this "charming trattoria" in the tiny historical town of Princeton is "like eating with an Italian family" – what with the "very attentive" (and very accented) waiters and "reasonably priced" "authentic" standards; however, the disenchanted dis the "pretty cheesy looking" interior and "so-so" fare.

Montrio L S M   23 | 21 | 22 | $42

414 Calle Principal (Franklin St.), Monterey, 831-648-8880

■ Located in a "fun setting" – a restored turn-of-the-century firehouse "away from the touristy wharf" – this Monterey "hot spot" (owned by the folks behind Rio Grill and Tarpy's Roadhouse) serves up a "creative" eclectic menu that mines the culinary repertoires of France, Italy and the Mediterranean for inspiration; "an interesting wine list" and "friendly staff" complete the experience.

Moss Beach Distillery L S M   15 21 16 $30
Beach Way & Ocean Blvd. (off Hwy. 1), Moss Beach, 650-728-5595

� "Amazingly romantic", this 1927 Moss Beach landmark "overlooking the Pacific" is most popular as a place "to snuggle under blankets on the deck" and watch the sun set into the sea; although debated, the "casual" American fare, e.g. calamari and cold beer, has improved in the last year and is always "good value"; N.B. it's rumored the place has its own ghost, but so far none of our surveyors has had the pleasure of making her acquaintance.

Navio L S M   – – – VE
Ritz-Carlton Hotel, 1 Miramonte Point Rd. (Hwy. 1), Half Moon Bay, 650-712-7000

With picture windows looking over Half Moon Bay, this large dining room in the recently opened Ritz-Carlton retreat is the spot for primo Pacific Ocean views; the seafood-oriented menu from chef Brian Bistrong (ex NY's Bouley Bakery) pairs with a California wine list; N.B. reservations are a must to get past the guard at the resort's entrance.

Nepenthe L S M   15 26 17 $29
Hwy. 1 (¼ mi. south of Ventana Inn & Spa), Big Sur, 831-667-2345

■ Situated on arguably the "most beautiful place on earth" affording "dramatic" vistas of the "misty cliffs of Big Sur for as far as you can see", the Coast's most famous and "fun" dive was once purchased "as a love nest for Orson Welles and Rita Hayworth"; the "average and overpriced food" (burgers and fries) is almost "beside the point", because no "visit to the area" is complete "without stopping for lunch" (or at the very least a drink on the terrace) and shooting a few "rolls of film."

Omei L S M   ▽ 24 14 17 $26
2316 Mission St. (King St.), Santa Cruz, 831-425-8458

■ "Oh my, it is so good" scream "surprised" surveyors, even though we told them not to be "fooled by the strip-mall setting" of this Santa Cruz Chinese; they agree that the "artfully presented and innovative" fare is some of the "best" they've "ever eaten"; "college-town service" and "not-much-to-look-at" decor do "leave a lot to be desired" – but "hey, we're here for the food."

Oswald's S   ▽ 26 19 23 $42
1547 Pacific Ave. (Cedar St.), Santa Cruz, 831-423-7427

■ This "sweet little place" "hidden" from the street "may be the best restaurant in Santa Cruz", thanks to "fabulous everything" – from the "consistently stellar" renditions of

Californian and European standards (think chocolate soufflé) to the welcoming owner to the "quaint building."

PACIFIC'S EDGE 🆂🅼   26 | 29 | 25 | $63 |
Highlands Inn, 120 Highland Dr. (Hwy. 1), Carmel, 831-622-5445

■ Voted the *Survey*'s No. 1 for Decor, courtesy of its "unparalleled view of the coast", this Carmel Highlander is "a must" whether you need a "romantic spot" or a place "for impressing business associates"; if the Californian–New French cuisine doesn't quite "keep up with the world-class" vista, it's still "beyond spectacular" (and the "prix fixe dinner with wine is gastronomic ecstasy"); expertly "courteous service" and an "impressive vino list" make this "a dining experience not to be missed."

Pasta Moon 🅻🆂🅼   23 | 18 | 20 | $35 |
315 Main St. (Mill St.), Half Moon Bay, 650-726-5125

■ Amici are over the moon when it comes to the "great pastas" and "inventive pizzas" that are "so much better than they expect from a small casual [Half Moon Bay] cafe"; the Italian eats "eclipse" the service, which, though often "caring", can also be "inattentive."

Pearl Alley Bistro 🅻🆂🅼   ▽ 24 | 21 | 21 | $35 |
110 Pearl Alley (Cedar St.), Santa Cruz, 831-429-8070

■ Alley cats strut over to this "always crowded" Santa Cruz bistro; change is a constant on the Eclectic menu that "features a different country's cuisine every month", but you can always rely on the "professional staff" and the "great" wine list (featuring selections like Wascally Wieslings and Can We Be Franc?) to keep things "fun."

Piatti 🅻🆂🅼   19 | 19 | 18 | $34 |
Sixth & Junipero Aves., Carmel, 831-625-1766
See review in North of San Francisco Directory.

Rio Grill 🅻🆂🅼   22 | 19 | 20 | $36 |
Crossroads Shopping Ctr., 101 Crossroads Blvd. (Rio Rd.), Carmel, 831-625-5436

◪ Judging from the lines, it's rio-lly clear that this "adorable" "Carmel hot spot" "has got the formula down pat" – "bold and assertive" Cal-Southwestern cooking, "truck-driver portions", a "jolly atmosphere" and "moderate prices"; while old-timers wax "what was [once] inventive is now tired" (and still "noisy"), most find it a welcome "alternative" to the "expensive" and "formal" dining spots of the area.

Robert's Bistro 🅻🆂🅼   ▽ 23 | 23 | 24 | $47 |
Crossroads Shopping Ctr., 217 Crossroads Blvd. (Rio Rd.), Carmel, 831-624-9626

■ "This could be Provence" fawn Francophile fans of chef-owner Robert Kincaid's "cozy romantic bistro" in Carmel, where a "warm friendly" staff serves "superlative", if somewhat "old-fashioned", French cuisine.

Roy's at Pebble Beach L S M 25 | 26 | 24 | $47
The Inn at Spanish Bay, 2700 17 Mile Dr. (Congress Rd.), Pebble Beach, 831-647-7423
■ "Open your eyes and you are in Hawaii" when you hit this Pebble Beach "mecca for relaxed dining"; culinary empire-builder "Roy Yamaguchi trains his chefs well", and the result is "exciting" Euro-Asian cuisine ("every morsel's a treasure to behold") that "doesn't disappoint" regular Roy-goers; of course, it doesn't hurt that there's a "view you can stare at forever", making this "a must at sunset."

Sardine Factory S M 22 | 22 | 22 | $44
701 Wave St. (Prescott Ave.), Monterey, 831-373-3775
■ For over 30 years, this seafood stalwart on historic Cannery Row has "maintained its status as one of the best in Monterey", thanks to "exceptional service" and "great fish"; outside offers the Bay views immortalized by John Steinbeck, while the interior contains a passel of fanciful interiors (from an "elegant" glass-domed gazebo to a Barbary Coast–like Captain's Room); even if it is "touristy" and charges incredibly "high prices", "you have to go once"; N.B. the 1,300-deep wine list is a novel unto itself.

Shadowbrook L S M – | – | – | M
1750 Wharf Rd. (Capitola Rd.), Capitola, 831-475-1511
Getting to this Continental-American institution perched on a hillside high above Capitola-by-the-Sea takes time, but the "tram ride to the restaurant is fun"; once there, the "stunning environment" of its old wooden house, surrounded by gardens on the banks of the Soquel Creek, is augmented by "great food and service" and live jazz; small wonder it's been a "very popular meeting place" since 1947.

Sierra Mar L S M ▽ 29 | 29 | 28 | $69
Post Ranch Inn, Hwy. 1 (30 mi. south of Carmel), Big Sur, 831-667-2800
■ Life doesn't get much better than sitting "on the edge of the world" and "living the high life" here at this swank eatery in Post Ranch Inn; while the "unbelievable views" of the Pacific Ocean make this "the most gorgeous dining room on the West Coast" and the 4,000-bottle "superlative wine list" is equally awe-inspiring, the "imaginative" Cal-French "food matches them both"; for the ultimate experience, just make sure to "get there before dark."

Stillwater Bar & Grill L S M ▽ 21 | 25 | 21 | $49
The Lodge at Pebble Beach, 17 Mile Dr. (Hwy. 1), Pebble Beach, 831-625-8524
◪ Golfers gush "you must have lunch at a window table overlooking the 18th hole" at this casual Pebble Beach

grill; but while they go on about the "good seafood", the skeptical snap "thank goodness for the setting, because the fare is nothing special" and "overpriced" as well.

Stokes Adobe 🅛🅢🅜 24 | 23 | 22 | $41

500 Hartnell St. (bet. Madison & Polk Sts.), Monterey, 831-373-1110

■ There's a lot for surveyors to be stoked about at this "lovely spot in Downtown Monterey": chef Brandon Miller's Mediterranean-inspired "Californian cuisine is cooked and served with flair", the 1833 "remodeled adobe" "building itself is quite impressive" and the "service couldn't be better"; although it lacks the "fancy trappings of the more expensive restaurants" of the region, admirers assert this is "probably the best."

Tarpy's Roadhouse 🅛🅢🅜 22 | 21 | 21 | $39

2999 Monterey-Salinas Hwy. (Canyon Del Rey Blvd.), Monterey, 831-647-1444

■ This "goofy" yet "friendly" "off-the-beaten-path" Cal-American roadhouse near the Monterey airport offers travelers a "cool location" for refueling; insiders suggest "stick to the comfort food that sticks to your ribs" and "sit on the patio" (the "planes overhead add to the charm").

Silicon Valley/Peninsula

F	D	S	C

Acorn, The LSM
18 | 17 | 19 | $36

1906 El Camino Real (Watkins Ave.), Atherton, 650-853-1906
◪ This longtime Atherton family-run "standby" still dishes up "well-executed" Mediterranean fare with "solid service" according to admirers; but former fans deride the "dated menu" and the "stuffy and staid" atmo of a place that's a "shadow of what it used to be."

Amber India LSM
25 | 19 | 20 | $28

Olive Tree Shopping Ctr., 2290 W. El Camino Real (Rengstorff Ave.), Mountain View, 650-968-7511
■ Diners don't mind that this "gem of a Peninsula" place is buried in a Mountain View strip mall; they just go for the "best Indian food, period" (including "unusual regional dishes") accompanied by "smart decor" and "professional service"; P.S. the "fantastic lunch buffet" is worth the "wait with Silicon Valley geeks."

Amici's East Coast Pizzeria LSM
18 | 11 | 16 | $16

790 Castro St. (High School Way), Mountain View, 650-961-6666
226 Redwood Shores Pkwy. (Twin Dolphin Dr.), Redwood City, 650-654-3333
69 E. Third Ave. (bet. El Camino Real & San Mateo Dr.), San Mateo, 650-342-9392
See review in San Francisco Directory.

Andale Taqueria LSM
19 | 12 | 12 | $12

6 N. Santa Cruz Ave. (Main St.), Los Gatos, 408-395-4244
21 N. Santa Cruz Ave. (Main St.), Los Gatos, 408-395-8997
209 University Ave. (bet. Emerson & Ramona Sts.), Palo Alto, 650-323-2939
"Burritos can become a weekly dietary staple" when they come from this "Mexican food chain", a series of "quick" counter-service joints where "everything is made from scratch" and is "a bargain" to boot; the popularity of the "healthy", "convenient, cheap eats" means it can be "hard to find a table sometimes."

Applewood Inn LSM
22 | 12 | 14 | $17

227 First St. (bet. Main & State Sts.), Los Altos, 650-941-9222
1001 El Camino Real (Menlo Ave.), Menlo Park, 650-324-3486
Applewood 2 Go SM
989 El Camino Real (Menlo Ave.), Menlo Park, 650-328-1556
903 El Camino Real (Castro St.), Mountain View, 650-940-1207
■ "Everyone finds something they love" at these den-like pie shops, whose "fantastic plump pizzas" come equipped

"with cool toppings" and "unbeatable crusts", plus a "good German beer selection" to wash it all down with.

A.P. Stump's 🄻🅂🄼　　24　24　22　$46
163 W. Santa Clara St. (bet. Almaden Blvd. & San Pedro St.), San Jose, 408-292-9928

■ This "upscale" sophisticate is "one of the tops in San Jose" say surveyors who stump for its "creative" Cal–New American "food cooked to perfection", "fantastic wine menu" and "exceptional service"; with "impressive decor" and "live jazz" Tuesday–Saturday imparting an air of "casual elegance", it's small wonder some sigh "too bad it's so far from SF" (though that doesn't stop "regulars, convention visitors and hockey fans" from crowding in).

Aqui Cal-Mex Grill 🄻🅂🄼　　22　17　16　$17
1145 Lincoln Ave. (bet. Minnesota Ave. & Willow St.), San Jose, 408-995-0381

■ "Funky" "Cal-Mex food with all the flavor and none of the fat" – along with margaritas from the "great tequila bar" – is the big "bang-for-the-buck" attraction of this Willow Glen "local favorite"; admittedly, it's a "casual" operation, but the "self-service is no problem"; amigos do advise sitting on the "sunny patio" to avoid the sometimes "noisy" interior.

Armadillo Willy's 🄻🅂🄼　　19　13　15　$18
10100 S. De Anza Blvd. (Stevens Creek Blvd.), Cupertino, 408-252-7427
1031 N. San Antonio Rd. (El Camino Real), Los Altos, 650-941-2922
878 Blossom Hill Rd. (Santa Teresa Blvd.), San Jose, 408-224-7427
Camden Park Plaza, 2071 Camden Ave. (Union Ave.), San Jose, 408-371-9033
995 Saratoga Ave. (Williams Rd.), San Jose, 408-255-7427
2260 Bridgepointe Pkwy. (Mariners Island Blvd.), San Mateo, 650-571-7427
2624 Homestead Rd. (San Tomas Expy.), Santa Clara, 408-247-1100
161 E. El Camino Real (Sunnyvale Saratoga Rd.), Sunnyvale, 408-245-5300

■ When the urge for "succulent ribs" hits, head to this local chain serving "belly-busting BBQ" and "authentic, hot smoked meats", accompanied by a "peanut cole slaw that sounds awful but is great"; being "very casual", this "dependable" stand is also "easy with kids."

A Tavola 🄻🅂🄼　　20　18　19　$33
716 Laurel St. (bet. Cherry & Olive Sts.), San Carlos, 650-595-3003

◪ Supporters call this San Carlos sibling of Nola and Mistral "completely underrated" for its "superb Italian classics" and eclectic Fusion fare (especially the "top-notch appetizers") served in a "cool yet comfortable" setting; but opponents observe a service "meltdown on busy nights", when the scene is "overcrowded with yuppies."

¡Ay Ay Ay! L M ▽ 19 | 15 | 19 | $22

301 State St. (2nd St.), Los Altos, 650-941-8226

◪ Fans favor this "fun Mexican" for "fresh and good ingredients" served in "large portions" on a "beautiful courtyard" in Downtown Los Altos, while snipers snarl the spot's "sub-par", with "prices way too high" for a cuisine with "no creativity"; even the simpatico say "eat outside or don't go."

Azuma Japanese Cuisine L S M ▽ 21 | 16 | 17 | $25

19645 Stevens Creek Blvd. (bet. Portal Ave. & Wolfe Rd.), Cupertino, 408-257-4057

■ "25-plus years of consistent quality and fair prices" keep Cupertino citizens coming to this "very authentic" Japanese where "big portions of sashimi" and "great sukiyaki" are faves; a few feel the traditional, tatami-booth "decor needs an upgrade."

Baccarat S M – | – | – | VE

Hotel Sofitel, 223 Twin Dolphin Dr. (Shoreline Dr.), Redwood City, 650-598-9000

Savvy Silicon Valleyites are betting that the recent arrival of executive chef Eric Truglas (ex Soleil) will turn this Redwood City veteran into a high roller; the new Provençal menu, featuring sea bass in Burgundy sauce and Grand Marnier soufflé, is served in an elegant dining room that caters to Hotel Sofitel business travelers by day and – thanks to its views of lights sparkling over the lagoon – romantics at night.

Baja Fresh Mexican Grill L S M 20 | 10 | 12 | $10

20735 Stevens Creek Blvd. (De Anza Blvd.), Cupertino, 408-257-6141
3990 El Camino Real (Arastradero Rd.), Palo Alto, 650-424-8599
Bernal Rd. Shopping Ctr., 117 Bernal Rd. Shopping Ctr. (Santa Teresa Blvd.), San Jose, 408-363-9400
1708 Old Oakland Rd. (Brokaw Rd.), San Jose, 408-436-5000

■ "Cheap and yummy" eats pack 'em in to the Peninsula outposts of this national "Mexican fast-food" chain where "wonderful fish tacos" ("even if you never liked them elsewhere") and "tasty salsa" provide "excellent value", especially for "lunch with kids."

Bandera S M 20 | 19 | 19 | $31

233 Third St. (Main St., off San Antonio Rd.), Los Altos, 650-948-3524

■ It's "not gourmet" and the service is "not so quick", but a menu of "super rotisserie chicken", "yummy ribs" and "great cornbread" keeps folks flocking to this "fun hangout", situated in a Los Altos Craftsman-style bungalow; although it's "kinda pricey", the "huge portions" ensure you'll make out like bandits.

Beauséjour **L S M**   ▽ 20 | 23 | 20 | $36

170 State St. (bet. 3rd & 4th Sts.), Los Altos, 650-948-1382
◪ Those seeking a sojourn are enamored of the "quiet, small" rooms that comprise this central Los Altos veteran, "patronized by senior citizens" for its "consistent" French fare ("the duck is as excellent as ever") and service; however, dissenters deem this "dowdy" dining experience "disappointing given its reputation."

Bella Luna **L S M**   17 | 17 | 17 | $28

233 University Ave. (bet. Emerson & Ramona Sts.), Palo Alto, 650-322-1846
◪ Among Luna-tics, this "charming little Italian bistro in Palo Alto" wins praise for "consistently good" cuisine ("out-of-sight" pasta), while the less moonstruck mope that the "non-memorable dishes" are "nothing special"; all agree the setting is "very pretty."

Bella Mia **L S M**   19 | 19 | 19 | $31

58 S. First St. (Willow St.), San Jose, 408-280-1993
■ "Get a seat upstairs" at this "straight-up Italian in Downtown San Jose", located in a "great old building" that's "good for big parties" ("watch for wedding receptions") and "business dinners"; and if some find the food a tad "tired", there's always "nice dining on the patio."

Bella Vista **M**   21 | 24 | 23 | $45

13451 Skyline Blvd. (5 mi. south of Rte. 92), Woodside, 650-851-1229
■ It's "worth the drive" to this "charming" Continental up the Santa Cruz Mountains near Woodside – an "awesome" location that's "spectacular on a fogless night"; most feel "the great view doesn't redeem food" that's "overpriced" and "only ok", but service that's "attentive without being annoying" and "warmth from the wood-burning fires" make "a nice retreat" for romantics and "out-of-towners."

Bistro Elan **L**   25 | 19 | 21 | $41

448 California Ave. (El Camino Real), Palo Alto, 650-327-0284
■ "The best-kept secret in Palo Alto" converts call this "sophisticated" bistro whose "fresh and creative" Cal-French fare, including "fantastic foie gras", "stands out" – especially when paired with the "good selection of wines by the glass" and served with elan by "friendly staff"; the "outdoor patio's a haven" for "the perfect long lunch."

Bistro Vida **L S**   20 | 20 | 21 | $32

641 Santa Cruz Ave. (El Camino Real), Menlo Park, 650-462-1686
◪ Passions run high over this Menlo Park French, a "typical 'in' spot" with a "most cordial host" presiding over

"intimate ambiance" enhanced by red walls; while patrons pack in for "good", "unpretentious bistro food" (it's "gotten more crowded lately"), skeptics shy away from the "tired menu" ("*frites* that are as flaccid as Bob Dole sans Viagra"), saying "just go to Left Bank" up the block.

Blue Chalk Cafe L M   15 | 15 | 15 | $26
630 Ramona St. (bet. Forest & Hamilton Aves.), Palo Alto, 650-326-1020

◪ When "Silicon Valley happy hour" arrives, this huge "hopping bar" in a 1927 Downtown Palo Alto landmark is "a place to go if you like dot-com" crowds and can "stick to the pool tables"; but while some find the Cajun/Creole "food is actually good", the "so-so" menu and "loud, loud, loud" scene chalk up few points with others, who sniff that BCC stands for "Blah Chump Cafe."

British Bankers Club L S M   12 | 16 | 12 | $23
1090 El Camino Real (Santa Cruz Ave.), Menlo Park, 650-327-8769

■ Menlo Park yuppies and singles "meet and greet" at this "basic burger bar" for a "great happy hour", attracted by the "patio and beer selection" in a "fun atmosphere"; but most agree the Eclectic "food and service don't match up to the surroundings."

Buca di Beppo S M   15 | 18 | 17 | $23
Pruneyard Shopping Ctr., 1875 S. Bascom Ave. (Campbell Ave.), Campbell, 408-377-7722
643 Emerson St. (bet. Forest & Hamilton Aves.), Palo Alto, 650-329-0665 L

■ "Mamma mia" sigh supporters of the Peninsula's "perennial birthday spot", a "good, cheap" Southern Italian duo that leaves customers "happily and painfully stuffed" from "gargantuan" family-style portions; "bring a sense of kitsch" to appreciate the "schmaltz, Sinatra and schlock" – and "bring the family" to help you clean your plate; P.S. "you have to be in the mood for noise" to enjoy it.

Buck's L S M   17 | 18 | 17 | $23
3062 Woodside Rd. (Cañada Rd.), Woodside, 650-851-8010

■ It's "worth standing in line" for a "hearty" American-style breakfast or weekend brunch at this "analog heaven for the digital crowd" in the heart of Woodside; "venture-capitalist groupies" and "local regulars" can also lunch or dine on "straightforward food served with whimsy" amid a "collector's paradise" of knickknacks crammed into every nook and cranny (just "don't trip over the dinosaur toys").

Cafe Borrone L S M   18 | 17 | 15 | $15
1010 El Camino Real (bet. Ravenswood & Santa Cruz Aves.), Menlo Park, 650-327-0830

■ Look to this "European-style cafe", "a Menlo Park mainstay", to see the beautiful people "hanging out" on "great patio seats"; the "lively young atmosphere" is always "bustling with students and a range of ages" sipping "frosted mochas to die for" and munching Californian "reasonable light meals" and "homemade desserts"; reading selections from the "fantastic book store next door" is de rigueur.

Cafe Brioche L S M   23 | 18 | 19 | $30

445 California Ave. (El Camino Real), Palo Alto, 650-326-8640
■ Though it's not brand-new, Palo Altans have recently made a "great discovery" of this "hidden diamond", a "small bistro that really cares about food"; "eating on the sidewalk", "great French onion soup" and Provençal "specials on the chalkboard" all add up to a spot that "feels like a bit of Europe"; small wonder it "fills up fast at lunch" and at "excellent brunch."

Café Marcella L S   23 | 18 | 22 | $39

368 Village Ln. (Santa Cruz Ave.), Los Gatos, 408-354-8006
◪ A "favorite" with the "CEO and VC crowd", this Provençal–Northern Italian packs 'em into its "fun, happy setting" with "great fish", "delicious pastas, pizzas and desserts" and "excellent, subtle service"; and if some say standards have "relaxed a bit", most maintain it's still "Los Gatos' best" – even if the "city buzz" makes it "too noisy to sustain a conversation."

Café Niebaum-Coppola L S M   16 | 22 | 15 | $33

473 University Ave. (bet. Cowper & Kipling Sts.), Palo Alto, 650-752-0350
◪ The latest in SV star power – Francis Ford Coppola's Southern Italian store-cafe-wine bar in Palo Alto – draws mixed reviews; fans give two thumbs-up to the "surprisingly good, fresh" food and "beautiful" setting filled with culinary and cinematic merchandise, while critics urge "stick to his movies" ("the kitchen needs help").

Cafe Prima Vera L   ▽ 21 | 18 | 19 | $33

Cornerstone Shopping Ctr., 15970 Los Gatos Blvd. (Blossom Hill Rd.), Los Gatos, 408-356-4902 S M
303 Almaden Blvd. (San Carlos St.), San Jose, 408-795-1200 M
1359 Lincoln Ave. (Minnesota Ave.), San Jose, 408-297-7929
Tech Museum of Innovation, 201 S. Market St. (Park Ave.), San Jose, 408-885-1094 S M
■ Its prima variety of "very good" Cal-Med "casual meals" characterizes this "upscale" San Jose chain; customers consider the "surprisingly lovely decor" conducive to "intimate" dining, even if prices are "getting expensive."

Cafe Pro Bono L S M   – | – | – | E

2437 Birch St. (California Ave.), Palo Alto, 650-326-1626
As the prices attest, nothing's for free at this "cozy nook"; nonetheless, this Italian-Med standby manages to please

Palo Alto's corporate lunchtime crowd; the signature Susan's Downfall – cheese-filled raviolis with almond sauce – is everyone's downfall.

Cafe Silan L S M   ▽ 18 14 16 $19

867 Santa Cruz Ave. (bet. Evelyn St. & University Dr.), Menlo Park, 650-326-5404

▨ This "small and casual" Menlo Parker has an "exotic" appeal for adventurous souls wanting to try "authentic" and "cheap" Kurdish cuisine; but naysayers name it a "major disappointment", and even advocates admit the "emphasis is on the food, not the decor or service."

Café Torre L M   20 16 20 $34

St. Joseph Pl. Shopping Ctr., 20343 Stevens Creek Blvd. (bet. De Anza Blvd. & Torre Ave.), Cupertino, 408-257-2383

■ It's "worth a trip" to this "charming" cafe off-the-beaten-path in Cupertino – "ok, it's in a strip mall" – for "wonderful Cal-Italian" fare (including "sumptuous mussels" and "humungous pasta portions") and "superb" wine bar offerings by the glass or flight (a "nifty idea for tasting and comparing"); but even boosters wish for a "bigger, more gracious locale."

Caffe Riace L S M   21 21 21 $33

200 Sheridan Ave. (bet. Birch St. & Park Blvd.), Palo Alto, 650-328-0407

■ "It is like having dinner with the family" at this hidden Palo Alto "slice of Italy", where "fresh creative entrees" exemplify the "terrific Sicilian" cuisine (you "can't beat the cannelloni" or the "fairly priced wines"); since it's so "pretty outside with the fountains", regulars recommend dining alfresco versus "squeezing into a tiny space" inside.

California Cafe Bar & Grill L S M   19 19 19 $32

Old Town Shopping Ctr., 50 University Ave. (Main St.), Los Gatos, 408-354-8118
Stanford Barn, 700 Welch Rd. (Quarry Rd.), Palo Alto, 650-325-2233
Valley Fair Shopping Ctr., 2855 Stevens Creek Blvd. (I-280), Santa Clara, 408-296-2233

■ This Bay Area chain has hit on a "tried-and-true formula that works" – offering "dependable" (what else?) Cal fare (like a "superb" version of the ubiquitous Chinese chicken salad) and "friendly service" in "classy and kid-friendly" digs; shopaholics say the setup is "better than what you usually find in a mall" (where they're often located), but convenience aside, there's "no other reason to step in."

Camranh Bay L S M   19 17 16 $26

201 E. Third Ave. (Ellsworth Ave.), San Mateo, 650-342-7577

▨ "Lovely floor-to-ceiling streetside windows" are just one draw at this Downtown San Mateo "white-tablecloth

Vietnamese" say supporters who lap up the "light, refined" "consistent Southeast Asian food"; critics call it "a place to be seen, not eat", baying about "bland" fare; still, it's "fun with friends", and the Thursday night jazz "is a definite plus."

Capellini L S M　　20　20　20　$32
310 Baldwin Ave. (B St.), San Mateo, 650-348-2296
■ "What a bargain" sing surveyors of this "underrated" San Mateo "meaty Northern Italian" whose "classy", "warm, inviting decor" inspires arias to "tasty bread" and "luscious" grilled fare; though a minority mutters the "noise level detracts from the experience", they're drowned out by those who feel "the food makes it worth it."

Carpaccio L S M　　20　19　19　$34
1120 Crane St. (Santa Cruz Ave.), Menlo Park, 650-322-1211
■ "You can always rely on a good affordable meal" at this "old-style Northern Italian", a "quiet, elegant neighborhood [Menlo Park] establishment" staffed by "personable, efficient servers"; admittedly, it seems like "nothing's ever new on the menu", but its classics are still "hard to beat."

Chantilly L M　　25　24　24　$50
3001 El Camino Real (Selby Ln.), Redwood City, 650-321-4080
◪ "High rollers celebrate" in the "dignified atmosphere" of Redwood City's "elegant" "event place" that's "a real winner" in its "beautiful new space"; though always "good for a business dinner", this French–Northern Italian also works whenever you want a "great experience in dining" fans feel – even if young bloods "yawn" the "tired and dated menu" is intended for "the older set."

Chart House S M　　17　19　19　$36
115 N. Santa Cruz Ave. (bet. Bean Ave. & Grays Ln.), Los Gatos, 408-354-1737
◪ The starry-eyed chart a course for the "romantic setting" of this steakhouse/seafooder, housed in a Los Gatos Victorian mansion ("ask to sit in the turret"), whose "good-sized portions" equal a "good value"; but skeptics steer clear, arguing that the food is "a little inconsistent" and the overall experience "overrated."

Chef Chu's L S M　　21　16　19　$26
1067 N. San Antonio Rd. (El Camino Real), Los Altos, 650-948-2696
■ "For 30 years", this Los Altos "good old standby" has set "the gold standard" in Silicon Valley for "fresh Chinese cuisine with a California influence", and if there's a touch of the "tourist trap" about it, "attentive service" helps keep it a "family favorite."

Chevys Fresh Mex 🅻🆂Ⓜ

13 | 13 | 14 | $19

*979 Edgewater Blvd. (bet. Beach Park Blvd. &
Port Royal Ave.), Foster City, 650-572-8441*
*2116 W. El Camino Real (Rengstorff Ave.), Mountain View,
650-691-9955*
*2907 El Camino Real (bet. Jefferson Ave. & Wilson St.),
Redwood City, 650-367-6892*
5305 Almaden Expy. (Blossom Hill Rd.), San Jose, 408-266-1815
1502 Saratoga Ave. (Atherton Ave.), San Jose, 408-871-9110
550 S. Winchester Blvd. (Moorpark Ave.), San Jose, 408-241-0158
204 S. Mathilda Ave. (Washington Ave.), Sunnyvale, 408-737-7395
See review in San Francisco Directory.

CHEZ TJ

26 | 23 | 25 | $63

*938 Villa St. (bet. Castro St. & Shoreline Blvd.), Mountain View,
650-964-7466*
■ Life's "really quite wonderful" at this "intimate", "romantic" dining destination tucked away in Mountain View; unafraid to "sometimes miss", "adventurous chef" Kirk Bruderer leads patrons through "outstanding" New French–New American prix fixe dinners amid the "fantastic ambiance" of a circa 1894 mansion; of course it's "very pricey" – but why carp when "everything is exquisite."

Cook's Seafood
Restaurant & Market 🅻Ⓜ

19 | 11 | 15 | $16

751 El Camino Real (Roble Ave.), Menlo Park, 650-325-0604
■ When trolling for seafood, the Menlo Park crowd finds "a treasure" at this "Gulf Coast–style" institution serving the "best fish and chips in the area", even if it is "order-at-the-counter fried food"; landlubbers "can't beat it for lunch" or "before a movie" because the fare, supplied from the adjoining fish market, is "so fresh" it lures them in.

Cool Café 🅻🆂

∇ 21 | 21 | 13 | $19

*Stanford University Cantor Arts Ctr., 328 Lomita Dr.
(Museum Way), Palo Alto, 650-725-4758*
■ The chance to "dine with Rodin" is the reason fans find Jesse Cool's latest Californian venture, located in Stanford University's Cantor Arts Center, the "best place to eat on the Peninsula" on sunny days; connoisseurs of all types admire the "artful view" of the sculpture garden while munching "great sandwiches and salads" and desserts paired with organic beers, wines and ports.

Dal Baffo 🅻Ⓜ

22 | 22 | 22 | $55

878 Santa Cruz Ave. (University Dr.), Menlo Park, 650-325-1588
■ For that "special night out", this "pricey" Menlo Park Continental – "old school and proud of it" – offers a "traditionally elegant" experience where "silky" service "complements" a "romantic setting" and "good retro cuisine"; "quiet, attentive" ambiance is augmented by

"good expensive wines" from a list that could be viewed as "too large to be usable" (1,050 labels).

Dashi L M   – | – | – | I
873 Hamilton Ave. (bet. Carlton Ave. & Willow Rd.), Menlo Park, 650-328-6868
Despite its unlikely location in a strip mall (near the Dumbarton Bridge), Sun Microsystems techies and other Menlo Parkers are already dashing over to this new, hip little Japanese; the appeal lies in the big, fresh pieces of sushi and creative rolls named after Silicon Valley towns.

Draeger's Market Bistro L S M   20 | 15 | 16 | $24
Draeger's Mkt., 1010 University Dr. (Santa Cruz Ave.), Menlo Park, 650-688-0694
◪ For "great food combined with great shopping", head to the "stylish dining room" located inside Menlo Park's gourmet grocer, where "fresh" American-Med fare fuels happy home chefs with "a tasty, [if] quick, meal"; however, the non-Market-oriented find it "noisy, pricey and crowded" ("why am I paying this much for a sandwich?").

Duck Club L S M   21 | 21 | 21 | $38
Stanford Park Hotel, 100 El Camino Real (University Dr.), Menlo Park, 650-330-2790
■ "If you love duck, you can't miss" at this "delightful surprise for a chain" (it's part of a brood hatched by Woodside Hotels); although the "wild game's the game", there's also a "varied" New American menu, "elegant atmosphere" and "good service"; P.S. the Bodega Bay and Monterey siblings feature "great views" of the coastline.

E&O Trading Co. L S M   18 | 21 | 17 | $32
96 S. First St. (San Fernando St.), San Jose, 408-938-4100
See review in San Francisco Directory.

EMILE'S   27 | 22 | 25 | $56
545 S. Second St. (bet. Reed & William Sts.), San Jose, 408-289-1960
■ "The first upscale restaurant in San Jose" remains an "old faithful" French, "nurturing longtime patrons with its atmosphere and delightful menus"; "no frills or pretense" here, "just perfect ingredients impeccably prepared" (don't miss "one of the world's finest" dessert soufflés); owner Emile Mooser, "as enthusiastic as ever", oversees the "outstanding service"; though "prices have escalated", the only question most have is "when can I go again?"

Empire Grill & Tap Room L S M   19 | 20 | 17 | $32
651 Emerson St. (bet. Forest & Hamilton Aves.), Palo Alto, 650-321-3030
■ "Have lunch in the lovely garden" command disciples of Downtown Palo Alto's "charming patio"-cum-restaurant

and bar; the pubby, "club-like atmosphere" "inside is so-so" (the "bartenders are comedians"), but the "great meat dishes" and "light meals" on the nouveau French–American menu are definitely "a notch above basic bar food."

Estampas Peruanas L S   ▽ 18 | 10 | 15 | $19

715 El Camino Real (bet. Brewster Ave. & Broadway), Redwood City, 650-368-9340

■ "If you can get over the location, you can't beat the food" at Redwood City's only Peruvian, tucked away in a modest storefront on the Peninsula's main strip-mall drag; it's a "friendly, family-oriented spot" offering "something different" in its "big portions of interesting" fish dishes.

Eulipia S   19 | 17 | 18 | $40

374 S. First St. (bet. San Carlos & San Salvador Sts.), San Jose, 408-280-6161

◪ Mixed critiques characterize this long-running San Jose Downtowner that's convenient "before or after theater"; fans "forget how good it is" for its Cal–New American cuisine ("innovative with some comfort food mixed in"), "comfortable ambiance" and "low-key" staff; but critics would rather not remember the "pricey soups and salads", "undistinguished atmosphere" and "problematic service" "if you appear to be a low-roller."

Evvia L S M   25 | 24 | 22 | $41

420 Emerson St. (bet. Lytton & University Aves.), Palo Alto, 650-326-0983

■ "Zorba would have loved this place" enthuse epicures about Palo Alto's "gourmet Greek" (sister to SF's Kokkari), a "highly addictive millionaire hot spot" that's "always a delight" thanks to a "succulent" menu that features "the Mediterranean's many treats" ("lamb never tasted so good"), a "cozy" "taverna setting" ("love that fireplace") and "enthusiastic service"; if it gets "noisy", think of it as the "ambiance reflecting the patrons' exuberance"; P.S. it's "tough to get a reservation", so take this "tip: eat at the bar."

Falafel's Drive-In L S M ⊅   – | – | – | I

2301 Stevens Creek Blvd. (bet. Bascom Ave. & I-880), San Jose, 408-294-7886

"Don't be frightened off by the non-decor" (a take-out window and a few picnic tables) at this offbeat San Jose stand marked by a funky retro sign; the drive-in offers falafel "to die for", especially when topped with the specialty spicy sauce; shakes and fries are must-tries too.

Faultline Brewing Company L M   16 | 17 | 16 | $27

1235 Oakmead Pkwy. (bet. Lakeside Dr. & Lawrence Expy.), Sunnyvale, 408-736-2739

■ A dot-com crowd heads to this "fun, noisy" "brewery in the heart of Silicon Valley" to meet "hip geeks after work";

located in an "unassuming Sunnyvale neighborhood", the patio is also a "good place to go with friends" for "consistent" Californian cuisine and homemade beers.

Faz ⬛S🅼   18 | 19 | 17 | $32

1108 N. Mathilda Ave. (Moffett Park Dr., off Hwy. 237), Sunnyvale, 408-752-8000
See review in San Francisco Directory.

Fiesta del Mar ⬛S🅼   ▽ 21 | 14 | 16 | $19

1005 Shoreline Blvd. (Terra Bella Ave.), Mountain View, 650-965-9354

Fiesta del Mar Too ⬛S🅼

735 Villa St. (Castro St.), Mountain View, 650-967-3525
◼ For "wonderful, authentic Mexican" munchies in Mountain View, amigos head to these offbeat eateries, consuming "good margaritas" and "great shrimp dishes" amid a literal fiesta of bright colors and knickknacks from south of the border; food "that's not too heavy" is the draw, even when it's "crowded on weekends."

Flea St. Café ⬛S   23 | 19 | 19 | $37

3607 Alameda de las Pulgas (Avy Ave.), Menlo Park, 650-854-1226
◼ Reviewers rave about owner Jesse Cool's "awesome organic" New American–Californian cuisine, served since 1982 in this Menlo Park location; the "fresh seasonal" approach, "put together in eclectic and rustic styles", is "simple but sophisticated", and while "vegetarian dishes are great", the menu "offers everything"; the "intimate", "homey atmosphere" is "warm and wonderful" (even if "the dining rooms remind me of my Aunt Ruth's").

Fook Yuen ⬛S🅼   23 | 12 | 15 | $26

195 El Camino Real (Millbrae Ave.), Millbrae, 650-692-8600
◼ The "dim sum rocks" at this "Hong Kong–style" Chinese that's set in Millbrae (but "feels like another country"), "close enough to SFO to enjoy a true meal before or after flying"; indeed, "come in with an empty stomach" and soon "you will be on a journey" to "a great variety [at] great prices"; however, even fans find the "factory setting" can be "fast-paced" and the "service poor."

Fuki Sushi ⬛S🅼   21 | 18 | 17 | $32

4119 El Camino Real (bet. Charleston & San Antonio Rds.), Palo Alto, 650-494-9383
◪ Most "excellent sushi" in a "serene setting" attracts advocates to this Palo Alto Japanese, whose "beautiful presentation" makes it a destination for "nice lunches" and "business power meals"; however, detractors decry the "pricey", "miniscule portions" and find service is "not so good"; N.B. a recent interior renovation may outdate the above decor score.

Gaylord India 🇱🇸🇲   18 | 16 | 16 | $30

1706 El Camino Real (Encinal Ave.), Menlo Park,
650-326-8761

See review in San Francisco Directory.

Gordon Biersch Brewery 🇱🇸🇲   14 | 15 | 14 | $24

640 Emerson St. (bet. Forest & Hamilton Aves.), Palo Alto,
650-323-7723
33 E. San Fernando St. (bet. 1st & 2nd Sts.), San Jose,
408-294-6785

◪ There's never a shortage of "frat boys gone dot-com types" to rave about these "rowdy" microbreweries in San Jose and Palo Alto, with their "fabulous" homemade suds and "fun atmosphere"; others opine "go for the beer and the scene, but leave to eat" because "the food is so over – even the [famed] garlic fries are old news."

Grandview 🇱🇸🇲   ▽ 20 | 12 | 16 | $24

1107 Howard Ave. (California Dr.), Burlingame,
650-348-3888

■ "Tell me a better Chinese for the money" demand devotees of this Burlingame grandee, whose "mixture of traditional and creative approaches" "makes you want to come back"; admittedly, "service can be iffy" and the "decor's [just] ok", but it's the perfect place "to bring family and friends" for a "filling Sunday afternoon affair" – "the lazy Susan spins faster than a DJ on speed."

Hawgs Seafood Bar 🇱🇸🇲   22 | 14 | 19 | $28

1700 W. Campbell Ave. (San Tomas Aquino Rd.), Campbell,
408-379-9555
150 S. Second St. (bet. San Fernando St. &
Paseo De San Antonio), San Jose, 408-287-9955

■ "Generous portions" of "fresh fish" in an "informal" atmosphere encourage landlubbers to gobble like hawgs at these "neighborhood" Campbell and San Jose seafood eateries; while most agree it's "worth the long wait" for the "delicious combos", the "noisy and crowded" atmo can be a downside; N.B. the Downtown SJ location is next to the SJ Repertory Theatre and offers a shuttle to the SJ Arena.

Higashi West 🇱🇲   22 | 20 | 19 | $35

632 Emerson St. (bet. Forest & Hamilton Aves.), Palo Alto,
650-323-9378

■ "The best sushi rolls around" at this "hip" Downtown Palo Alto "celebrity hangout", known for "creative" "California-type" raw fish concoctions as well as "non-traditional Japanese food" and "great selection of sake", all served in a modern "industrial Asian decor"; some chafe at the "small expensive portions" ("you'll wonder if you ate – bill says yes, tummy says no"), but the consensus says it's "worth it."

Hobee's L S M

17 | 12 | 16 | $16

Pruneyard Shopping Ctr., 1875 S. Bascom Ave. (bet. Campbell & Hamilton Aves.), Campbell, 408-369-0575
Oaks Shopping Ctr., 21267 Stevens Creek Blvd.
(opp. De Anza College), Cupertino, 408-255-6010
2312 Central Expy. (Rengstorff Ave.), Mountain View,
650-968-6050
4224 El Camino Real (Monroe Dr.), Palo Alto, 650-856-6124
67 Town and Country Village (Embarcadero Rd.), Palo Alto,
650-327-4111
680 River Oaks Plaza (Montague Expy.), San Jose, 408-232-0190
800 Ahwanee Ave. (Mathilda Ave.), Sunnyvale, 408-524-3580

◪ "Go for the wholesome breakfast or not at all" to this "glorified coffee shop" chain, "the obligatory brunch place" to its fans; however, others opine this "Denny's for hippies" is "starting to be boring": the "food sounds good, but always disappoints" after "long waits", with the "legendary" blueberry coffee cake "the only redeeming item."

Hong Kong Flower Lounge L S M

21 | 15 | 14 | $28

51 Millbrae Ave. (El Camino Real), Millbrae, 650-692-6666
560 Waverley St. (bet. Hamilton & University Aves.), Palo Alto, 650-326-3830

◪ Whether they're in Millbrae or Palo Alto, disciples drop by this duo for some "dim sum heaven" at lunch and an "extensive selection" of "excellent Hong Kong–style food" – either choosing the "great live seafood in tanks" or letting the kitchen "make special dishes"; though some snap "the bloom is off this flower", citing "weird decor" and servers who "flunk the attitude test", the "hordes spilling out the door are the best proof" it's "worth it."

Iberia L S M

21 | 21 | 19 | $41

1026 Alma St. (bet. Oak Grove & Ravenswood Aves.), Menlo Park, 650-325-8981

■ Since it "moved from Portola Valley" to "a nice location in Menlo Park", it's "now convenient" to savor the "superb Spanish food with a personality" served at this "cute place"; though service can be "slow", the "exciting menu" makes it a "great getaway" "for the adventuresome."

I Fratelli L S M

19 | 18 | 19 | $31

388 Main St. (bet. 1st & 2nd Sts.), Los Altos, 650-941-9636
See review in San Francisco Directory.

Il Fornaio L S M

19 | 20 | 19 | $33

327 Lorton Ave. (bet. Burlingame Ave. & California Dr.), Burlingame, 650-375-8000
520 Cowper St. (bet. Hamilton & University Aves.), Palo Alto, 650-853-3888
Hyatt Sainte Claire, 302 S. Market St. (San Carlos St.), San Jose, 408-271-3366
See review in San Francisco Directory.

Isobune Sushi 🅛🅢🅜   `16` `13` `14` `$23`

1451 Burlingame Ave. (El Camino Real), Burlingame, 650-344-8433
See review in San Francisco Directory.

Jocco's 🅛🅜   `24` `17` `22` `$38`

236 Central Plaza (bet. 2nd & 3rd Sts.), Los Altos, 650-948-6809
■ "Don't tell anyone" urge fans of this "favorite in Downtown Los Altos" whose "friendly neighborhood feel" encourages them to come consume "wonderful" "very rich" New American "comfort food" – including "incredible desserts" – and to "laugh with friends" (you'll have to, since the "close tables" can make it "too noisy" to talk).

JOHN BENTLEY'S 🅛   `26` `21` `24` `$50`

2991 Woodside Rd. (bet. Cañada & Whiskey Hill Rds.), Woodside, 650-851-4988
■ "Keep it a secret so we can get in" beg believers in chef-owner John Bentley's establishment, "a true jewel of the Peninsula" that "feels like Vermont in charming Woodside"; the "innovative" New American dishes are "consistently excellent", matched with a "great wine list" and delivered with "friendly and professional service"; while the "cozy, romantic" setting – a bright red old firehouse – wins kudos, even fans find it "a pity" the dining room is "so small."

Joy Luck Place 🅛🅢🅜   `–` `–` `–` `M`

Cupertino Village, 10911 N. Wolfe Rd. (Homestead Rd.), Cupertino, 408-255-6988
On weekends, you'll find long lines for "excellent dim sum" at one of the "best Chinese in Silicon Valley" – a huge standby located in a Cupertino Asian mall; while it's fun to pick a variety of dishes from carts as they roll by, the seafood entrees are superlative too.

Juban 🅛🅢🅜   `18` `16` `15` `$28`

1204 Broadway (bet. California Dr. & El Camino Real), Burlingame, 650-347-2300
712 Santa Cruz Ave. (El Camino Real), Menlo Park, 650-473-6458
◩ Would-be barbecue barons head to this "interactive" Japanese Menlo Park and Burlingame pair whose main attraction is "delightful hibachi cooking" of "grill-it-yourself" seafood and meats (including "tasty Kobe beef"); though it can be "pricey for a family night out" and some say it's "more effort than it's worth", "kids love it", and at least eating here "won't kill your diet."

JZ Cool 🅛🅢🅜   `17` `14` `15` `$20`

827 Santa Cruz Ave. (bet. Crane St. & University Dr.), Menlo Park, 650-325-3665
■ The way Jesse Cool cooks "gourmet quick meals" is the "way you wish you cooked at home" – but with her "very casual", "all organic" "healthy deli" in Menlo Park, you

don't have to; the "excellent soups" and other "delicious" items can be "pricey", yet all agree it's "a great lunch spot" that's particularly "good for solo dining."

Kabul ⬛S🅼   22 | 17 | 18 | $27

San Carlos Plaza, 135 El Camino Real (Hull St.), San Carlos, 650-594-2840
833 W. El Camino Real (bet. Mary & Pastoria Aves.), Sunnyvale, 408-245-4350
■ "You will go home happy" if you "bring your appetite" to one of the Peninsula's few Afghani eateries to sample some "unique fare"; the "best lamb chops anywhere", "killer" kebabs and "delicious veggie (pumpkin) dishes" brought to table by "competent" servers all add up to "a fabulous meal for the money."

Kathmandu West ⬛S🅼   ▽ 15 | 9 | 13 | $20

20916A Homestead Rd. (Hollenbeck Ave.), Cupertino, 408-996-0940
■ Silicon Valley's only "authentic Nepalese" – situated in a Cupertino strip mall – features a modest dining room where techies go for the "very good lunch buffet" loaded with "homestyle cooked food" that's "similar to Indian without the heat"; "warm and friendly service" is an added bonus.

Kingfish ⬛S🅼   – | – | – | M

201 S. B St. (2nd Ave.), San Mateo, 650-343-1226
Named for the legendary Louisiana governor Huey 'Kingfish' Long, this newcomer to Downtown San Mateo's dining scene is making quite a splash with its New Orleans–style seafood (complete with a raw bar); Crescent City decor and live blues music dress up the former brewpub digs.

Krungthai ⬛S   24 | 14 | 16 | $21

580 N. Winchester Blvd. (Dorcich St.), San Jose, 408-248-3435 🅼
642 S. Winchester Blvd. (Moorpark Ave.), San Jose, 408-260-8224
■ No matter which Winchester Boulevard location they frequent, fans "love this place", insisting it serves the "best Thai food south of San Francisco" – "creative" and "excellently prepared" – "and if you like it hot and spicy, they will gladly accommodate you"; no wonder this duo can get "very crowded."

Kuleto's Trattoria ⬛S🅼   18 | 19 | 18 | $36

1095 Rollins Rd. (Broadway), Burlingame, 650-342-4922
◩ "So convenient to the airport" sums up the appeal of this "standard Italian" in Burlingame where frequent fliers fuel up and suits "do business" thanks to perks like an "affordable wine list", a "nice interior" and valet parking at both lunch and dinner; however, "disappointing food and service" dismay some diners.

La Cumbre Taqueria ⏻ⓢⓜ

| 21 | 9 | 13 | $10 |

28 N. B St. (bet. 1st & Tilton Aves.), San Mateo, 650-344-8989
See review in San Francisco Directory.

La Fiesta ⓢⓜ

| – | – | – | M |

240 Villa St. (Calderon Ave.), Mountain View,
650-968-1364
Silicon Valleyites head to this off-the-beaten-path Mexican in Mountain View, because despite the warehouse-complex locale, it always looks like a fiesta is going on inside or on the patio; "great authentic" fare, including "magical salsas and margaritas" and a homemade mole sauce, keeps amigos happy – and there's a "kids welcome" mat out too.

La Fondue ⓢⓜ

| 22 | 24 | 20 | $44 |

14510 Big Basin Way (bet. 3rd & 4th Sts.), Saratoga,
408-867-3332
■ "Indulgence incarnate" is on the menu, "but you have to work for it" at Downtown Saratoga's "perfect fondue" Swiss – a "very romantic" yet "fun place" that looks like a cross between "a King Arthur fetish" and a "Harry Potter delight"; "if you can get reservations", seasoned dippers suggest allowing "extra time for this experience" or dropping in "just for dessert"; P.S. "bring your gold card."

LA FORÊT ⓢⓜ

| 28 | 26 | 27 | $57 |

21747 Bertram Rd. (Almaden Rd.), San Jose, 408-997-3458
■ "Excellent game", "outstanding service" and an "exceptional setting" on a creek bank make this "very fancy" San Jose French situated in an old boarding house "well worth the drive" for a "special celebration"; even if there's a lingering feeling that the menu is "getting pricey", this "out-of-the-way gem" remains the "absolute favorite" of many Francophiles.

L'Amie Donia

| 25 | 18 | 20 | $47 |

530 Bryant St. (bet. Hamilton & University Aves.), Palo Alto,
650-323-7614
◩ Chef-owner Donia Bijan's "creative" bistro is "a friend" (albeit an "expensive" one) to Palo Altans seeking "fantastic French comfort food"; those in-the-know "sit at the counter and watch" the cooks create "classics from the Left Bank" and "delicious original dishes"; otherwise, it's "impossible to talk" because the "tables are so close together"; N.B. patio seats provide another option.

La Pastaia ⏻ⓢⓜ

| 21 | 22 | 22 | $40 |

Hotel De Anza, 233 W. Santa Clara St. (Almaden Blvd.),
San Jose, 408-286-8686
◩ When sports lovers need a pre-Arena place to eat, they head to this "lovely" Italian in Downtown San Jose; it's the "best restaurant near the Shark Tank", serving "always consistent and tasty" dishes amid "gorgeous decor" thanks

to a recent redo; less enthusiastic fans, on the other hand, find the food "reliable but not imaginative."

Lark Creek **L S M**

| 23 | 23 | 22 | $43 |

50 E. Third Ave. (bet. El Camino Real & San Mateo Dr.), San Mateo, 650-344-9444
See review in North of San Francisco Directory.

La Taqueria **L M ⧸**

| 23 | 9 | 13 | $11 |

15 S. First St. (Santa Clara St.), San Jose, 408-287-1542
See review in San Francisco Directory.

Late for the Train **L S M**

| 17 | 16 | 18 | $21 |

150 Middlefield Rd. (Willow Rd.), Menlo Park, 650-321-6124
■ Get a "glimpse of the '60s" at this "kitschy", "different" Menlo Park Californian with a heavy organic/vegetarian slant and "apple butter at all the tables"; "wholesome" types enjoy the "down-to-earth", "healthy-but-not-too-healthy" fare served in the "living room" setting as well as "on the patio"; "modest prices" add to the appeal.

Le Bistro **L M**

| – | – | – | E |

207 W. Main Ave. (Hale Ave.), Morgan Hill, 408-782-2505
Morgan Hillers are already abuzz about this cozy little bistro with a bay window overlooking Main Street and walls awash in sunny yellows; chef/co-owner Mohamed Rabhaa deals in ambitious American dishes, with hints of Italian influences thrown in; the creative menu also includes a sprinkling of vegetarian entrees.

Left at Albuquerque **L S M**

| 15 | 15 | 15 | $23 |

1100 Burlingame Ave. (California Dr.), Burlingame, 650-401-5700
Pruneyard Shopping Ctr., 1875 S. Bascom Ave. (bet. Campbell & Hamilton Aves.), Campbell, 408-558-1680
445 Emerson St. (bet Lytton & University Aves.), Palo Alto, 650-326-1011
◪ An "impressive tequila bar" and "generous portions" of "solid Southwestern cuisine" keep hombres heading to this "always packed" Bay Area mini-chain to "hang out" amid "classic roadhouse decor"; but critical compadres say they "should have kept going" instead of turning in here: it's "too loud to talk", and "the food is nothing special."

Left Bank **L S M**

| 21 | 21 | 19 | $38 |

635 Santa Cruz Ave. (Doyle St.), Menlo Park, 650-473-6543
See review in North of San Francisco Directory.

Le Mouton Noir **S M**

| 23 | 23 | 23 | $53 |

14560 Big Basin Way (bet. 4th & 5th Sts.), Saratoga, 408-867-7017
◪ Devotees of this "classical French" veteran housed in a Saratoga Victorian deem it "one of the tops in the area" and rave about executive chef Seth Fiertl's "outstanding" "flavorsome food"; there are "disappointed" diners in the

ranks, however, who call it "overpriced" and a "shadow of its former self"; despite the division, solid scores side with supporters who "can't wait till next time."

LE PAPILLON L S M   28 | 26 | 28 | $57

410 Saratoga Ave. (Kiely Blvd.), San Jose, 408-296-3730
■ With accolades such as "flawless" and "unforgettable" describing this "creative and modern" "standard for fine French in the South Bay", it should come as no surprise that San Jose gourmets "go here to impress"; chef Scott Cooper's food is "exceptional", "the tasting menu is a tour de force", service is "unparalleled" ("low-key yet prompt") and the wine cellar is "excellent", causing converts to sigh "I just wish I lived closer."

Le Poisson Japonais ● S M   – | – | – | VE

642 Ramona St. (bet. Forest & Hamilton Aves.), Palo Alto, 650-330-1147
Owner Kenji Seki (of LA's Chinois on Main) schmoozes with customers at his cutting-edge Japanese newcomer, Palo Alto's of-the-moment 'in' spot, where dressing to kill is de rigueur; the beautiful people are buzzing about the extensive sake list and the miso-marinated sea bass and sushi platters devised by chef Naoki Uchiyama (ex Spago Beverly Hills); N.B. the late-night dining – a rarity in the Valley – is a plus.

Lion & Compass L M   20 | 19 | 20 | $38

1023 N. Fair Oaks Ave. (Weddell Dr.), Sunnyvale, 408-745-1260
■ "Ground zero for Silicon Valley" is this Sunnyvale "landmark", lionized by its fans for serving "fresh, well-done" New American food in an "airy atmosphere" that encourages workaholics to "relax on weekend evenings" while serving as a "place to be seen" for weekday lunch.

Long Life Noodle Company & Jook Joint L S M   13 | 11 | 11 | $15

Stanford Shopping Ctr., 393 Stanford Shopping Ctr. (Sand Hill Rd.), Palo Alto, 650-324-1110
See review in San Francisco Directory.

Los Gatos Brewing Co. L S M   19 | 19 | 18 | $29

130G N. Santa Cruz Ave. (Grays Ln.), Los Gatos, 408-395-9929
■ An "excellent selection of brews on tap" and "better food than most beer joints" distinguish this "upscale" New American in Downtown Los Gatos; "surprised" supporters swear the "very noisy" hangout offers "something for everyone" – "family fare", "nice [Sunday] brunch" and a "meat market" on weekends.

Lucy's Tea House L M ⊭   – | – | – | I

180 Castro St. (Villa St.), Mountain View, 650-969-6365
This tiny Taiwanese teahouse is tucked down an alley off Mountain View's Castro Street, where an enclosed patio

equipped with big wicker seats encourages lingering over fragrant homemade hot and cold beverages (like bubble teas, a Chinese classic made with tapioca pearls) and sandwiches, including a variety of vegetarian options; N.B. don't miss the tea-flavored ice creams and milkshakes.

MacArthur Park **L S M**   17 | 18 | 17 | $32
See review in San Francisco Directory.

Maddalena's/Café Fino **L M**   – | – | – | E
544 Emerson St. (bet. Hamilton & University Aves.), Palo Alto, 650-326-6082
Palo Alto impresario Fred Maddalena's culinary combo is Silicon Valley's "best-kept secret"; a "movie crowd" comes for "fine old-style service" and "romantic dining upstairs" in his namesake Italian restaurant; next door, the art deco cafe is a "great supper jazz club with decent food" and "an amazing old-world bartender" who pours drinks while patrons dance up a discreet storm.

Mandarin Gourmet **L S M**   23 | 21 | 20 | $28
420 Ramona St. (University Ave.), Palo Alto, 650-328-8898
■ The "sophisticated setting" and "attractive presentation" of "excellent food" make this Palo Alto "Chinese with a light touch" "nice enough for a date"; voters also appreciate the "reasonable prices" and "quick service" – in case that date is a dud.

Mango Cafe **M**   19 | 12 | 14 | $18
435 Hamilton Ave. (bet. Cowper & Waverley Sts.), Palo Alto, 650-324-9443
■ Going to this "cozy, casual" Palo Alto cafe for "Caribbean treats" is like taking an "inexpensive" "trip to the islands"; get ready for "addictive jerk chicken" ("remember the fire extinguisher"), "goat stew to spice up your taste buds" and "fabulous" "fish bowl–size smoothies"; P.S. it's "a great place for vegetarians" too.

Max's Opera Cafe **L S M**   16 | 15 | 16 | $23
1250 Old Bayshore Hwy. (Airport Blvd.), Burlingame, 650-342-6297
Stanford Shopping Ctr., 711 Stanford Shopping Ctr. (El Camino Real), Palo Alto, 650-323-6297
See review in San Francisco Directory.

Max's Restaurant **L S M**   16 | 13 | 16 | $22
1000 El Camino Real (Ralston Ave.), Belmont, 650-592-6290 ◖
1001 El Camino Real (Lexington Ave.), Redwood City, 650-365-6297
Westgate Ctr., 1620 Saratoga Ave. (bet. Atherton & Campbell Aves.), San Jose, 408-379-8886
See review in San Francisco Directory.

Mei Long L S M
▽ 26 22 24 $34

867 E. El Camino Real (Bernardo Ave.), Mountain View, 650-961-4030

■ Ardent admirers of this "classy" "Chinese-French fusion" spot located in an "obscure" Mountain View strip mall declare that it "deserves more attention" for its "innovative dishes", "exquisite presentation and service", "excellent wine list" and "formal, quiet surroundings."

Mio Vicino L S M
21 15 17 $25

384 E. Campbell Ave. (bet. Central & Harrison Aves.), Campbell, 408-378-0335
1140-8 Lincoln Ave. (bet. Meredith Ave. & Willow St.), San Jose, 408-286-6027
1290 Benton St. (Monroe St.), Santa Clara, 408-241-9414

◪ This popular Italian trio draws "crowds" for its "large portions" of "tasty", if "garlicky", pastas and pizza, "quick service", "reasonable prices" and "convenient locations"; "service and decor need work", but amici don't mind.

Mistral L S M
20 20 18 $34

370-6 Bridge Pkwy. (Marine World Pkwy.), Redwood Shores, 650-802-9222

■ The "high-tech digerati" compete for the "best outdoor seats on the Peninsula" at this "suburban" Cal-Italian (a relative of Nola and A Tavola) with an "urban" menu that rivals the "waterfront view"; there may be "too many pagers and dot-commers" in the "big lunchtime crowd", but it "definitely fills a need for Redwood Shores residents."

Miyake L S M
17 13 14 $21

10650 S. De Anza Blvd. (Bollinger Rd.), Cupertino, 408-253-2668
140 University Ave. (High St.), Palo Alto, 650-323-9449

■ "Come for the party" at these "untraditional" Japanese where "great inexpensive sushi" served on boats attracts "lots of Stanford students" who help transform the hangout into a "fun disco scene at night"; "if only I were 18 again" lament older folks who like the "cheap" eats but not the "unbearable noise" at Palo Alto (Cupertino is quieter).

Nola L S M
18 21 16 $31

535 Ramona St. (bet. Hamilton & University Aves.), Palo Alto, 650-328-2722

■ "Young" singles enjoy a "taste of New Orleans" at this "popular" Palo Alto Cajun-Creole that makes you "feel like you're in the Big Easy" with its "party atmosphere" and balconied courtyard; the "so-so" food and "disappearing" service are "secondary" to the "scene"; best advice: "come for the mating game" and "very good drinks."

Original Joe's ◐ L S M
19 14 19 $24

301 S. First St. (San Carlos St.), San Jose, 408-292-7030
See review in San Francisco Directory.

Orlo's L S M
▽ 23 | 28 | 23 | $36

Hayes Mansion, 200 Edenvale Ave. (Marjohn Blvd.), San Jose, 408-226-3200

■ The "best hidden restaurant in San Jose" can be found at Hayes Mansion, a "historic" structure built in 1905 and now a conference center; touting a "romantic atmosphere", "beautiful furnishings" and "excellent" Med fare, it's perfect for a "special night out", belle epoque style.

Osteria L M
22 | 15 | 18 | $31

247 Hamilton Ave. (Ramona St.), Palo Alto, 650-328-5700

■ "Delicious", "reliably al dente" pasta and other "fairly priced" "simple dishes" are why locals love this "old-time" Northern Italian in Palo Alto; it's also why they put up with the "crowds", "close tables" and "inconsistent service."

Palo Alto Sol L S M
▽ 21 | 16 | 19 | $21

408 California Ave. (El Camino Real), Palo Alto, 650-328-8840

■ "California Avenue finally gets a superb Mexican venue" cheer compadres of this Palo Alto "find" where "you'll fantasize about the food" – "generous servings" of "*bueno* mole", "inventive enchiladas" and other "authentic" eats; N.B. the menu boasts 20 south-of-the-border beers.

Pancho Villa Taqueria L S M
23 | 10 | 15 | $10

365 S. B St. (bet. 3rd & 4th Aves.), San Mateo, 650-343-4123
See review in San Francisco Directory.

Paolo's L M
23 | 24 | 22 | $45

River Park Tower, 333 W. San Carlos St. (Woz Way), San Jose, 408-294-2558

☑ "Fancy" and "elegant" describe this San Jose Italian, an "old standard" (since 1958) that "can always be relied upon for a great meal" amid "soft surroundings"; however, a handful of former fans feel the landmark is "losing it": "food isn't as great as it should be at those prices."

Passage to India L S M
– | – | – | M

1991 W. El Camino Real (bet. Escuela & Rengstorff Aves.), Mountain View, 650-969-9990

Now in bigger and brighter digs, this favorite offers a gourmet Northern Indian repertoire; dot-commers and families gladly make the passage to Mountain View for the daily lunch and weekend dinner buffets that are a real deal, and once there they save room for the array of sweets devised by the dedicated dessert chef from India.

Peninsula Fountain & Grill L S M – | – | – | M

Stanford Shopping Ctr., 180 El Camino Real (University Ave.), Palo Alto, 650-327-3141
566 Emerson St. (Hamilton Ave.), Palo Alto, 650-323-3131
A true Palo Alto "institution" since 1923, this "hometown diner" is beloved for "terrific milkshakes" (its nickname

isn't the 'Creamery' for nothing) and "surprising gourmet specials"; ever-popular for weekend brunch, it keeps hungry patrons patiently waiting outside for a seat at the fountain counter or in a booth.

Perry's Palo Alto L S M   15 | 15 | 16 | $27
546 University Ave. (Cowper St.), Palo Alto, 650-326-0111
See review in San Francisco Directory.

Piatti L S M   19 | 19 | 18 | $34
Stanford Shopping Ctr., 2 Stanford Shopping Ctr. (El Camino Real), Palo Alto, 650-324-9733
See review in North of San Francisco Directory.

Pigalle L S M   ∇ 21 | 21 | 20 | $41
27 N. Santa Cruz Ave. (Main St.), Los Gatos, 408-395-7924
■ "Ooh-la-la", does this "quaint, romantic" bistro bring "a bit of France" to Downtown Los Gatos with its murals of *la vie parisienne* decorating the "charming room" and a "wonderful" "menu combining old and new French" fare; all in all, it's "a great value"; N.B. a prix fixe lunch and dinner are also offered.

Pisces S M   25 | 21 | 22 | $53
1190 California Dr. (Broadway), Burlingame, 650-401-7500
◪ "Why go to the city when Pisces is here?" ask admirers of Michael Mina's "high-caliber" Burlingame seafooder (sibling to SF's Aqua) situated in a "small, renovated train stop"; the majority is hooked on the "exciting and creative" finfare, but a school of dissenters decries "wallet-deflating" prices for "inadequate portions"; all agree "this place needs a bigger space", as it gets "cramped" and "noisy."

Plumed Horse M   22 | 22 | 22 | $50
14555 Big Basin Way (4th St.), Saratoga, 408-867-4711
■ "Dated but delicious" sums up reviewer reaction to this "old-world" New French–Californian in Saratoga where the "monied middle-aged" set goes "to be seen" and to enjoy "wonderful" food "without attitude", as well as an "amazing wine list" and "knowledgeable staff"; P.S. the "rustic lodge-like bar" is "fun" "for drinks."

Pluto's L S M   18 | 12 | 13 | $13
482 University Ave. (Cowper St.), Palo Alto, 650-853-1556
See review in San Francisco Directory.

Red Tractor Cafe L S M   15 | 14 | 14 | $13
El Paseo De Saratoga Shopping Ctr., 1320 El Paseo De Saratoga (bet. Campbell & Saratoga Aves.), San Jose, 408-374-2222
See review in East of San Francisco Directory.

Restaurant Umunhum ▧   ▽ 18 | 17 | 16 | $45 |

699 Almaden Expy. (Via Valiente), San Jose, 408-927-8773
◪ Intrepid surveyors have uncovered a "surprising find" in a South San Jose strip mall – this "eclectic" International–Pacific Rim offering "innovative entrees" and a "good wine list"; less-impressed patrons, however, say the "inconsistent" kitchen "tries hard but does not execute well" – "it still has a ways to go for what you pay."

Rue de Paris ▧▧   ▽ 21 | 18 | 21 | $39 |

19 N. Market St. (Santa Clara St.), San Jose, 408-298-0704
◪ Amateur detectives favor this "very intimate" San Jose French that stages "mystery dinners", applauding the "delicious dishes" and "nice new sidewalk tables"; skeptics cite "overpriced, average food" and a "poor location" as evidence you should try elsewhere.

Scott's ▧▧▧   18 | 18 | 18 | $35 |

2300 E. Bayshore Rd. (Embarcadero Rd.), Palo Alto, 650-856-1046
185 Park Ave. (bet. Almaden Blvd. & Market St.), San Jose, 408-971-1700
◼ One of a regional chain of "formula fish" and steak spots, this Downtowner is noted for "pricey" fare you can always "count on being fresh and cooked right"; "pleasant but not distinctive", it "goes over swimmingly well" with the corporate crowd "at lunch" thanks to "attentive service" and "pleasant atmosphere."

SENT SOVI ▧   26 | 23 | 24 | $64 |

14583 Big Basin Way (5th St.), Saratoga, 408-867-3110
◼ "NASDAQ may have crashed", but this Saratoga survivor "remains a top pick" in many a foodie's portfolio; the "romantic", "unpretentious" New French is "a destination restaurant" where "gustatory pleasure" is delivered by chef David Kinch, a "rising genius" who takes "dramatic risks while keeping less adventurous diners happy"; a few feel the experience is "overpriced", but many more maintain it's "worth a long drive."

71 Saint Peter ▧▧   ▽ 23 | 17 | 22 | $37 |

71 N. San Pedro St. (bet. Santa Clara & St. John Sts.), San Jose, 408-971-8523
◼ It's "amazing" that "such wonderful food can come from such a small open kitchen" declare disciples of this "romantic", "intimate" Mediterranean in Downtown San Jose; "reasonable prices", a "helpful staff" and patio seating (definitely your best bet on warm nights) enhance the "delightful experience."

Shiok! Singapore Kitchen ▧▧   ▽ 19 | 14 | 17 | $20 |

1137 Chestnut St. (Santa Cruz Ave.), Menlo Park, 650-838-9448
◼ "Deserves a try" opine enthusiasts of this "authentic" Singaporean in Menlo Park, featuring a "fascinating

mixture of flavors" that "tastes like homemade"; "service needs to improve", but "spicy food lovers" aren't deterred.

Sinaloa Cafe L S   ∇ 21 | 13 | 15 | $21 |

19210 Monterey Rd. (Peebles Ave.), Morgan Hill, 408-779-9740

◼ The Peña family runs this modest Morgan Hill Mexican, known for four decades for its "terrific, authentic food"; amigos also "come for the margaritas", which are a specialty of the *casa*.

Soleil L S M   – | – | – | E |

The Westin Hotel, 675 El Camino Real (bet. Embarcadero Rd. & University Ave.), Palo Alto, 650-321-4422

The few voters who've frequented this Palo Alto New French–Mediterranean in the Westin Hotel say it delivers "excellent food" from a seasonal menu to guests and locals alike; an umber palette permeates the decor and the open kitchen gives diners a glimpse of the action.

Spago Palo Alto L S M   24 | 23 | 21 | $55 |

265 Lytton Ave. (Bryant St.), Palo Alto, 650-833-1000

☑ Still a "Silicon hot spot", this "beautiful" Bay Area link in the Wolfgang Puck chain brings a "glamorous Hollywood feel to Palo Alto"; both the food and the atmosphere are "sophisticated yet casual" Californian, attracting "corporate types" as well as the "technology crowd"; it takes some hits for being "too noisy", "too snooty" and "too expensive", but it's still "the place to go if you want to impress."

Spiedo Ristorante L S M   17 | 17 | 19 | $36 |

151 W. Santa Clara St. (bet. Almaden Blvd. & San Pedro St.), San Jose, 408-971-6096

223 Fourth Ave. (bet. B St. & Ellsworth Ave.), San Mateo, 650-375-0818

☑ It's the "convenient location" and "great value" – more so than the "average" to "very good" food – that draw professionals to these San Jose and San Mateo Meds that have an "airy feeling" about them.

Steamer's Grillhouse L S M   19 | 21 | 18 | $37 |

Old Town Shopping Ctr., 31 University Ave. (bet. Elm & Main Sts.), Los Gatos, 408-395-2722

☑ This recently relocated Los Gatos fish house has been a "local favorite for seafood since the early 1980s", so naturally, there's debate about whether it is "great in its new location" or "lost its way while crossing the road"; regardless, it now attracts the "working crowd with a loud bar", and lunch remains "a value."

St. Michael's Alley L S   ∇ 22 | 17 | 20 | $34 |

806 Emerson St. (Homer Ave.), Palo Alto, 650-326-2530

◼ Patron saints extol the virtues of this "tiny" Californian tucked away in Palo Alto – "a fun and creative menu", a strong wine list, "wonderful service" and a "welcoming, warm atmosphere"; "pleasant outdoor dining" encourages many to find it up their alley.

Stoddard's L S M ▽ 18 17 18 $27

111 S. Murphy Ave. (Evelyn Ave.), Sunnyvale, 408-733-7824
■ When the Sunnyvale high-tech set wants "excellent beers", they head to this brewpub to get some "bustling atmosphere" with their suds; if the "standard" American "snack" food isn't always a hit, "you'll keep coming back" for the live music.

Straits Cafe L S M 22 18 17 $31

3295 El Camino Real (Ventura Ave.), Palo Alto, 650-494-7168
See review in San Francisco Directory.

Su Hong Menlo Park L S M 19 13 18 $22

1039 El Camino Real (bet. Oak Grove & Valparaiso Aves.), Menlo Park, 650-323-6852

Su Hong To Go L S M

630 Menlo Ave. (Santa Cruz Ave.), Menlo Park, 650-322-4631
◨ "Huge portions" of Chinese food ("scrumptious" vs. "mediocre") await at this "casual" Menlo Parker with "good prices"; some participants proclaim that the to-go operation is "almost better than dining in", since "the food outshines the service."

Tapestry L M 22 21 21 $44

Soda Work Plaza, 11 College Ave. (Main St.), Los Gatos, 408-395-2808
◨ "Artistic surroundings" and a "lovely" heated patio attract the "beautiful people" of Los Gatos to this "out-of-the-way, but more-than-worth-the-drive" Californian in a "converted house that is just a bit too cramped for comfort"; food-wise, "a fusion of flavors explodes in your mouth", and service is "competent and friendly"; those who find it too "noisy" "go at non-peak times."

Tarragon L M ▽ 16 21 18 $36

140 S. Murphy Ave. (bet. Evelyn & Washington Aves.), Sunnyvale, 408-737-8003
◨ The "lovely decor" and "impressive bar area" are the highlights of this Downtown Sunnyvale Californian that otherwise seems to have "lost its spark"; reactions to the food range from "not bad, not great" to "very low quality-to-price ratio"; your call as to whether it's "worthy of its location on cute Murphy Avenue."

3 Fish L S M 16 15 16 $31

888 El Camino Real (bet. Oak Grove & Santa Cruz Aves.), Menlo Park, 650-326-2633
◨ Surveyors say there's "nothing exciting" about this New England–style seafooder in Menlo Park, just "good fresh

fish" served in "an open, bright environment"; there's also talk that it "has gone downhill since it opened" – perhaps it's still "evolving."

Tied House
Cafe & Brewery 🆛🆂🅼　　14｜13｜14｜$24

954 Villa St. (bet. Castro St. & Shoreline Blvd.), Mountain View, 650-965-2739
San Pedro Sq., 65 N. San Pedro St. (Santa Clara St.), San Jose, 408-295-2739

■ Silicon Valleyites tie one on at this duo of microbreweries doling out "decent beer" and "pub-quality" Cal-American grub ("if you stick to the ribs and onion rings, you'll be okay"); the crowd can get "noisy", especially in the "bar area that attracts singles on Friday night", but the "comfortable" *biergarten*-style patio provides refuge.

Tony & Alba's Pizza 🆛🆂🅼　　–｜–｜–｜I

619 Escuela Ave. (El Camino Real), Mountain View, 650-968-5089
Originally a mom-and-pop pie parlor, this operation has blossomed into a Mountain View institution; fans flock here for pizzas bearing a medium-thick crust and a variety of toppings (try the Tony's Special for a bit of everything) in sizes that range from personal to huge; pastas, salads and sandwiches are also on the menu.

Trellis 🆛🅼　　–｜–｜–｜E

1077 El Camino Real (Santa Cruz Ave.), Menlo Park, 650-326-9028
Boasting big picture windows and an open kitchen, this "brand-new" addition to the Menlo Park dining scene comes from Kurt Ugur, also managing partner of Cafe Pro Bono; from the large banquettes diners can watch executive chef Doug McGraw's "wonderful" Italian specialties take shape.

231 Ellsworth 🆛🅼　　24｜22｜22｜$50

231 S. Ellsworth Ave. (bet. 2nd & 3rd Aves.), San Mateo, 650-347-7231

■ Dining sophisticates swear this recently "redone" New American "tucked away in San Mateo" is "superb in every way" – from the "exciting, well-executed menu" to the "best wine list on the Peninsula" to the "beautiful new dining room" with a "supper-club feel"; "SF prices", however, mean many save it for a "special occasion."

University Coffee Café 🆛🆂🅼　　15｜16｜12｜$15

271 University Ave. (bet. Bryant & Ramona Sts.), Palo Alto, 650-322-5301

■ Get "a warm buzz" at this "cool", "always busy" Cal cafe in Downtown Palo Alto where "excellent" roasted-in-house coffee plus "yummy fruit smoothies" and other "fine snacks" sustain caffeine fiends; "grab an outdoor table" on "Sunday mornings with the paper" or simply sip and "watch the world walk by."

Viaggio Ristorante 🅛🆂   18 | 21 | 18 | $42

14550 Big Basin Way (4th St.), Saratoga, 408-741-5300

◪ "A sea of sophistication" is how happy campers describe this "charming" Saratoga Mediterranean that "fulfills expectations" with "consistent" food, "beautiful decor" and "professional" service; a handful of frustrated foes feels it "aspires to greatness but doesn't make it."

Village Pub, The 🅛🆂🅜   – | – | – | E

2967 Woodside Rd. (Whiskey Hill Rd.), Woodside, 650-851-1294

It takes a village – tony-yet-quaint Woodside, in this case – to anticipate the reopening of a favorite meeting spot; bearing the pedigree of an ex PlumpJack manager and chef, it now offers Med–New American fare, including game in season, in a contemporarily clubby atmosphere.

Viognier 🅛🆂🅜   24 | 22 | 22 | $46

Draeger's Mkt., 222 E. Fourth Ave. (bet. B St. & Ellsworth Ave.), San Mateo, 650-685-3727

◧ Dining in the "elegant room" above Draeger's in "sleepy San Mateo" "makes you feel like you're part of some secret society", but it's no secret this "exquisite" Med is "America's best restaurant in a supermarket"; the combination of chef Scott Giambastiani's "outstanding food", an "excellent wine selection" and "knowledgeable, professional service" means it "never disappoints."

White Rock Cafe 🅛   ▽ 16 | 12 | 16 | $25

3116 Alum Rock Ave. (White Rd.), San Jose, 408-729-4843

◧ "East San Jose gets haute cuisine": in a "neighborhood not noted for fine dining", this Cal-French is "surprisingly good", especially its five-course prix fixe; but the real draw is when owner Michiko Boccara cooks on Friday nights.

Wild Hare 🆂🅜   21 | 21 | 20 | $46

1029 El Camino Real (bet. Menlo & Santa Cruz Aves.), Menlo Park, 650-327-4273

◧ Carnivores make a beeline to chef-owner Joey Altman's "wild indeed" "mountain lodge" in "mellow" Menlo Park, where the "bold, assertive flavors" of "exotic meats" (bison, ostrich, etc.) as well as the "personality" of TV's *Bay Cafe* chef "shine through" the "cosmopolitan ambiance"; while the hoopla doesn't always impress, the "culinary adventure" makes a visit "worth the drive from SF."

Willow Street
Wood-Fired Pizza 🅛🆂🅜   19 | 15 | 17 | $22

20 S. Santa Cruz Ave. (Main St.), Los Gatos, 408-354-5566
Westgate Ctr., 1554 Saratoga Ave. (bet. Graves Ave. & Prospect Rd.), San Jose, 408-871-0400
1072 Willow St. (Lincoln Ave.), San Jose, 408-971-7080

◧ There's always a "steady crowd" at this "easygoing" chain of South Bay "yuppie pizza parlors"; partisans particularly "love the open kitchen" where you can watch the cooks create "consistently good", innovative pies (Thai chicken, anyone?) along with "amazing garlic bread" and other "cheap" eats; while it offers a varied Cal-Italian menu, somehow folks always manage to order "the same thing."

Woodside Bakery & Cafe L S M | 20 | 15 | 15 | $24 |
3052 Woodside Rd. (Cañada Rd.), Woodside, 650-851-0812
■ It "smells so wonderful" inside this "nice breakfast place" in Woodside, a "local treat" that's "great for morning coffee" and "homemade pastries"; wood-fired pizzas and International fare mean it's also "a favorite" for lunch, especially on the "great outdoor patio in summer"; neighbors sigh "we need more places like this."

Yamin Win L M | – | – | – | M |
305 Second St. (bet. San Antonio Rd. & Whitney St.),
Los Altos, 650-941-9293
"Exotic flavors in a neighborhood restaurant" sums up this Los Altos Burmese located in a Downtown mini-mall: you're sure to win by "trying the variety of salads" (including tea leaf) or letting proprietor San Lin guide you through the inexpensive menu, prepared from her family's recipes.

Zao Noodle Bar L S M | 15 | 13 | 15 | $17 |
261 University Ave. (Ramona St.), Palo Alto, 650-328-1988
See review in San Francisco Directory.

Zibibbo L S M | 22 | 21 | 18 | $39 |
430 Kipling St. (bet. Lytton & University Aves.), Palo Alto,
650-328-6722
☑ "Be sure to go with a crowd of plate passers", because this "cavernous", "hip place to see-and-be-seen" in Palo Alto (sister to SF's LuLu and Azie) specializes in "family-style" portions of "creative" Med cuisine (don't miss the "marvelous" "fire-roasted mussels"); "disappointed" diners note the "noise" and "mediocre service" "get in the way of great food"; N.B. a new wine bar now serves 60 varieties by the glass.

Indexes

CUISINES
LOCATIONS
SPECIAL FEATURES

Indexes list the best of many within each category.

All restaurants are in the City of San Francisco unless otherwise noted (E=East of San Francisco; N=North of San Francisco; S=South of San Francisco; SV= Silicon Valley/Peninsula).

CUISINES

Afghan
Helmand
Kabul/SV

American (New)
A.P. Stump's/SV
Avenue 9
bacar
Big Four
Bistro Ralph/N
Bollinger/E
Boonville Hotel/N
Brannan's Grill/N
Cafe Beaujolais/N
Cafe La Haye/N
Cafe Lolo/N
Celadon/N
Chaz
Chenery Park
Chez TJ/SV
Cielo/S
Cobalt Tavern
Cosmopolitan Cafe
Cypress Club
Deuce/N
Dot
Duck Club/E/N/S/SV
Eulipia/SV
Feast/N
First Crush
Flea St. Café/SV
Fog City Diner
French Laundry/N
Gary Danko
Ginger Island/E
Globe
Gordon's Hse. of Fine Eats
Indigo
Infusion Bar
Jianna
Jocco's/SV
John Bentley's/SV
Johnfrank
Julius' Castle
Kenwood/N
Lark Creek/E/SV
Lark Creek Inn/N
Le Bistro/SV
Liberty Cafe
Lion & Compass/SV
Los Gatos Brewing/SV
Mecca
Meetinghouse
Miss Millie's
MoMo's

Mustards Grill/N
955 Ukiah/N
Northstar
Olema Inn/N
One Market
Paragon
Park Grill
Perlot
Postrio
Restaurant 301/N
Rick's
Rotunda
Roux/N
Skates on the Bay/E
Slow Club
Station House Café/N
Tastings/N
Town's End
2223
231 Ellsworth/SV
Universal Cafe
Village Pub/SV
Wild Hare/SV
Woodward's Garden
Yabbies Coastal Kit.
Zin/N
zuzu/N

American (Regional)
Duarte's Tavern/S
Eastside West
Le Krewe
Miramonte/N
Rocco's Seafood
3 Fish/SV
Yankee Pier/N

American (Traditional)
Anzu
Autumn Moon/E
Avenue Grill/N
Balboa Cafe
Bandera/SV
Beach Chalet Brew.
Bette's Oceanview/E
Bittersweet Bistro/S
Bix
Blue
Blue Plate
Boulevard
Brazen Head
Bubba's Diner/N
Buckeye Roadhse./N
Buck's/SV
Café Esin/E

Cuisine Index

Cafe Flore
Cafe For All Seasons
Calistoga Inn/N
Casa Orinda/E
Cheesecake Factory
Chloe's Cafe
Cliff House
Compass Rose
Curve Bar
Delancey St.
Dine
Dipsea Cafe/N
Dottie's True Blue
Draeger's/SV
Ella's
Empire Grill/SV
FatApple's/E
Felix & Louie's/N
Firewood Café
Fly Trap
Gordon Biersch
Gordon Biersch/SV
Gordon's/N
Half Moon Bay/S
Hard Rock Cafe
Hayes St. Grill
It's Tops Coffee
Jimtown Store/N
Kate's Kitchen
Kelly's Mission Rock
Kensington Circus Pub/E
Lark Creek/E/SV
Lark Creek Inn/N
Liverpool Lil's
MacArthur Park
MacArthur Park/SV
Magnolia Pub
Mama's Royal/E
Mama's/Washington Sq.
Mel's Drive-In
Moose's
Mo's Burgers
Moss Beach/S
Nepenthe/S
OakTown Cafe/E
Parkside Cafe/N
Perry's
Perry's/SV
Planet Hollywood
Pluto's
Pluto's/SV
Pork Store Cafe
Potrero Brewing
Red Tractor Cafe/E/SV
Rick & Ann's/E
Rutherford Grill/N
Sam's Anchor Cafe/N

Sam's Grill
Sand Dollar/N
Sears Fine Food
Shadowbrook/S
Stoddard's/SV
Tarpy's Roadhse./S
Tied House/SV
Tommy's Joynt
Townhouse/E
21st Amendment Brew.
Twenty Four

Asian
Asia de Cuba
AsiaSF
Azie
Betelnut Pejiu Wu
Bridges/E
Brix/N
Carême Room
Charlie Hong Kong/S
Citrus Club
Clouds Downtown/S
Compass Rose
Crustacean
Dragon Well
E&O Trading
E&O Trading/SV
Eos
Flying Fish Grill/S
Grasshopper/E
Hawthorne Lane
House
Long Life Noodle
Long Life Noodle/E/SV
Oritalia
Pairs/N
Ponzu
Roy's/Pebble Bch./S
Sake Tini/N
Silks
Straits Cafe
Straits Cafe/SV
Tin-Pan Asian Bistro
Tonga Room
Venture Frogs
Watergate
Xanadu/E
Yamin Win/SV
Zao Noodle Bar
Zao Noodle Bar/SV

Bakeries
Arizmendi Bakery
Arizmendi Bakery/E
Cheese Board/E
Citizen Cake
Downtown Bakery/N

Emporio Rulli/N
Gayle's Bakery/S
Liberty Cafe
Model Bakery/N
Town's End
Woodside Bakery/SV

Barbecue
Armadillo Willy's/SV
Brother-in-Law's BBQ
Brother's Korean
Buckeye Roadhse./N
Coriya Hot Pot
Everett & Jones BBQ/E
Foothill Cafe/N
Hahn's Hibachi
Juban/SV
Koryo/E
Livefire Grill
Livefire Grill/N
MacArthur Park
MacArthur Park/SV
Memphis Minnie's

Belgian
Frjtz Fries

Bolivian
Peña Pachamama

Brazilian
Terra Brazilis

Burmese
Irrawaddy Burmese
Mandalay
Nan Yang Rockridge/E
Yamin Win/SV

Cajun/Creole
Blue Chalk Cafe/SV
Catahoula/N
Elite Cafe
Le Krewe
Nola/SV
PJ's Oyster Bed

Californian
Academy Grill
Ahwahnee Din. Rm./E
Albion River Inn/N
Alta Mira/N
Applewood Inn/N
A.P. Stump's/SV
Aqui Cal-Mex/SV
AsiaSF
Asqew Grill
Avenue Grill/N
Backflip
Bay Wolf/E

Bistro Elan/SV
Blackhawk Grille/E
Blue Plate
Boonville Hotel/N
Bridges/E
Bucci's/E
Cactus Cafe/N
Cafe Borrone/SV
Cafe Kati
Cafe Monk
Café Mozart
Cafe Prima Vera/SV
Café Torre/SV
California Cafe/E/N/SV
Carnelian Room
Carneros/N
Charles Nob Hill
Charlie's
Chateau Souverain/N
Cheers
Chez Panisse/E
Chez Panisse Café/E
Christopher's/E
Cielo/S
Citizen Cake
Cityscape
Clouds Downtown/S
Convivio/S
Cool Café/SV
Covey/S
Desiree
Domaine Chandon/N
Duarte's Tavern/S
El Paseo/N
Emma
Enrico's Sidewalk Cafe
Erna's Elderberry/E
Eulipia/SV
Faultline Brewing/SV
Flea St. Café/SV
Flying Fish Grill/S
Foothill Cafe/N
Fournou's Ovens
Gabriella Café/S
Garden Court
Garibaldis/Presidio
Garibaldis/College/E
General's Daughter/N
Glen Ellen Inn/N
Grand Cafe
Grasing's/S
Hawthorne Lane
House
Indigo
Insalata's/N
Italian Colors/E
Jardinière

Taiwan/E
Tommy Toy's
Ton Kiang
Yank Sing
Yuet Lee

Coffeehouses
Cafe Borrone/SV
Caffe Centro
University Coffee/SV

Coffee Shops/Diners
Bette's Oceanview/E
Bubba's Diner/N
Diner/N
Dipsea Cafe/N
Hobee's/SV
It's Tops Coffee
JoAnn's Cafe/S
Mama's Royal/E
Max's Diner
Max's Diner/E
Max's Opera Cafe
Mel's Drive-In
Peninsula Fountain/SV
Sears Fine Food

Continental
Alta Mira/N
Anton & Michel/S
Bella Vista/SV
Caprice/N
Dal Baffo/SV
Hotel Mac/E
Ovation
Rest. at Stevenswood/N
Shadowbrook/S

Cuban
Asia de Cuba

Delis/Sandwich Shops
Cafe Citti/N
East Coast West Deli
Gayle's Bakery/S
Jimtown Store/N
JZ Cool/SV
Max's Diner
Max's on the Square
Max's Opera Cafe
Max's Opera Cafe/SV
Merenda
Moishe's Pippic
Saul's/E

Dim Sum
Fook Yuen/SV
Harbor Village
Hong Kong Flower/SV
Jade Villa/E

Koi Palace/S
Mayflower
Restaurant Peony/E
Taiwan
Taiwan/E
Ton Kiang
Yank Sing

Eclectic/International
Andalu
British Bankers Club/SV
Britt-Marie's/E
Bubble Lounge
Cafe Cuvée
Cafe La Haye/N
Carta
Charlie's
Chow
Firefly
Hayes & Vine Wine
Mendo Bistro/N
Mixx/N
Pangaea/N
Park Chow
Pearl/N
Pearl Alley/S
Rest. Umunhum/SV
Soizic/E
Spettro/E
Stars
Stinson Beach Grill/N
Townhouse/E
Venus/E
Wappo Bar Bistro/N
Woodside Bakery/SV

English
Kensington Circus Pub/E
Lovejoy's Tea Rm.
Pelican Inn/N

Eritrean
Massawa

Ethiopian
Blue Nile/E
Rasselas

French
Auberge du Soleil/N
Basque Cultural Ctr./S
Basque Nueva Cocina
Beauséjour/SV
Brix/N
Cafe Beaujolais/N
Café Fanny/E
Cafe Jacqueline
Café Mozart
Campton Place

Carême Room
Casanova/S
Chantilly/SV
Chateau Souverain/N
Christophc/N
Citron/E
Clémentine
El Paseo/N
Emile's/SV
Fresh Cream/S
Galette
Guernica/N
Jardinière
Julius' Castle
La Forêt/SV
La Vie
L'Olivier
Luna Park
Piaf's
Plouf
Restaurant LuLu
Rue de Main/E
Rue de Paris/SV
Scala's Bistro
Ti Couz
V Rest. & Wine
Waterfront
Zax

French (Bistro)
Absinthe
À Côté/E
Alamo Square
Anjou
Baker St. Bistro
Bistro Clovis
Bistro Elan/SV
Bistro Jeanty/N
Bistro Vida/SV
Bizou
Black Cat
Bocca Rotis
Bouchon/N
Butler & Chef
Cafe Bastille
Cafe Brioche/SV
Café Claude
Cafe de la Presse
Cafe de Paris/L'Entrecôte
Café Marcella/SV
Café Rouge/E
Chapeau!
Charcuterie/N
Christophe/N
Clémentine
Florio
Foreign Cinema
Fringale

girl & the fig/N
Hyde St. Bistro
Jojo/E
La Folie
L'Amie Donia/SV
La Note/E
Le Bistrot
Le Central Bistro
Le Charm
Left Bank/E/N/SV
Le Mouton Noir/SV
Montrio/S
Nizza La Bella/E
Pigalle/SV
Robert's Bistro/S
Savor
South Park Cafe
Syrah/N
Voulez-Vous/E
White Rock Cafe/SV
Zazie

French (New)
Alfy's/N
Applewood Inn/N
Azie
Baccarat/SV
Bistro Liaison/E
Charles Nob Hill
Chaya Brasserie
Chaz
Chez TJ/SV
Club XIX/S
Domaine Chandon/N
Elisabeth Daniel
Erna's Elderberry/E
Fifth Floor
Fleur de Lys
Gary Danko
Grand Cafe
Isa
Kenwood/N
La Folie
La Rue/E
La Toque/N
Le Colonial
Le Papillon/SV
Madrona Manor/N
Marché aux Fleurs/N
Marinus/S
Masa's
mc^2
Meritage/N
955 Ukiah/N
Ovation
Pacific's Edge/S
Pastis
Pinot Blanc/N

Plumed Horse/SV
Rendezvous Inn/N
Restaurant 301/N
Ritz-Carlton Din. Rm.
Rubicon
Sent Sovi/SV
Sierra Mar/S
Suleil/SV
Terra/N
Tommy Toy's
Watergate

Fusion
A Tavola/SV
Azie
Brix/N
EOS
House
Mei Long/SV
Oritalia
Roy's
Roy's/Pebble Bch./S
Soizic/E
Straits Cafe
Straits Cafe/SV

German
Schroeder's
Suppenküche
Tommy's Joynt
Walzwerk

Greek
Evvia/SV
Kokkari Estiatorio

Hamburgers
Balboa Cafe
Barney's
Barney's/E
Burger Joint
Hard Rock Cafe
It's Tops Coffee
Liverpool Lil's
Magnolia Pub
Mel's Drive-In
Moose's
Mo's Burgers

Hawaiian
Rick's
Tita's

Hungarian
Hungarian Sausage

Indian
Ajanta/E
Amber India/SV
Breads of India/E
Ganges

Gaylord India
Gaylord India/SV
Indian Oven
Lotus Cuisine of India/N
Maharani
Passage to India/SV
Shalimar
Vik's Chaat Corner/E
Zaika/E
Zante's

Indonesian
Rice Table/N

Italian
(N=Northern; S=Southern;
N&S=Includes both)
Acquerello (N)
Albona Rist. (N)
Alioto's (S)
Allegro (N&S)
Antica Trattoria (N&S)
Aperto (N&S)
Avanti/S (N&S)
Baldoria (N&S)
Bella Luna/SV (N&S)
Bella Mia/SV (N&S)
Bella Trattoria (N&S)
Bistro Don Giovanni/N (N&S)
Bocca Rotis (N&S)
Bontà Rist. (N&S)
Brazio/E (N)
Bruno's (N&S)
Buca di Beppo (S)
Buca Giovanni (N&S)
Cafe Citti/N (N)
Cafe 817/E (N)
Café Fanny/E (N)
Café Marcella/SV (N)
Café Niebaum-Coppola (S)
Café Niebaum-Coppola/SV (S)
Cafe Pro Bono/SV (N&S)
Cafe Riggio (N&S)
Café Tiramisu (N)
Café Torre/SV (N&S)
Caffe Delle Stelle (N)
Caffè Greco (N&S)
Caffe Macaroni (S)
Caffe Riace/SV (S)
Caffe Sport (S)
Capellini/SV (N)
Capp's Corner (N&S)
Carpaccio/SV (N)
Casanova/S (N&S)
Chantilly/SV (N)
Convivio/S (N&S)
Cucina Jackson Fillmore/N (N)
Delfina (N&S)

Cuisine Index

Della Santina's/N (N)
E'Angelo (N)
Emma (N&S)
Emmy's Spaghetti (N&S)
Emporio Rulli/N (N&S)
Faz (N&S)
Faz/E/SV (N&S)
Felix & Louie's/N (N&S)
Fior d'Italia (N)
Florio (N&S)
Frantoio/N (N)
Gabriella Café/S (N)
Giorgio's Pizza (N&S)
Gira Polli (N&S)
Gira Polli/N (N&S)
Green Valley Cafe/N (N)
I Fratelli (N&S)
I Fratelli/SV (N&S)
Il Davide/N (N)
Il Fornaio (N)
Il Fornaio/E/N/S/SV (N)
Italian Colors/E (N&S)
Jackson Fillmore (N&S)
Julius' Castle (N)
Kuleto's (N&S)
Kuleto's/SV (N&S)
La Felce (N)
Laghi (N)
La Ginestra/N (S)
La Pastaia/SV (N&S)
La Villa Poppi (N)
Little Joe's (N&S)
L'Osteria del Forno (N)
Luna Park (N&S)
Macaroni Sciue Sciue (S)
Maddalena's/SV (N&S)
Mangiafuoco (N)
Marin Joe's/N (N&S)
Mario's Bohemian Cigar (N)
Mazzini Trattoria/E (N&S)
Merenda (N)
Meritage/N (N)
Mescolanza (N)
Mezza Luna/S (S)
Michelangelo (N&S)
Mio Vicino/SV (N&S)
Mistral/SV (N&S)
Montrio/S (N&S)
Mucca/N (N&S)
Nizza La Bella/E (N)
Nob Hill Café (N&S)
North Beach (N&S)
Oliveto Cafe/E (N)
Original Joe's (N&S)
Original Joe's/SV (N&S)
Osteria (N)
Osteria/SV (N)
Palatino (N&S)

Palio d'Asti (N&S)
Pane e Vino (N)
Paolo's/SV (N&S)
Parma (N)
Pasta Moon/S (N&S)
Pasta Pomodoro (N&S)
Pasta Pomodoro/E/N (N&S)
Pazzia (N&S)
Pesce (N)
Piatti/E/N/S/SV (N&S)
Piazza D'Angelo/N (N&S)
Postino/E (N)
Prego Rist. (N&S)
Prima/E (N)
Puccini & Pinetti (N&S)
Ristorante Bacco (N&S)
Ristorante Fabrizio/N (N)
Ristorante Ideale (N&S)
Ristorante Milano (N)
Ristorante Umbria (N&S)
Rose Pistola (N)
Rose's Café (N)
Salute Rist./E/N (N&S)
Santi (N&S)
Scala's Bistro (N&S)
Spiedini/E (N)
Spiedo Rist./SV (N&S)
Splendido (N&S)
Stinking Rose (N)
Terra/N (N)
Tomatina/N (S)
Tommaso's (S)
Tratt. La Siciliana/E (S)
Trattoria Contadina (N&S)
Tra Vigne/N (N&S)
Trellis/SV (N&S)
Tuscany/N (N)
Uva/N (N&S)
Venezia/E (N&S)
Venticello (N)
Via Centro/E (N)
Via Vai (N&S)
Vicolo (N&S)
Vivande Porta Via (N&S)
Zinzino (N&S)
Zuni Cafe (N)
zuzu/N (N)

Japanese
Ace Wasabi's
Anzu
Azuma/SV
Backflip
Blowfish, Sushi
Chaya Brasserie
Dashi/SV
Ebisu
Fuki Sushi/SV

Godzila Sushi
Grandeho's Kamekyo
Hamano Sushi
Hana/N
Higashi West/SV
Hotei
Isobune Sushi
Isobune Sushi/E/SV
Juban
Juban/SV
Kabuto Sushi
Kirala/E
Kyo-Ya
Le Bistrot
Le Poisson Japonais/SV
Maki
Mifune
Miyake/SV
O Chamé/E
Ozumo
Robata Grill & Sushi/N
Sanraku Four Seasons
Sushi Groove
Sushi Ran/N
Sushi to Dai For/N
Tachibana/E
Takara
Ten-Ichi
Tokyo Go Go
Uzen/E
We Be Sushi
Yokoso Nippon
Yoshida-Ya
Yoshi's/Jack London/E

Jewish
East Coast West Deli
Max's Diner
Max's Diner/E
Max's on the Square
Max's Opera Cafe
Max's Opera Cafe/SV
Moishe's Pippic
Saul's/E

Korean
Brother's Korean
Hahn's Hibachi
Koryo/E

Kurdish
Cafe Silan/SV

Malaysian
Shiok! Singapore Kit./SV

Mediterranean
Academy Grill
Acorn/SV
Arlequin Food to Go
Bay Wolf/E

Bistro Aix
Bittersweet Bistro/S
Bucci's/E
Café Esin/E
Cafe Gibraltar/S
Cafe Monk
Cafe Prima Vera/SV
Cafe Pro Bono/SV
Caffè Museo
Carneros/N
Carrara's/E
Cetrella Bistro/S
Chez Nous
Chez Panisse/E
downtown/E
Draeger's/SV
Enrico's Sidewalk Cafe
Fandango/S
Faz
Faz/E/SV
Fournou's Ovens
42 Degrees
Frascati
Garibaldis/Presidio
Garibaldis/College/E
Insalata's/N
Lalime's/E
La Mediterranée
La Mediterranée/E
Lapis
La Scene Café
Ledford House/N
Lucy's Cafe/N
Manzanita/N
Mezze/E
Mikayla/Casa Madrona/N
Mistral/N
Mixx/N
Montrio/S
Ondine/N
Orlo's/SV
Palomino
paul K
PlumpJack Cafe
PlumpJack Cafe/N
Ritz-Carlton Terrace
Rivoli/E
Salute Rist./E
Savor
71 Saint Peter/SV
Soleil/SV
Spiedo Rist./SV
Stars
Stokes Adobe/S
Truly Mediterranean
Verbena/E
Via Centro/E
Viaggio Rist./SV

Cuisine Index

Village Pub/SV
Viognier/SV
Willow Wood Market/N
Zaré
Zax
Zibibbo/SV
Zodiac Club
Zuni Cafe

Mexican/Tex-Mex
Andale Taqueria/SV
Aqui Cal-Mex/SV
¡Ay Ay Ay!/SV
Baja Fresh/SV
Cactus Taqueria/E
Cafe Marimba
Casa Aguila
Chevys Fresh Mex
Chevys Fresh Mex/E/N/S/SV
Doña Tomás/E
El Balazo
El Palomar/S
Fiesta del Mar/SV
Guaymas/N
Joe's Taco Lounge/N
Juan's Place/E
La Cumbre Taqueria
La Cumbre Taqueria/SV
La Fiesta/SV
La Palma
La Rondalla
Las Camelias/N
La Taqueria
La Taqueria/SV
Maya
Maya/N
Mom is Cooking
Palo Alto Sol/SV
Pancho Villa
Pancho Villa/SV
Picante Cocina/E
Primo Patio Cafe
Roosevelt Tamale
Sinaloa Cafe/SV
Taqueria Cancun

Middle Eastern
Falafel's Drive-In/SV
Kan Zaman
La Mediterranée
La Mediterranée/E
Truly Mediterranean

Moroccan
Kasbah Moroccan/N

Nepalese
Kathmandu West/SV

Noodle Shops
Charlie Hong Kong/S
Citrus Club
Hotei
Long Life Noodle
Long Life Noodle/E/SV
Mifune
Tin-Pan Asian Bistro
Zao Noodle Bar
Zao Noodle Bar/SV

Nuevo Latino
Alma

Pacific Rim
butterfly
Jordan's/E
Rest. Umunhum/SV

Pakistani
Shalimar

Persian
Maykedah

Peruvian
Estampas Peruanas/SV

Pizza
Amici's
Amici's/N/SV
Applewood Inn/SV
Arizmendi Bakery
Arizmendi Bakery/E
Café Niebaum-Coppola
Café Niebaum-Coppola/SV
Cheese Board/E
Firewood Café
Frantoio/N
Giorgio's Pizza
Il Fornaio
Il Fornaio/E/N/S/SV
La Ginestra/N
L'Osteria del Forno
Mescolanza
Mio Vicino/SV
Nob Hill Café
North Beach Pizza
North Beach Pizza/E
Pasta Moon/S
Pauline's Pizza
Pazzia
Pizza Rustica/E
Pizzetta 211
Postrio
Tomatina/N
Tommaso's
Tony & Alba's Pizza/SV
Uva/N
Via Vai

Vicolo
Willow Street Pizza/N/SV
Woodside Bakery/SV
Zachary's Chicago Pizza/E
Zante's
Zinzino

Polynesian
Tonga Room
Trader Vic's/E

Pub Food
Calistoga Inn/N
Gordon Biersch
Gordon Biersch/SV
Half Moon Bay/S
Liverpool Lil's
Magnolia Pub
Pelican Inn/N
Potrero Brewing
Tied House/SV
21st Amendment Brew.

Russian
Katia's Russian Tea Rm.

Seafood
Alamo Square
Alioto's
Aqua
A. Sabella's
Barbara's Fishtrap/S
Chart House/S/SV
Cook's Seafood/SV
Crow's Nest/S
Crustacean
downtown/E
Eastside West
Farallon
Flying Fish Grill/S
Great Eastern
Hawgs Seafood/SV
Hayes St. Grill
Hong Kong Flower/SV
House
Koi Palace/S
Little River Inn/N
Mayflower
McCormick & Kuleto's
Navio/S
Pacific Café
Pesce
Pier 23 Cafe
Pisces/SV
PJ's Oyster Bed
Plouf
Red Herring
Ritz-Carlton Terrace
Rocco's Seafood

Rose Pistola
Sam's Grill
Sardine Factory/S
Scoma's
Scoma's/N
Scott's/E/SV
Skates on the Bay/E
Spenger's/E
Station House Café/N
Steamer's Grillhouse/SV
Stillwater/S
Swan Oyster Depot
Tadich Grill
Thanh Long
3 Fish/SV
Ti Couz
Twenty Four
Waterfront
Yabbies Coastal Kit.
Yankee Pier/N
Yuet Lee

Singaporean
Shiok! Singapore Kit./SV
Straits Cafe
Straits Cafe/SV

South African
Joubert's

South American
Destino
Estampas Peruanas/SV
girl & the gaucho/N
Le Krewe
Miramonte/N
Peña Pachamama
Terra Brazilis

Southern/Soul
Biscuits & Blues
Catahoula/N
Everett & Jones BBQ/E
Kate's Kitchen
Kingfish/SV
Le Krewe
Memphis Minnie's
Nola/SV
Powell's Place

Southwestern
Cactus Cafe/N
Left at Albuquerque
Left at Albuquerque/E/SV
Rio Grill/S

Spanish
Alegrias, Food From Spain
Basque Nueva Cocina
B44

César/E
Esperpento
Guernica/N
Iberia/SV
Picaro
Ramblas
Thirsty Bear Brewing
Timo's
Zarzuela

Steakhouses
Alfred's Steak Hse.
Bighorn Grill/E
Brazio/E
Carmel Chop Hse./S
Chart House/S/SV
Cole's Chop Hse./N
Crow's Nest/S
Harris'
House of Prime Rib
Izzy's Steak
John's Grill
Morton's
Mucca/N
Rutherford Grill/N
Scott's/E/SV
Vic Stewart's/E

Swiss
La Fondue/SV
Matterhorn Swiss

Taiwanese
Coriya Hot Pot
Lucy's Tea Hse./SV
Taiwan
Taiwan/E

Tapas
À Côté/E
Alegrias, Food From Spain
AsiaSF
Basque Nueva Cocina
butterfly
César/E
Cha Cha Cha
Charanga
Chez Nous
Destino
Esperpento
girl & the gaucho/N
Grasshopper/E
Iberia/SV
Isa
Oritalia
Piaf's
Picaro
Ramblas
Thirsty Bear Brewing

Timo's
Zarzuela

Tearooms
Compass Rose
Frjtz Fries
Lovejoy's Tea Rm.
Lucy's Tea Hse./SV
O Chamé/E

Thai
Ara Wan/N
Basil
Cha Am Thai
Dusit Thai
Khan Toke Thai
King of Thai
Krungthai/SV
Manora's Thai
Marnee Thai
Narai
Neecha Thai
Phuping/E
Plearn Thai/E
Royal Thai
Royal Thai/N
Thai House
Thanya & Salee
Thep Phanom
Yukol Place

Tibetan
Lhasa Moon

Vegetarian
(*Vegan)
Flea St. Café/SV
Fleur de Lys
Greens
Herbivore*
Joubert's
Late for the Train/SV
Long Life Vegi/E
Millennium
Ravens/N*
Three Seasons

Vietnamese
Ana Mandara
Camranh Bay/SV
Golden Turtle
La Vie
Le Cheval/E
Le Colonial
Le Soleil
Slanted Door
Thanh Long
Tu Lan
Vi's/E

LOCATIONS

SAN FRANCISCO

Bernal Heights
Angkor Borei
Blue Plate
Dusit Thai
Emmy's Spaghetti
Hungarian Sausage
Liberty Cafe
Palatino
Taqueria Cancun
Zante's

Castro
Blue
Cafe Cuvée
Cafe Flore
Chow
Firewood Café
La Mediterranée
Ma Tante Sumi
Pasta Pomodoro
Thai House
Tin-Pan Asian Bistro
Tita's
2223
Zao Noodle Bar

Chinatown
Brandy Ho's
Empress of China
Great Eastern
House of Nanking
Hunan Home's
R & G Lounge
Yuet Lee

Civic Center
Chevys Fresh Mex
Indigo
Max's Opera Cafe
Mel's Drive-In
Millennium
Stars
Venture Frogs

Cow Hollow
Baker St. Bistro
Balboa Cafe
Betelnut Pejiu Wu
Bontà Rist.
Brazen Head
Cafe de Paris/L'Entrecôte
Charlie's
Eastside West
Left at Albuquerque

Liverpool Lil's
Merenda
Pane e Vino
Perry's
PlumpJack Cafe
Prego Rist.
Rose's Café
Via Vai
Yoshida-Ya

Downtown
Alfred's Steak Hse.
Anjou
Anzu
Aqua
Asia de Cuba
B44
Biscuits & Blues
Bix
Bubble Lounge
Cafe Bastille
Café Claude
Cafe de la Presse
Café Tiramisu
Campton Place
Carnelian Room
Cha Am Thai
Cheesecake Factory
Chevys Fresh Mex
Cityscape
Compass Rose
Cypress Club
E&O Trading
Elisabeth Daniel
Farallon
Faz
Fifth Floor
Firewood Café
First Crush
Fleur de Lys
Garden Court
Gaylord India
Globe
Grand Cafe
Harbor Village
Hunan
John's Grill
Kokkari Estiatorio
Kuleto's
La Scene Café
Le Central Bistro
Le Colonial
L'Olivier

EAST OF SAN FRANCISCO

Alameda
Chevys Fresh Mex

Albany
Britt-Marie's
Christopher's
Nizza La Bella

Berkeley
Ajanta
Barney's
Bette's Oceanview
Bistro Liaison
Blue Nile
Breads of India
Cactus Taqueria
Café Fanny
Café Rouge
Cambodiana
César
Cha Am Thai
Cheese Board
Chez Panisse
Chez Panisse Café
downtown
FatApple's
Ginger Island
Jimmy Bean's
Jordan's
Juan's Place
Kirala
Lalime's
La Mediterranée
La Note
La Rue
Long Life Noodle
Long Life Vegi
Mazzini Trattoria
North Beach Pizza
O Chamé
Paragon Bar
Picante Cocina
Plearn Thai
Rick & Ann's
Rivoli
Santa Fe
Saul's
Shen Hua
Skates on the Bay
Spenger's
Taiwan
Tratt. La Siciliana
Venezia
Venus
Via Centro
Vik's Chaat Corner

Voulez-Vous
Xanadu
Zachary's Chicago Pizza
Zaika

Danville
Blackhawk Grille
Brazio
Bridges
Faz
Piatti

El Cerrito
FatApple's

Emeryville
Bucci's
Chevys Fresh Mex
Townhouse
Trader Vic's

Hayward
Everett & Jones BBQ
Rue de Main

Kensington
Kensington Circus Pub

Lafayette
Duck Club
Postino

Livermore
Chevys Fresh Mex
Wente Vineyards

Oakland
À Côté
Arizmendi Bakery
Autumn Moon
Barney's
Battambang
Bay Wolf
Cactus Taqueria
Cafe 817
Carrara's
Citron
Doña Tomás
Everett & Jones BBQ
Garibaldi/Presidio
Grasshopper
Isobune Sushi
Italian Colors
Jade Villa
Jojo
Koryo
Le Cheval
Little Shin Shin
Mama's Royal

Mendocino County
Albion River Inn
Boonville Hotel
Cafe Beaujolais
Ledford House
Little River Inn
MacCallum House
Mendo Bistro
Moosse Cafe
955 Ukiah
Pangaea
Ravens
Rendezvous Inn
Rest. at Stevenswood
St. Orres

Mill Valley
Avenue Grill
Buckeye Roadhse.
Cactus Cafe
Dipsea Cafe
El Paseo
Frantoio
Gira Polli
Joe's Taco Lounge
La Ginestra
Piatti
Piazza D'Angelo
Robata Grill & Sushi
Willow Street Pizza

Napa
Bistro Don Giovanni
Brix
Carneros
Celadon
Chevys Fresh Mex
Cole's Chop Hse.
Foothill Cafe
Mustards Grill
Napa Valley Wine
Pairs
Pearl
Sake Tini
Tuscany
Uva

Novato
Chevys Fresh Mex

Olema
Olema Inn

Ross
Marché aux Fleurs

Rutherford
Auberge du Soleil
La Toque
Rutherford Grill

San Anselmo
Alfy's
Bubba's Diner
Cucina Jackson Fillmore
Insalata's

San Rafael
Amici's
Il Davide
Kasbah Moroccan
Las Camelias
Lotus Cuisine of India
Pasta Pomodoro
Rice Table
Royal Thai
Salute Rist.
Sushi to Dai For

Santa Rosa
Cafe Lolo
Chevys Fresh Mex
Feast
Hana
John Ash & Co.
Mariposa
Mistral
Mixx
Syrah
zuzu

Sausalito
Alta Mira
Ara Wan
Christophe
Guernica
Mikayla/Casa Madrona
Ondine
Scoma's
Sushi Ran

Sebastopol/Valley Ford
Lucy's Cafe
Willow Wood Market

Sonoma
Cafe La Haye
Della Santina's
Deuce
General's Daughter
Maya
Meritage
Piatti
Rest. at Sonoma Mission

Sonoma Coast
Duck Club

St. Helena
Green Valley Cafe
Meadowood Grill

Campbell
Buca di Beppo
Hawgs Seafood
Hobee's
Left at Albuquerque
Mio Vicino

Cupertino
Armadillo Willy's
Azuma
Baja Fresh
Café Torre
Hobee's
Joy Luck Place
Kathmandu West
Miyake

Foster City
Chevys Fresh Mex

Los Altos
Applewood Inn
Armadillo Willy's
¡Ay Ay Ay!
Bandera
Beauséjour
Chef Chu's
I Fratelli
Jocco's
Yamin Win

Los Gatos
Andale Taqueria
Café Marcella
Cafe Prima Vera
California Cafe
Chart House
Los Gatos Brewing
Pigalle
Steamer's Grillhouse
Tapestry
Willow Street Pizza

Menlo Park
Acorn
Applewood Inn
Bistro Vida
British Bankers Club
Cafe Borrone
Cafe Silan
Carpaccio
Cook's Seafood
Dal Baffo
Dashi
Draeger's
Duck Club
Flea St. Café
Gaylord India

Iberia
Juban
JZ Cool
Late for the Train
Left Bank
Shiok! Singapore Kit.
Su Hong
3 Fish
Trellis
Wild Hare

Millbrae
Fook Yuen
Hong Kong Flower

Morgan Hill
Le Bistro
Sinaloa Cafe

Mountain View
Amber India
Amici's
Applewood Inn
Chevys Fresh Mex
Chez TJ
Fiesta del Mar
Hobee's
La Fiesta
Lucy's Tea Hse.
Mei Long
Passage to India
Tied House
Tony & Alba's Pizza

Palo Alto
Andale Taqueria
Baja Fresh
Bella Luna
Bistro Elan
Blue Chalk Cafe
Buca di Beppo
Cafe Brioche
Café Niebaum-Coppola
Cafe Pro Bono
Caffe Riace
California Cafe
Cool Café
Empire Grill
Evvia
Fuki Sushi
Gordon Biersch
Higashi West
Hobee's
Hong Kong Flower
Il Fornaio
L'Amie Donia
Left at Albuquerque
Le Poisson Japonais
Long Life Noodle

MacArthur Park
Maddalena's/Café Fino
Mandarin Gourmet
Mango Cafe
Max's Opera Cafe
Miyake
Nola
Osteria
Palo Alto Sol
Peninsula Fountain
Perry's
Piatti
Pluto's
Scott's
Soleil
Spago Palo Alto
St. Michael's Alley
Straits Cafe
University Coffee
Zao Noodle Bar
Zibibbo

Redwood City
Amici's
Baccarat
Chantilly
Chevys Fresh Mex
Estampas Peruanas
Max's on the Square
Mistral

San Carlos
A Tavola
Kabul

San Jose
A.P. Stump's
Aqui Cal-Mex
Armadillo Willy's
Baja Fresh
Bella Mia
Cafe Prima Vera
Chevys Fresh Mex
E&O Trading
Emile's
Eulipia
Falafel's Drive-In
Gordon Biersch
Hawgs Seafood
Hobee's
Il Fornaio
Krungthai
La Forêt
La Pastaia
La Taqueria
Le Papillon
Max's on the Square

Mio Vicino
Original Joe's
Orlo's
Paolo's
Red Tractor Cafe
Rest. Umunhum
Rue de Paris
Scott's
71 Saint Peter
Spiedo Rist.
Tied House
White Rock Cafe
Willow Street Pizza

San Mateo
Amici's
Armadillo Willy's
Camranh Bay
Capellini
Kingfish
La Cumbre Taqueria
Lark Creek
Pancho Villa
Spiedo Rist.
231 Ellsworth
Viognier

Santa Clara
Armadillo Willy's
California Cafe
Mio Vicino

Saratoga
La Fondue
Le Mouton Noir
Plumed Horse
Sent Sovi
Viaggio Rist.

Sunnyvale
Armadillo Willy's
Chevys Fresh Mex
Faultline Brewing
Faz
Hobee's
Kabul
Lion & Compass
Stoddard's
Tarragon

Woodside
Bella Vista
Buck's
John Bentley's
Village Pub
Woodside Bakery

SPECIAL FEATURES

(Restaurants followed by a † may not offer
that feature at every location.)

Breakfast
(See also Hotel Dining)
Absinthe
Autumn Moon/E
Bette's Oceanview/E
Bubba's Diner/N
Buck's/SV
Butler & Chef
Cafe Borrone/SV
Cafe de la Presse
Cafe 817/E
Café Fanny/E
Cafe Flore
Caffè Greco
Casa Aguila
Chloe's Cafe
Citizen Cake
Desiree
Dipsea Cafe/N
Dottie's True Blue
Downtown Bakery/N
Draeger's/SV
Duarte's Tavern/S
Ella's
Emporio Rulli/N
FatApple's/E
Frjtz Fries
Gordon's/N
Harbor Village
Hobee's/SV
It's Tops Coffee
Jimmy Bean's/E
Jimtown Store/N
JoAnn's Cafe/S
La Mediterranée†
La Note/E
Mama's Royal/E
Mama's/Washington Sq.
Model Bakery/N
Pork Store Cafe
Red Tractor Cafe/E†
Rick & Ann's/E
Rose's Café
Savor
Sears Fine Food
Station House Café/N
Town's End
Universal Cafe
University Coffee/SV
Venus/E
Woodside Bakery/SV
Zazie

Brunch
(Best of many)
Absinthe
Autumn Moon/E
Baccarat/SV
Bette's Oceanview/E
Bistro Vida/SV
Buckeye Roadhse./N
Buck's/SV
Cafe Brioche/SV
Cafe Cuvée
Cafe Marimba
California Cafe/E†
Carême Room
Chloe's Cafe
Dottie's True Blue
Draeger's/SV
Ella's
Empire Grill/SV
Flea St. Café/SV
Frjtz Fries
Garden Court
General's Daughter/N
Harbor Village
Hobee's/SV
Hong Kong Flower/SV
Il Fornaio†
Insalata's/N
Kate's Kitchen
La Mediterranée†
La Note/E
Lark Creek/E†
Late for the Train/SV
Mama's Royal/E
Mama's/Washington Sq.
Mazzini Trattoria/E
Mel's Drive-In†
Mikayla/Casa Madrona/N
Miss Millie's
MoMo's
Moose's
Moss Beach/S
Napa Valley Grille/N
Navio/S
Pacific
Pasta Moon/S
Perry's/SV†
Piazza D'Angelo/N
Pigalle/SV
Postrio
Primo Patio Cafe

Red Tractor Cafe/E†
Restaurant LuLu
Rick & Ann's/E
Rio Grill/S
Ritz-Carlton Terrace
Rose's Café
Sam's Anchor Cafe/N
Schroeder's
Soleil/SV
St. Michael's Alley/SV
Ton Kiang
Top of the Mark
Town's End
2223
Universal Cafe
University Coffee/SV
Viognier/SV
Waterfront
Wente Vineyards/E
Woodside Bakery/SV
XYZ
Yank Sing†
Zazie
Zibibbo/SV
Zuni Cafe

Buffet Served

(Check prices, days and times)
Academy Grill
Ahwahnee Din. Rm./E
Amber India/SV
Anzu
Carême Room
Cliff House
Coriya Hot Pot
Duck Club/SV†
Empress of China
Garden Court
Gaylord India†
House of Nanking
Irrawaddy Burmese
Jordan's/E
Kathmandu West/SV
Le Soleil
Little Joe's†
Lotus Cuisine of India/N
MacArthur Park/SV†
Mikayla/Casa Madrona/N
Navio/S
Pacific
Passage to India/SV
Pelican Inn/N
Rest. at Meadowood/N
Ritz-Carlton Terrace
Robata Grill & Sushi/N
Salute Rist./E†
Tommy's Joynt
Top of the Mark

Business Dining

Alfred's Steak Hse.
Anzu
A.P. Stump's/SV
Aqua
Azie
bacar
Baccarat/SV
Big Four
Bizou
Boulevard
Buck's/SV
Café Torre/SV
Campton Place
Carpaccio/SV
Chantilly/SV
Chart House/SV†
Chaya Brasserie
Cosmopolitan Cafe
Cypress Club
Dal Baffo/SV
Dine
Duck Club/SV†
Emile's/SV
Evvia/SV
Farallon
Faz†
Fior d'Italia
Fly Trap
Fournou's Ovens
Gordon's Hse. of Fine Eats
Harris'
Hawthorne Lane
House of Prime Rib
Iberia/SV
Il Fornaio/SV†
Infusion Bar
Izzy's Steak
John's Grill
Kokkari Estiatorio
Kuleto's/SV
Kyo-Ya
La Forêt/SV
Lark Creek/SV†
Le Central Bistro
Le Mouton Noir/SV
Lion & Compass/SV
Mandarin Gourmet/SV
Masa's
Maya
mc²
Moose's
Morton's
OakTown Cafe/E
One Market
Orlo's/SV
Osteria/SV

Special Feature Index

Le Papillon/SV
Le Poisson Japonais/SV
Liberty Cafe
Maddalena's/Café Fino/SV
Manzanita/N
Marché aux Fleurs/N
Max's Diner/E†
Maya/N
Meetinghouse
Memphis Minnie's
Meritage/N
Mezze/E
Millennium
Miramonte/N
Mucca/N
Navio/S
Nizza La Bella/E
Nola/SV
One Market
Ozumo
Palatino
Pane e Vino
Pangaea/N
Paolo's/SV
Pearl/N
Pesce
Piazza D'Angelo/N
Pinot Blanc/N
Ravenous/N†
Restaurant LuLu
Rick & Ann's/E
Ristorante Ideale
Roux/N
Rue de Paris/SV
Sake Tini/N
Saul's/E
71 Saint Peter/SV
Soizic/E
Spiedo Rist./SV†
St. Michael's Alley/SV
Tied House/SV†
Ton Kiang
Trader Vic's/E
Tra Vigne/N
Trellis/SV
Vik's Chaat Corner/E
Vivande Porta Via
Voulez-Vous/E
Waterfront
We Be Sushi†
Wente Vineyards/E
Wild Hare/SV
Yank Sing†
Zibibbo/SV

Child-Friendly

(Besides the normal fast-food places; * indicates children's menu available)
Alioto's*
Anzu*

Applewood Inn/SV†
Aqui Cal-Mex/SV
Armadillo Willy's/SV†
A. Sabella's*
Autumn Moon/E
Avanti/S*
Baja Fresh/SV†
Barney's†
Beach Chalet Brew.*
Bella Mia/SV
Bette's Oceanview/E*
Bittersweet Bistro/S*
Bocca Rotis*
Brazio/E*
Bubba's Diner/N*
Buca di Beppo/SV†
Buckeye Roadhse./N
Buck's/SV*
Cactus Cafe/N*
Cafe Riggio*
Capp's Corner*
Casa Orinda/E
Chart House/SV†
Chez Panisse Café/E*
Chow*
Convivio/S*
Deuce/N*
Draeger's/SV*
Duck Club/SV†
El Palomar/S*
Everett & Jones BBQ/E†
FatApple's/E†
Faz/SV†
Felix & Louie's/N*
Fiesta del Mar/SV†
Hana/N*
Harbor Village
Insalata's/N*
Isobune Sushi†
JZ Cool/SV
Left Bank/SV†
Lovejoy's Tea Rm.*
Max's Diner†
Max's on the Square†
Max's Opera Cafe†
Mazzini Trattoria/E*
Mel's Drive-In†
Montrio/S*
Original Joe's/SV†
Oswald's/S*
Pacific's Edge/S
Pairs/N*
Park Chow
Perry's†
Piatti/N†
Picante Cocina/E
Pluto's*

Red Tractor Cafe/E*
Restaurant Peony/E
Rick & Ann's/E*
Ritz-Carlton Din. Rm.*
Rutherford Grill/N*
Sardine Factory/S
Shadowbrook/S*
Spenger's/E
Spettro/E*
Splendido*
Tomatina/N
Tonga Room*
Yankee Pier/N
Yoshida-Ya
Zao Noodle Bar†

Dancing
(Check days and times)
AsiaSF
Backflip
Biscuits & Blues
Cafe de Paris/L'Entrecôte
Cityscape
Compass Rose
Crow's Nest/S
Enrico's Sidewalk Cafe
Jordan's/E
Maddalena's/Café Fino/SV
Mezza Luna/S
Paragon Bar/E
Peña Pachamama
Plumed Horse/SV
Shanghai 1930
Sno-Drift
Tonga Room
Top of the Mark
Zaika/E

Delivery/Takeout
(D=delivery, T=takeout)
Absinthe (T)
Alegrias, Food From Spain (T)
Alfred's Steak Hse. (T)
Antica Trattoria (T)
Asia de Cuba (T)
A Tavola/SV (D,T)
Autumn Moon/E (T)
Avenue Grill/N (T)
Baker St. Bistro (T)
Basque Nueva Cocina (T)
Beauséjour/SV (T)
Bella Vista/SV (T)
B44 (T)
Bighorn Grill/E (T)
Bistro Aix (T)
Bistro Liaison/E (T)
Bistro Ralph/N (T)
Bistro Vida/SV (D,T)

Bizou (T)
Black Cat (T)
Brazio/E (T)
British Bankers Club/SV (T)
Buca Giovanni (D,T)
Buckeye Roadhse./N (T)
Cafe Beaujolais/N (T)
Cafe Brioche/SV (T)
Café Esin/E (T)
Cafe Gibraltar/S (T)
Cafe La Haye/N (T)
Cafe Lolo/N (T)
Café Marcella/SV (T)
Cafe Monk (T)
Café Rouge/E (T)
Cafe Silan/SV (T)
Caffe Riace/SV (D,T)
Casanova/S (T)
Casa Orinda/E (T)
Charanga (T)
Chenery Park (T)
Chez Nous (T)
Christopher's/E (T)
Cliff House (T)
Clouds Downtown/S (T)
Cosmopolitan Cafe (T)
Delfina (T)
Doña Tomás/E (T)
downtown/E (T)
Duck Club/N†
E&O Trading/SV (T)
Eastside West (T)
Eulipia/SV (T)
Evvia/SV (D)
Fandango/S (T)
Feast/N (T)
Flea St. Café/SV (T)
Florio (T)
Flying Fish Grill/S (T)
Fringale (T)
Frjtz Fries (T)
Garibaldis/Presidio†
General's Daughter/N (T)
girl & the fig/N (T)
girl & the gaucho/N (T)
Glen Ellen Inn/N (T)
Globe (T)
Gordon's/N (D,T)
Gordon's Hse. of Fine Eats (T)
Greens (T)
Hotel Mac/E (T)
House of Prime Rib (T)
Indigo (T)
Insalata's/N (T)
Isa (T)
Izzy's Steak (D,T)
Jianna (T)

Jordan's/E (T)
Kasbah Moroccan/N (T)
Kingfish/SV (T)
La Forêt/SV (T)
Lark Creek/E†
Le Bistrot (T)
Left Bank/N†
Le Poisson Japonais/SV (D,T)
Luna Park (T)
Marché aux Fleurs/N (T)
Ma Tante Sumi (T)
Mazzini Trattoria/E (T)
Meadowood Grill/N (T)
Mezza Luna/S (T)
Millennium (T)
Miramonte/N (T)
Mistral/N (T)
Mistral/SV (T)
Montrio/S (T)
Moosse Cafe/N (T)
Mucca/N (T)
955 Ukiah/N (T)
Nizza La Bella/E (T)
Nola/SV (D,T)
Pacific (T)
Pangaea/N (T)
Paolo's/SV (T)
Pastis (T)
Pearl/N (T)
Pesce (T)
Pigalle/SV (T)
Pinot Blanc/N (T)
PJ's Oyster Bed (D,T)
Plouf (T)
Ravenous/N†
Ravens/N (T)
Restaurant LuLu (T)
Restaurant 301/N (T)
Rio Grill/S (T)
Rivoli/E (T)
Rose Pistola (T)
Roux/N (T)
Roy's (T)
Rue de Paris/SV (T)
Rutherford Grill/N (T)
Sake Tini/N (T)
Santi/N (T)
71 Saint Peter/SV (T)
Sierra Mar/S (T)
Splendido (T)
Station House Café/N (T)
St. Michael's Alley/SV (T)
Stoddard's/SV (T)
Stokes Adobe/S (T)
Syrah/N (T)
Tapestry/SV (T)
Tarragon/SV (T)

3 Fish/SV (D,T)
Townhouse/E (T)
Tra Vigne/N (D,T)
Trellis/SV (T)
Viaggio Rist./SV (T)
Vic Stewart's/E (T)
Village Pub/SV (T)
Viognier/SV (T)
Wappo Bar Bistro/N (D,T)
Wente Vineyards/E (T)
Wild Hare/SV (T)
Wine Spectator/N (D,T)
Yabbies Coastal Kit. (T)
Yankee Pier/N (T)
Zarzuela (T)
Zibibbo/SV (T)
Zin/N (T)
Zuni Cafe (T)

Dining Alone

(Other than hotels and places
with counter service)
Absinthe
Bistro Jeanty/N
Burger Joint
Butler & Chef
Cafe Bastille
Cafe Brioche/SV
Café Claude
Cafe de la Presse
Cafe Flore
Café Torre/SV
Caffe Centro
Caffè Greco
Caffè Museo
Casa Aguila
César/E
Chez TJ/SV
Citizen Cake
Dal Baffo/SV
Empire Grill/SV
Enrico's Sidewalk Cafe
Eos
Evvia/SV
FatApple's/E
Flea St. Café/SV
Frjtz Fries
Hahn's Hibachi
Hotei
House of Nanking
Jimtown Store/N
Kabuto Sushi
L'Amie Donia/SV
La Note/E
Le Bistrot
Left Bank/SV†
Mario's Bohemian Cigar
Matterhorn Swiss

Mifune
Model Bakery/N
Mo's Burgers†
Pasta Pomodoro†
Pluto's†
Red Tractor Cafe/E†
Rose's Café
Sears Fine Food
Suppenküche
Tachibana/E
Ti Couz
Tommaso's
Tommy's Joynt
Tu Lan
Viognier/SV
Vivande Porta Via
Wild Hare/SV
Yoshi's/Jack London/E
Zazie
Zibibbo/SV

Entertainment

(Call for days and times of performances)
Albion River Inn/N (piano)
Alegrias (flamenco/guitar)
Ana Mandara (jazz)
Angkor Wat (dancers)
Anzu (piano)
A.P. Stump's/SV (jazz)
AsiaSF (illusionists)
Azie (DJ)
bacar (jazz)
Backflip (DJ)
Beach Chalet Brew. (jazz)
Big Four (piano)
Biscuits & Blues (blues)
BIX (jazz)
Black Cat (jazz)
Bollinger/E (varies)
Bruno's (jazz)
butterfly (DJ/jazz)
Cafe Bastille (jazz)
Café Claude (jazz)
Café Niebaum-Coppola (jazz)
Carta (jazz/piano)
Chantilly/SV (piano/violin)
Cityscape (jazz)
Cobalt Tavern (jazz)
Cole's Chop Hse./N (jazz)
Compass Rose (varies)
Convivio/S (jazz)
Cosmopolitan Cafe (blues/jazz)
Crow's Nest/S (bands/comedy)
Cypress Club (jazz)
Destino (flamenco/tango)
downtown/E (jazz)

Eastside West (jazz)
El Palomar/S (vocals)
Emmy's Spaghetti (guitar)
Enrico's Sidewalk Cafe (jazz)
Faultline Brewing/SV (bands)
Faz (jazz/piano)
42 Degrees (jazz trio)
Ganges (Indian)
Gordon Biersch/SV†
Gordon's Hse. of Fine Eats (jazz)
Guaymas/N (mariachi)
Half Moon Bay/S (blues/jazz)
Harris' (jazz/piano)
Hawthorne Lane (piano)
Hungarian Sausage (jazz/piano)
Infusion Bar (funk/jazz/rock)
Italian Colors/E (guitar)
Jardinière (jazz duo)
John's Grill (jazz)
Jordan's/E (swing)
Kan Zaman (belly dancer)
Kasbah/N (belly dancer)
Katia's (accordion/guitar)
Kelly's (bands/blues/jazz)
Kingfish/SV (blues)
La Note/E (jazz)
La Rondalla (mariachi)
La Rue/E (jazz)
Le Colonial (jazz)
Ledford House/N (jazz)
Left Bank/N†
Little River/N (classical guitar)
Maddalena's/SV (jazz)
Madrona Manor/N (jazz)
Maharani (sitar)
Marinus/S (jazz)
Max's Opera Cafe (vocals)
Mecca (jazz/R&B)
Mezza Luna/S (varies)
Mistral/SV (jazz)
Moose's (jazz)
Navio/S (jazz)
One Market (jazz/piano)
Oswald's/S (classical guitar)
Ovation (guitar/piano)
Pacific's Edge/S (jazz)
Paolo's/SV (piano/vocals)
Pearl Alley/S (guitar)
Peña Pachamama (world)
Perlot (piano)
Piaf's (cabaret/piano)
Pier 23 Cafe (varies)
Plumed Horse/SV (bands/piano)
Ponzu (DJ)
Prima/E (jazz/piano)
Rasselas (blues/jazz)
Rick's (Hawaiian)

Ritz-Carlton Din. Rm. (harp)
Ritz-Carlton Terrace (jazz)
Rose Pistola (jazz)
Rue de Paris/SV ("murder" mysteries)
Sake Tini/N (varies)
Santa Fe/E (piano)
Saul's/E (varies)
Schroeder's (polka)
Shadowbrook/S (jazz)
Shanghai 1930 (jazz)
Station House Café/N (jazz)
Stoddard's/SV (jazz/reggae)
Straits Cafe/SV†
Tarragon/SV (jazz)
Thanya & Salee (DJ)
Tied House/SV†
Timo's (flamenco/guitar)
Tonga Room (bands)
Top of the Mark (jazz/swing)
Townhouse/E (jazz)
21st Amendment Brew. (jazz)
Twenty Four (jazz)
Uva/N (guitar)
Viaggio Rist./SV (piano)
Wappo Bar/N (Brazilian/jazz)
Waterfront (jazz trio)
Yoshi's/Jack London/E (jazz)
Zuni Cafe (piano)

Fireplaces

Albion River Inn/N
Alta Mira/N
Anton & Michel/S
Applewood Inn/N
Auberge du Soleil/N
Baccarat/SV
Backflip
Bella Mia/SV
Bella Vista/SV
Big Four
Bistro Don Giovanni/N
Bistro Jeanty/N
Bittersweet Bistro/S
Bollinger/E
Boonville Hotel/N
Brannan's Grill/N
Brazio/E
Brix/N
Caprice/N
Casanova/S
Casa Orinda/E
Cetrella Bistro/S
Chantilly/SV
Chart House/S†
Chateau Souverain/N
Chez TJ/SV
Cielo/S

Cliff House
Club XIX/S
Covey/S
Crow's Nest/S
Dal Baffo/SV
Della Santina's/N
Domaine Chandon/N
Duck Club/N†
El Paseo/N
Erna's Elderberry/E
Evvia/SV
Foreign Cinema
French Laundry/N
Fresh Cream/S
Half Moon Bay/S
Harris'
House of Prime Rib
Iberia/SV
Il Fornaio/E†
John Ash & Co./N
Joubert's
Kenwood/N
Kokkari Estiatorio
Lark Creek/N†
La Toque/N
Ledford House/N
Left at Albuquerque/E†
Left Bank/N†
Le Mouton Noir/SV
Lion & Compass/SV
Livefire Grill
Los Gatos Brewing/SV
MacArthur Park
MacCallum House/N
Madrona Manor/N
Manka's Inverness/N
Marinus/S
Mezza Luna/S
Mezze/E
Mikayla/Casa Madrona/N
Moosse Cafe/N
Mucca/N
Navio/S
Nepenthe/S
Oliveto Cafe/E
Orlo's/SV
Ovation
Pacific
Pairs/N
Park Chow
Pelican Inn/N
Peña Pachamama
Piatti/E†
Piazza D'Angelo/N
Pinot Blanc/N
Plouf
Plumed Horse/SV

Special Feature Index

PlumpJack Cafe/N†
Potrero Brewing
Prima/E
Ravenous/N†
Ravens/N
Red Herring
Rest. at Meadowood/N
Rest. at Stevenswood/N
Rio Grill/S
Robert's Bistro/S
Rutherford Grill/N
Salute Rist./E†
Sardine Factory/S
Scott's/SV†
Shanghai 1930
Sierra Mar/S
Skates on the Bay/E
Sno-Drift
Spago Palo Alto/SV
Stokes Adobe/S
Tapestry/SV
Tarpy's Roadhse./S
Tarragon/SV
Venticello
Vic Stewart's/E
Viognier/SV
Wild Hare/SV
Wine Spectator/N

Historic Places
(Year opened; *building)
1830s Stokes Adobe/S*
1848 La Forêt/SV*
1849 Tadich Grill
1860 Mucca/N*
1862 Boonville Hotel/N
1862 General's Daughter/N*
1863 Cliff House
1867 Cafe de Paris/L'Entrecôte*
1867 Sam's Grill
1876 Woodward's Garden*
1880 OakTown Cafe/E*
1881 Madrona Manor/N
1882 Calistoga Inn/N
1882 MacCallum House/N*
1882 Wine Spectator/N*
1884 Terra/N*
1886 Fior d'Italia
1886 Chart House/SV*
1886 Cole's Chop Hse./N*
1890 Spenger's/E
1890 Deuce/N*
1893 Schroeder's
1893 Cafe Beaujolais/N*
1901 downtown/E
1902 Chez TJ/SV*
1904 Compass Rose*

1905 Orlo's/SV*
1907 Emma*
1908 John's Grill*
1909 Garden Court*
1911 Hotel Mac/E*
1912 Capp's Corner*
1912 Carême Room
1912 Swan Oyster Depot
1914 Balboa Cafe
1915 Jordan's/E*
1917 Manka's Inverness/N
1917 Napa Valley Wine/N*
1917 Tarpy's Roadhse./S*
1919 Sardine Factory/S*
1920 Sam's Anchor Cafe/N
1922 Julius' Castle
1922 Roosevelt Tamale
1924 Big Four*
1924 Farallon*
1925 Beach Chalet Brew.*
1925 John Bentley's/SV*
1927 Ahwahnee Din. Rm./E
1927 Alta Mira/N*
1927 Blue Chalk Cafe/SV*
1927 Moss Beach/S
1928 Alfred's Steak Hse.
1933 Sears Fine Food
1934 Duarte's Tavern/S
1934 Trader Vic's/E
1935 Alioto's
1935 Tommaso's
1937 Buckeye Roadhse./N
1937 Original Joe's
1939 Little River Inn/N
1940 Bruno's
1940 Cetrella Bistro/S*
1945 Tonga Room
1947 Tommy's Joynt
1949 Nepenthe/S
1952 It's Tops Coffee
1956 Ondine/N
1959 Enrico's Sidewalk Cafe
late 1800's Miramonte/N*
late 1800's Vic Stewart's/E*

Hotel Dining
Abigail Hotel
  Millennium
Ahwahnee Hotel
  Ahwahnee Din. Rm./E
Albion River Inn
  Albion River Inn/N
Alta Mira Hotel
  Alta Mira/N
Applewood Inn
  Applewood Inn/N
Auberge du Soleil Inn
  Auberge du Soleil/N

Special Feature Index

Johnfrank
Jojo/E
Kabuto Sushi
Kirala/E
Kokkari Estiatorio
Le Colonial
Left Bank/N†
Le Poisson Japonais/SV
Luna Park
Manzanita/N
Mazzini Trattoria/E
mc²
Mecca
Miramonte/N
Moose's
Mucca/N
Mustards Grill/N
Nizza La Bella/E
Nola/SV
Oliveto Cafe/E
Pearl Alley/S
Perry's†
Piazza D'Angelo/N
Plouf
PlumpJack Cafe
Postrio
Restaurant LuLu
Ritz-Carlton Din. Rm.
Rose Pistola
Rose's Café
Roy's
Santi/N
Slanted Door
Spago Palo Alto/SV
Sushi Groove
Sushi Ran/N
Tokyo Go Go
Tra Vigne/N
Universal Cafe
Via Centro/E
Village Pub/SV
Wild Hare/SV
Yankee Pier/N
Zibibbo/SV
Zodiac Club
Zuni Cafe

Jacket Required
Acquerello
Aqua
Bix
Campton Place
Carnelian Room
Chantilly/SV
Club XIX/S
Elisabeth Daniel
French Laundry/N
La Folie

Masa's
Ovation
Pacific's Edge/S
Tommy Toy's

Late Dining – After 12:30
(All hours are AM)
Absinthe (1)
bacar (1)
Backflip (2)
Black Cat (2)
Bouchon/N (1)
Brazen Head (1)
Brother's Korean†
butterfly (1)
Globe (1)
Great Eastern (1)
It's Tops Coffee (3)
King of Thai (1:30)
Koryo/E (2)
La Rondalla (3)
Liverpool Lil's (1)
Mel's Drive-In†
North Beach Pizza†
Original Joe's/SV†
Rasselas†
Taqueria Cancun†
Tommy's Joynt (1:45)
Yuet Lee (3)

Meet for a Drink
(Most top hotels and the
following standouts)
Absinthe
Ana Mandara
Avenue Grill/N
Azie
bacar
Balboa Cafe
Bandera/SV
Beach Chalet Brew.
Betelnut Pejiu Wu
Bistro Don Giovanni/N
Bistro Vida/SV
Bix
Boulevard
British Bankers Club/SV
Bruno's
Bubble Lounge
Cafe Bastille
Café Claude
Cafe Flore
Café Rouge/E
Carnelian Room
César/E
Charlie's
Clouds Downtown/S

Cosmopolitan Cafe
Cypress Club
Domaine Chandon/N
E&O Trading
Eastside West
Empire Grill/SV
Enrico's Sidewalk Cafe
Eos
Farallon
Faultline Brewing/SV
First Crush
Foreign Cinema
42 Degrees
Gordon Biersch
Gordon's Hse. of Fine Eats
Hayes & Vine Wine
Infusion Bar
Jardinière
Johnfrank
Kensington Circus Pub/E
Kokkari Estiatorio
Lapis
Le Colonial
Left Bank/N†
Los Gatos Brewing/SV
Magnolia Pub
Mazzini Trattoria/E
mc^2
Mecca
MoMo's
Moose's
Nizza La Bella/E
Nola/SV
One Market
Pairs/N
Palio d'Asti
Pearl Alley/S
Perry's
Potrero Brewing
Restaurant LuLu
Rose Pistola
Roy's
Sake Tini/N
Sam's Anchor Cafe/N
Slow Club
Spago Palo Alto/SV
Splendido
Stars
Suppenküche
Thirsty Bear Brewing
Tied House/SV
Timo's
Tokyo Go Go
Townhouse/E
Trader Vic's/E
21st Amendment Brew.
2223

Viaggio Rist./SV
Waterfront
Wine Spectator/N
Zibibbo/SV
Zodiac Club
Zuni Cafe

Noteworthy Newcomers
À Côté/E
Alma
Andalu
Asia de Cuba
Basque Nueva Cocina
Bistro Liaison/E
Carmel Chop Hse./S
Carneros/N
Cetrella Bistro/S
Chenery Park
Dashi/SV
Desiree
downtown/E
East Coast West Deli
Emmy's Spaghetti
Frjtz Fries
Galette
girl & the gaucho/N
Grasshopper/E
Isa
Kingfish/SV
La Rue/E
Le Bistro/SV
Le Bistrot
Le Krewe
Le Poisson Japonais/SV
Manzanita/N
Miramonte/N
Navio/S
Oritalia
Ozumo
Pairs/N
Paragon Bar/E
Pesce
Ramblas
Rest. at Stevenswood/N
Roux/N
Sake Tini/N
Three Seasons
Trellis/SV
231 Ellsworth/SV
Via Centro/E
Village Pub/SV
V Rest. & Wine
zuzu/N

Offbeat
Ace Wasabi's
Albona Rist.
Angkor Wat

AsiaSF
Backflip
Blue Nile/E
Buca di Beppo/SV†
Cafe Silan/SV
Caffe Sport
Casa Orinda/E
Catahoula/N
Cha Cha Cha†
Cypress Club
Dot
Falafel's Drive-In/SV
Fritz Fries
Hungarian Sausage
Irrawaddy Burmese
Isobune Sushi†
Jimtown Store/N
Joubert's
Kan Zaman
Kathmandu West/SV
Katia's Russian Tea Rm.
Khan Toke Thai
La Palma
La Rondalla
Lhasa Moon
Lovejoy's Tea Rm.
Lucy's Tea Hse./SV
Maharani
Mango Cafe/SV
Maykedah
Moss Beach/S
Peña Pachamama
Spettro/E
St. Orres/N
Trader Vic's/E
Walzwerk
Yamin Win/SV
Yoshi's/Jack London/E

Outdoor Dining

(G=garden; P=patio;
S=sidewalk; T=terrace;
W=waterside)
Acorn/SV (P)
À Côté/E (P)
Albion River Inn/N (W)
Alfy's/N (P)
Alta Mira/N (T)
Anton & Michel/S (P)
Applewood Inn/N (T)
A.P. Stump's/SV (P,S)
Aqui Cal-Mex/SV (P)
Auberge du Soleil/N (T)
Autumn Moon/E (G)
Backflip (P)
Baker St. Bistro (S)
Baldoria (S)

Barbara's Fishtrap/S (P)
Barney's (P)
Bay Wolf/E (T)
Bella Mia/SV (P)
B44 (P,S)
Bighorn Grill/E (P)
Bistro Aix (P)
Bistro Don Giovanni/N (P,I)
Bistro Elan/SV (G,P)
Bistro Jeanty/N (P)
Bistro Liaison/E (P)
Bittersweet Bistro/S (G,P)
Black Cat (S)
Blackhawk Grille/E (P,T,W)
Blue Plate (G,P)
Bollinger/E (P)
Bouchon/N (P)
Brazio/E (T,W)
Bridges/E (G,P)
British Bankers Club/SV (P)
Brix/N (P)
Cafe Bastille (S,T)
Cafe Borrone/SV (P)
Cafe Brioche/SV (S)
Café Claude (S,T)
Cafe de Paris/L'Entrecôte (P,S,T)
Cafe Flore (P,S)
Cafe Gibraltar/S (T)
Cafe Prima Vera/SV (P)
Caffè Greco (S)
Caffe Riace/SV (P)
Calistoga Inn/N (T)
Caprice/N (W)
Carneros/N (P)
Casanova/S (P)
Celadon/N (T,W)
César/E (P)
Cetrella Bistro/S (T)
Charlie's (P)
Chart House/SV†
Chateau Souverain/N (P)
Cheesecake Factory (T)
Chow (G)
Cielo/S (P,T,W)
Citron/E (P)
Club XIX/S (P,W)
Cole's Chop Hse./N (T,W)
Convivio/S (P)
Cool Café/SV (P)
Covey/S (G,P,T,W)
Crow's Nest/S (P,W)
Della Santina's/N (G,P)
Deuce/N (G,P)
Dipsea Cafe/N (P,W)
Domaine Chandon/N (T,W)
Doña Tomás/E (P)
Duck Club/E†
El Paseo/N (P)

Empire Grill/SV (G,P)
Emporio Rulli/N (P,S)
Enrico's Sidewalk Cafe (P,S)
Erna's Elderberry/E (T)
Faultline Brewing/SV (P,W)
Faz†
Feast/N (P,S)
Flea St. Café/SV (P)
Foreign Cinema (P)
42 Degrees (G,P)
Frantoio/N (G,P)
French Laundry/N (P)
Fresh Cream/S (W)
Frjtz Fries†
Gabriella Café/S (P)
Galette (T)
General's Daughter/N (P)
girl & the fig/N (P)
Glen Ellen Inn/N (P,W)
Gordon's/N (P,S)
Grasing's/S (P)
Guaymas/N (P,W)
Half Moon Bay/S (P,W)
Hawgs Seafood/SV (P)
Herbivore (P)
Hobee's/SV†
Hyde St. Bistro (S)
Iberia/SV (P)
Il Davide/N (P,S)
Il Fornaio†
Isa (P)
Italian Colors/E (P)
Jimtown Store/N (P)
John Ash & Co./N (P,T)
Julius' Castle (T)
Kelly's Mission Rock (P,W)
Kenwood/N (G)
La Fondue/SV (P)
La Forêt/SV (W)
L'Amie Donia/SV (P)
La Note/E (G)
La Pastaia/SV (P)
Lapis (T,W)
Lark Creek/E†
La Rue/E (P)
Late for the Train/SV (G,P)
Le Charm (P)
Le Colonial (P)
Ledford House/N (W)
Left Bank/E†
Le Mouton Noir/SV (P)
Lion & Compass/SV (P)
Liverpool Lil's (P,S)
Madrona Manor/N (T)
Marché aux Fleurs/N (P)
Marinus/S (P,T)
Mariposa/N (G)
Meadowood Grill/N (T)

Meritage/N (G,P)
Millennium (G)
Miramonte/N (P)
Miss Millie's (P)
Mistral/N (P,W)
Mistral/SV (P,W)
MoMo's (P)
Moosse Cafe/N (P,W)
Moss Beach/S (P)
Mucca/N (P,W)
Nepenthe/S (P)
Nizza La Bella/E (S)
Nola/SV (P)
O Chamé/E (P)
Olema Inn/N (G,P)
Orlo's/SV (P,W)
Palomino (P,W)
Paolo's/SV (P,T,W)
Park Chow (P)
Pastis (P)
Pearl/N (P)
Pearl Alley/S (P)
Piatti/E†
Piazza D'Angelo/N (P)
Picante Cocina/E (P)
Pier 23 Cafe (G,T,W)
Pinot Blanc/N (P)
Plouf (S,T)
PlumpJack Cafe/N†
Postino/E (P)
Potrero Brewing (P,T)
Prima/E (P,S)
Primo Patio Cafe (P)
Ravenous/N†
Rest. at Meadowood/N (P,T)
Rest. Umunhum/SV (P)
Rick & Ann's/E (G,P)
Rio Grill/S (P)
Ristorante Fabrizio/N (P)
Ritz-Carlton Terrace (T)
Rose Pistola (S)
Rose's Café (S)
Roux/N (P)
Roy's/Pebble Bch./S (P)
Rue de Paris/SV (P)
Rutherford Grill/N (P)
Salute Rist./E†
Sam's Anchor Cafe/N (T,W)
Santa Fe/E (G,P)
Santi/N (P)
Savor (G,P)
Sent Sovi/SV (P)
71 Saint Peter/SV (P)
Shadowbrook/S (P)
Sierra Mar/S (T,W)
Sinaloa Cafe/SV (P)
Spago Palo Alto/SV (G,P,T)
Spiedini/E (P)

Splendido (T,W)
Station House Café/N (G,P)
Steamer's Grillhouse/SV (P)
Stillwater/S (W)
Stinson Beach Grill/N (P)
Stoddard's/SV (P)
Straits Cafe/SV†
Tapestry/SV (P)
Tarpy's Roadhse./S (P)
Tastings/N (P)
Tomatina/N (P)
Townhouse/E (P)
Town's End (P)
Trader Vic's/E (W)
Tra Vigne/N (G,T)
Tropix/E (P)
Tuscany/N (P)
Twenty Four (P)
Universal Cafe (P)
Uva/N (P)
Via Centro/E (S)
Viaggio Rist./SV (P)
Via Vai (P)
Vic Stewart's/E (P)
Voulez-Vous/E (T)
Wappo Bar Bistro/N (G,P)
Waterfront (P,W)
Wente Vineyards/E (P)
Willow Wood Market/N (P)
Wine Spectator/N (T)
Woodside Bakery/SV (P)
Yankee Pier/N (P)
Zazie (G,P)
Zibibbo/SV (G,P)
Zinzino (P,S)
Zuni Cafe (S)

Parties & Private Rooms

(Any nightclub or restaurant charges less at off-times; * indicates private rooms available)

Acquerello*
Ahwahnee Din. Rm./E*
Alfred's Steak Hse.*
Alfy's/N*
Alioto's*
Alta Mira/N*
Ana Mandara*
Angkor Wat*
Anton & Michel/S*
A.P. Stump's/SV*
Asia de Cuba*
AsiaSF*
A Tavola/SV*
Auberge du Soleil/N*
Autumn Moon/E*
Avenue Grill/N*

Azie
Backflip*
Baldoria*
Basque Cultural Ctr./S*
Bay Wolf/E*
Bella Mia/SV*
Bella Vista/SV*
Betelnut Pejiu Wu*
Big Four*
Bighorn Grill/E*
Blackhawk Grille/E*
Bollinger/E*
Boulevard*
Brazio/E*
Bridges/E*
British Bankers Club/SV*
Brix/N*
Bubba's Diner/N
Buca Giovanni*
Buckeye Roadhse./N*
Cafe Bastille*
Cafe Beaujolais/N*
Cafe Kati*
Cafe Lolo/N*
Café Marcella/SV
Cafe Monk*
Café Mozart*
Cafe Riggio*
Café Rouge/E^x
Caffe Delle Stelle*
Calistoga Inn/N*
Caprice/N*
Carnelian Room*
Carneros/N*
Carpaccio/SV
Casanova/S*
Casa Orinda/E*
Catahoula/N*
Cetrella Bistro/S*
Chantilly/SV*
Charles Nob Hill*
Chart House/SV†
Chaya Brasserie
Chaz*
Chenery Park*
Chez TJ/SV*
Christopher's/E*
Cielo/S*
Citron/E*
Cityscape
Cliff House*
Club XIX/S*
Covey/S*
Cypress Club*
Dal Baffo/SV*
Deuce/N*
Domaine Chandon/N

Passage to India/SV
Pasta Moon/S*
Pastis
Pearl/N
Pelican Inn/N*
Peninsula Fountain/SV†
Perry's†
Piaf's
Piazza D'Angelo/N*
Pigalle/SV*
Pinot Blanc/N*
Pisces/SV
Plumed Horse/SV*
PlumpJack Cafe*
Ponzu*
Postrio*
Potrero Brewing*
Prima/E*
R & G Lounge
Red Herring*
Rest. at Meadowood/N*
Rest. at Sonoma Mission/N*
Restaurant LuLu*
Restaurant Peony/E*
Restaurant 301/N
Rick's*
Rio Grill/S*
Ritz-Carlton Din. Rm.*
Rotunda*
Roux/N
Roy's
Rubicon*
Sake Tini/N
Salute Rist./E*
Sam's Grill*
Santa Fe/E*
Sardine Factory/S*
Scala's Bistro
Sent Sovi/SV*
Shadowbrook/S*
Shanghai 1930ˣ
Silks*
Sno-Drift*
Soizic/E*
Spago Palo Alto/SV*
Spenger's/E*
Splendido*
Stars*
St. Michael's Alley/SV
Stoddard's/SV*
Stokes Adobe/S*
Tapestry/SV
Tarragon/SV
Terra/N*
Thirsty Bear Brewing*
Tomatina/N*
Tommy Toy's*

Tonga Room
Tony & Alba's Pizza/SV*
Top of the Mark
Trader Vic's/E*
Tra Vigne/N*
Trellis/SV*
21st Amendment Brew.*
Twenty Four*
2223*
231 Ellsworth/SV*
Uva/N*
Venticello
Venus/E
Via Centro/E
Viaggio Rist./SV*
Vic Stewart's/E*
Village Pub/SV*
Viognier/SV*
Walzwerk*
Wappo Bar Bistro/N*
Waterfront*
Wente Vineyards/E*
Wild Hare/SV*
Wine Spectator/N*
Woodward's Garden*
Xanadu/E*
Yankee Pier/N
Yank Sing†
Yoshida-Ya*
Yoshi's/Jack London/E*
Zarzuela*
Zibibbo/SV*
Zodiac Club

People-Watching
Ace Wasabi's
Ana Mandara
Asia de Cuba
AsiaSF
Avenue Grill/N
Balboa Cafe
Bandera/SV
Betelnut Pejiu Wu
Bix
Blowfish, Sushi
Bouchon/N
Boulevard
Cafe Bastille
Cafe Borrone/SV
Café Claude
Cafe Flore
Café Niebaum-Coppola
Caffe Centro
Caffè Greco
Carême Room
Cha Cha Cha†
Clouds Downtown/S
Dot

downtown/E
Eastside West
Empire Grill/SV
Enrico's Sidewalk Cafe
Evvia/SV
Foreign Cinema
Gordon Biersch
Grasshopper/E
Jardinière
Johnfrank
Left at Albuquerque†
Left Bank/N†
Mario's Bohemian Cigar
Mecca
Moose's
Mustards Grill/N
Nola/SV
Perry's†
Postrio
Restaurant LuLu
Rose's Café
Sam's Anchor Cafe/N
Spago Palo Alto/SV
Stoddard's/SV
Sushi Groove
Tin-Pan Asian Bistro
Tokyo Go Go
Tra Vigne/N
2223
Village Pub/SV
Wild Hare/SV
Zibibbo/SV
Zuni Cafe

Power Scenes

Aqua
Asia de Cuba
bacar
Big Four
Blackhawk Grille/E
Boulevard
Buck's/SV
Carpaccio/SV
Charles Nob Hill
Cypress Club
Dal Baffo/SV
downtown/E
Evvia/SV
Fifth Floor
Fleur de Lys
Fly Trap
Hawthorne Lane
Il Fornaio/SV†
Jardinière
Le Central Bistro
Le Colonial
Le Poisson Japonais/SV
Lion & Compass/SV

mc^2
Moose's
One Market
Park Grill
Postrio
Ritz-Carlton Din. Rm.
Rubicon
Soleil/SV
Spago Palo Alto/SV
Spiedo Rist./SV†
Tommy Toy's
Village Pub/SV
Viognier/SV
Wild Hare/SV

Pre-Theater/
Early-Bird Menus

(Call to check prices,
days and times)
Absinthe
Alamo Square
Anjou
Anzu
Avenue 9
Caffe Delle Stelle
Campton Place
Chapeau!
Christophe/N
Clémentine
First Crush
girl & the fig/N
Grand Cafe
Hyde St. Bistro
Jardinière
Juban
La Scene Café
Le Mouton Noir/SV
Millennium
Oritalia
paul K
Postrio
Robert's Bistro/S
Scala's Bistro
Stars
Suppenküche
Terra Brazilis

Prix Fixe Menus

(Call to check prices,
days and times)
Ahwahnee Din. Rm./E
Alamo Square
Alfy's/N
Anjou
Anzu
Aqua
Auberge du Soleil/N

Pubs/Bars/ Microbreweries

Quiet Conversation

Elisabeth Daniel
El Paseo/N
Fifth Floor
Fournou's Ovens
Gary Danko
Hotel Mac/E
Iberia/SV
Julius' Castle
Lalime's/E
La Toque/N
La Villa Poppi
Le Mouton Noir/SV
L'Olivier
Madrona Manor/N
Masa's
Ma Tante Sumi
Napa Valley Wine/N
O Chamé/E
Oswald's/S
Pacific's Edge/S
Park Grill
Pelican Inn/N
Pigalle/SV
Postino/E
Rue de Main/E
Sent Sovi/SV
Silks
St. Orres/N
Zaré
Zax

Raw Bars

Absinthe
bacar
Bistro Vida/SV
Bouchon/N
Cafe de Paris/L'Entrecôte
Café Rouge/E
Eastside West
Elite Cafe
Emma
Faz/SV†
Fog City Diner
Foreign Cinema
Globe
Grasshopper/E
House†
Jianna
Kingfish/SV
Le Bistrot
Le Central Bistro
Livefire Grill†
McCormick & Kuleto's
Meritage/N
MoMo's
Navio/S
Olema Inn/N
Pesce

Pisces/SV
Plouf
Red Herring
Restaurant LuLu
Rocco's Seafood
Station House Café/N
Stillwater/S
Stinson Beach Grill/N
Swan Oyster Depot
Tachibana/E
3 Fish/SV
Ti Couz
Twenty Four
Yabbies Coastal Kit.
Yankee Pier/N
Zibibbo/SV
Zuni Cafe

Reservations Essential

Acquerello
Ahwahnee Din. Rm./E
Albona Rist.
Alegrias, Food From Spain
Ana Mandara
Anton & Michel/S
Aqua
Asia de Cuba
Auberge du Soleil/N
Autumn Moon/E
Baker St. Bistro
Basque Cultural Ctr./S
Bella Vista/SV
B44
Bistro Liaison/E
Bix
Bizou
Blackhawk Grille/E
Bontà Rist.
Cafe Beaujolais/N
Cafe Lolo/N
Café Mozart
Calistoga Inn/N
Caprice/N
Catahoula/N
Celadon/N
Chantilly/SV
Chez Panisse/E
Chez Panisse Café/E
Christophe/N
Cielo/S
Club XIX/S
Cole's Chop Hse./N
Duck Club/S†
Erna's Elderberry/E
Firefly
Fleur de Lys
French Laundry/N
Gary Danko

Glen Ellen Inn/N
Helmand
John Bentley's/SV
Kokkari Estiatorio
La Fondue/SV
L'Amie Donia/SV
La Rue/E
La Toque/N
La Villa Poppi
L'Olivier
Madrona Manor/N
Manka's Inverness/N
Marinus/S
Mariposa/N
Matterhorn Swiss
Mistral/SV
Mucca/N
Napa Valley Wine/N
Olema Inn/N
Orlo's/SV
Ovation
Pacific's Edge/S
Pastis
Pisces/SV
Plouf
PlumpJack Cafe†
Postino/E
Ravenous/N†
Rest. at Stevenswood/N
Ritz-Carlton Din. Rm.
Ritz-Carlton Terrace
Roux/N
Roy's
Roy's/Pebble Bch./S
Sierra Mar/S
St. Orres/N
Tastings/N
Venticello
Wild Hare/SV
Wine Spectator/N
Yoshi's/Jack London/E
Zaré

Romantic Places

Acquerello
Ahwahnee Din. Rm./E
Anton & Michel/S
Applewood Inn/N
Auberge du Soleil/N
Beauséjour/SV
Bella Vista/SV
Big Four
Bistro Elan/SV
Bistro Vida/SV
Cafe Brioche/SV
Cafe Jacqueline
Café Mozart
Café Torre/SV

Caffe Riace/SV
Carnelian Room
Casanova/S
Chantilly/SV
Chez Panisse/E
Chez TJ/SV
Christophe/N
Citron/E
Covey/S
Cypress Club
Dal Baffo/SV
Domaine Chandon/N
Duck Club/N†
Elisabeth Daniel
El Paseo/N
Emile's/SV
Erna's Elderberry/E
Fifth Floor
Flea St. Café/SV
Fleur de Lys
French Laundry/N
Fresh Cream/S
Gabriella Café/S
Ganges
Gary Danko
Greens
Guernica/N
Il Davide/N
Indigo
Jardinière
John Ash & Co./N
John Bentley's/SV
Julius' Castle
Kasbah Moroccan/N
Katia's Russian Tea Rm.
Khan Toke Thai
La Folie
La Fondue/SV
La Forêt/SV
Lalime's/E
L'Amie Donia/SV
Lark Creek/N†
La Toque/N
La Villa Poppi
Le Mouton Noir/SV
Le Papillon/SV
L'Olivier
MacCallum House/N
Madrona Manor/N
Maharani
Manka's Inverness/N
Marché aux Fleurs/N
Marinus/S
Masa's
Matterhorn Swiss
Meetinghouse
O Chamé/E
Olema Inn/N

Ondine/N
Osteria/SV
Ovation
Pacific's Edge/S
Perlot
Pigalle/SV
Rest. at Meadowood/N
Ritz-Carlton Din. Rm.
Ritz-Carlton Terrace
Robert's Bistro/S
Roy's/Pebble Bch./S
Rue de Main/E
Rue de Paris/SV
Sent Sovi/SV
71 Saint Peter/SV
Sierra Mar/S
Silks
Soleil/SV
St. Michael's Alley/SV
St. Orres/N
Tarragon/SV
Terra/N
Venticello
Viognier/SV
Waterfront
Wente Vineyards/E
Woodward's Garden
Yoshida-Ya
Zaré
Zax

Senior Appeal

Acorn/SV
Acquerello
Alfred's Steak Hse.
Alioto's
Anton & Michel/S
A. Sabella's
Bella Vista/SV
Big Four
Buca Giovanni
Buck's/SV
Cafe For All Seasons
Charles Nob Hill
Cole's Chop Hse./N
Covey/S
Dal Baffo/SV
Draeger's/SV
Duck Club/N†
Emile's/SV
FatApple's/E
Fior d'Italia
Fleur de Lys
Fly Trap
Garden Court
Harris'
Hayes St. Grill
Hobee's/SV

Hotel Mac/E
House of Prime Rib
Izzy's Steak
John's Grill
La Felce
La Ginestra/N
Lalime's/E
Le Bistrot
Marin Joe's/N
Masa's
Morton's
Osteria
Rotunda
Rue de Main/E
Sardine Factory/S
Scoma's†
Sears Fine Food
Tadich Grill
Vic Stewart's/E

Singles Scenes

Backflip
Balboa Cafe
Bandera/SV
Beach Chalet Brew.
Betelnut Pejiu Wu
Biscuits & Blues
Bix
Blowfish, Sushi
Blue Chalk Cafe/SV
British Bankers Club/SV
Bruno's
Bubble Lounge
butterfly
Cafe Bastille
Cafe Borrone/SV
Café Claude
Cafe Flore
Charlie's
Clouds Downtown/S
Elite Cafe
El Palomar/S
Faultline Brewing/SV
Foreign Cinema
Frjtz Fries†
Gordon Biersch
Gordon's Hse. of Fine Eats
Guaymas/N
Infusion Bar
Johnfrank
Los Gatos Brewing/SV
Luna Park
Mecca
MoMo's
Nola/SV
Palomino
Paragon
Pearl Alley/S

Perry's†
Pier 23 Cafe
Potrero Brewing
Sam's Anchor Cafe/N
Slow Club
Stoddard's/SV
Thirsty Bear Brewing
Tied House/SV
Tokyo Go Go
2223
Zibibbo/SV
Zuni Cafe

Sleepers
(Good to excellent food,
but little known)

Angkor Borei
Applewood Inn/N
Ara Wan/N
Arlequin Food to Go
Avanti/S
Azuma/SV
Baccarat/SV
Beauséjour/SV
Bittersweet Bistro/S
Brazio/E
Café Esin/E
Cafe Gibraltar/S
Cafe Prima Vera/SV†
Cambodiana/E
Carême Room
Charcuterie/N
Chaz
Cielo/S
Convivio/S
Covey/S
Destino
Deuce/N
Dusit Thai
El Palomar/S
Feast/N
Fiesta del Mar/SV
Flying Fish Grill/S
Gabriella Café/S
Glen Ellen Inn/N
Grandview/SV
Green Valley Cafe/N
Guernica/N
Hana/N
Irrawaddy Burmese
Jordan's/E
La Palma
La Villa Poppi
Ledford House/N
Lotus Cuisine of India/N
MacCallum House/N
Marinus/S
Mei Long/SV

Mo's Burgers†
Mucca/N
Narai
955 Ukiah/N
Omei/S
Orlo's/SV
Oswald's/S
Pairs/N
Palo Alto Sol/SV
Pangaea/N
Pazzia
Pearl/N
Pearl Alley/S
Phuping/E
Pigalle/SV
Pizzetta 211
Ravens/N
Rendezvous Inn/N
Rest. at Stevenswood/N
Restaurant 301/N
Rice Table/N
Robert's Bistro/S
Rue de Paris/SV
71 Saint Peter/SV
Sierra Mar/S
Sinaloa Cafe/SV
Stillwater/S
St. Michael's Alley/SV
Syrah/N
Thanya & Salee
Tratt. La Siciliana/E
Venus/E
Willow Wood Market/N
Yukol Place

Tasting Menus
Acquerello
Ahwahnee Din. Rm./E
Alfy's/N
Anzu
Aqua
Auberge du Soleil/N
Azie
Bridges/E
Cafe Kati
Café Tiramisu
Campton Place
Chapeau!
Charles Nob Hill
Club XIX/S
Cypress Club
Domaine Chandon/N
Duck Club/E†
Elisabeth Daniel
Erna's Elderberry/E
Fifth Floor
First Crush
Fleur de Lys

French Laundry/N
Gary Danko
Isa
Jardinière
Kasbah Moroccan/N
La Folie
La Forêt/SV
Lark Creek/N†
La Rue/E
La Toque/N
La Villa Poppi
Le Mouton Noir/SV
Le Papillon/SV
Le Poisson Japonais/SV
Little Shin Shin/E
Madrona Manor/N
Masa's
mc^2
Mistral/N
Navio/S
Oliveto Cafe/E
Ondine/N
Pacific's Edge/S
Paolo's/SV
Paragon Bar/E
Perlot
Pinot Blanc/N
Pisces/SV
Rest. at Meadowood/N
Rest. at Sonoma Mission/N
Ritz-Carlton Din. Rm.
Roy's
Rubicon
Sardine Factory/S
Sent Sovi/SV
Silks
Soleil/SV
Spiedini/E
Tastings/N
Tommy Toy's
Tratt. La Siciliana/E
231 Ellsworth/SV
Uzen/E
V Rest. & Wine
Zaré

Tea Service
Citizen Cake
Compass Rose
Dragon Well
Garden Court
Katia's Russian Tea Rm.
Lovejoy's Tea Rm.
Lucy's Tea Hse./SV
O Chamé/E
Ritz-Carlton Din. Rm.
Rotunda

Watergate
Yank Sing

Teenagers & Other Youthful Spirits
Barney's
Fiesta del Mar/SV†
Fog City Diner
Fuki Sushi/SV
Hard Rock Cafe
Hobee's/SV
Left at Albuquerque/SV†
Long Life Noodle/SV†
Max's on the Square†
Max's Opera Cafe
Mel's Drive-In†
Mo's Burgers
Planet Hollywood
Rutherford Grill/N
Sardine Factory/S

Teflons
(Get lots of business, despite so-so food, i.e. they have other attractions that prevent criticism from sticking)
Beach Chalet Brew.
Cafe de la Presse
Chevys Fresh Mex†
Cliff House
Gordon Biersch
Hard Rock Cafe
Kasbah Moroccan/N
Kelly's Mission Rock
Long Life Noodle
Mel's Drive-In
Pier 23 Cafe
Sam's Anchor Cafe/N
Spenger's/E
Tommy's Joynt
Tonga Room

Theme Restaurants
Hard Rock Cafe
Kasbah Moroccan/N
Maharani
Max's Diner†
Max's Opera Cafe
Max's Opera Cafe/SV
Napa Valley Wine/N
Planet Hollywood
Spenger's/E
Stinking Rose

Valet Parking
Absinthe
Albona Rist.
Alfred's Steak Hse.

Special Feature Index

Greens
Higashi West/SV
Jardinière
John Ash & Co./N
Julius' Castle
Kyo-Ya
La Folie
La Forêt/SV
Lark Creek/N†
La Toque/N
Le Mouton Noir/SV
Le Poisson Japonais/SV
Mandarin
Marinus/S
Masa's
mc^2
Morton's
Napa Valley Wine/N
Orlo's/SV
Pacific's Edge/S
Rest. at Sonoma Mission/N
Ritz-Carlton Din. Rm.
Ritz-Carlton Terrace
Roy's
Roy's/Pebble Bch./S
Sent Sovi/SV
Sierra Mar/S
Silks
Solcil/SV
Spago Palo Alto/SV
Tommy Toy's
Village Pub/SV
Wild Hare/SV

Wine/Beer Only

Acquerello
Alegrias, Food From Spain
Alfy's/N
Andalu
Angkor Wat
Antica Trattoria
Aperto
Applewood Inn/N
Avanti/S
Baker St. Bistro
Baldoria
Bay Wolf/E
Bistro Aix
Bistro Clovis
Bistro Elan/SV
Bistro Liaison/E
Bistro Ralph/N
Bocca Rotis
Bontà Rist.
Boonville Hotel/N
Buca Giovanni
Cafe Beaujolais/N
Cafe Brioche/SV

Café Claude
Café Esin/E
Cafe For All Seasons
Cafe Jacqueline
Cafe Kati
Cafe La Haye/N
Cafe Lolo/N
Café Marcella/SV
Café Mozart
Café Torre/SV
Celadon/N
Cha Cha Cha†
Chapeau!
Charanga
Chaz
Chez Nous
Chez Panisse/E
Chez Panisse Café/E
Chez TJ/SV
Christophe/N
Citron/E
Convivio/S
Cucina Jackson Fillmore/N
Delfina
Desiree
Destino
Diner/N
Domaine Chandon/N
Duck Club/S†
Elisabeth Daniel
El Paseo/N
Eos
Firefly
Flying Fish Grill/S
Frascati
French Laundry/N
Frjtz Fries
Gabriella Café/S
Galette
Gira Polli
girl & the gaucho/N
Glen Ellen Inn/N
Gordon's/N
Grandview/SV
Grasing's/S
Grasshopper/E
Greens
Hayes & Vine Wine
Herbivore
House
Hyde St. Bistro
I Fratelli
Indian Oven
Isa
Jackson Fillmore
Jocco's/SV
Joe's Taco Lounge/N

Special Feature Index

Winning Wine Lists

Special Feature Index

Special Feature Index

Special Feature Index

ALPHABETICAL PAGE INDEX*

* All restaurants are in the City of San Francisco unless otherwise noted (E=East of San Francisco; N=North of San Francisco; S=South of San Francisco; and SV=Silicon Valley.

Alphabetical Page Index

Alphabetical Page Index

Alphabetical Page Index

Alphabetical Page Index

Alphabetical Page Index

Alphabetical Page Index

Alphabetical Page Index

Alphabetical Page Index

Wine Vintage Chart 1985–2000

This chart is designed to help you select wine to go with your meal. It is based on the same 0 to 30 scale used throughout this *Survey*. The ratings (prepared by our friend **Howard Stravitz**, a law professor at the University of South Carolina) reflect both the quality of the vintage and the wine's readiness for present consumption. Thus, if a wine is not fully mature or is over the hill, its rating has been reduced. We do not include 1987, 1991–1993 vintages because they are not especially recommended for most areas.

	'85	'86	'88	'89	'90	'94	'95	'96	'97	'98	'99	'00
WHITES												
French:												
Alsace	24	18	22	28	28	26	25	23	23	25	23	25
Burgundy	24	24	18	26	21	22	27	28	25	24	25	–
Loire Valley	–	–	–	26	25	22	24	26	23	22	24	–
Champagne	28	25	24	26	29	–	24	27	24	24	–	–
Sauternes	22	28	29	25	27	–	22	23	24	24	–	20
California:												
Chardonnay	–	–	–	–	–	21	26	22	25	24	25	–
REDS												
French:												
Bordeaux	26	27	25	28	29	24	26	25	23	24	22	25
Burgundy	23	–	22	26	29	20	26	27	25	23	26	–
Rhône	25	19	26	29	28	23	25	22	24	28	26	–
Beaujolais	–	–	–	–	–	–	22	20	24	22	24	–
California:												
Cab./Merlot	26	26	–	21	28	27	26	24	28	23	26	–
Zinfandel	–	–	–	–	–	26	24	25	23	24	25	–
Italian:												
Tuscany	26	–	24	–	26	23	25	19	28	24	25	–
Piedmont	25	–	25	28	28	–	24	26	28	26	25	–